PCs made easy

STAGE 4

A PRACTICAL COURSE

caps
lock

PCs made easy

STAGE 4

A PRACTICAL COURSE

PUBLISHED BY THE READER'S DIGEST ASSOCIATION LIMITED
LONDON NEW YORK SYDNEY MONTREAL

PCS MADE EASY
A PRACTICAL COURSE – STAGE 4

Published by the Reader's Digest Association Limited, 2001

The Reader's Digest Association Limited
11 Westferry Circus, Canary Wharf, London E14 4HE
www.readersdigest.co.uk

We are committed to both the quality of our products and the service we provide to our customers, so please feel free to contact us on 08705 113366, or by email at cust_service@readersdigest.co.uk
If you have any comments about the content of our books, you can contact us at gbeditorial@readersdigest.co.uk

For Reader's Digest
Series Editor: Christine Noble
Assistant Editor: Caroline Boucher
Art Editor: Julie Bennett

Reader's Digest General Books
Editorial Director: Cortina Butler
Art Director: Nick Clark

PCs made easy was created and produced for The Reader's Digest Association Limited by De Agostini UK Ltd, from material originally published as the Partwork *Computer Success Plus*.

Printing and binding: Printer Industria Gráfica S.A., Barcelona

ISBN 0 276 42634 7

CONTENTS

caps
lock
shift
control

Windows

Using the StartUp folder

To make your computer load the programs you need to use as soon as you turn it on, just add shortcuts to the StartUp menu.

The StartUp menu might already contain a few programs that Microsoft Office uses, so don't delete them.

You might have noticed an extra folder within the Start menu's Programs folder called StartUp. Although it can be opened and used just like any other folder, StartUp has a special function: any program placed within it will automatically run whenever the computer boots up.

This allows you to start your favourite programs automatically each time you switch on the computer. Just put a shortcut to the program into this folder and you no longer need to spend time hunting around for the programs you most commonly use.

In every other way, the StartUp folder behaves like any other folder; you can add or remove items by using the Taskbar Properties dialog box (see opposite). However, you will not be able to delete the folder because Windows uses it in its boot-up process.

● What you might find

Click on the Start menu, then Programs and then select StartUp. You might find that it already contains some items. Don't worry if you don't recognize them – some programs place items in this folder as part of their installation process. Some versions of Microsoft Office, for example, install Find Fast, a small indexing program that runs as soon as Windows starts.

Some graphics cards also include special utilities that they install in the StartUp folder. Although it's possible to remove these items, it's safest to leave them in place.

● Adding your own programs

It's easy to add your own program shortcuts to the folder. Once you have done so, these shortcuts will enable the associated programs to start up at the same time as Windows. This can be handy if you regularly use a single program, such as Word or Excel. But be careful: the more items you put in the StartUp folder, the longer Windows takes to load, so stick to the programs that you most often use.

There's another very good use for this folder. If you add a shortcut to a document, the program that created it will start with the document automatically opened and ready for you to work on. For example, imagine a simple 'to do' list created in Notepad. Save the list as to-do.txt in your *PCs made easy* folder file and place a shortcut for it in the StartUp folder. Now, whenever Windows restarts, your list will pop up as a reminder.

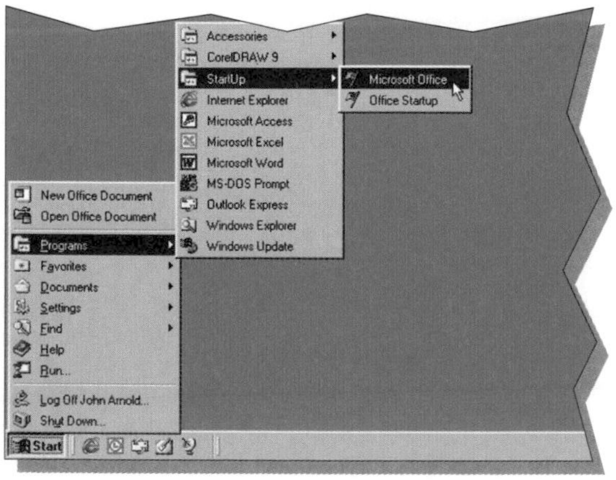

You can check what programs are already in your StartUp folder by calling it up from the Programs folder.

WHAT IT MEANS

BOOT UP

The term 'boot up' refers to the process that commences when you switch on your computer. Before Windows or any other program starts up, the computer runs its own tiny built-in program to check whether crucial components are working correctly. After the computer boots up, it will load Windows and then you can begin work.

Adding a program to StartUp

In this exercise we'll show you how to place the Calculator program in the StartUp folder so that it opens automatically every time Windows starts up.

1 Select the Settings folder from the Start menu and click on the Taskbar & Start Menu option.

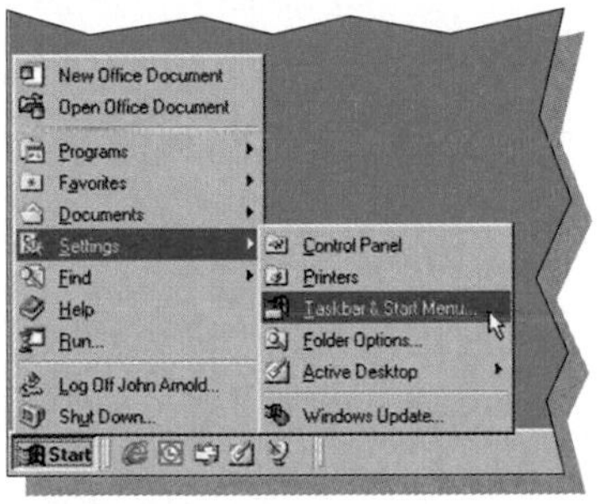

2 The Taskbar Properties dialog box appears. Click on the Start Menu Programs tab and then press the Add button in the Customize Start menu section.

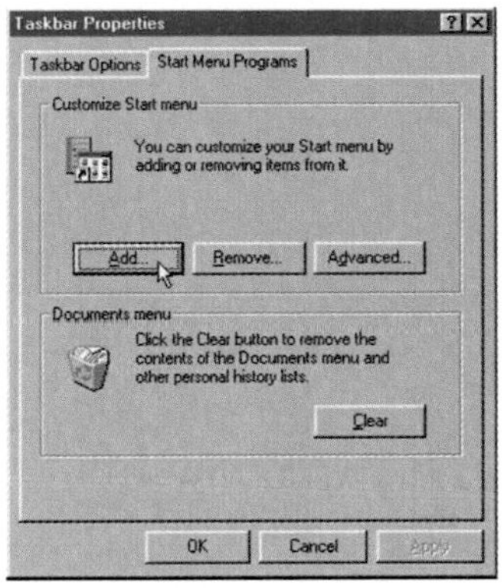

3 The Create Shortcut dialog box appears, requesting the path (see Stage 1, page 23) of the program. To find this, press the Browse button.

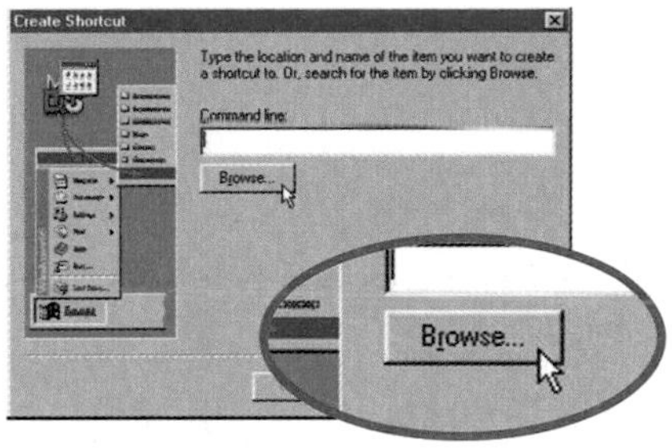

4 Use the Browse dialog box to locate the Calc program, which you will find in the Windows directory. Click on it once to highlight it and then press the Open button.

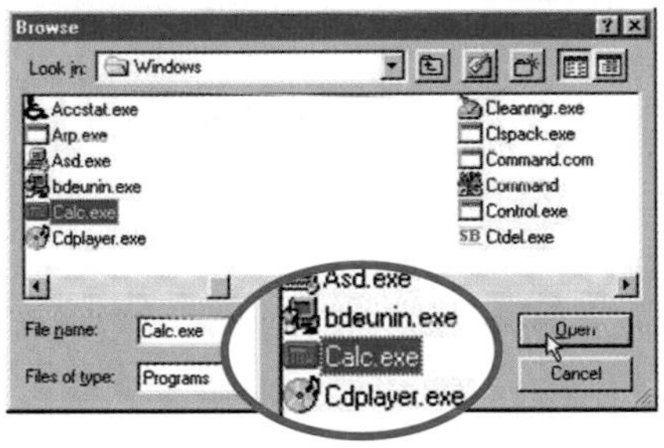

5 You'll return to the Create Shortcut dialog box, with the path entered for you. Press the Next button.

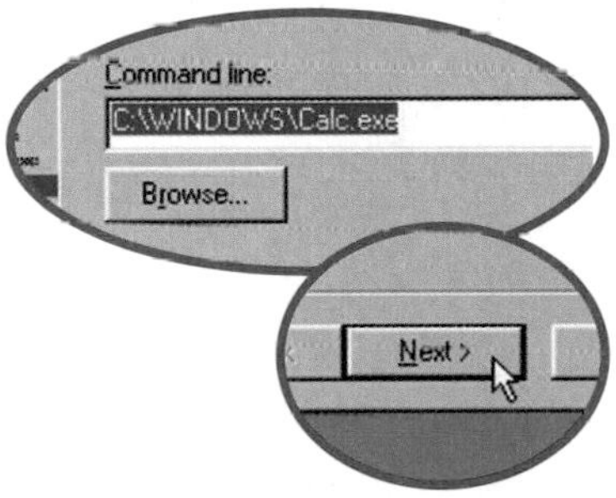

6 Windows now needs to know where you want the shortcut to go. Locate the StartUp folder and click on it once to select it. Then press the Next button.

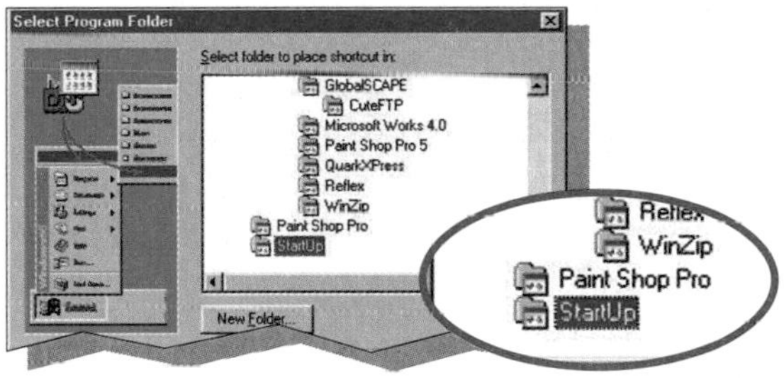

7 You will be asked to type in a name for your shortcut. In our example we've simply called it 'Calculator'. Click the Finish button.

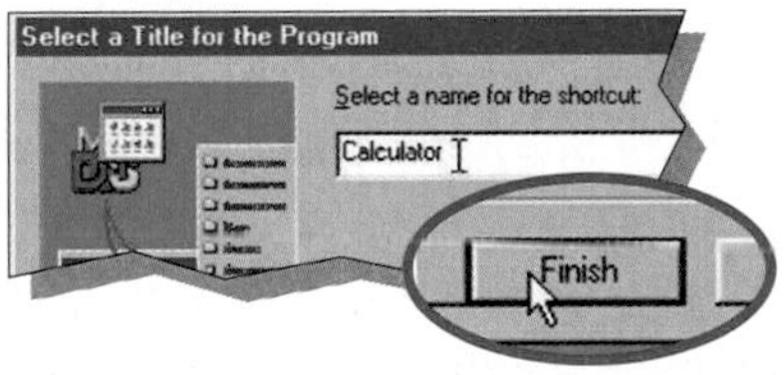

8 Go to the Start menu and select Programs, then StartUp. You'll see that the Calculator option is sitting inside the StartUp folder.

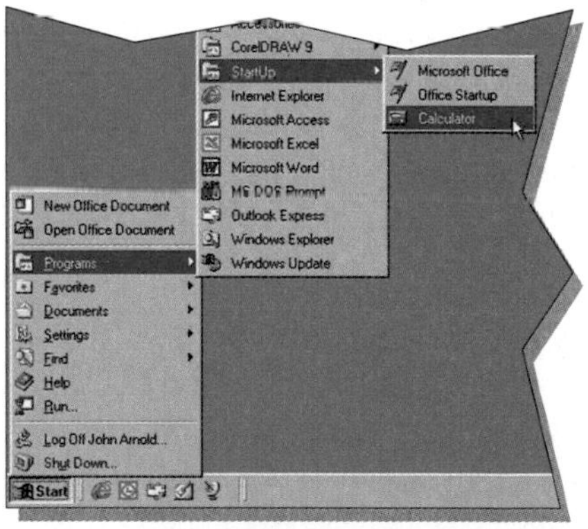

HOW TO FIND FILES

If you want to add an item to the StartUp folder, but you're unsure of where to find it (Step 4), you can use Windows' built-in Find command (see Stage 2, pages 8-9). Windows can tell you the path of all files that contain a particular word. (Be careful, however, as some programs don't include their full name in their file name – Calculator is called Calc, for example.)

In the Taskbar Properties dialog box select the Start Menu Programs tab and then the Advanced button (see Step 2). You can then view the Start Menu in the Windows Explorer format. Double-click through the Start Menu's folders until you find the shortcut for the program you are looking for. Right-click on it and select Properties from the pop-up menu. Under the Shortcut tab the path for your shortcut will be shown in the Target text box. Make a note of this and then use it when browsing (as in Step 4).

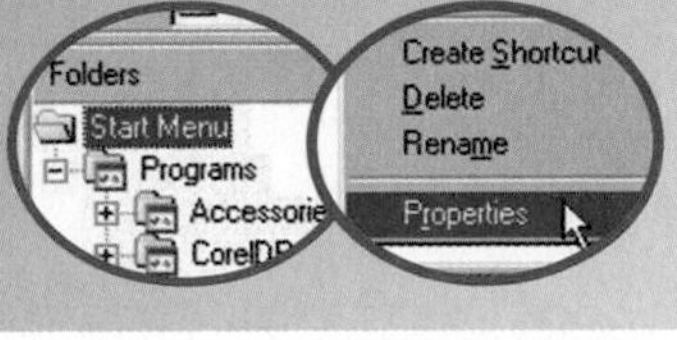

9 Now restart your PC. As soon as Windows has finished loading, the Calculator program will start up automatically.

When Windows crashes

Windows is a vast program. It has a heavy, constant workload, ensuring that different programs and hardware all work together. Sometimes, however, things go wrong.

It is a fact of computer life that all computers go wrong at some point. Most of the time they reliably carry out the instructions contained in programs – such as Word and CorelDRAW – but sometimes a small problem in a program causes the computer to stop working. A hardware fault can also have the same effect.

This type of crash usually affects just the program you are currently using, but it can also affect other programs. In the worst case, Windows itself might stop working properly.

Despite their serious nature, these crashes are rarely disastrous. A basic knowledge of what causes them, and what to do if they occur, will help you to survive most crashes.

● What causes crashes?

If your computer does crash, any one of several factors may be to blame: some program files might have become damaged ('corrupted' in computer jargon); new hardware might not be set up properly; or – much more rarely – a badly written program might behave in a way that accidentally affects other programs and/or Windows itself.

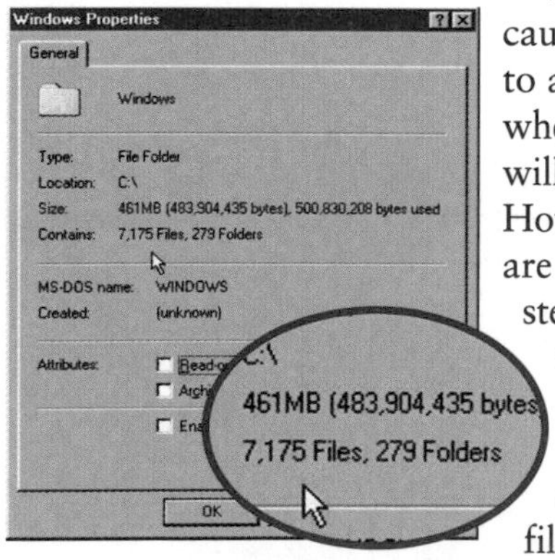

Windows is a very complicated system composed of thousands of files. Crashes can be caused by a small part of a file being damaged.

Whatever the cause, it's hard to anticipate when a crash will occur. However, there are some handy steps you can take to help minimize the chances of program file corruption. These are covered in What to do to avoid Windows crashes, opposite.

Crashes are frightening, but just restarting the program or Windows usually works.

There are several types of crash, varying in severity, the actions Windows takes if they arise and the options open to you. We'll cover them in order of severity.

● Program crashes

First, there are the crashes that involve only one program. If Windows detects that a program is misbehaving, it will tell you that it has no option other than to shut it down. Follow Windows' instructions – it's usually a simple matter of pressing the Close button. Unfortunately, you will lose any unsaved information in the documents that you were working on.

You might find that one program appears to lock up, even though Windows does not detect it. If so, you can shut down an unresponsive program yourself (see page 12 for information on how to do this). In all

WHAT IT MEANS

CRASH

If your computer or a program stops working when you haven't shut it down, it is said to have crashed. Crashes often cause problems: you might lose unsaved work, documents might become damaged or Windows itself might be affected.

With certain types of crash, your mouse pointer completely freezes, so the mouse movements have no effect on the pointer.

cases where a program crashes, it is best to restart Windows as soon as possible. This fresh start helps to flush out parts of Windows that have become temporarily corrupted in the computer's memory.

● Windows crashes

It's important to see if a single program has crashed, or if Windows itself has problems. If your computer locks up, try to switch to another program. Try clicking on other windows on your screen, or press the [Alt] and [Tab] keys together to switch away from the frozen program. If you can successfully switch to windows that work normally, you have a frozen program and you can follow the advice overleaf.

If, however, you cannot switch to other windows, it is likely that Windows itself has crashed. You might also find that the mouse doesn't work: clicking on buttons or menu options might have no effect, or the mouse pointer might also be completely frozen. In this case you will have to shut down and restart the computer.

A few crashes – fortunately much rarer – will leave you with a completely black screen, often with just a small flashing line in the top left corner. Once again, your only option is to restart your computer.

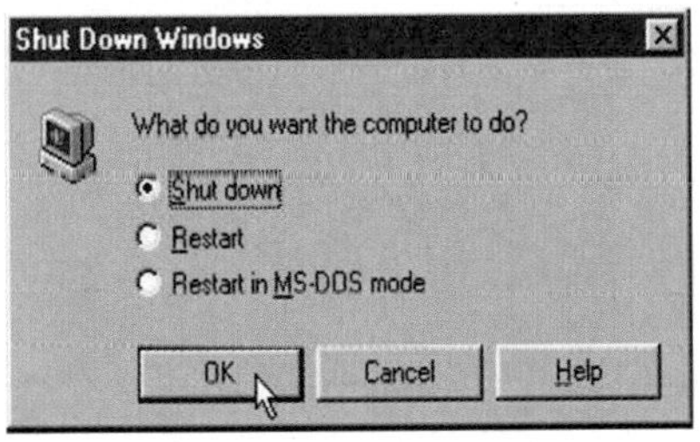

To minimize the chances of accidentally damaging computer files, shut down the computer properly.

● Forcing a restart

The trickiest part is shutting down your computer when you cannot get to the shut down option on the Start button. This often occurs with serious Windows crashes.

In this case (and only in this case), you should press [Ctrl]+[Alt]+[Del]. This special keyboard shortcut is used to restart the computer. You might have to wait a while before the computer restarts and you might even have to press the shortcut twice. If this fails, there is no option other than switching the computer off and then back on. This is the only time that you can ignore the proper shut down procedure (left).

In a very small number of cases, the crash will even restart the computer without giving you any warning or prompting from Windows. The only option here is to wait for Windows to return.

When the computer restarts, it will run through some routine checks. After certain types of crash your computer might suggest running the ScanDisk tool (see Stage 3, pages 8-9). This checks the computer's hard disk for errors, indicating damaged files which could stop Windows and its programs working. If your computer doesn't run this check automatically, it's a good idea to do it yourself as soon as possible after a crash.

When this screen appears, do NOT switch off your PC. Windows is busy saving files to the hard disk.

Only when you see this screen is it OK to switch off your PC. On some newer computers, Windows switches the computer off at this stage.

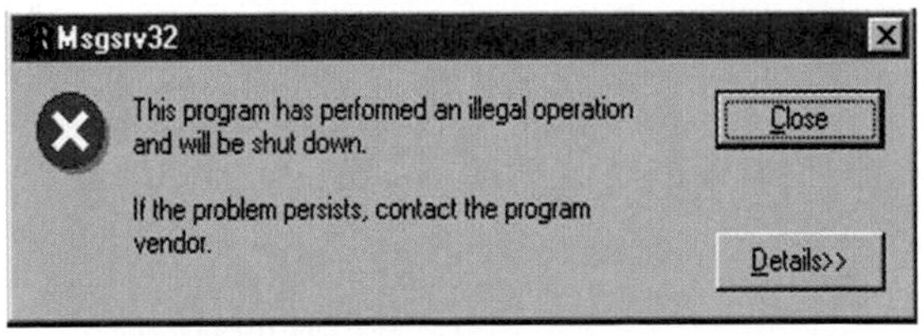

Windows will sometimes shut down a program it suspects is about to cause damage. The program could be an application such as Word or Excel, or part of Windows itself, as shown here.

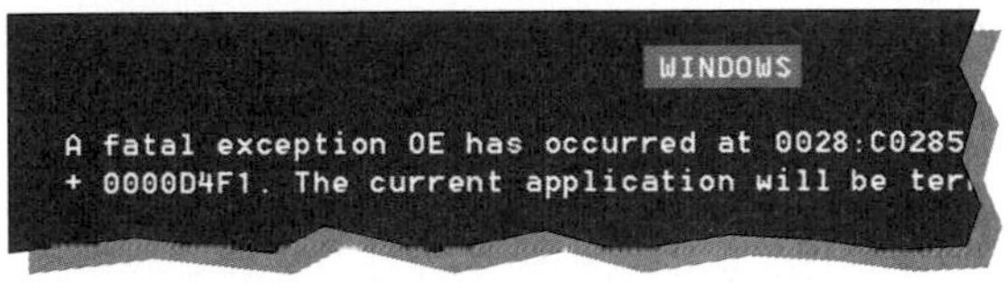

Sometimes the crash can be so severe that the Windows screen disappears altogether. This text-only blue screen reports a problem in one part of the Windows system; once again, Windows must shut down the offending program.

CHECKPOINT ✔

WHAT TO DO TO AVOID WINDOWS CRASHES

You can minimize the risk of your computer crashing by following a few simple guidelines:

✔ Only quit programs by clicking the Close button or by selecting Exit from the File menu.
✔ Always shut down Windows properly and wait until it is safe before turning off the computer (left).
✔ Never move or delete files or folders in the Windows folder; these are the heart of the Windows operating system and your computer can go seriously wrong if you alter them.
✔ If crashes seem to affect a particular program, contact its manufacturer's technical support department.
✔ If a program is slowing down or the hard disk is particularly busy, give the system a chance to catch up with itself. Trying to hurry it will increase the risk of a crash.

If a program stops responding

TELLING WHETHER a program has crashed is actually more difficult than you might think. Some programs appear to be dead and unresponsive, when in fact they are just busy processing a lot of information.

This is particularly the case when you ask a program to perform complex operations on large files. It will need time to work through the task. The program can appear to be frozen when it's actually busy on your behalf.

You can get Windows to close programs that are busy but it's bad practice. If you force them to close, you might cause a real crash or even corrupt files on the hard disk. If you suspect that a program has crashed because it has frozen, you should look for a few tell-tale signs. Many programs use a status line at the bottom of the screen to show progress when performing long operations. Look for these: if you can see the indicator changing, it's unlikely that the program has crashed.

● Problem files

If a program always crashes when you are working on a particular document, the problem probably lies with the document rather than the program.

Some programs are particular about the structure of documents and tend to freeze if they don't see the information they expect when opening documents. Try to re-save the document with a new file name or file type.

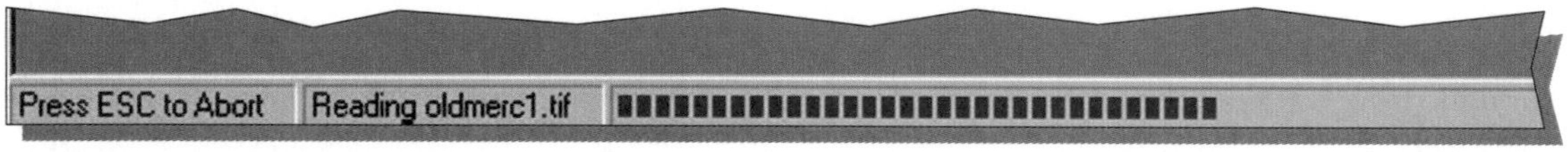

If a program fails to respond to your mouse clicks, it's possible that the program is merely busy on your last command. Check that the progress indicators show activity. The program shown above is opening a very large graphics file; blue rectangles are added as the file is opened.

CLOSING A FROZEN PROGRAM

For situations where a particular program seems to have stopped responding, Windows provides a way to stop the program and remove it from the computer's memory.

Start by pressing the [Ctrl]+[Alt]+[Del] keys together. This is the same keyboard shortcut to use when it is necessary to restart the computer after Windows itself has crashed (see page 11). When Windows hasn't crashed, this shortcut pops up the Close Program dialog box (right).

There are two main options available to you. Pressing the Shut Down button will close Windows altogether, and is equivalent to selecting the Shut down option from the Start menu. Here we use the End Task button to close the frozen program.

The Close Program dialog box has a list of programs that are currently running. This list will vary from computer to computer, depending on the options installed and the software that's running. It will almost certainly include several programs that you might never have heard of; don't worry, these are programs that Windows uses to perform important tasks behind the scenes. They are listed towards the bottom of the list.

In our example, the Windows Calculator program appears to have frozen. Next to the Calculator item in the list is a phrase that Windows has added: 'Not responding'. This shows that Windows has tried to check that the Calculator program is still working properly and has received no reply. Select the frozen program by clicking on it to highlight it, then press the End Task button.

Windows will now try to force the program to close. Sometimes you will instantly see the program disappear from the screen at the same time as the Close Program dialog box closes. At other times the program proves harder for Windows to close and you might see another dialog box, which asks you to confirm your decision.

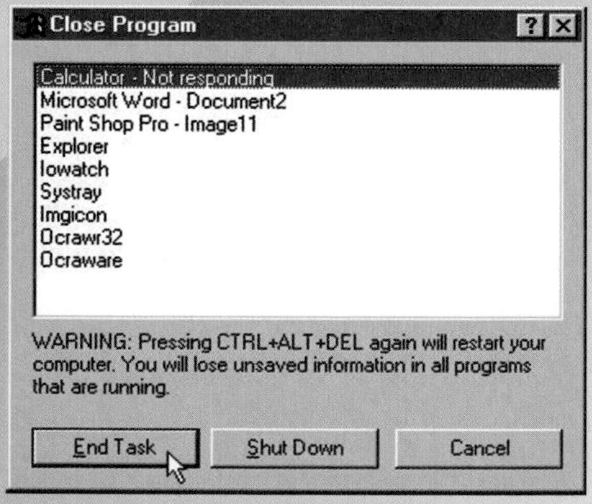

If you press the [Ctrl]+[Alt]+[Del] shortcut when the screen above is showing, you will restart your computer. However, unsaved work in open programs will be lost. For example, changes to Word Document2 and Paint Shop Pro Image11 will be lost.

PC TIPS

Because you can never predict a crash, you should act on the basis that one might occur at any time. It's therefore vital to make sure that you save your files frequently.

Many programs, such as Word and Excel, will save your work automatically every five minutes. However, you should get into the habit of saving files manually to cover programs that don't save automatically.

Files can become damaged during a crash, so you should always back them up – especially the very important ones.

Solving persistent crashes

Sometimes a particular program keeps crashing. In this instance a possible solution might be a full reinstallation of the program.

IRREGULAR AND unconnected crashes are nothing to worry about – as long as your computer restarts without problems and ScanDisk doesn't report any disk errors. However, if your computer suffers persistent and frequent crashes, you need to take action as soon as possible. If the crashes concern several programs or Windows itself (and you have followed the advice below), seek expert help. If you have a persistent problem with one particular program, your first course of action should be to reinstall it. Here we show you a step-by-step guide to removing Windows programs.

1 Click on the Start button and select the Settings folder from the pop-up menu, then choose Control Panel from the list of options.

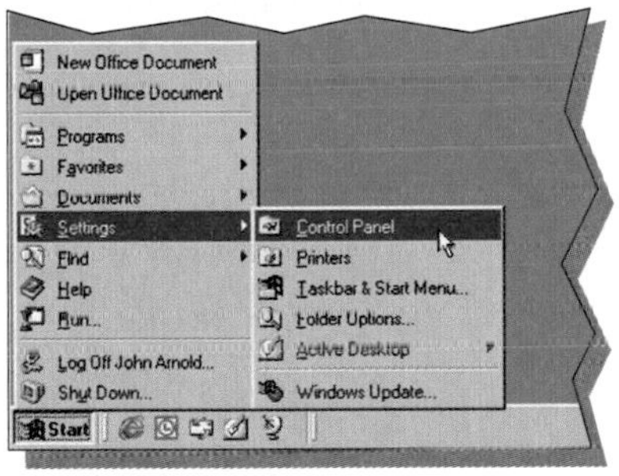

2 When the Control Panel window opens, find the Add/Remove Programs icon and double-click on it.

3 You will see the Add/Remove Programs Properties dialog box. Select the Install/Uninstall tab at the top of the dialog box and you will see a list of software that has been installed on your computer. Locate the program that is persistently crashing. We've demonstrated this exercise with Sound Blaster Live! Value. Click on the program name and click on the Add/Remove button.

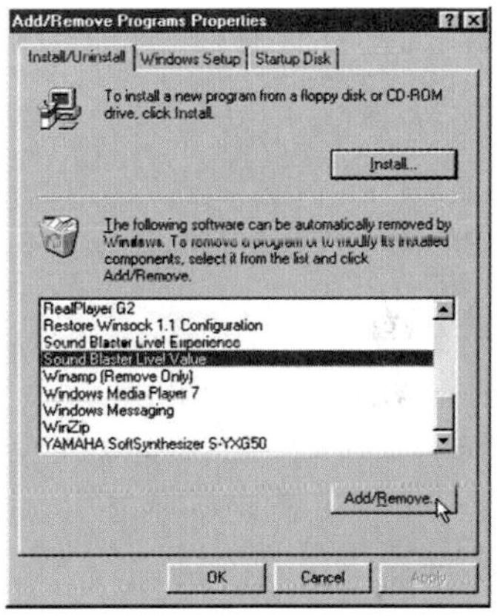

4 Depending on the software, you will now see a dialog box that asks you to confirm that you want to continue the deinstallation. Click on Yes.

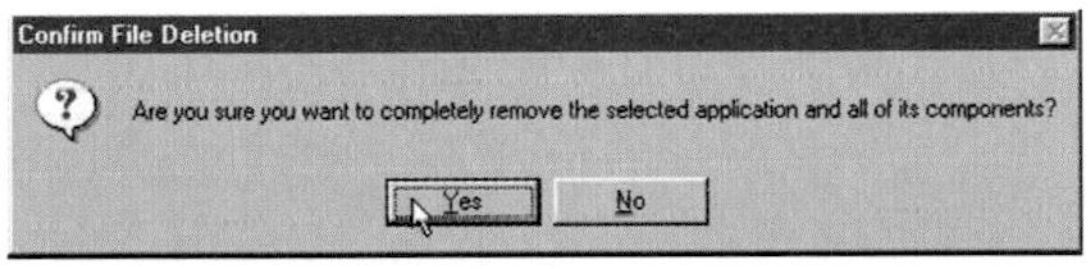

Confirm File Deletion
Are you sure you want to completely remove the selected application and all of its components?
Yes
No

5 The removal process is usually quite quick and will be accompanied by a message or status bar to show progress.

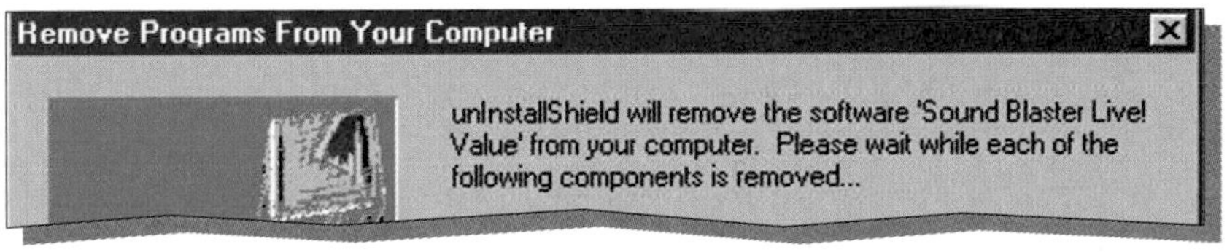

Remove Programs From Your Computer
unInstallShield will remove the software 'Sound Blaster Live! Value' from your computer. Please wait while each of the following components is removed...

IF ALL ELSE FAILS

Computers that frequently crash or fail to restart properly almost certainly have major problems. Even if you find that you can work most of the time without trouble, ignoring the crashes inevitably risks bigger problems. In such cases, you need an expert to help out, as you might need to reinstall Windows.

Starting with a fresh Windows installation solves problems that have built up over time. This is because each new program or piece of hardware that you add to your computer also adds more files to Windows. Over a period of time, Windows can lose track of important files.

The process of reinstallation is complicated, however, so make sure you get the help of a knowledgeable person. (A computer dealer will charge for this help.)

6 Now reinstall the program from your original floppy disks or CD-ROM. Follow the same steps as you did originally. For instance, most installation programs run automatically when you insert their CD-ROM into your computer. Remember to reinstate any customized settings you had.

7 Once the software has been reinstalled, restart your computer (the installation program might do this automatically). Then check the program thoroughly: try to make the old problems appear. If the problem hasn't gone away, it's likely that you will need to get expert help (see If all else fails, left).

Using the Active Desktop

One of the main features of Windows is the Active Desktop. But are you getting the most out of it? Here we look at the advanced features that make your PC and the Internet interact closer than ever before.

One aspect of the Windows Active Desktop is the ability to add your favourite Web pages to your Desktop. You can also add items from Microsoft Active Desktop gallery.

While Windows 98 represented a subtle shift in the modern computer interface over its predecessor, Windows 95, the Active Desktop was a radical step forward. This was partly in terms of look and feel, but much more significantly in terms of what can only be called interface philosophy. Instead of treating the PC as a self-sufficient, stand-alone machine, it embraces the ethos of the Web – that all systems, regardless of type, can be seen as nodes on a massive network, each one sending and receiving information, and playing its own part as a small cog in a vast, information-rich wheel.

● Shifting emphasis

It's important to understand this shift in emphasis in order to get the most out of the Active Desktop. Put simply, it takes your choice of content from the Web and puts it on your Desktop – or rather embeds it within your Desktop. All that blank space, which hitherto was only fit for cluttering up with files and shortcuts, can become a living, breathing maelstrom of information and your chosen Multimedia content.

Instead of attractive (but passive) wallpaper, you can specify a Web page as your background: your customized Excite or Yahoo! page, perhaps, or one of the many excellent news sites, such as CNN. You can subscribe to such a page, which means that your system can retrieve updates as and when you connect to the Web. These pages aren't accessed by a browser in the usual way; they are embedded within their own windows that are actually a part of the Desktop.

● Computer active

The Active Desktop doesn't provide an extra button on your Taskbar, nor do you have your regular browser toolbars. Instead, you navigate the site, or indeed the Web at large, solely via

WINDOWS 95 AND THE ACTIVE DESKTOP

If you are using Windows 95, you can still try out the Active Desktop. By installing Internet Explorer 5 on your PC, you will get most of the Active Desktop features of Windows 98. Go to www.microsoft.com to download Internet Explorer from the Microsoft Web site.

links within the Web pages themselves – another example of how closely your browser is now integrated within your operating system. You can also access the Web by typing a Web address into the Address box in any folder or via Windows Explorer, rather than its Internet cousin. This allows you to see Web-accessed pages in the directory tree in the left-hand menu. You can copy or move them around your hard disk as with any file.

● Your own choice

Depending on your version of Internet Explorer, you could have many Web pages, each in its own window, plus an active channel (see Accessories or Channels? box, below), mini-screens with regular headline updates, or Java applets (small downloadable programs created with the Java programming language), such as a 3D clock.

You can also schedule your PC to dial into the Web and make all the updates at preset times, for example, first thing in the morning. This ties into your PC's task-scheduling features and is the ideal way of keeping your various programs up to date with a standard dial-up connection. Again, this can profoundly change the way you view your PC, turning it into your first port of call for in-depth information that is updated more often than a daily newspaper.

You can also customize your Desktop settings so that using your computer feels more like browsing the Web: file and folder titles are underlined like hyperlinks and can be opened with a single click. To see a preview of a file in the adjacent folder window, simply pass the mouse over the top.

Incredibly, you can also customize each and every folder, for example by adding a picture background, by editing its own HTML script, which you can access via the folder customization wizard.

This isn't for the faint-hearted, however: there is some complex HTML in there, and while it's very easy to restore the defaults, it certainly pays to be extremely wary.

When your Desktop is set to Web-browsing style (above, left), just passing the mouse over an icon will make it active, so one click will open the folder or start the program. If you have activated channels (above, right), the Channel guide is a good starting point, as it provides a comprehensive guide to all available channels.

PC TIPS

Toggling desktops

You may not want to work with the Active Desktop all the time. It is extremely easy to toggle between the Active Desktop and the 'classic' version by right-clicking on the Desktop and simply turning it off and on. You have a choice of how you work with it, too. Simply customize the settings in the appropriate dialog boxes to suit (see the exercise on page 17).

ACCESSORIES OR CHANNELS?

Microsoft made a significant change to Internet Explorer when it upgraded from version 4 to version 5. Instead of the Channels that Internet Explorer 4 introduced, Microsoft included Web Accessories in version 5. Despite the difference in names, the two systems are broadly similar. Channels are special Web sites created by their authors to work directly with Internet Explorer 4. If you use Internet Explorer 4, you get a Channel bar that lists a basic set of channels and you can add more at any time.

However, Channels didn't take off as well as Microsoft hoped, and so it moved to Web Accessories. These are small, quick-to-download programs designed to work with Internet Explorer. Web authors have created a wide variety of Web Accessories for their sites. For example, The New York Times uses one to provide extra news information, and AltaVista has an interesting Web Accessory that can translate Web pages between five languages.

The channel bar provided with Internet Explorer 4 comes with a selection of channels. To add or replace channels, click on the channel guide at the top of the channel bar to connect to the channels area of Microsoft's Web site, where you can select channels.

Using the Active Desktop means connecting to the Internet more often. The Dial-up Connection dialog box will appear in between clicking on a channel on the Active Desktop and actually logging on to the current site to fetch the information. This makes the Active Desktop a little cumbersome.

Adding a Web page to your Desktop

There are different ways of accessing the numerous Active Desktop settings, of which the following is just one. And remember, there is no correct setup – you can customize as much, or as little, as you want. Here we show you how to make a web page appear as part of the Windows Desktop.

1 Right-click anywhere on your Desktop. Select Active Desktop and then Customize my Desktop.

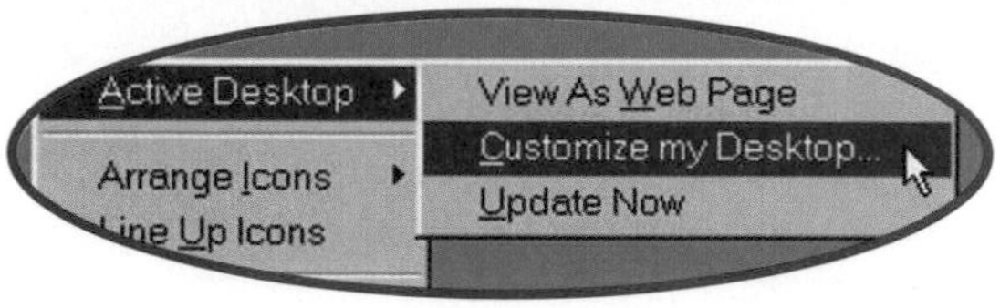

PC TIPS

By default, Windows will dial up and connect to the Internet at 3am to update the page you have subscribed to. To alter the setting, click the Customize Subscription button in the dialog box, as in Step 4, and use the Subscription Wizard.

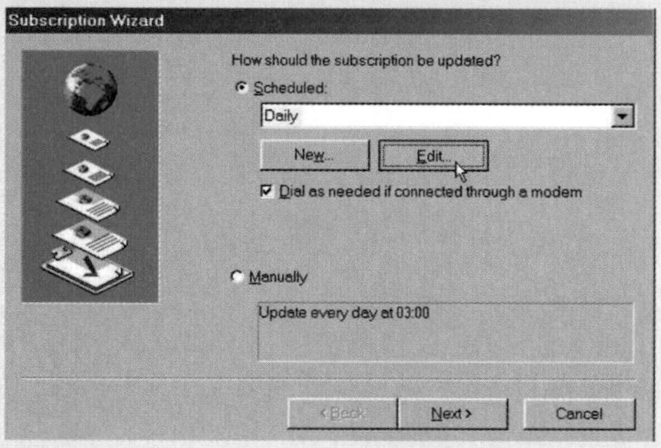

2 In the Display Properties dialog box, click the Web tab and select the View my Active Desktop as a web page option. Click the New button. In the dialog box that pops up, click No.

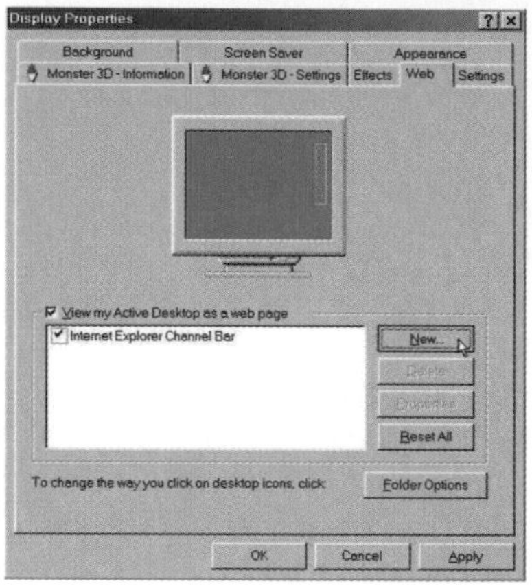

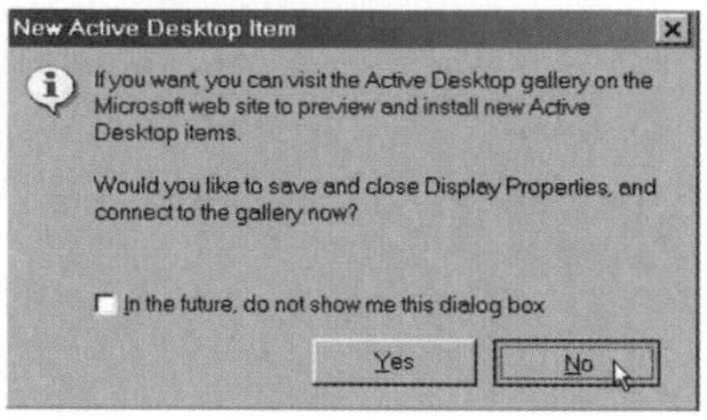

3 Various Web sites offer Active Desktop content. CNN is particularly good: type in its web address – http://www.cnn.com – and click OK.

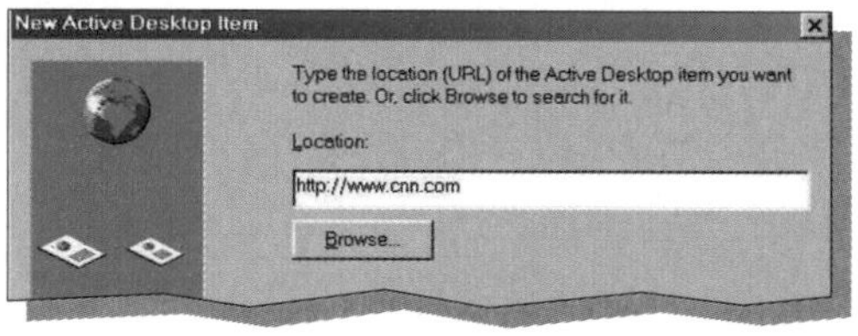

4 Click the OK button in the dialog box that appears.

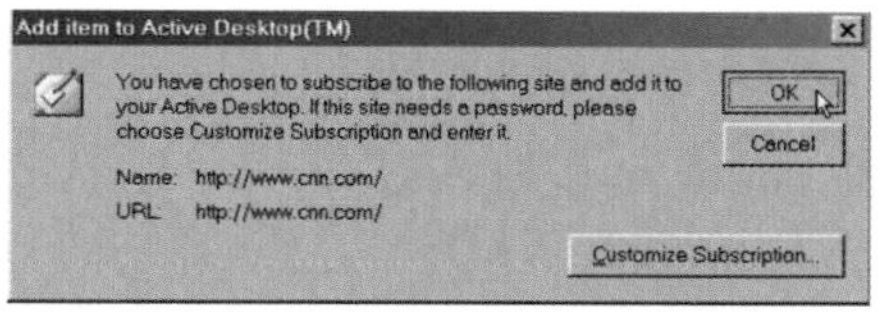

5 Windows will use your modem to connect to the Internet, download the subscribed pages and then automatically log off.

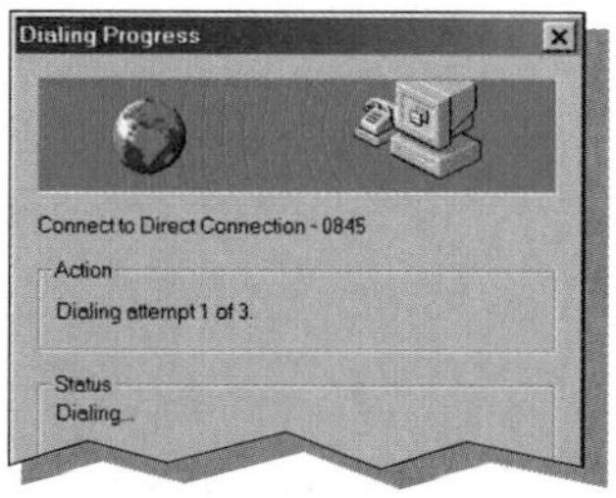

6 Now customize the folder settings: click the Folder Options button in the Display Properties dialog box, and click on the Yes button to switch to the appropriate window.

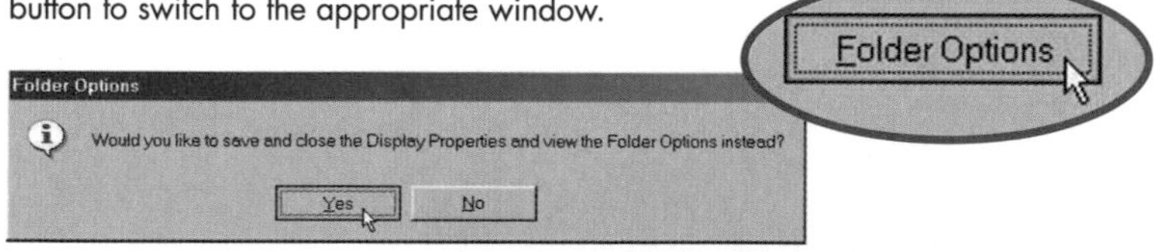

7 Your Active Desktop will appear in the background and the Folder Options dialog box will also appear. The Custom option will already be checked. Select the Web style option instead and press the OK button.

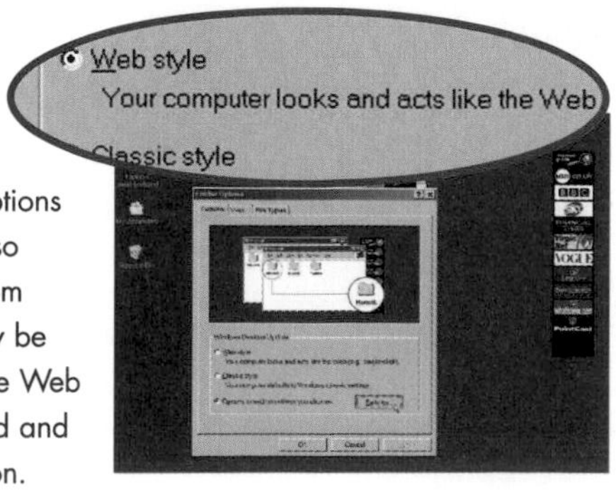

8 The Active Desktop now appears, with a CNN Web page window. Note: there's no browser, so navigate the Web site by clicking the page's hyperlinks.

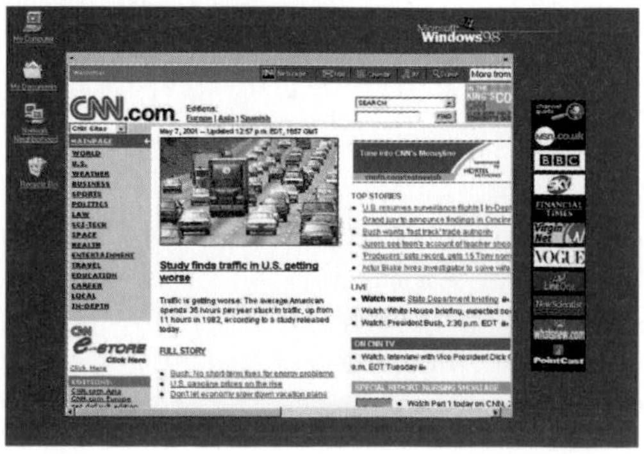

Adjusting Active Desktop items

You can fine-tune Active Desktop items to make them work better on a home computer that only connects to the Web via a telephone line.

1 For this exercise, we'll download some Active Desktop material from Microsoft's online gallery. Right-click on the Desktop and select Active Desktop from the pop-up menu. Then click the Customize my Desktop command.

2 On the Web tab of the Display Properties dialog box, click the New button. When asked if you want to connect to the Active Desktop gallery on the Microsoft Web site, click the Yes button.

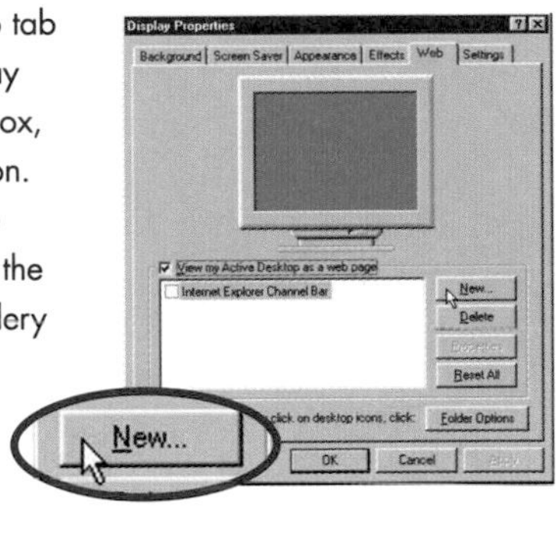

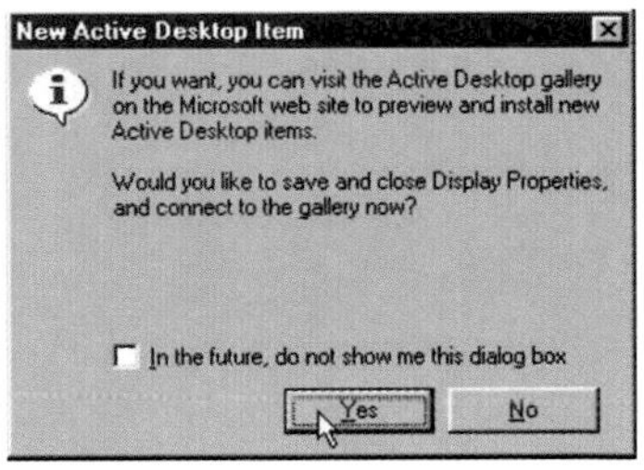

3 Your PC will connect to the Internet, start Internet Explorer and load the relevant page from the Microsoft site. Click on cool utilities on the left to see what Active Desktop items are available. Click on an item. We've chosen Comic Clock. A sample preview appears.

4 Click the Add to Active Desktop link and then the Yes button when Windows asks you to confirm.

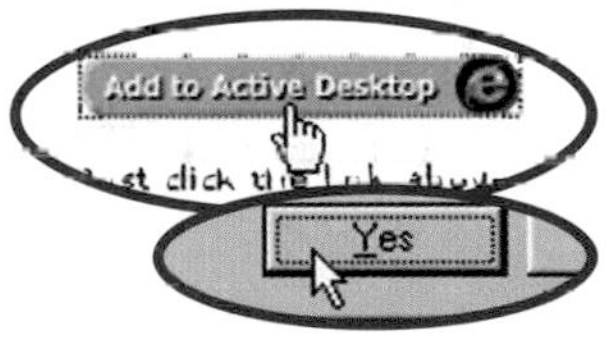

5 Click OK when the Add item to Active Desktop(TM) dialog box appears and the Comic Clock will download.

6 You can now disconnect from the Internet and your Comic Clock will appear on your Desktop. To fine-tune the way the Comic Clock works, move the mouse over the top of its window until you see a small grey bar appear at the top. Click the small down-pointing arrow and select Properties from the menu.

7 Click the Download tab of the Properties dialog box that appears. This lets you control the way that this Active Desktop item updates via the Internet. It's always worth checking these settings, as many are only appropriate for situations where you are online almost permanently, or where you have a very high speed connection.

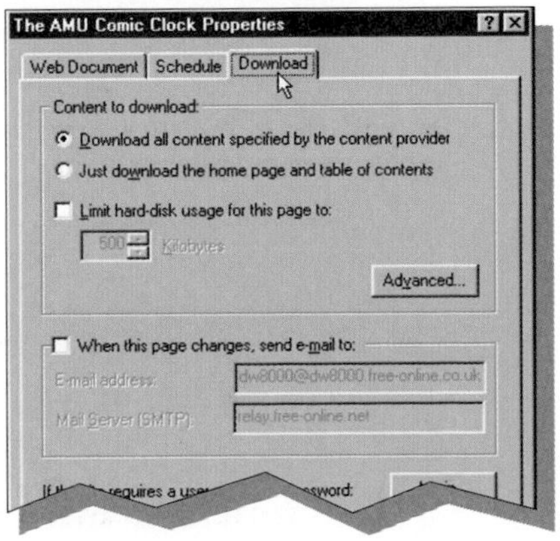

8 As an example, click the Advanced button and use the dialog box that appears to make sure that the sound and video option is not ticked. By experimenting with these settings for each Active Desktop item, you can get the right balance between full Multimedia content and your Internet connection costs.

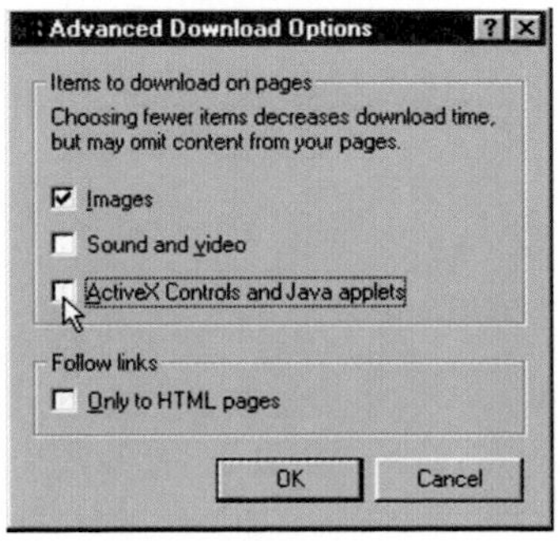

Dial-up networking

Windows' dial-up networking provides a quick and easy method of connecting to the Internet that works with any software.

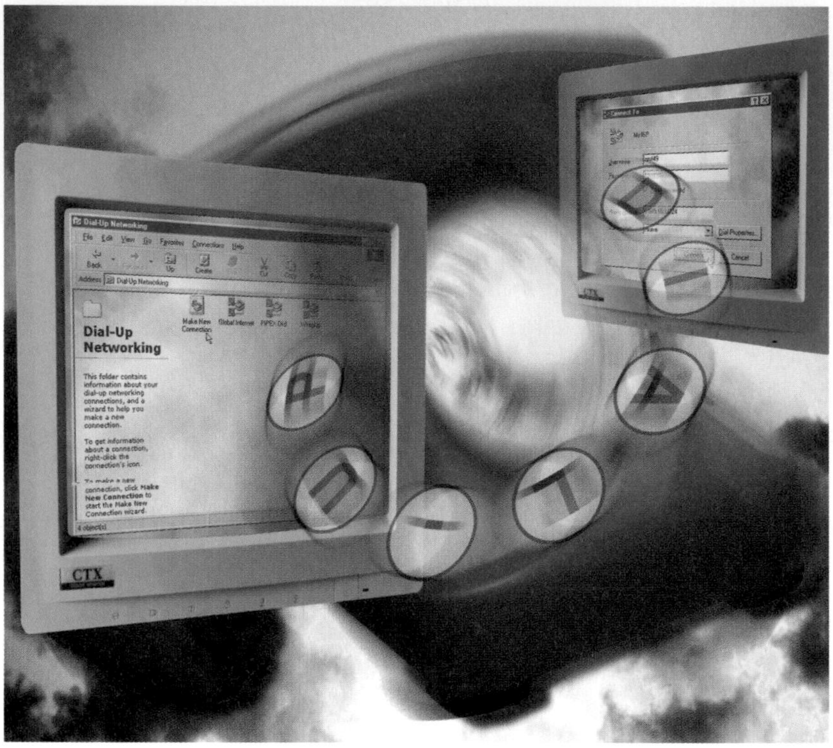

Dial-up networking is a generic alternative to ISP software for connecting to another PC or the Internet over the telephone line.

Dial-up networking is one of the most useful components of Windows. It allows anyone with a modem to gain access to shared information on another computer. You can use dial-up networking to connect to any computer as long as the computer you are dialling is set up to receive incoming calls. The Internet is the classic example of a network you access by dialling, via an Internet service provider. In fact, the primary use for the dial-up networking tool – as far as home users are concerned – is providing a quick and easy connection to the Internet.

● Linking to the Internet

When you first open an account with an Internet service provider (ISP), you'll be provided with all the information you need to connect to the Internet. Often, particularly with content-driven ISPs, such as CompuServe and AOL, you will also be given some specific software that connects you to the Internet and allows you to use email and the Web.

If you try to use a program that includes its own Internet software, however, you may experience problems. If the program cannot recognize your existing ISP connection, and it needs to be connected to the Internet in order to work, you will be unable to use the program. This applies particularly to games and some other programs that have their own connection methods.

● Easier access

Dial-up networking solves the problem by giving you a means to access the Internet that will be understood by any and all software. By entering just a few details – most importantly the telephone number to be dialled by the modem – you create an Internet connection that can be used at any time by simply double-clicking on its shortcut. You can even tell the software to remember your user name and password so that you don't have to type it in every time (or you can choose not to do this – it depends how security-conscious you are).

Because of the universal nature of dial-up networking, most ISPs now recommend it as the best way to connect to the Internet, and all provide details of how to set it up for their service. Also, because dial-up networking is part of Windows, programs that need to connect to the Internet can access the dial-up connection and start it automatically.

Dial-up networking is particularly useful for games and other programs that need to be connected to the Internet in order to work. It enables them to bypass any ISP software and go directly to the modem.

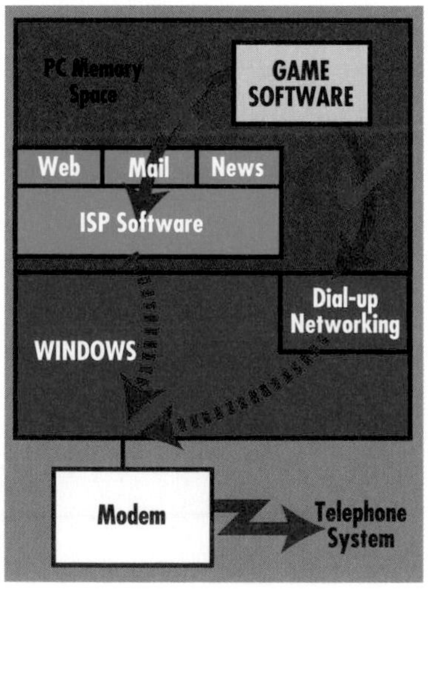

TWO WAYS TO CONNECT

With some ISPs, such as CompuServe or AOL, a dial-up networking connection is installed with their proprietary software when you set up your account. Although connecting to the Internet via these ISPs is normally achieved through this software, you can also connect by double-clicking on the relevant connection icon in the Dial-Up Networking folder.

Set up a dial-up networking connection

Here we show you how to establish a dial-up networking connection to an Internet service provider's computer. When completed, you'll have an automatic shortcut connection to the Internet.

1 Double-click on the My Computer icon on the Desktop, and then double-click on the Dial-Up Networking folder. If the folder is not present, you will need to install it (see Install the software box, below).

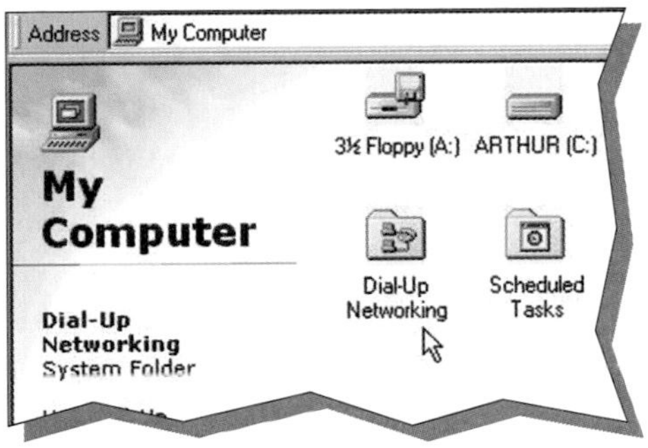

2 If you already have dial-up connections established on your computer, you will see them listed here. To create a new connection, double-click on the Make New Connection icon. This will start the dial-up connection wizard.

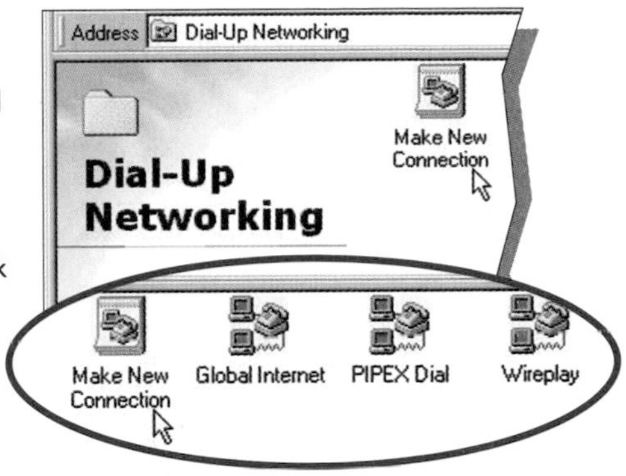

3 On the first page of the wizard, type a name for your connection (such as the name of your ISP) and make sure your modem is selected. To be able to choose it from the list, the modem must already have been installed. When you've chosen, click the Next button to continue.

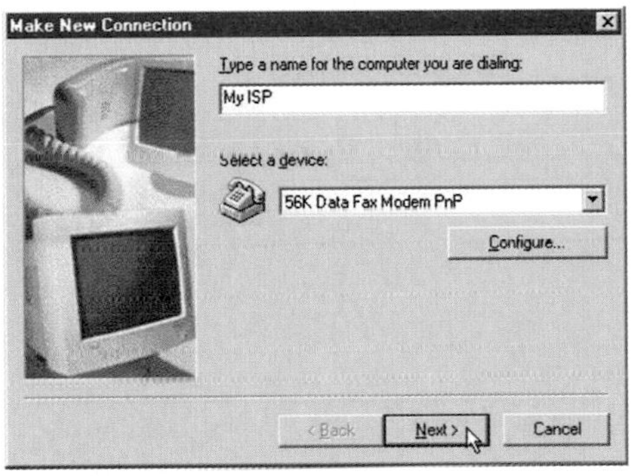

4 Now type in the telephone number your modem needs to phone in order to connect to your ISP. If you do not know this number, consult the documentation that came with your ISP subscription. Also make sure to specify the country you are dialling from and then press the Next button.

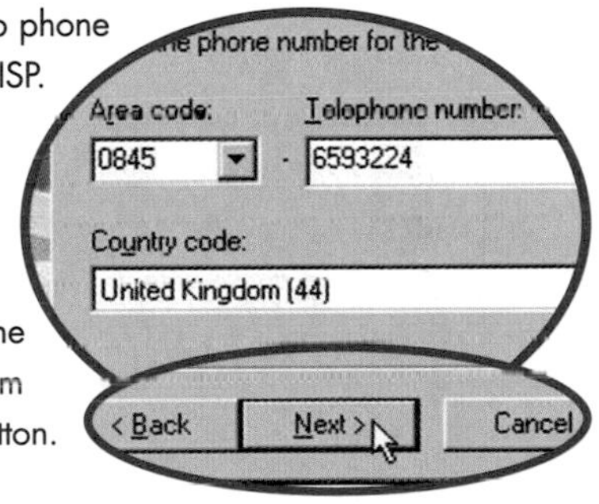

5 The next page confirms the choices you have made, and on clicking the Finish button you will have created a new dial-up networking connection. However, many ISPs will also instruct you to make various changes to the default connection properties. To do so, right-click on the new connection icon in the Dial-Up Networking folder and choose Properties from the pop-up menu.

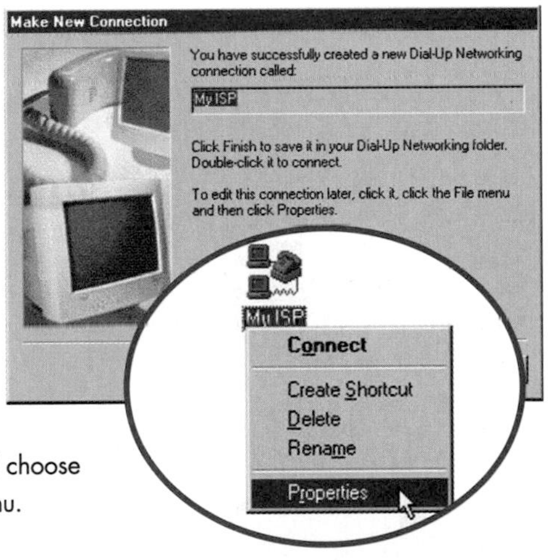

6 Any changes that need to be made will be fully explained by your ISP. The most common alterations occur on the Server Types page, and also on the window accessed via the TCP/IP Settings button. The options on these pages are highly technical, and there is no need to know all about them; just follow your ISP's instructions exactly.

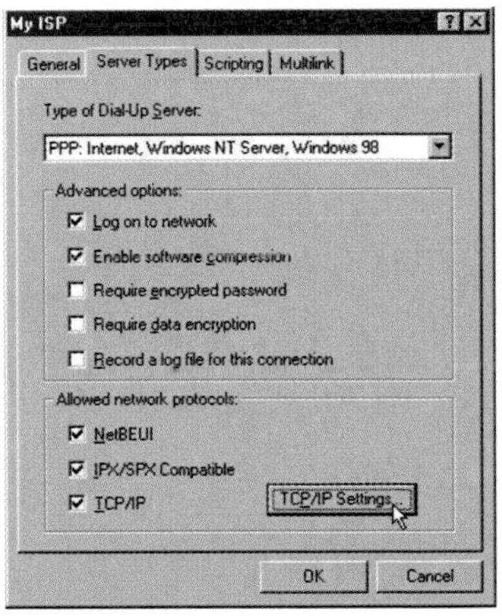

7 When your dial-up networking connection is complete, you can double-click on it to connect. At this point you will need to enter your user name and password.

The main connection icon cannot be moved from the Dial-Up Networking folder, but you can make a shortcut to it by dragging and dropping the connection on to the Desktop.

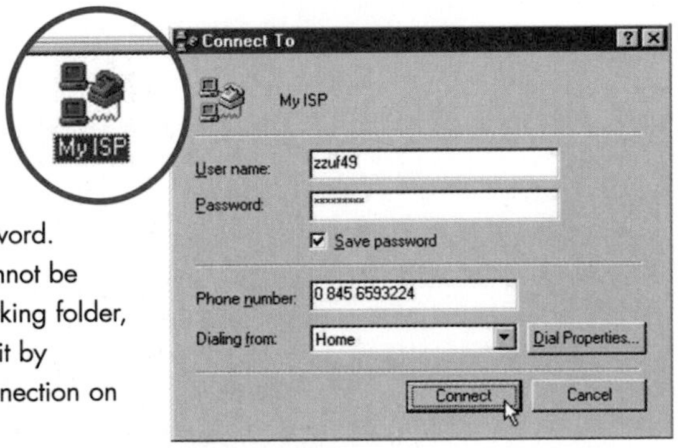

INSTALL THE SOFTWARE

If dial-up networking is not installed on your computer, insert your Windows CD-ROM and wait for it to autostart. When it does, select the Add/Remove Software option, then the Communications category and press the Details button. Put a tick in the Dial-Up Networking check box and then press the OK button on both windows. The software will now be installed.

Introducing Windows Millennium Edition

Is your PC living in the past? Windows Millennium Edition (Me) brings many of the advantages of Windows 2000 to home PC users, as well as providing an easier-to-use operating system.

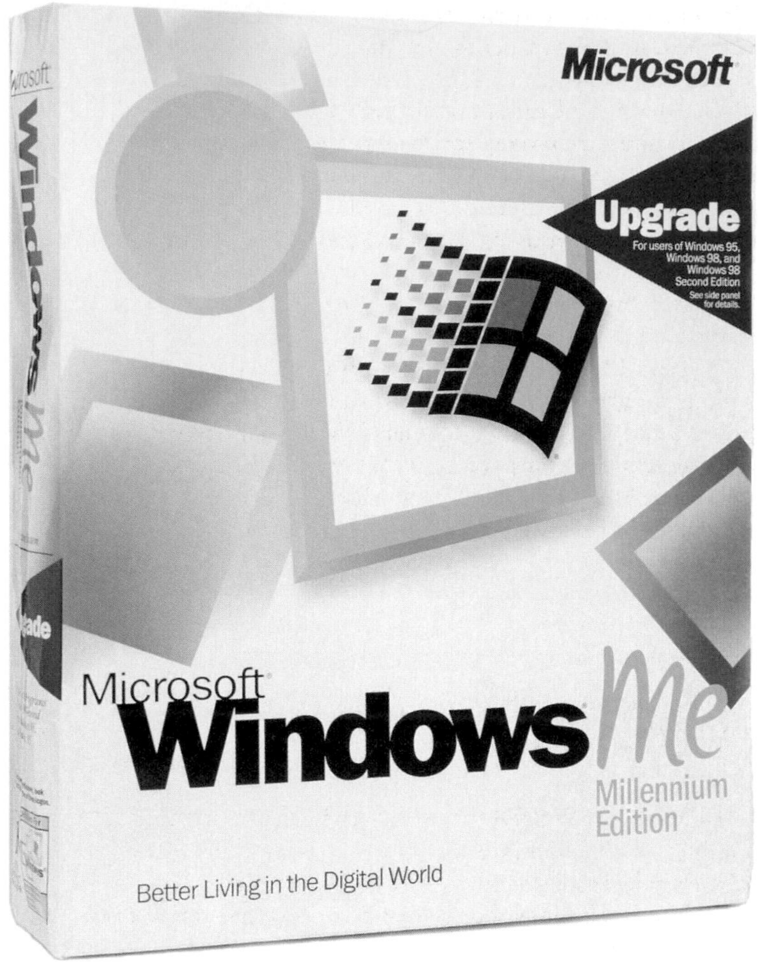

Windows Me looks and works much like Windows 98, but with extra intelligence to make home computing more productive.

While Windows 98 remains the main operating system for many home and small-business users, larger businesses had an early taste of 21st-century computing with Microsoft's Windows 2000. Although Windows 2000 combined increased reliability with new features, there were compatibility problems for many types of hardware add-ons and games for home PCs. Although it was possible to upgrade to Windows 2000, it could be an expensive choice, requiring new hardware in some cases. With Windows Millennium Edition (Me), Microsoft plugged the gap between the two operating systems.

● Windows make-over

Windows Me gives you some of the improvements of Windows 2000 but without the hardware and software headaches. It replaces Windows 98, and if you have bought a PC recently, it probably came with Windows Me installed.

With Windows Me, the Desktop looks different, but this is mostly cosmetic. There's a new set of icons and, although the names and functions are virtually identical, they have an enhanced 3D appearance. There's also a new, deep blue Desktop colour, replacing the dull green of Windows 95 and 98.

● Smarter Windows

Windows Me shares some of Windows 2000's built-in intelligence; it can alter the entries on the Start menu to reflect the programs you use most often, simplifying the Start menu so that it focuses on your favourite programs without your having to rearrange it by hand. If you find this feature confusing, switch it off.

Also, when you first open the Control Panel, it contains seven of the most used Panel icons, including Display, Date/Time and Add/Remove Programs. To see the full set of icons, there's a clickable link on the left of the Control Panel window. Like Windows 2000, there's also a Control Panel icon dedicated to digital cameras and scanners.

WINDOWS ME

Windows Me closely follows the format of Windows 98, at least for the purposes of the average user. Therefore, unless indicated otherwise, all the exercises in *PCs made easy* work on both operating systems, with only minor differences in screen layout.

● New accessories and games

One area where Windows Me does make a leap forward is in PC Multimedia. The most obvious is Windows Media Player 7, a single program that can play CDs, MP3s, music videos and tune into Internet radio. It can also record CDs to the hard disk. As well as playing popular sound files, such as MP3s and Windows sound files (.WAV), it also plays and records a format that Microsoft is trying to popularize on the Internet: Windows Media Audio (WMA) files. These offer similar file sizes and sound quality to MP3s.

If you have a video camera and video capture hardware you can use the new Windows Movie Maker software to edit your videos. However, the sheer amount of data contained in digital video means that you need a fairly powerful PC – typically 400MHz or faster.

Windows Me's Games folder has a total of 11 games. The additions are mostly Internet games, such as Backgammon and Checkers (draughts), which can also be played over a home network if you have two or more PCs. For fans of faster-moving action, there's a 3D pinball game, too. Windows Me comes with the latest versions of Microsoft's Internet Explorer Web browser and Outlook Express email software.

Windows Me also brings some office features to the home PC. For example, many homes have two PCs – one for the kids and one for the parents. The home networking software lets you share a modem so that, as long as one of your home PCs has a modem and Internet connection, all your PCs can surf the Internet at the same time.

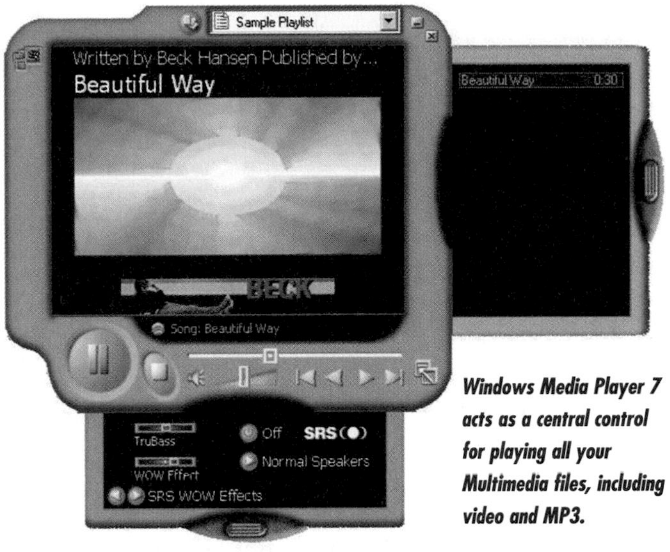

Windows Media Player 7 acts as a central control for playing all your Multimedia files, including video and MP3.

WHATEVER NEXT

Microsoft claims that the next version of Windows for PCs, to be called Windows XP, combines the stability of the Windows 2000 operating system and the wide-ranging software and hardware support of Windows Millennium Edition into a single operating system (OS). Hardware and software developers got plenty of notice by Microsoft, which means that all hardware drivers and other software ought to be fully compatible with all PCs, whether used for home or business.

Under the hood

The more hardware and software you add to your PC, the more unstable it becomes – but Windows Me has a solution.

ALTHOUGH WINDOWS Me is a direct descendant of Windows 98, Microsoft has tried to make it more reliable. It may lack the robust and stable Windows 2000 underpinnings, but it keeps tabs on the vital system files that badly written software might try to overwrite. The aim is to tackle the frustrating problem of a PC gradually becoming less reliable over time.

Often a Windows 95 or 98 PC works fine when the operating system is newly installed, but it gradually becomes less reliable as you install more software or hardware, which you will inevitably do. Ironically, the hardware is often still working perfectly. The problem is that each new program or piece of hardware copies across system files. Sometimes, poor programming means that good system files are overwritten with out-of-date or 'bugged' versions.

To help users manage the new features, Windows Me keeps much better track of its previous states and makes them more accessible. The System Restore tool lets you revert to a specific date. This means that if you notice problems starting to appear after you have installed some software, you can automatically go back to the state before the software was installed.

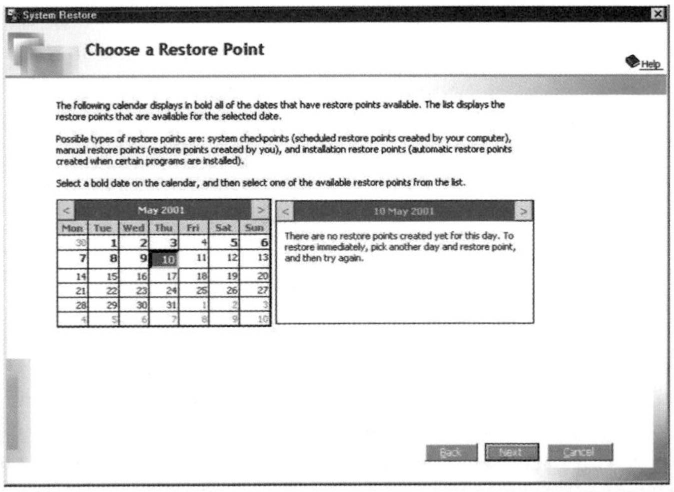

The System Restore tool can help you overcome software problems by choosing a specific date on which your PC was working well and reverting to that state.

Upgrading to Windows Me

Windows Me combines a cosmetic make-over with useful improvements and new features, such as the ability to roll back changes if they don't work, but is it worth spending the money to upgrade your computer?

Although Windows 2000 was the first Windows operating system (OS) for the new millennium, it's a business OS that is not intended for home PC users. Despite the confusingly similar name, Windows Millennium Edition (also known as Windows Me) is the right upgrade for most Windows 98 users.

Unlike Windows 2000, Windows Me is still compatible with all the games software and miscellaneous hardware add-ons that work with Windows 98. It's also much cheaper to upgrade – around £70, instead of £175 for Windows 2000.

● Should you upgrade?

Windows Me is a useful, although not ground-breaking, upgrade to Windows 98. If you're not sure whether it's worth upgrading, refer to pages 20-21 and 25 for a brief outline of what's been added. While there are some new utilities, games and Multimedia programs, other features, such as the home networking software, won't be of any benefit if you only have one PC at home.

By contrast, if you're still working with Windows 95, upgrading to Windows Me is certainly worthwhile. It brings all the advantages of Windows 98, such as more effective use of the hard disk, useful system file-checking utilities and better games support, plus the new Windows Me extras discussed on pages 20-21.

● Before you start

Even before you buy the Windows Me upgrade package, you should check your PC's specifications against the minimum requirements of the new OS (see Hardware needed box, right). Note that the specifications given by Microsoft are the bare minimum requirements. This means that Windows Me will run quite slowly on a PC with such a basic specification. If you do want to upgrade an old Windows 95 PC to Windows Me, this is an important factor to bear in mind. In fact, Windows Me will almost certainly run at a slower rate than Windows 95 on the same PC, so if you have a slow Windows 95 PC, you should upgrade the hardware at the same time. More realistic requirements for Windows Me than those specified are a PC with a processor running at 400MHz or faster, 64MB of RAM and a hard disk of 8GB or more, which will leave plenty of space for programs and documents. Of course, any modern PCs with Pentium III or equivalent chips running at 750MHz or more make perfect Windows Me machines.

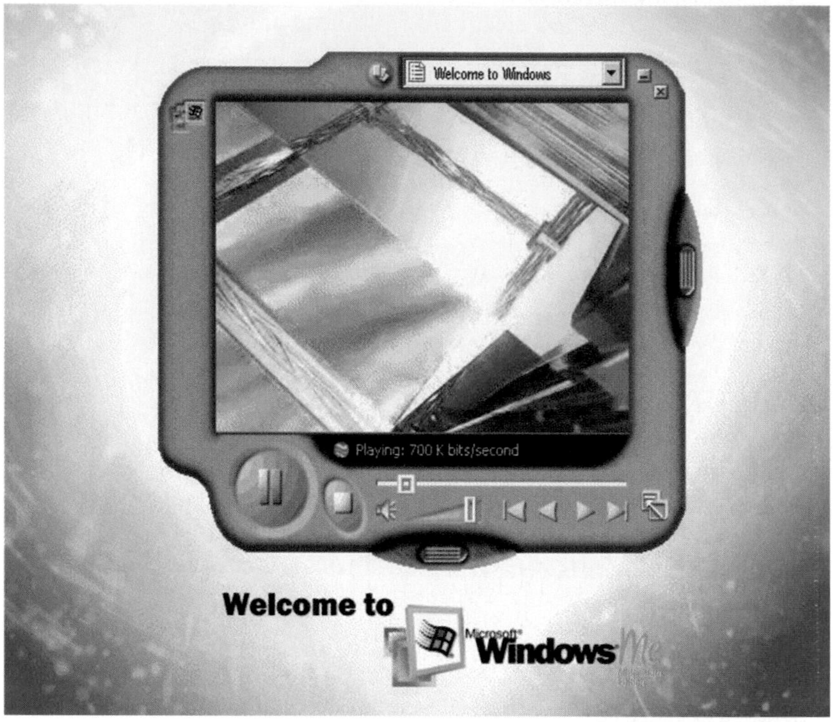

The updated media player is a more capable one as it is able to play many more formats, including sound and video.

● Memory requirements

In recent years, 600+MHz PCs with 64MB or even 128MB of memory have become very affordable. Microsoft creates its new operating systems to exploit the constant increase in PC performance – that's why minimum system

HARDWARE NEEDED

To use Windows Me you need a PC with at least:
- ● A Pentium or equivalent processor with a clock speed of at least 150MHz
- ● 32MB of memory minimum (64MB is preferable)
- ● A hard disk with at least 350MB free space
- ● A CD-ROM or DVD-ROM drive
- ● A VGA or better graphics card and monitor
- ● A keyboard and mouse

requirements always creep up with each new OS. If you want to gauge the likely performance of your PC with Windows Me, try visiting a large computer store and look for a demonstration model with a basic specification which is running Windows Me. This exercise should give you some idea of how your own PC would perform with Windows Me. The upgrade package comes with Windows Me on CD-ROM and a short booklet that covers the upgrading basics.

● Blank floppies and CDs

To be on the safe side, you should also have a readily available blank floppy disk (used to create a new Windows Startup disk) and the CD-ROMs that came with any hardware add-ons. Although the CDs might not be required – Windows Me includes drivers for much more hardware than Windows 95 or 98 – it's better to have them ready to hand rather than scrabbling around to find them during the upgrade process.

A completely fresh installation

Simply upgrading your Windows 95 or 98 PC to Windows Me is the easiest option (see page 24), but starting from scratch with a completely fresh installation also has its advantages.

MICROSOFT HAS TRIED to make the Windows Me installation process as reliable and easy as possible. The process shown on page 24 works perfectly well on most PCs. The big advantage of this approach is that all your programs and hardware will work just as well after the upgrade as before.

However, there is a potential downside for some PCs. For example, a PC that has had many dozens of programs, games and hardware add-ons installed and removed over a year or two tends to have a bloated Windows Registry. This is a system file that's vital to the way Windows works. It gets bigger with each new program or hardware addition, and often the uninstall options don't remove their Registry entries. Over time, the redundant and out-of-date entries slow the PC down and can even lead to crashes.

Many PC experts prefer an alternative upgrade process. A fresh installation of Windows Me – one where absolutely no aspect of the previous Windows 95 or 98 installation, nor any programs, nor any extra hardware remains – means the Registry is brand new. The only way to achieve this is to reformat the hard drive, thereby creating a completely blank disk – no Windows, no programs and no software. Before embarking on this boat-burning exercise, make sure that you have all the disks (floppy or CD) required to reinstall all your software and applications. Also, you should back up all your data files.

Once the hard disk is reformatted, Windows Me can be installed from the CD-ROM. After this, all software programs can be installed from their original CD-ROMs. Any extra hardware that Windows Me didn't recognize on its installation can be installed using their CD-ROMs. Finally, all documents can be copied onto the hard disk from the backups.

This process sounds drastic and it's certainly more labour-intensive, but it results in a more stable and faster PC. The Windows Me Quick Start Guide booklet includes instructions on creating a fresh installation of Windows Me.

If you install a completely fresh version of Windows Me, you will have to reinstall all your software from its CD-ROMs. This can be a very time-consuming process.

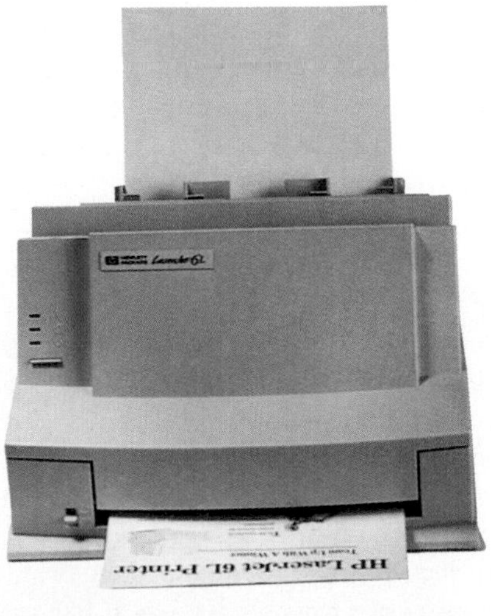

Be prepared for the fact that Windows Me might not immediately recognize all your hardware, such as joysticks, printers and so forth. When this happens, you should reinstall the drivers from the CD-ROMs that were supplied with the hardware.

Installing Windows Me

With few precautions, you can install Windows Me as easily as any other piece of software.

1 Start your computer as usual. Close down any programs that have started up automatically and then back up your documents (see PC Tips box, below). Run a virus detector as an additional precaution.

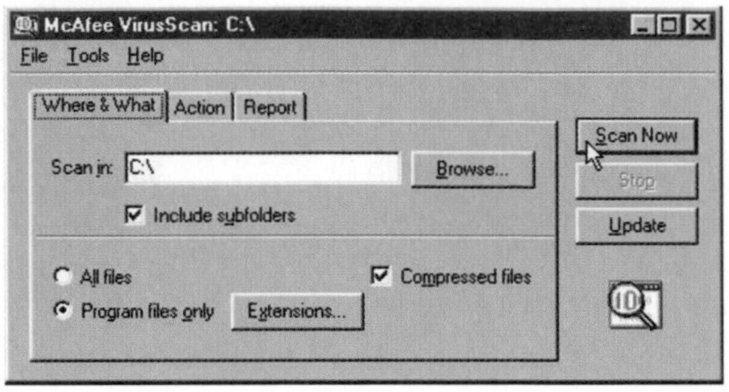

2 Close any programs running in the Taskbar's System Tray. Most can be closed by right-clicking on their icon and selecting Exit or Disable from the menu. If no such option appears, double-click on the icon and look for Exit or Disable in the dialog box that appears. Some programs – such as the Windows Task Scheduler – cannot be closed, but these can be safely ignored.

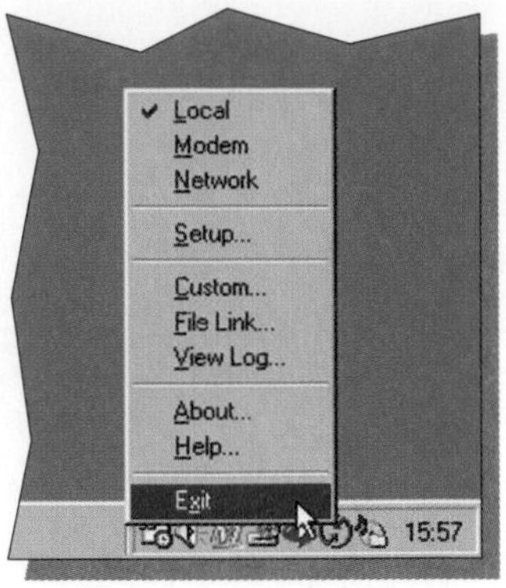

3 Insert the Windows Me CD into your PC's CD-ROM drive. After a few moments and a quick check of the version of Windows you are currently using, Windows asks if you want to upgrade. Click the Yes button.

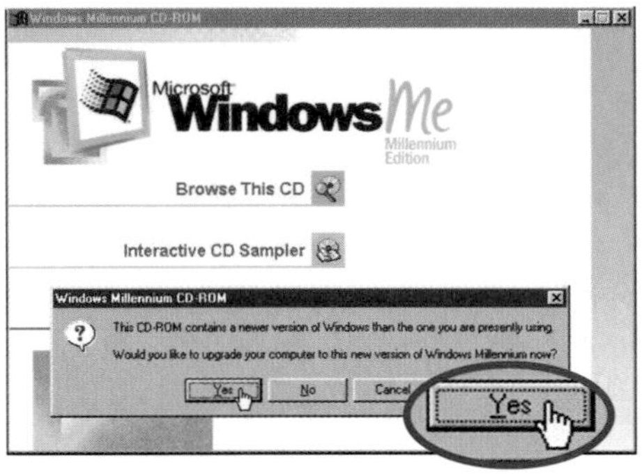

4 Work through the Windows Setup process. After a few opening screens, you will be asked if you want to keep your old Windows system files. Unless you are very tight for hard disk space, select the Yes option. Windows Me then keeps these files on your hard disk, allowing you to revert to your old OS if things go wrong.

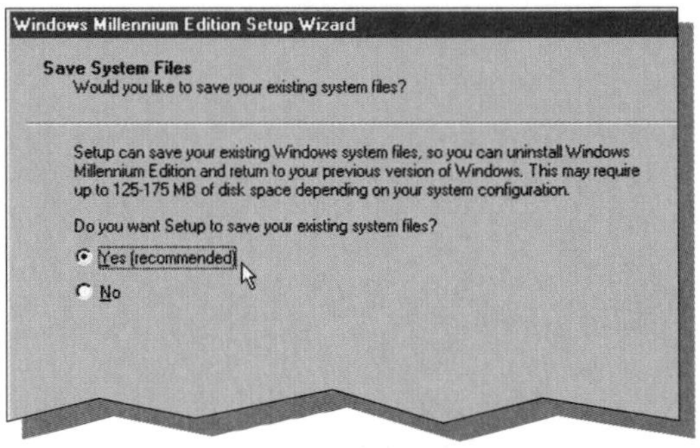

5 Insert the blank floppy disk when the setup program prompts you to create a Windows Startup disk. You should rarely, if ever, need this disk, but it can often get your PC started should it later develop problems.

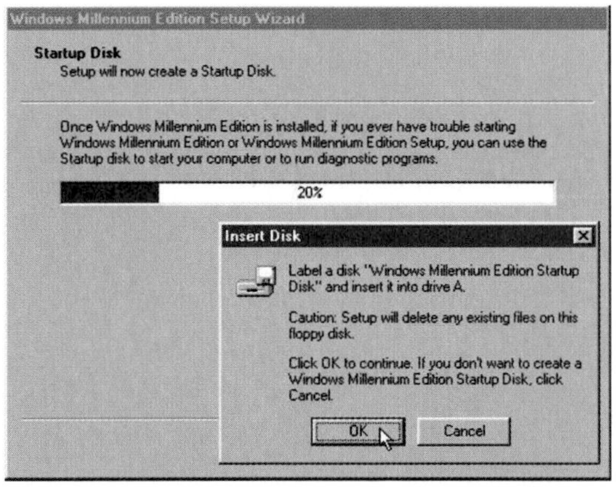

6 The lengthy file copying and upgrade process now takes place. After the first batch of copying, the Setup Wizard will restart the PC automatically, so you can leave the PC unattended. After around half an hour or so, Windows Me starts and checks the hardware. If you are prompted, insert any of your hardware's CDs.

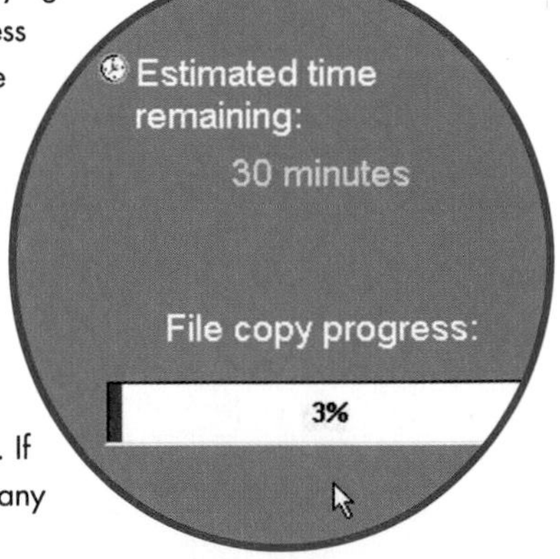

7 When the process is over, Windows Me restarts and automatically loads a Welcome movie with the new multimedia player. Once that's over, check to see that all your hardware works as before. If something doesn't appear to work, install its drivers from the device's CD-ROM.

PC TIPS

Backing up

Although the upgrade process looks easy, installing a new operating system is a risky business. There's always a possibility that the PC won't work properly afterwards. For this reason, you must back up all your important documents before starting. Don't forget to back up other documents that might not be stored in your My Documents folder, such as your Word or Excel templates. In fact, the safest tactic is to back up all your folders as well as My Documents (see Stage 2, pages 24-25).

A quick tour of Windows Me

Once Windows Me is installed and running, spend a little time looking around the system to see what's new and what's changed.

1 When you upgrade a Windows 95 or 98 PC to Windows Me, most of your old settings should remain in place; this includes the dull, green Windows 98 backdrop. To change to the Windows Me settings, open the Display Properties dialog box and select the Windows Standard scheme.

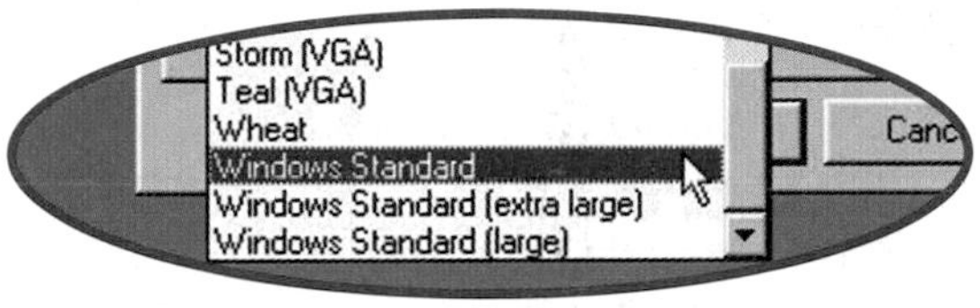

2 You will now see the Windows Me Desktop make-over as it's meant to look (right), with a blue background to complement the redesigned Desktop icons, a selection of which are shown below.

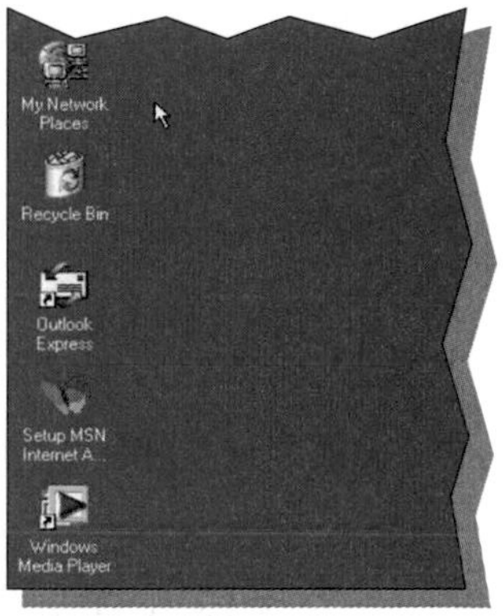

3 Next, open the Control Panel. In this case, our previous Windows 98 setup displayed the icons alone without the Web page view, and Windows Me has inherited this setting. Select Folder Options from the Tools menu.

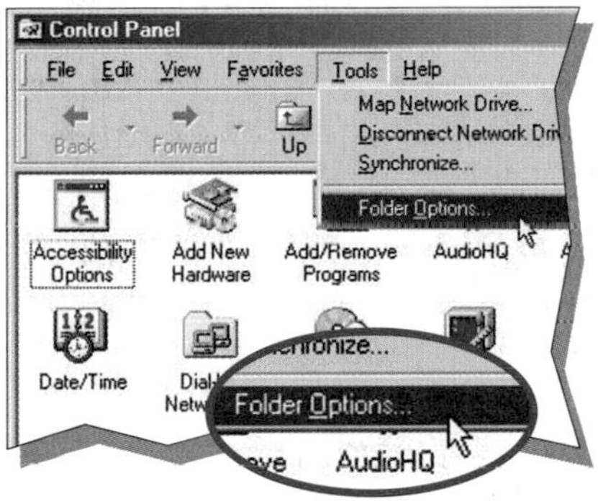

4 Select the Enable Web content in folders option and click the OK button. Now the Control Panel is displayed with only the most commonly used icons showing. The link contained within the information panel on the left lets you view all the icons as and when you want.

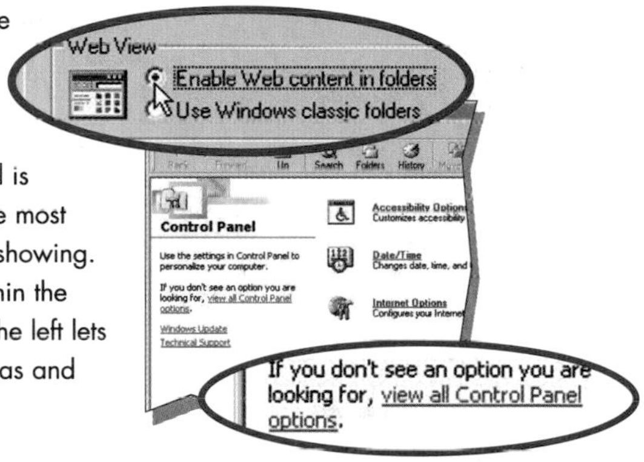

5 Now that Web content in folders is switched on, similar information panels appear in other folders. The My Computer folder includes a link that lets you switch to the My Documents folder with a single click, for example. The aim of these links is to let you switch quickly to the folders you use most often.

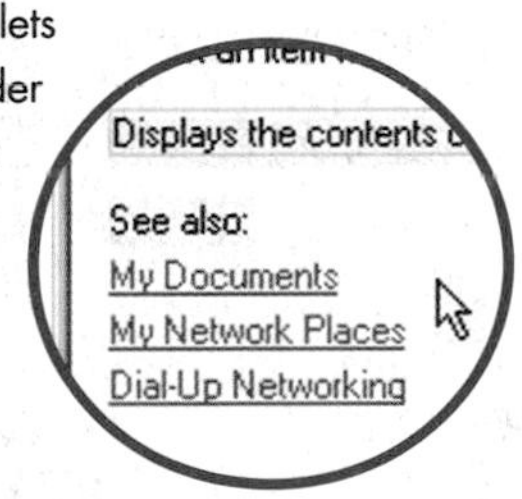

6 Browse through the menus and you'll find new games – including new variations of classic games that you can play across the Internet. There are also some new entries in the Accessories folder, including a Wizard for setting up home networking and the MSN Messenger Service.

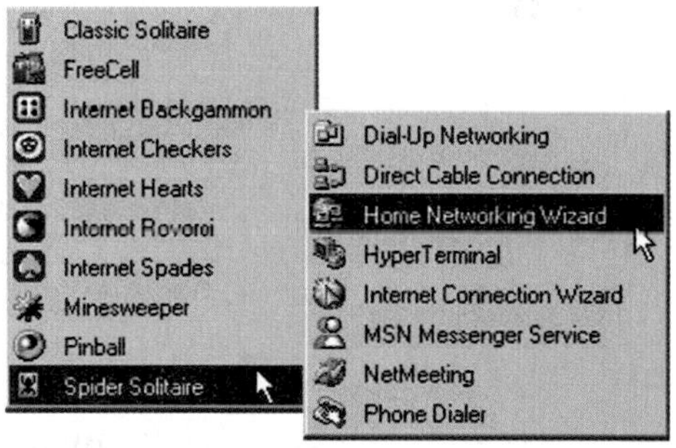

7 Some of the other Accessories have gained useful new features. For example, in the Open and Save dialog boxes of Notepad, Paint and Wordpad, a new panel of buttons lets you switch to different locations instead of having to dig through the usual folder list.

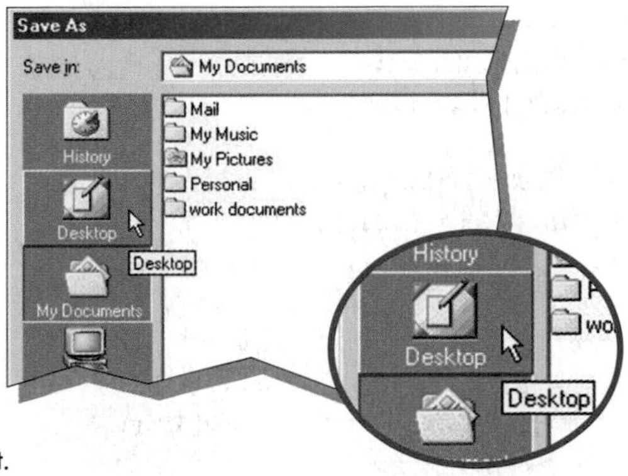

8 When you select Shut Down from the Start menu, you'll see a redesigned Shut Down dialog box. It works as before, but there's no longer an option to restart your PC in MS-DOS mode.

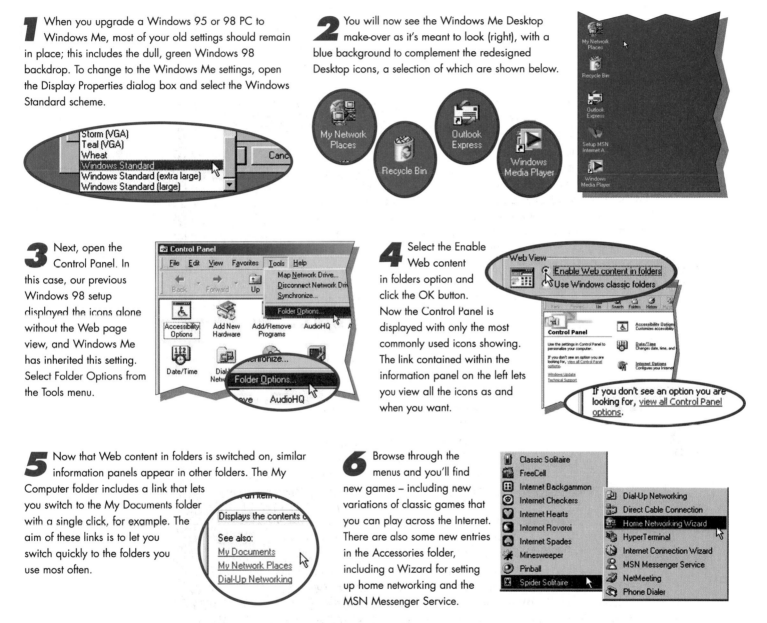

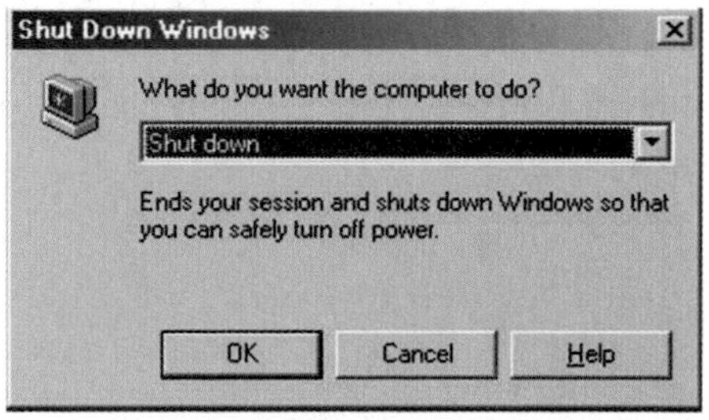

Searching with Windows Me

If you've lost track of a document, you don't have to click through dozens of folders to find it. Even if you can't remember what it's called, the Search command can normally dig it out in a few minutes.

If you have organized your files and documents into folders (see Stage 1, pages 18-21), it should usually be easy to find and keep track of all your work. All you need to do is look in the appropriate folder instead of poring through one stuffed with dozens of unrelated files.

However, if you can't quite remember where you stored a document, then the more folders you have used, the more clicking you have to do. Or perhaps you can remember a phrase in a letter, without recalling which letter it's in. When such circumstances arise, it's best to forget browsing and try searching instead.

With the introduction of Windows Me, Microsoft has revamped the Windows 98 Find command. It now uses panels in the style of Internet Explorer for the search query and the results. It's also easier to customize, allowing you to choose which columns to display and which to hide in the search results panel.

● Search queries

At the heart of any search program or command is the query – your choice of data to use in the search. Once you've set the query, you tell Windows to search and the search command checks files against it.

The simplest queries are those where you know the name of the file and just want to locate it without wading through lots of folders. Just type in the file name and click Search Now and you will get a list of all files on your hard disk that match that name. However, the real power of the Search command comes from its ability to check lots of extra information. For example, if you can't remember the name of a file, you can search for all documents that include a particular phrase. Or you can search for all documents that you modified in the last week.

The Search command lets you try out and then combine these many different query options, allowing you to fine-tune your query – perfect for those times when the first search turns up too many positive matches.

The revamped Search command in Windows Me offers plenty of scope for keeping track of your files and documents.

● Finding space wasters

The Search command has many uses, including housekeeping. If, for instance, you use a lot of scanned images but disk space is tight, search for all image files over a certain size, look through the search results and delete or archive unnecessary files.

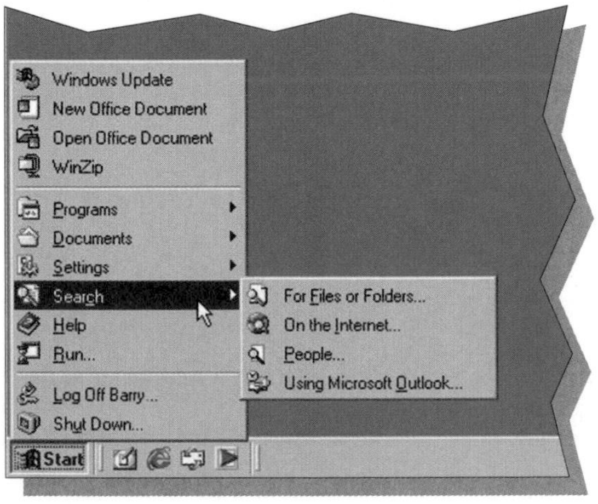

The Search command is located on the Start menu and has a sub-menu that lets you look for different types of items.

Setting up search queries in Windows Me

Save time by setting up search queries to avoid having to browse through your hard disk folders to find important documents and files. You can also save a search query for use later.

1 Bring up the Search window by clicking on the Start button, then on Search and then on For Files or Folders. The simplest search is one that looks for text in the file name. Type the text into the first box on the left of the window and then select the part of your computer's hard disk that you want to search from the Look in box.

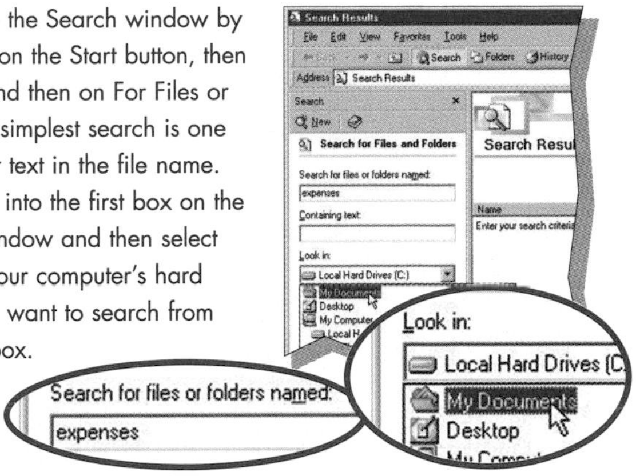

2 Click the Search Now button and Windows searches the hard disk. Within seconds all matches are located and displayed in the Search Results panel on the right. If you click on any of the matches, full details are shown in the panel at the top of the window.

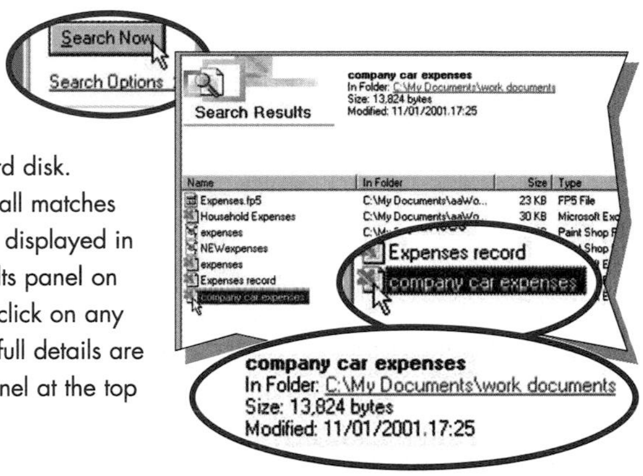

3 If you can't remember anything about the name of a document, but can remember a phrase you used in its text, try searching for that instead. Clear text from the first box and type the words into the Containing text box before clicking Search Now.

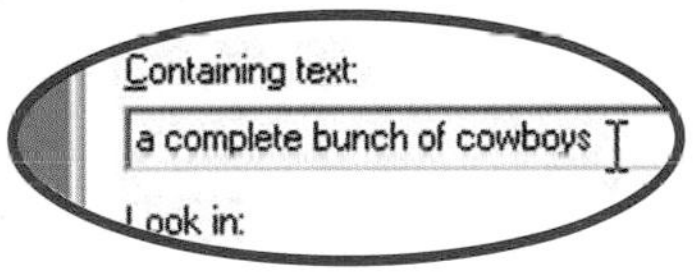

4 On large hard disks with thousands of documents, text searches can take a while. Try refining the search further. First, click the Search Options link on the left to see more query options.

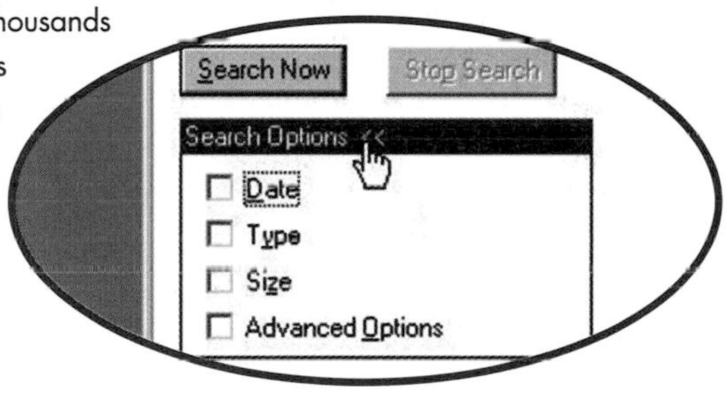

5 You can use any or all of the different types of data to fine tune your search queries. For instance, if you want to find all TIF images that are over 10MB in size, tick the Size box in the Search Options panel and adjust the figure to 10000. Next type '*.TIF' into the Search for files or folders named box (the asterisk acts as a wildcard character so that every file ending in .TIF will be checked). Click the Search Now button.

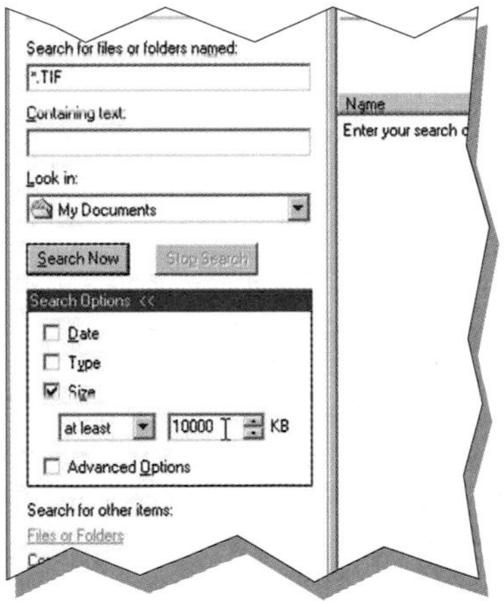

6 The results panel lists the files that match. Select any of them and a thumbnail view appears in the top panel. If you're trying to save space on your hard disk, and if you're sure you can safely erase the file, simply press the [Delete] key.

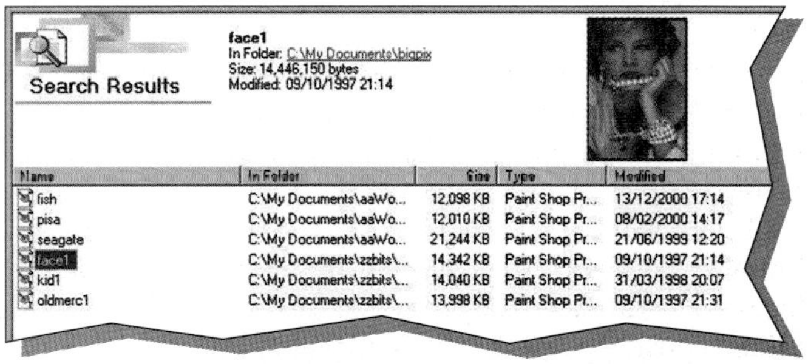

7 You can combine as many different options as you like in the query panel. You can also build up your query one item at a time. This is perfect for initial searches that yield too many hits – such as searching for a file name with 'letter' in it. Use the Type box when you want to search for documents created by a particular program.

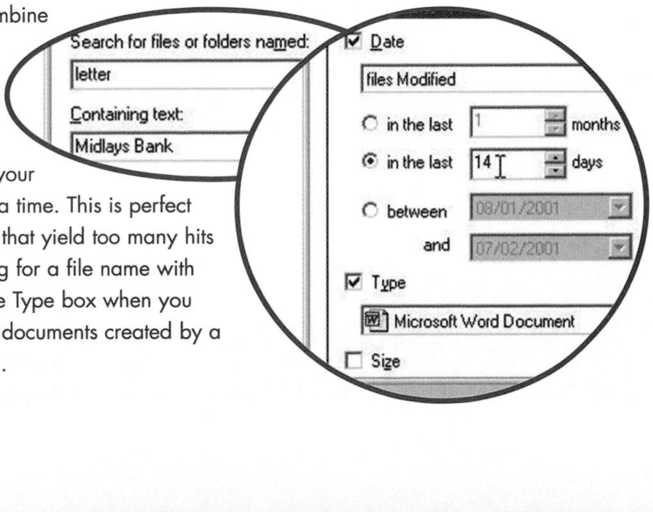

PC TIPS

If you often repeat the same Search – for example, to find all of your work documents that have been modified in the last month – then you can save the Search query, to use again and again. To do this, simply select Save Search in the File menu after you have completed the original search.

Software

Microsoft® Word

Microsoft® Excel

CorelDRAW™

Customizing your toolbars

Microsoft Word usually displays two toolbars, but it can show more. You can even create your own customized toolbar to help you use the program more effectively.

The beauty of using a mouse with Windows programs is that you don't need to scroll through a long list of menu options to look for a tool or command. Almost all programs have a row of one-click buttons that cover the most commonly used commands. These buttons are combined into toolbars.

Word is no different: it has two toolbars displayed at the top of the screen, just under the menu bar. These are the Standard and Formatting toolbars. They allow you to select many of Word's commands with just a single click of the mouse button. Many of the buttons you can see on the Standard and Formatting toolbars are similar to those in Excel, CorelDRAW and many other Windows programs.

For example, the buttons on the Standard toolbar include basic commands, such as Open, Save, Print, Cut, Paste and Help. These commands are not directly related to changing the appearance or formatting of the text in your documents manually. For that, you use the buttons on the Formatting toolbar, where you'll find commands such as Bold, Italics and Underline.

● Other tools

There are also other toolbars available within Word. Some appear automatically: the Drawing toolbar – which has lots of buttons for drawing shapes and lines on your page – appears whenever you press the Drawing button on the Standard toolbar.

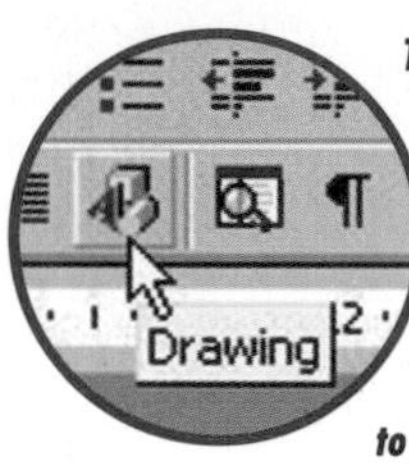

The Drawing tools in Word let you create shapes, change them and fill them with colour. Click on the Drawing button to bring up the toolbar.

There are also other toolbars which you can switch on or off by selecting the Toolbar command on the View menu. By turning on the toolbars in this way, you can

WHAT IT MEANS

SUBSCRIPT AND SUPERSCRIPT

Subscript and superscript are the terms used to describe text characters that sit below or above the line on which normal text sits. The trademark symbol (as in CorelDRAW$_{TM}$*) is a subscript character.*

make any of them appear permanently. This can be useful if you're frequently changing from one activity to another and don't like the toolbars appearing and disappearing. We show Word's extra toolbars below. You will find some with buttons that help you to jazz up your documents and some that are more suitable for business users as they include buttons for producing forms and working with database information, which are rarely used by home PC users.

● Make your own toolbars

Word also allows you to create custom toolbars. This is particularly useful if you find you use a variety of buttons from a number of different toolbars. By combining your favourite buttons into one personalized toolbar, you can work much more quickly and efficiently.

If you don't want to create a whole new toolbar from scratch, you can just add extra buttons to Word's existing toolbars. For example, if you often use the **subscript and superscript** options, it helps to have these available on an accessible toolbar.

One useful way to gain more screen space for your Word document is to combine the Standard and Formatting toolbars into a single toolbar containing your most used buttons. The newest version of Word (Word 2000) does this for you (see page 44).

Introducing Word's other toolbars

Drawing

The Drawing toolbar allows you to draw simple diagrams and pictures using Word's drawing tools. There are pre-set shapes for you to choose, which you can then adjust and colour however you want.

Picture

This toolbar allows you to brighten up your letters, essays and other documents by inserting graphics. Pictures can be imported into Word from other programs, such as Paint or CorelDRAW, and then adjusted in size once they are in place on the page.

Tables and Borders

This toolbar lets you format and create simple tables with borders around them. You can even put borders or frames around individual words in the text if you want.

WordArt

The WordArt toolbar provides lots of options for creating special text effects. These are great for producing banners or greetings cards or anything where you want the text to really stand out.

More advanced toolbars

There are special toolbars that can help you to create more complex documents.

Reviewing

This feature allows you to track changes made to your document and to undo them. It also lets you add comments and highlights which aren't for other readers.

Web

The most recent versions of Word were created with the Internet in mind. You can easily add in links to the World Wide Web using this toolbar, and even access your Web browser options.

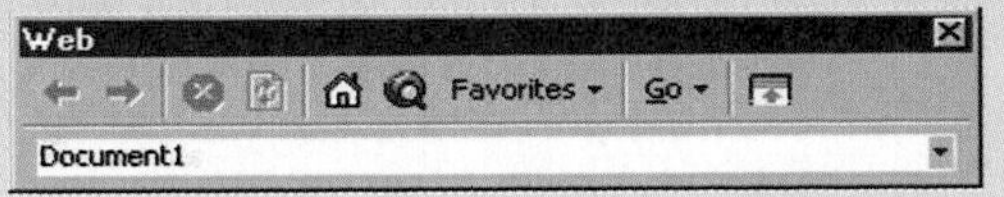

Database

The Database toolbar is for inserting and altering complex tables. It is of more use to business rather than home users.

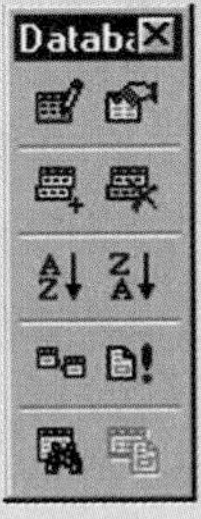

Visual Basic

Visual Basic is a simple programming language for use in conjunction with Word. Unless you're a programmer, you're unlikely to find these commands useful.

Control toolbox

This toolbar allows you to insert objects, such as check boxes and radio buttons, into your document, which can be particularly useful when creating forms or linked files, for instance.

Forms

This toolbar is similar to the Control toolbox, except that it is dedicated to creating a variety of forms. If your document has a form in it, the information can be transferred to other programs, such as Microsoft Excel.

Arranging the toolbars

You don't have to accept the on-screen arrangement of toolbars that comes with Word. It's easy to put the tools you want where you want.

THE STANDARD and Formatting toolbars that Word displays by default can be moved anywhere on the screen. If you move a toolbar to one of the screen's other edges, it will lock against that edge. When a toolbar is not positioned at an edge, it is said to be floating. You can re-shape a floating toolbar so that it occupies a more convenient area on screen.

1 Let's bring up one of the hidden toolbars on screen. From the View menu, select Toolbars and choose the AutoText toolbar (AutoText is a system of customization that allows you to enter frequently used text or pictures at the press of a button). The new toolbar (right) will appear, floating on screen.

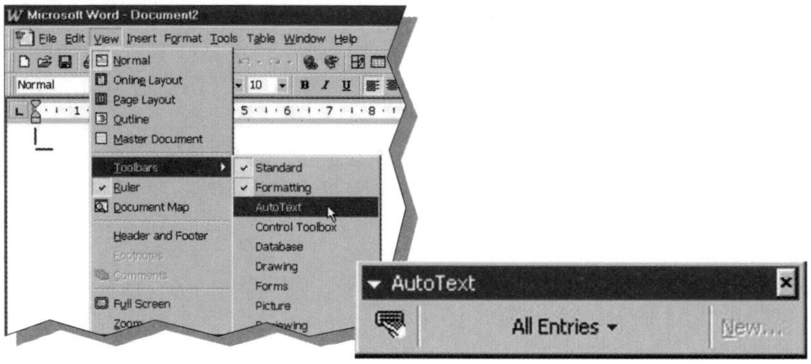

2 You can move a toolbar around by clicking on the blue bar and holding down the left mouse button; if you now move the mouse, the toolbar will also move. Release the mouse button when you have moved it to its new location.

3 If you want to change the shape of a floating toolbar, move your cursor to the edge of the toolbar until it changes into a double-headed arrow. Keep your finger on the left mouse button, move the cursor up and down, and the toolbar changes shape.

4 You can close a toolbar by clicking on the standard 'X' button in the top right-hand corner. You get the toolbar back by using the View menu again (see step 1).

5 To move an existing toolbar, click on the two vertical grey bars at the far left of the toolbar and keep your mouse button pressed down.

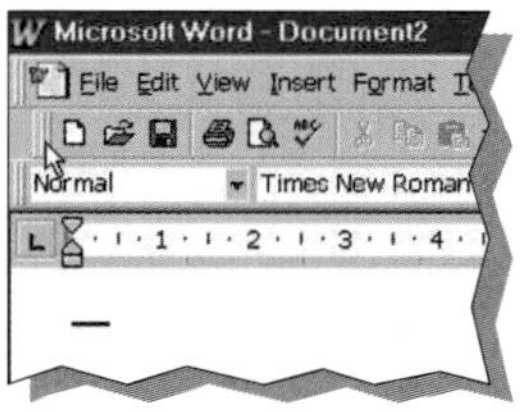

6 Move the mouse down and to the right and you will find that the toolbar moves with the mouse. Release the mouse button and the toolbar will appear as a floating toolbar, just like the AutoText toolbar in Steps 1 and 2.

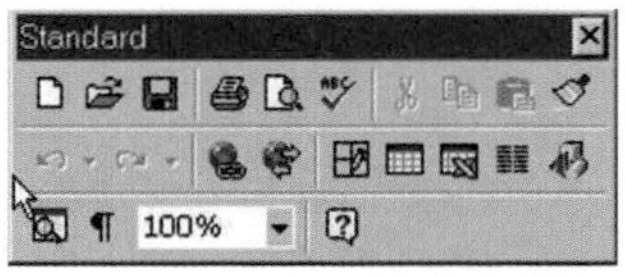

7 To lock a toolbar back in place, move it to one of the edges of the Word window; when you release the mouse button, the bar will lock in place, either vertically or horizontally.

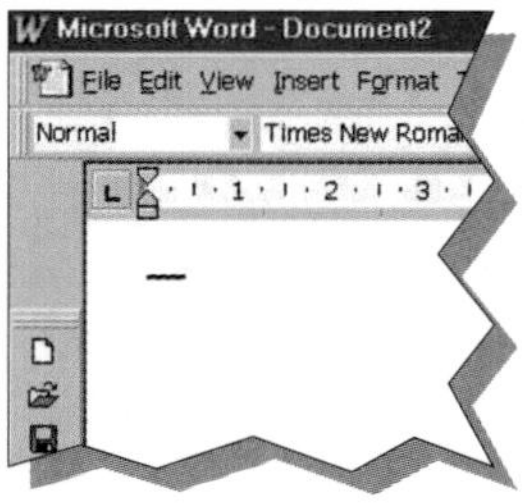

8 You can even put two toolbars on the same line. Just move a floating toolbar to the right of an existing toolbar. (You should only do this if there seems to be enough space for the extra buttons.)

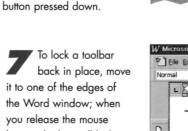

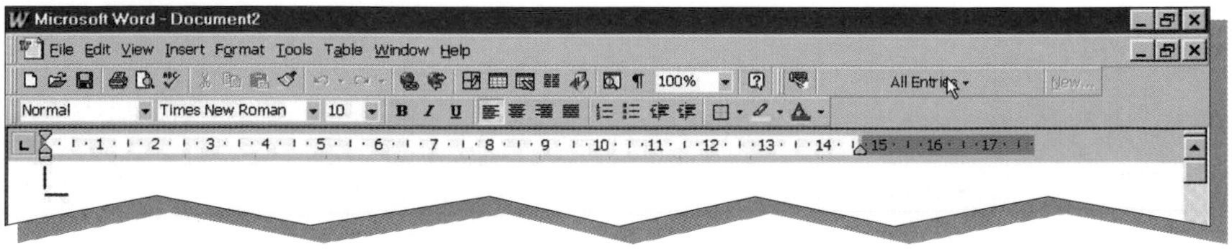

PC TIPS

Toolbars for your templates

In Stage 1, pages 36-39, we showed you how to create templates to use as the basis for similar documents. You can also add different toolbar setups to different templates. You could then have, for example, a template for invoices, with lots of formatting buttons; or a template for shopping lists with lots of tables buttons, and so on. Just arrange the toolbar to your liking and save the template as you usually do.

How to customize the toolbars

As well as controlling which toolbars are displayed on screen, you can also create your own customized toolbar containing your choice of buttons.

1 Here we remove the Insert Microsoft Excel Worksheet button (which is next to the Insert Table button). Hold down the [Alt] key, click on the button on the toolbar and drag it away from the bar. When you let go of the mouse, the button will have been removed from the toolbar.

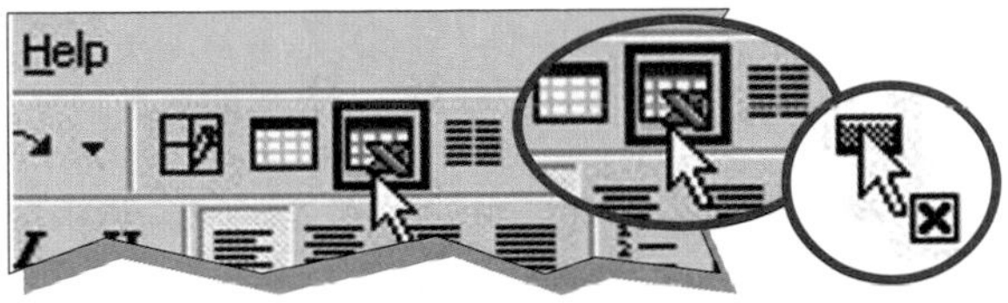

2 To add new commands to a toolbar, go to the View menu, select Toolbars and then choose Customize.

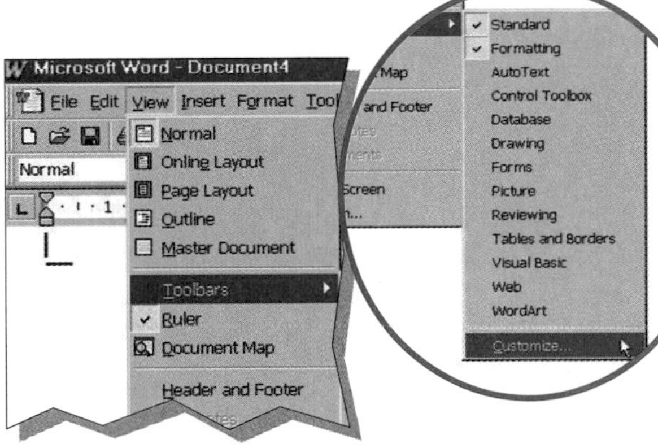

3 Select the Toolbars tab at the top of the window. Make sure that the Standard toolbar is highlighted in the Toolbars list and then select the Commands tab.

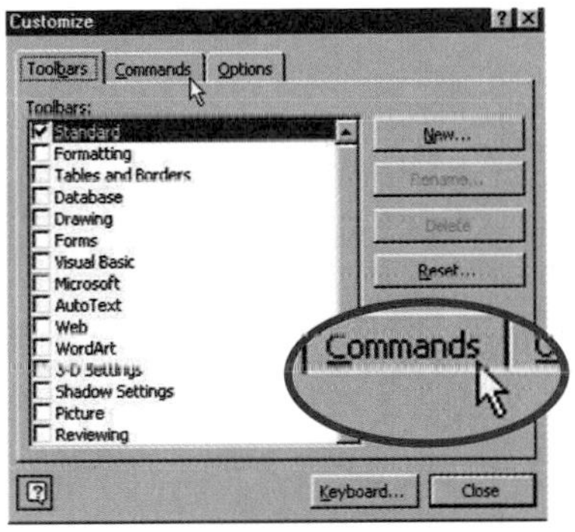

4 We are going to add a **Save All** button. Click on File in the Categories list, and scroll down the Commands list until you find the Save All command.

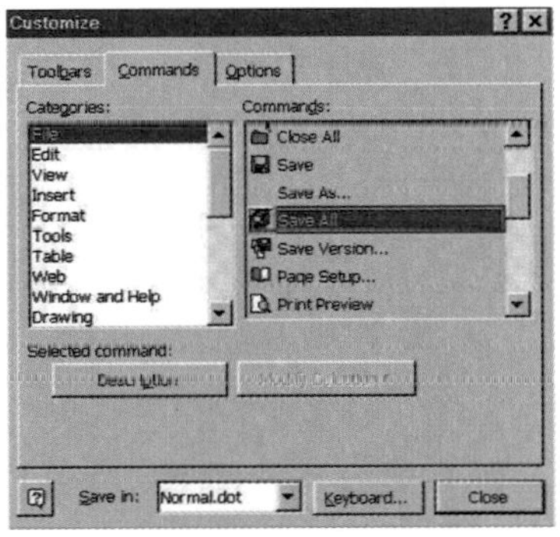

WHAT IT MEANS

SAVE ALL

This command saves changes to all the Word documents that are currently open. The normal Save command saves the changes only in the document that you are working on.

5 Click on the Save All button and drag it on to the toolbar. A vertical black bar will appear as you drag the button to show you where the button will appear when you drop it.

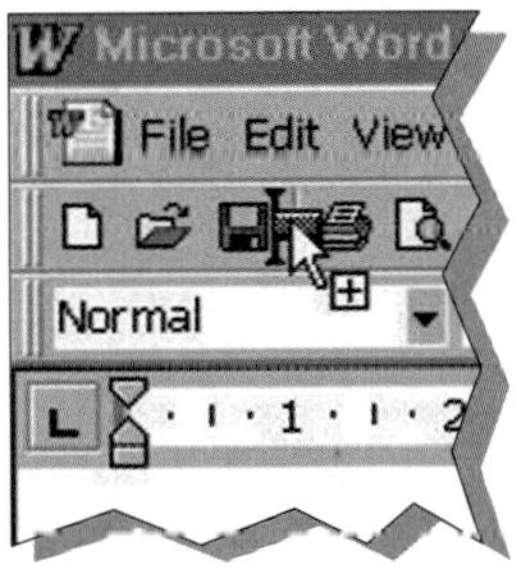

6 To move buttons from one toolbar to another, use the [Alt] key as shown in Step 1, but drag the button to a new position on another toolbar instead.

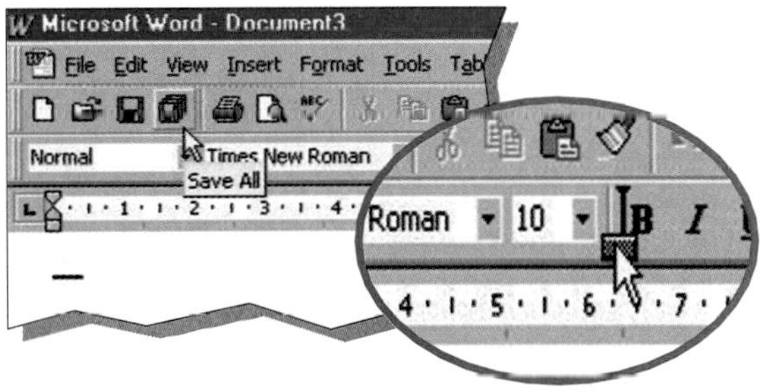

7 As you move more and more buttons to a single toolbar, you might find it convenient to delete a whole toolbar. This can free space and let you see more of your document. Go to the View menu, select the Toolbars option and then Customize. Click on the Toolbars tab, select the toolbar you want to delete and press the Delete button. You'll find this can be done only with custom toolbars; the default toolbars can be altered, but they cannot be deleted altogether.

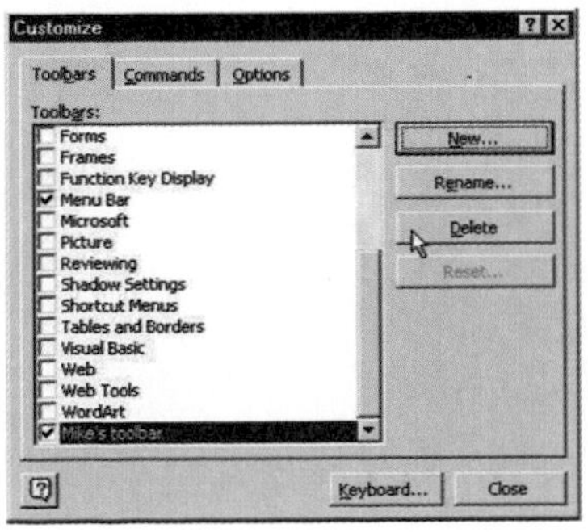

8 To hide one of the default toolbars so that it no longer appears on your Word screen, turn it into a floating toolbar by dragging it from the top of the screen into the main area of the Word screen (as in Step 6 on page 32), then simply click on the close button at the top right of the toolbar.

PC TIPS

Default settings

If you get a little too trigger-happy when deleting buttons and toolbars, you can reset things to the way they were when you first installed Word. Simply go to the View menu, click on Toolbars, then Customize and ensure that the Toolbars tab is selected. From there, click on the toolbar you want to reset, press the Reset button and all the toolbar settings you have changed will be reset to their original state.

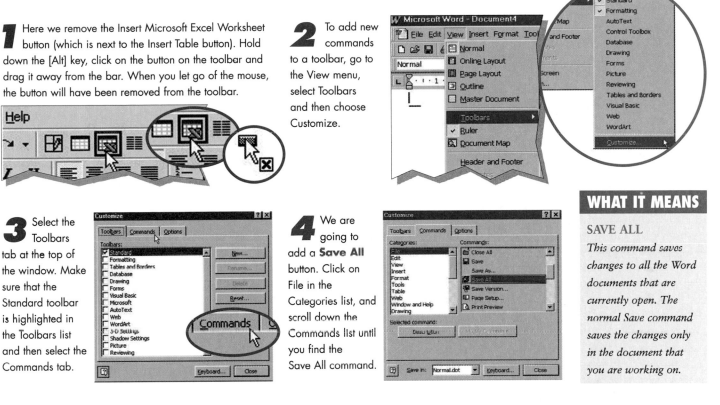

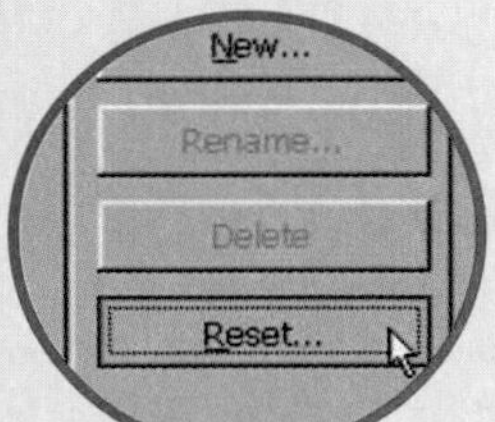

Customizing your menus

Word offers you plenty of ways to customize its settings so that it works in the way you prefer. Here we show you how to alter the menu options to suit your needs.

We have already seen how to customize Word's toolbars (see pages 30-33). By adding and removing buttons from the standard toolbars, as well as creating brand new toolbars, we have shown you how to alter Word's toolbar options to suit the way you work. Exactly the same thing can also be done with the drop-down menus and their options.

This means that, depending on what settings you choose, you can alter your own copy of Word so much that it can become almost unrecognizable to other users, while at the same time working to your exact specifications and preferences.

● Adding to a menu

There are nine built-in, drop-down menus displayed on the menu bar. Although their contents might seem fixed, these menus can all be altered just as easily as altering toolbars, and by using the same tools. The Customize window, with its list of Categories and Commands, makes adding a new command to a menu a simple case of dragging and dropping the command. Moving a command from menu to menu or deleting one entirely is just as easy to do.

● Changing and moving menus

The same principles can be applied to a whole menu, allowing you to delete it or move it wherever you want. You can add any of the pre-set menus to the menu bar. You can even create multiple instances of the same menu that offer different options.

It is also possible to create custom menus that house their own commands. This is useful if you want to keep your most commonly used functions in one menu or if you want to create a new set of commands.

In our exercise opposite, we show how to add a line spacing command to the Format menu. This is an operation that usually takes a number of separate mouse clicks to activate, so if you use it regularly you can save a lot of time. We also show how to add this command to the menu bar, where it will be available with a click or two of the mouse. The same principle applies to other commands, so with only a little tinkering, you can quickly create your own made-to-measure menus.

PC TIPS

Children's menus

Younger computer users may have some difficulty finding their way around Word's normal menus, especially the longer ones. So why not set up their own, simplified menu containing a sub-set of the most important commands? It could include just Open, Save and Print.

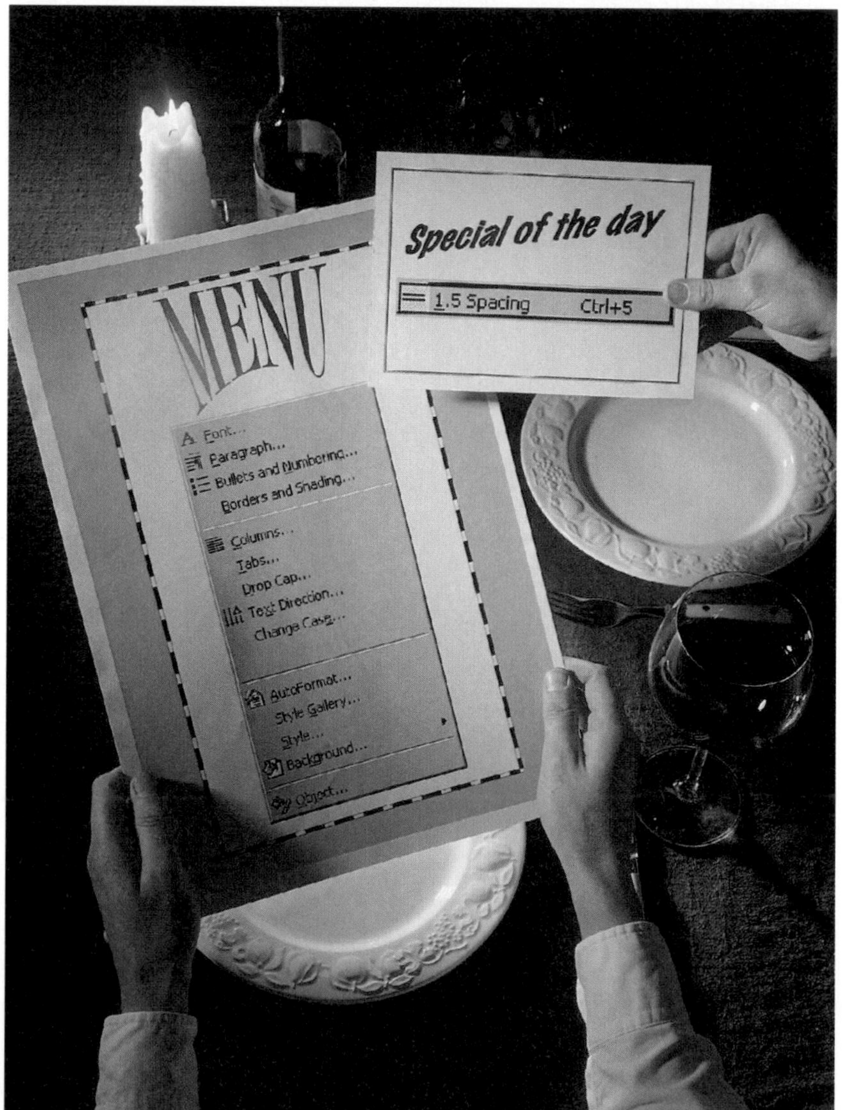

Adding a menu option

In this example, we show how to add a useful command to the Format menu or even create a whole new menu. The same principles apply to adding other options.

1 We are going to customize the Format menu by adding an option for 1.5 line spacing (you could just as easily add double line spacing if you prefer). Ordinarily, this function can be accessed only by going through a number of sub-menus, but we'll put the option directly on the Format menu. Start by clicking on Customize in the Tools menu.

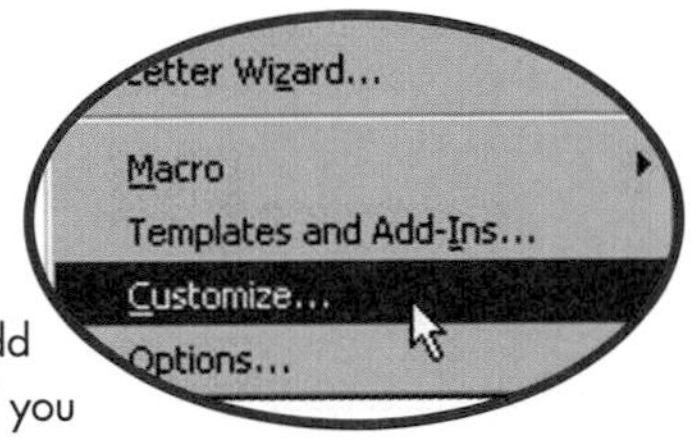

2 When the Customize dialogue box appears, click on the Commands tab. This gives a list of Categories on the left and Commands on the right. Line spacing is in the Format category, so click on that and scroll down the commands list to find 1.5 Spacing.

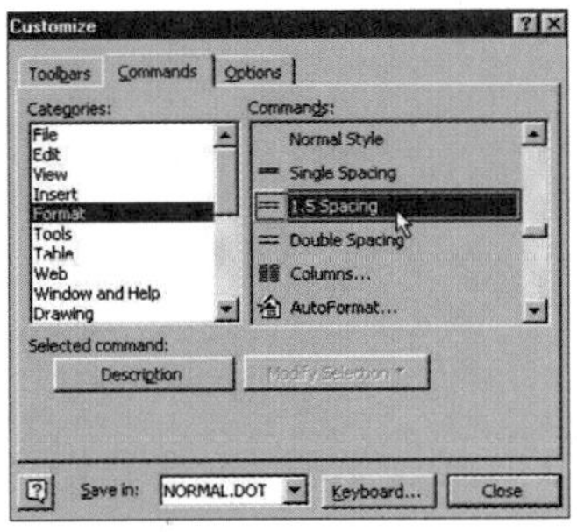

PC TIPS

You can change menus as much and as often as you like because you can always return to the original menus very easily. Go to the Built-in Menus option, near the bottom of the Categories list. This shows you all the standard menus and you can then drag and drop your choice onto the toolbar and use it to replace your customized version.

3 Drag the 1.5 Spacing command over the Format menu button and the full menu will drop down. If you keep your finger on the mouse button you'll find that a black horizontal line appears in the menu options. This indicates where the new menu option will appear when you let go of the mouse. Place the 1.5 Spacing command on the Format menu by letting go of the mouse button. When you've finished, you can close the Customize dialogue box.

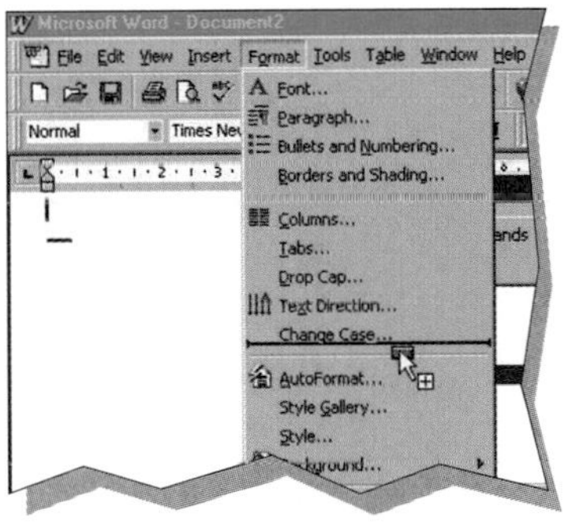

4 Type some text into a blank document, highlight it and then go to the Format menu. You will now see your new menu option. Select it and your text will reflect the new format.

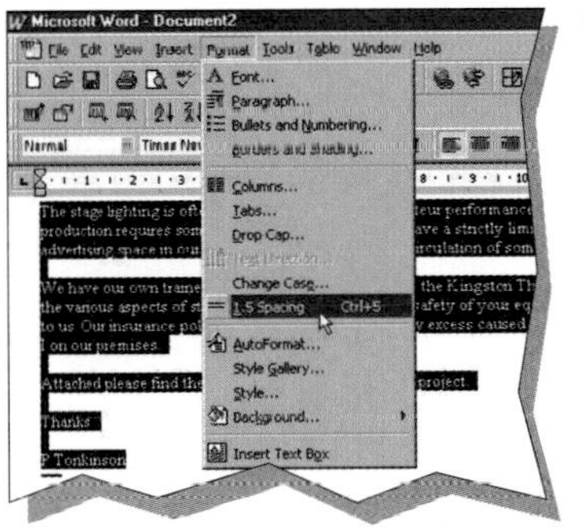

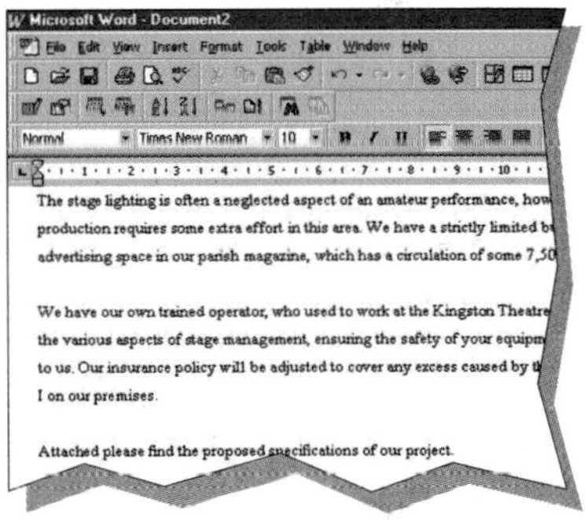

5 To move an existing menu command, open the Customize dialog box and find the menu command (see Step 2). Then drag and drop it to a different position on the menu or to a different menu entirely. To delete a command, drag and drop it from the menu on to the main Word document.

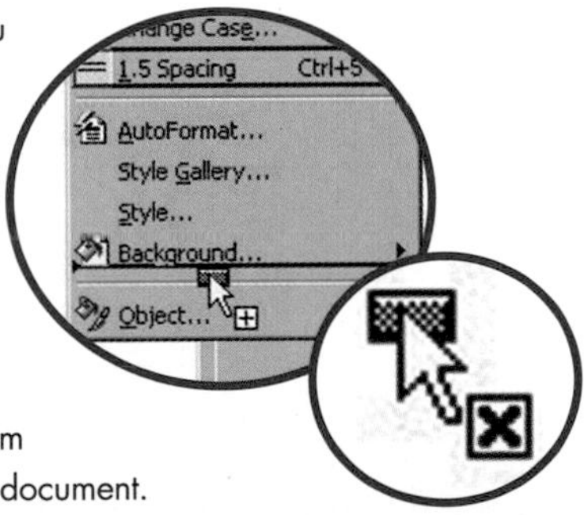

6 A whole menu can be deleted in the same manner, just by dragging and dropping the menu's name from the toolbar onto the main Word document. Here we are deleting the Format menu.

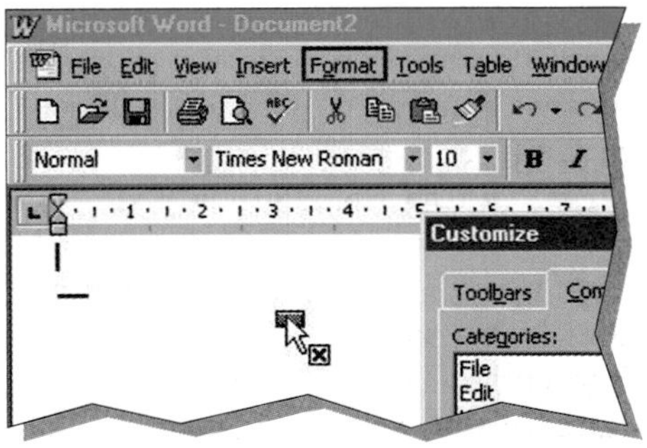

7 If you want to create a completely new menu, go right to the end of the Categories list in the Customize dialogue box and select the New Menu entry. Drag it onto the toolbar next to an existing menu.

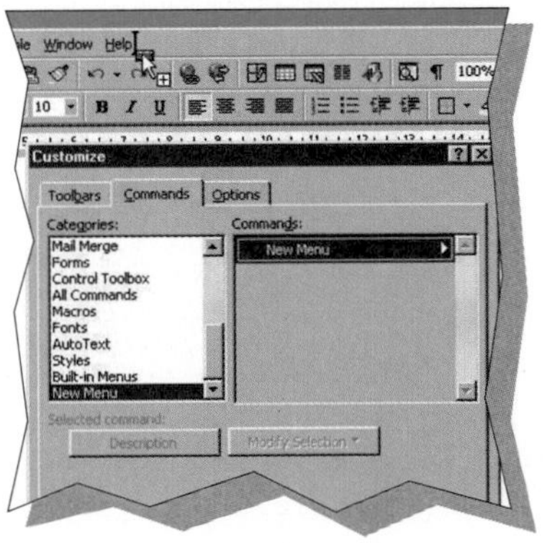

8 The new menu is simply called New Menu. To change it to something more meaningful, click on it with the right mouse button. A list of options appears and you can type a suitable word into the Name text box.

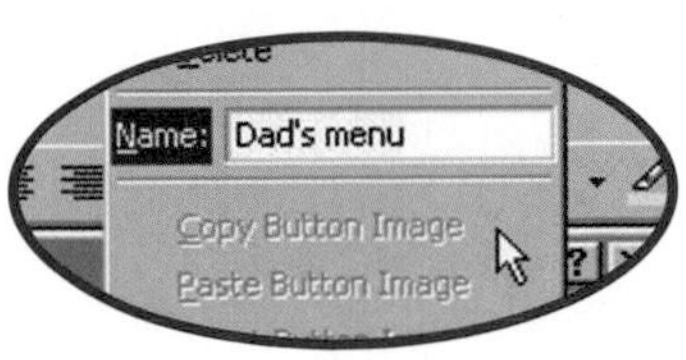

9 Now you can use exactly the same procedure we showed in Steps 2-3 to add commands to your new menu.

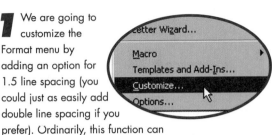

Seeing more in Word

If you'd like to clear your screen of clutter and make more space for your documents, why not make use of Word's Full Screen option?

Your screen doesn't have to be cluttered with icons and tools. There are various ways of sweeping them from your screen to leave you a clean, uncluttered space to work in.

If your computer has a 14- or 15-inch monitor, you might find that there's not always a lot of space to display your document. This is especially true if you are working with a screen resolution of 640x480. With a complex program such as Word, a great deal of the screen is taken up with toolbars, buttons and scrollbars, leaving a much smaller area for typing. For example, with a 640x480 resolution screen and a 14-inch monitor, Word provides a 12x27cm area for typing, out of a possible 20x28cm. This is just 42 per cent of the total screen area.

● Removing toolbars

If you want to see more of your letters and documents, there are several ways to get a larger area to work in. The Windows Taskbar is normally set to appear on top of whichever program you are using, but you can switch this off very easily (see Stage 2, pages 14-17). This gives you a little more room at the bottom of the screen.

You can also try closing the toolbars to stop them from appearing on the screen (see pages 30-33). This isn't a perfect option – you lose access to many useful buttons – but you will be able to see just how much of the typing area you lose to them (below). A much better idea is to use Word's Full Screen mode. This provides a blank screen to type on. Select the Full Screen option from the View menu. To return to the normal view, press the [Esc] key, or press the Close Full Screen button on the tiny floating toolbar (the only distraction that appears on screen).

● Switching your views

You can switch views, depending on the type of work you are doing, for example, using full screen views when typing and switching to normal mode to add style and formatting with the toolbars and menus. Full Screen mode

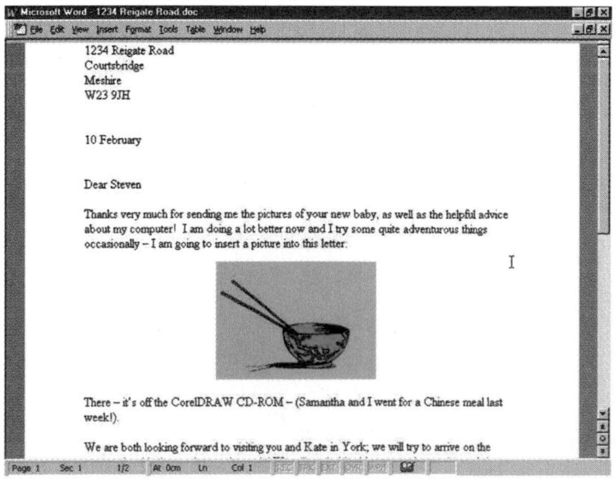

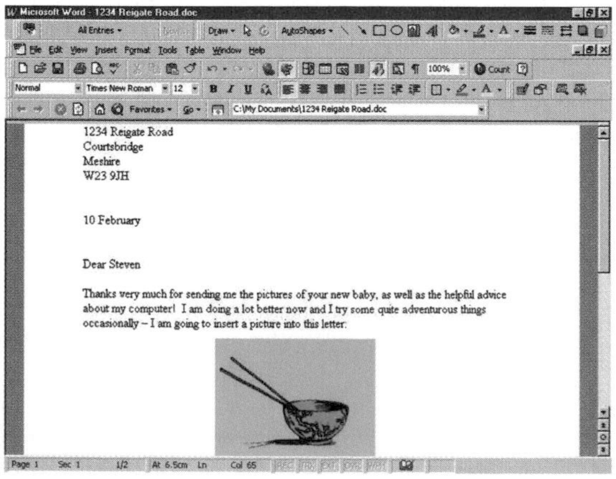

The Word screen (near left) has more toolbars than usual on display but, when compared with the other screen (far left), it shows clearly how much screen space is lost if you keep too many toolbars on the screen.

gives you a lot of extra space but, without menus or toolbars, you'll need to find other ways to access Word's editing and formatting options (see Shortcuts, right). There are two methods: the first is to click the right mouse button and Word produces a menu of frequently used commands for you to choose from.

The other option is to make the menus visible only when you need them. Move your pointer to the top of the screen and the menu bar appears. Select the Word menu and command you want and then the menu bar will disappear, restoring your full screen view.

SHORTCUTS

Keyboard shortcuts are especially useful when you're in Full Screen mode. You get quick access to common commands without having to move your mouse at all. It doesn't matter that you can't see the menus – the commands will still work perfectly. Here are some very useful shortcuts.

[Ctrl]+[N]	New	[Ctrl]+[C]	Copy
[Ctrl]+[O]	Open	[Ctrl]+[X]	Cut
[Ctrl]+[S]	Save	[Ctrl]+[V]	Paste
[Ctrl]+[P]	Print	[Ctrl]+[B]	Bold
[Ctrl]+[Z]	Undo	[Ctrl]+[I]	Italics
[Ctrl]+[A]	Select all	[Ctrl]+[U]	Underline

PC TIPS

Full Screen Button

If you find you use Full Screen mode a lot, you might want to add it as a button to one of the toolbars. On pages 30-33, we described how to customize Word's toolbars.

Here's how to add the Full Screen Mode button: from the View menu, select Toolbars and choose the Customize option. From the dialog box that now appears, choose the Commands tab and select the View category. The list on the right shows the commands that are in the View menu: scroll down to the Full Screen button (see below) and drag it onto one of the toolbars.

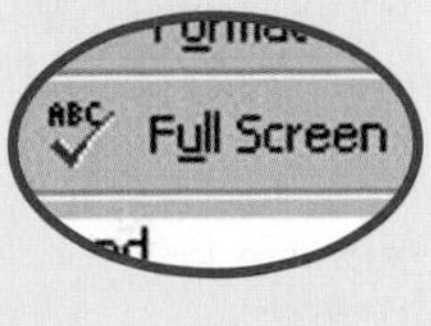

Using Word's Full Screen view

Seeing more of your document on the screen can help you prepare your work more quickly and clearly – it's easy to get a full screen view of your work in progress.

1 Here's a Word document as it normally appears. As you can see, space for several lines of text is taken up by the working parts of the Word window, such as the title bar, menu bar, two toolbars and status line. All of these considerably reduce the space you have for working on your document.

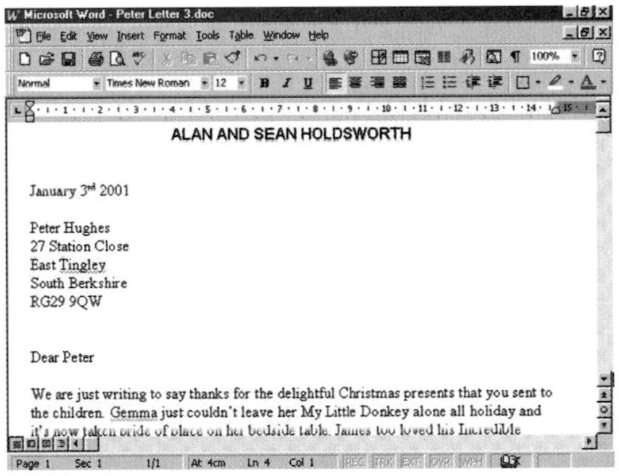

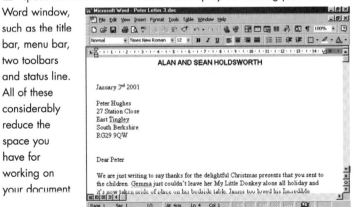

2 To see the difference that Full Screen mode can make, go to the View menu and select the Full Screen command.

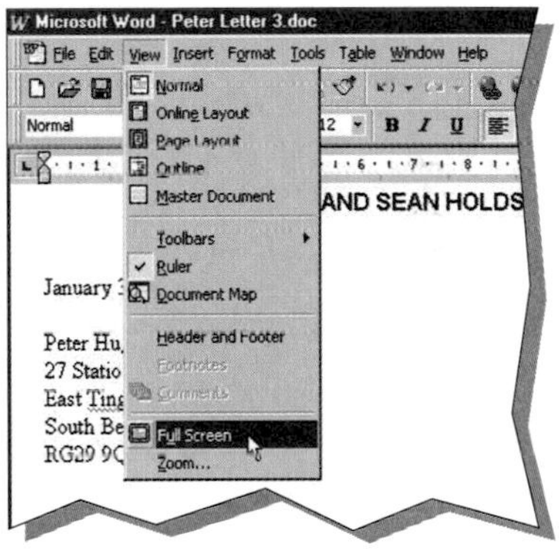

3 You will now see your document taking up the whole of the screen. All of the screen clutter has disappeared, leaving just one small floating toolbar. This view will help you to concentrate on the document itself. We can now see a lot more of our letter on screen.

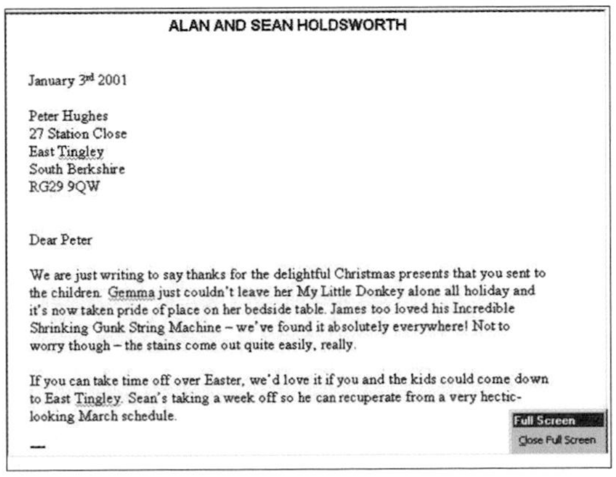

4 Move the mouse pointer to the top of the screen and you will see Word's menu bar automatically reappear (right). Choose your commands and the menu bar will automatically disappear again. To switch back out of Full Screen mode, click on the Close Full Screen option on the floating toolbar. Pressing [Esc] also moves you back to the normal viewing mode.

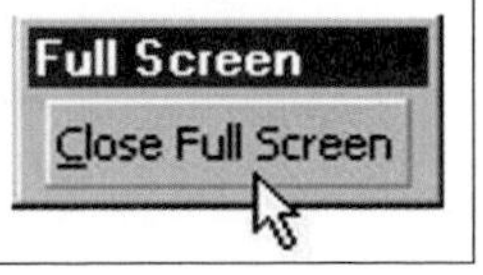

Using fields in Word

Fields are powerful, flexible tools that enable you to set up coded instructions so Word can carry out a variety of operations automatically.

We've already seen how useful fields can be when setting up a mail merge (Stage 3, pages 50-53). In that example, we put several fields in a document as place markers in order to tell Word where we wanted names and address details inserted. However, there are many other ways to use fields.

● Field uses

In very simple terms, fields are coded instructions that Word can recognize, act upon and then replace with the appropriate text or numbers. The big advantage is that once you have set up a field, you can use it to import information any time you want to work on the document, thus updating it automatically. At the simplest and most common level, you can add fields that update data that is readily available on your computer: for example, inserting today's date or automatically updating page numbers.

HIDDEN FIELDS

Apart from mail merging, you will be surprised at just how often you have used fields already – probably without even knowing it. For example, more than half of the items on the Insert menu are field-related, even though the relevant dialog boxes don't mention the fact and the codes are normally hidden from view.

If you wish, you can ask Word to show you any field codes on the page (see page 40). The fields are very easy to spot as they are enclosed on either side by curly brackets – { thus } – which are known as braces (right). However, you can't just type a field code on to a page. You must apply it in the correct way from the relevant dialog box.

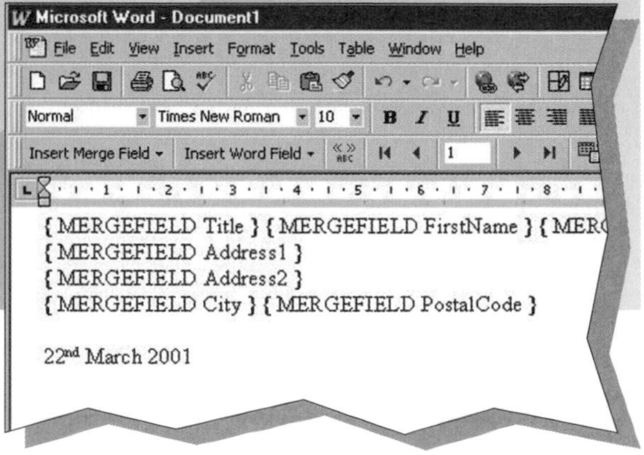

PC TIPS

Selecting Fields in the View menu provides all the options in one place, although many options are also available from specific dialog boxes. While these are not always as flexible, they can be easier to use, notably Mail Merge Helper (in the Tools menu) and the Index and Tables dialog box in the Insert menu. The fields and options available through the Field dialog box are useful, but mainly for advanced users.

● Advanced calculations

At a more complex level, fields can be used to co-ordinate multiple documents or documents with multiple parts. Mail merge is an obvious example of this, as name and address fields can call up the relevant details from a separate data document and produce personalized letters for a bulk mailing.

Even more advanced fields are used when you create indexes, tables of contents, footnotes and figure references, for example, in long or complex documents. However, the basic principle is that Word lets you mark any relevant text or figures in the document. It is then able to tabulate or index the entries automatically.

You can cross-reference documents in a similar way, perhaps creating a field that refers the reader to another part of the document. You can even add a link that takes the reader there with a single click.

Word also has more advanced fields that look similar to the functions used in Microsoft Excel. In fact, Word is able to use fields to work out quite complex formulae that employ other, sometimes variable, factors also enclosed in fields. For example, using fields you can create a table of sales figures that adds itself up. It could even work out gross sales and profits and then insert the results in places that you have marked elsewhere in the document.

● See what's possible

Most of the examples above are quite involved applications for a word processor because they embrace spreadsheet formula components, such as functions and operators as well as tables, bookmarks and so on. Have a look at the Field dialog box (below) to see what is possible and you'll get an idea of how complicated it can be.

The more complex uses for fields will be covered later in the course, but over the next two pages we will deal with a couple of the more basic and widely applicable ones.

The Field dialog box

To get an idea of how powerful and complex fields can be, call up the Field dialog box from Word's Insert menu. Click on each category in turn and you will see a description of the function underneath the Field codes panel.

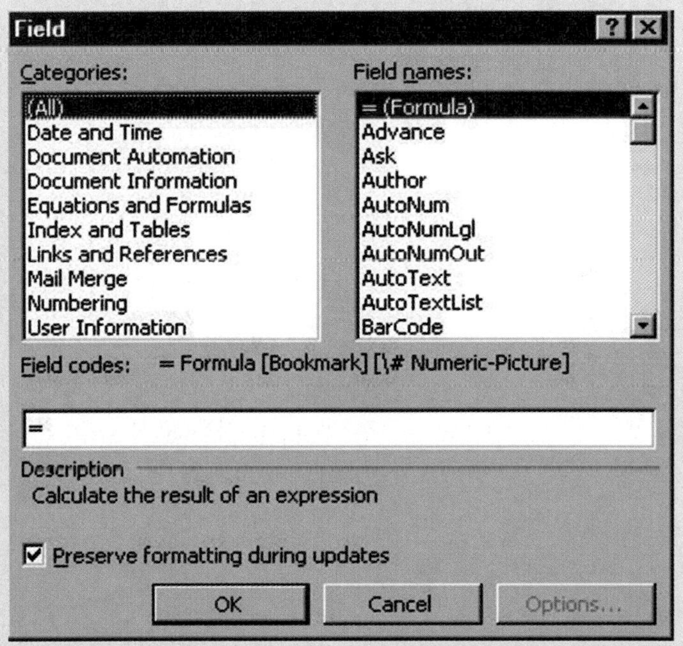

Date and Time
This inserts the date and/or time the document was created, the current date, the total editing time, the date the document was last printed or saved and the current time. Customize the date/time display by clicking on the Options button.

Document Automation
This is a complex collection of functions. Compare allows you to assess the results of other fields – you could set it to trawl through a list of customers and find those with a credit rating above a set amount. The other Document Automation functions are much more advanced and are mainly for business users.

Document Information
This calls in information specified elsewhere in Word, such as the numbers of words in the current document.

Equations & Formulas
This inserts spreadsheet-style formulae.

Index & Tables
These are used to create an index or a list of contents across one or more documents, and also mark the relevant entries. These features can be extremely useful and save time.

Links & References
This allows you to insert bookmarked text, a hyperlink or a picture into a document.

Mail Merge
An advanced feature for documents.

Numbering
Lets you number paragraphs and paragraph sections as well as enter additional numerical information, such as how many times a document has been saved.

User Information
This lets you insert information that comes from the Options dialog box. For example, if you have already typed your address details into Word's Options dialog box, you can insert them as a field instead of retyping them every time you need them (see pages 40-41).

Adding time, date and page fields

Here we'll see how to set up a document that automatically inserts the date and time it was printed and correctly numbers the pages.

1 Open a new document in Word. Click on the Insert menu and select Date and Time. The dialog box that pops up contains settings for various time and date formats. These show how the information will appear in your document. Click on the style that you want to use and then click OK.

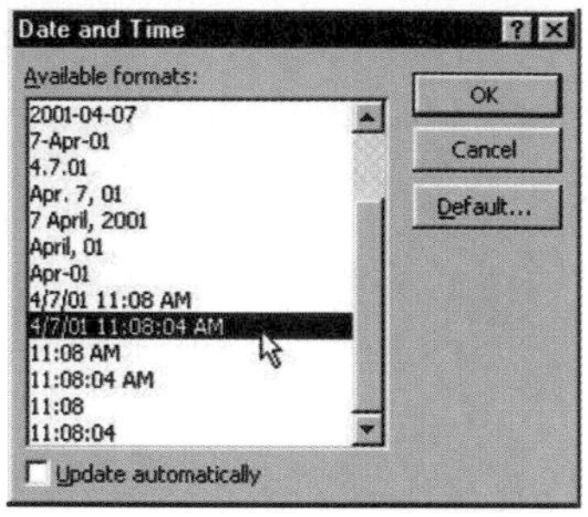

2 This puts a field in the document, displaying the date and time that you entered it. Save the page, close it, and open it again (here we have left it for several hours). Click on the field to select it and press the [F9] key to update the time and date information.

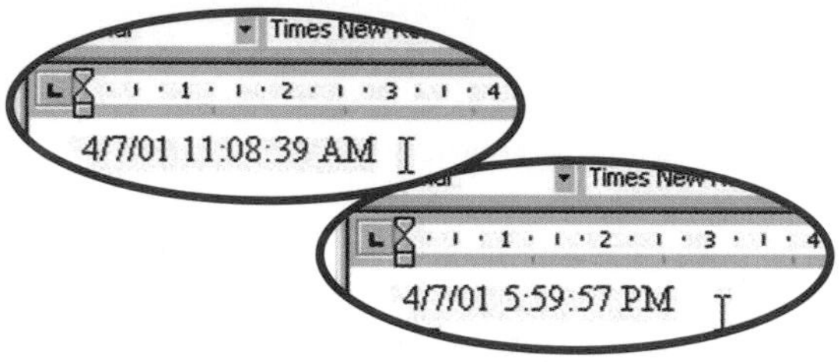

PC TIPS

Once you have created a field, you can treat it as if you had typed in the data yourself. This means you can cut and paste it, delete part of it or do anything you would do to normal text.

3 Now select Options from the Tools menu. Click the View tab and put a tick in the Field codes box. Press the OK button to return to your document. You can now see the field that is generating the updated time/date stamp. However, whenever you print out the page, you'll see that it's always the date and time that prints, not the field code. Now hide the codes by repeating the procedure and unticking the Field codes box before you click OK.

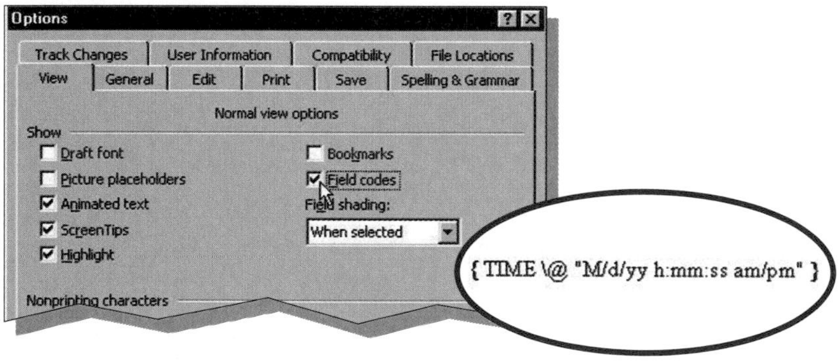

4 Go to the Insert menu again. Now select Page Numbers. Ensure that the Position box is set to Bottom of page (Footer) and that the Show number on first page option is checked. The Alignment box should show Right, to position the number to the right of the page. Click the OK button.

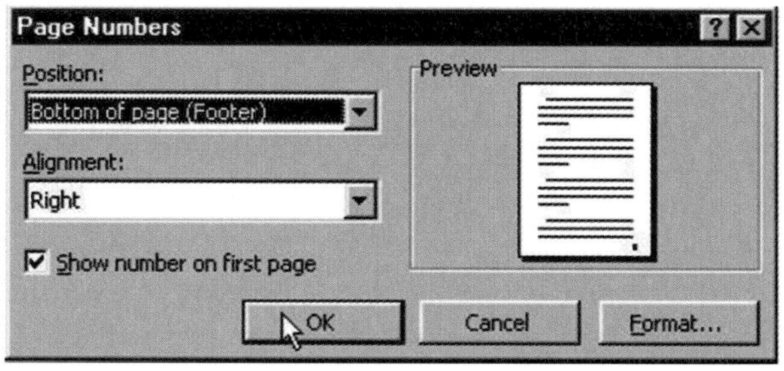

5 You will see that you now have a small page number at the bottom right of the page. You'll notice that it's grey and that you can't select it with the mouse pointer (as you can with other text in your document). That's because it's in a special part of the page, called a footer (see opposite).

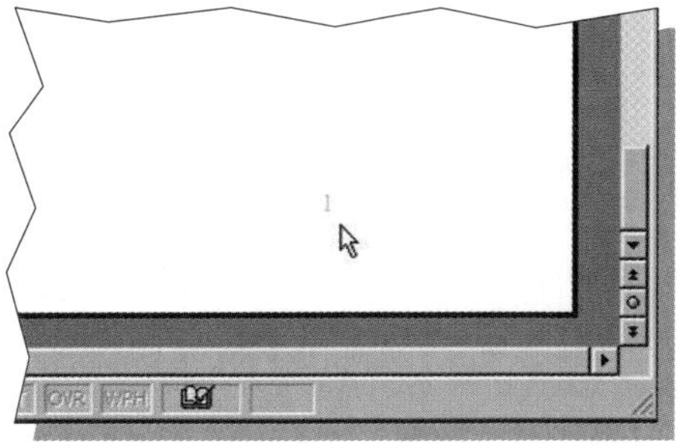

6 Now let's create a new page to see how it numbers automatically. Go to the Insert menu and select the Page Break option. In the dialog box that appears (below left), leave the default Insert Page break and click OK. When you return to your document, scroll down to the bottom of the new page and you'll see that the number 2 has automatically been inserted.

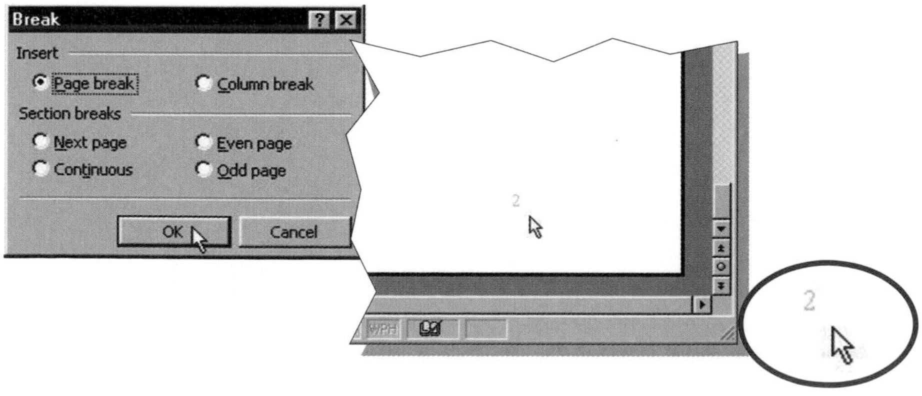

Entering user information

Here we create a letter that customizes itself, taking the User Information on the PC and inserting the name and address at the top.

WHAT IT MEANS

HEADER AND FOOTER

Headers and footers are special areas at the top and bottom of the page. They can be edited from the View menu. They are usually used for longer documents to put running heads at the top of the page, or page numbers at the bottom.

1 Create a new page and, from the Tools menu, select Options and click the User Information tab. This may already be filled in, but if it isn't, add your name, initials and address information; then click the OK button at the bottom of the screen.

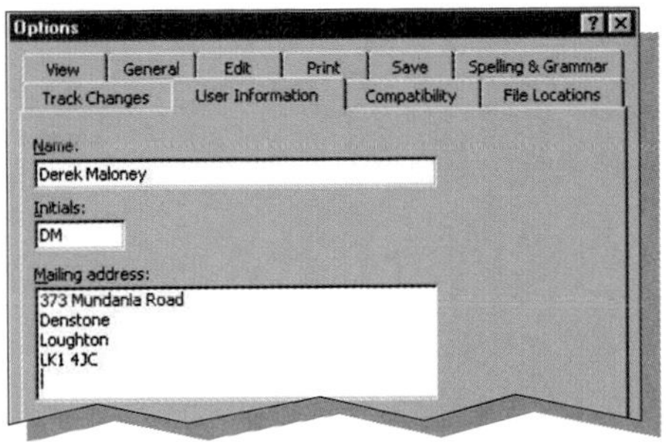

2 Now select Field from the Insert menu. In the dialog box that appears, look under Categories and select User Information. Under Field names, select UserAddress. Click OK. The field will retrieve the address from your User Information and place it on the page.

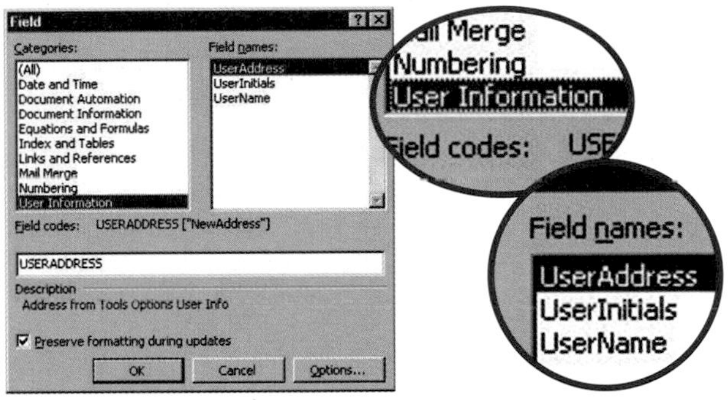

3 You must tab each line of the address to move it over to the right. Underneath place a suitable Date and Time field, as you did opposite. Type in, or copy and paste, enough text to resemble a letter and then add a few blank lines at the bottom.

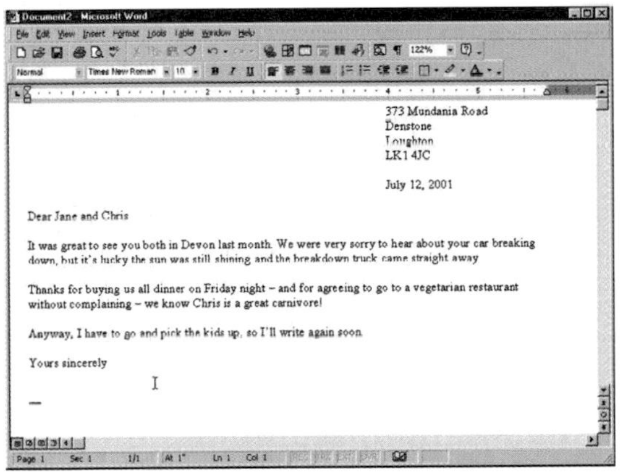

4 Call up the Field dialog box and select User Information again. This time choose UserName under Field names and click OK. The field will automatically retrieve the name from your User Information and place it on the page.

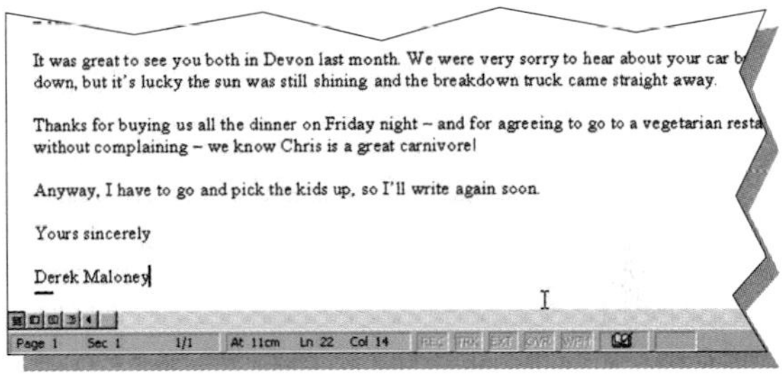

5 Now let's add a number to the bottom of the page. This time, we'll make it tell the reader whether to expect any more pages, which is very useful when faxing letters. Go to the View menu and select **Header and Footer**. A toolbar pops up and gives you a header, so click the Switch between Header and Footer button on the toolbar to put in a footer. Click on the Insert AutoText button and select Page X of Y. Click Close.

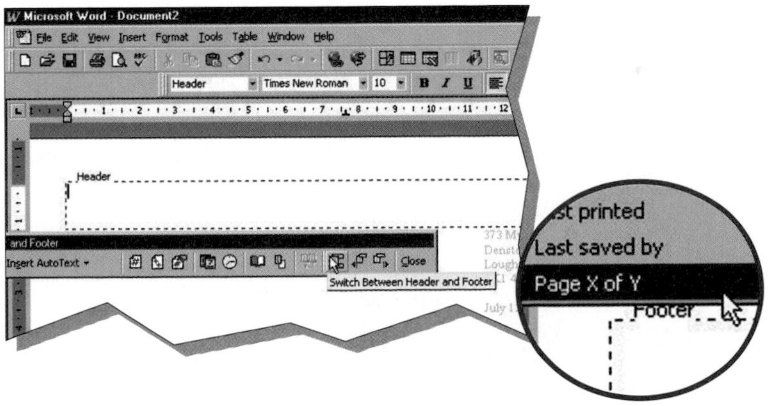

6 At the bottom of the page you will now see Page 1 of 1. If you add another page the first page will then say Page 1 of 2, and the second, Page 2 of 2. Word will update this automatically as you add more pages. If you want to apply a different font style to this text, double-click on it and you will be able to see the footer and then call up the Header and Footer toolbar again. You can now highlight and format this text as usual.

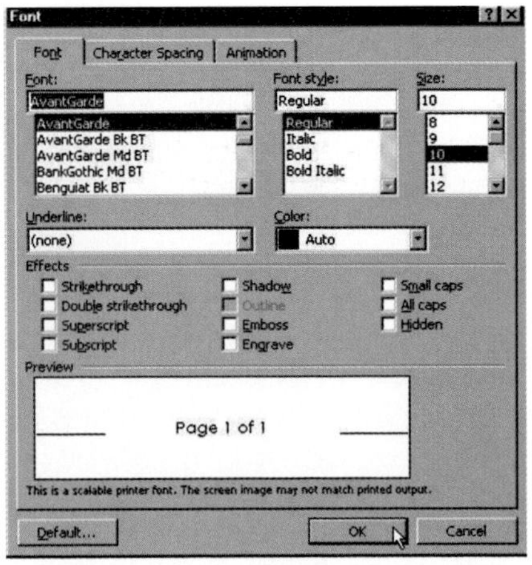

Saving files as HTML

Save Word documents in this special format and you'll be able to create your own Web pages for the Internet straight from your word processor.

HTML stands for HyperText Markup Language, a name that sounds as if it had been invented specifically to put people off. But, if you ignore the technical-sounding Hyper and Language, the name explains exactly what it's all about: text markup.

In very simple terms, HTML is a series of codes that allow you to mark text so that it can then be understood by a Web browser and displayed on-screen. You can create an HTML file in various ways. For example, you could use Web editor or Notepad (see Stage 3, pages 154-157). However, one of the simplest methods is to use Word.

● How Word uses codes

At the simplest level, HTML codes specify that a section of text exists in, say, bold or italic. At its most complex, the code can be used to create a page that is full of pictures and tables.

Word already uses its own, similar codes in much the same way. When you format an ordinary document, Word assigns codes to the file. It hides these codes from you but your keyboard commands add and remove them.

When you select Save As in a Word document, you are given a choice of alternative file types for your document. Pick one of these and Word will convert its own codes to suit the file type you have chosen. One of these available file types is HTML.

● Creating pages

In theory, all you have to do to create a Web page is to take a Word document and save it as HTML. However, Word can do a lot of things which HTML can't, and so complicated documents might not display properly. Tables often do not work, and formatting and justification might become confused.

On the opposite page, we'll show you how easy it is to save a Word file in HTML form, and we'll outline some of the limitations. Word also has a helpful Wizard to take you through the process and provide a flexible template from which to start.

WEB EDITORS

Although many people – even professionals – use a word processor to create pages for the Internet, there are dozens of specialized Web editors. Many are shareware (free programs, at least for a time), while others are add-ons for PCs or desktop-publishing programs.

Most Web editors include a text editor with automated functions for adding components, such as pictures and hyperlinks, plus a viewer to see the finished product. This is essential because it shows how a page will appear in the browser. Examples include Luckman Interactive's WebEdit and Sausage Software's HotDog (as shareware).

However, some editors employ what is known as **WYSIWYG** (see What it Means box, right) which allows you to create a Web page and see the results immediately – without the need for a viewer. Word, to some extent, is a WYSIWYG Web editor.

WHAT IT MEANS

WYSIWYG

WYSIWYG stands for What You See Is What You Get – in other words, what you see on screen looks exactly the same as the output version. Traditionally, this would have meant the version printed on paper, but today, the final output could just as easily be a Web site.

Experimenting with HTML pages

Here we see how to create a simple document, save it in HTML format and view the result. We also explore some limitations of HTML.

IF YOU HAVE prepared a document that you would like to be included in a Web site, the simplest way to see if it works is to save it as an HTML file and view it using your Web browser software (such as Netscape Navigator or Microsoft Internet Explorer). The result might be perfectly acceptable, although it can look slightly different from the document you would get if you printed out the page. Here we look at what kind of results you can expect.

PC TIPS

To avoid some of the problems where an HTML page created in Word doesn't look quite right in your Web browser, you can use Word's Web Page Wizard. Choose New from the File menu. The usual New dialog box appears. Click the Web pages tab and then double-click on the Web Page Wizard icon. Word will now create a page with three ready-made place holders for the information for your Web page. Just follow the instructions to complete the page. Note: if the Web Page Wizard icon does not appear in your New dialog box, you will have to add it from your Microsoft Word CD-ROM.

1 Let's suppose that you have created a document with some inserted images and some formatted text. For our example, we've just inserted a piece of clipart, added a headline and then simply formatted a short list of contents modelled on a newsletter. It doesn't matter how complex your page is for the purposes of this exercise.

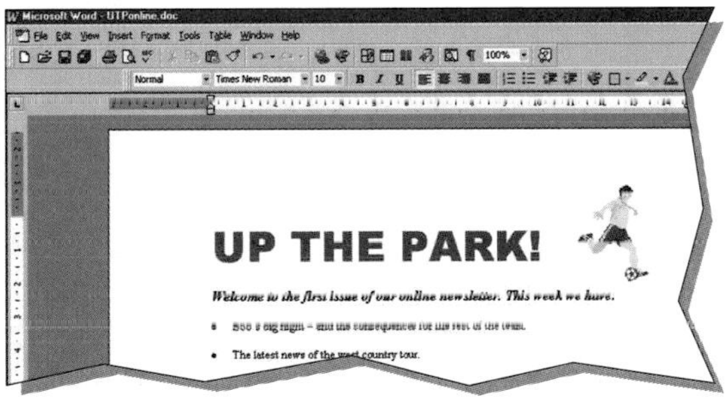

2 To save the file in HTML format, select Save As from the File menu. In the Save As dialog box, select a location in the Save in box, enter a file name, then drag down the Save As type list and choose HTML. Word will add a .htm extension to your file name. Click Save.

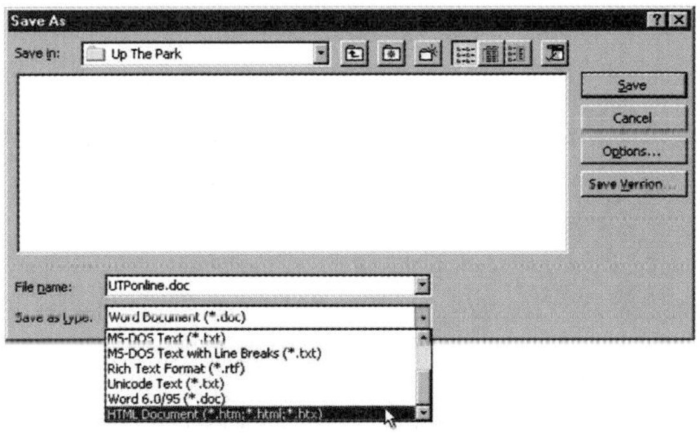

3 Open up your browser (in our case we are using Netscape Navigator) and select Open Page from the File menu.

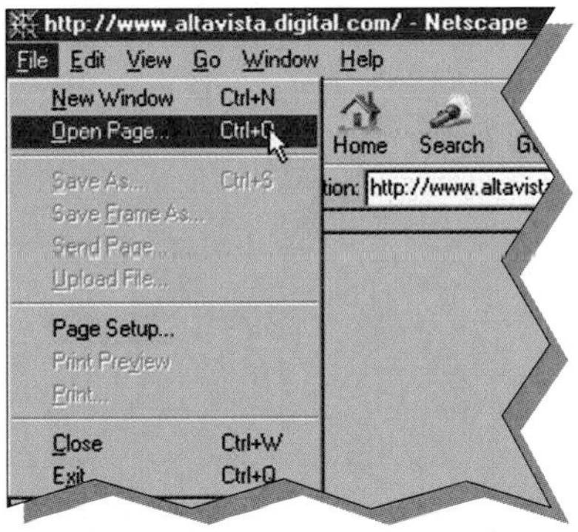

4 Find your file on your hard disk by pressing the Choose File button (below). Then use the Open dialog box (right) to find and select the file you created in Step 2.

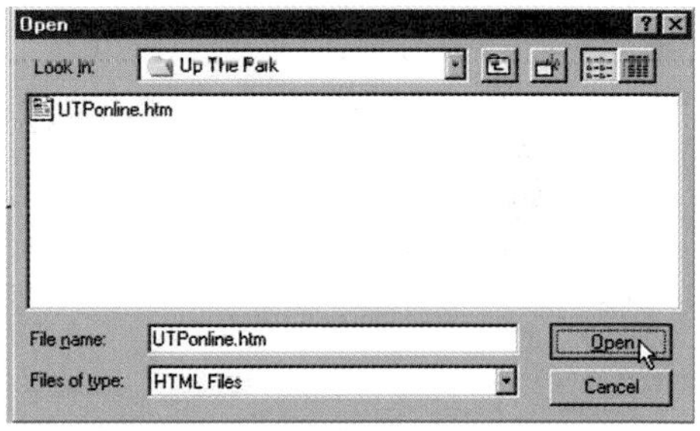

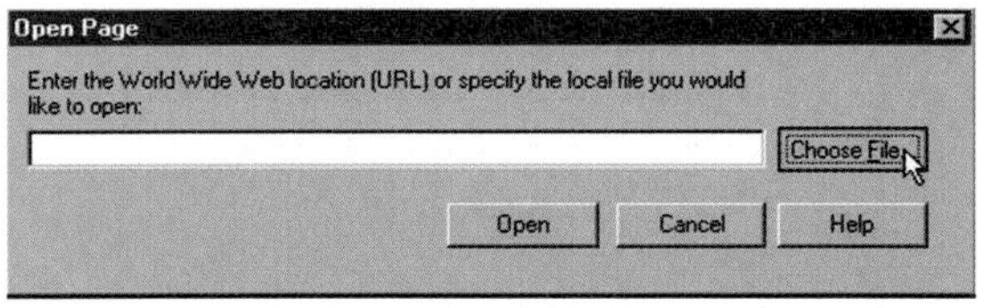

5 Your file name and its location will now be displayed in the Open Page dialog box. Click Open to confirm your choice.

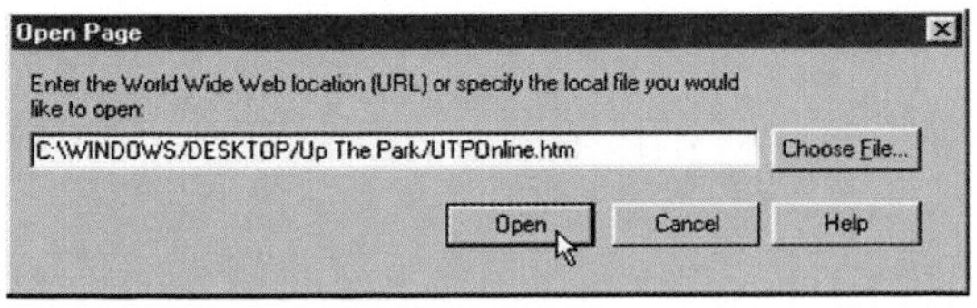

6 Depending on how complicated your page is, you might well see subtle differences in the result displayed by your browser (see PC Tips, left). In our example, the headline and the picture have swapped places, and there is a larger gap between this and the rest of the text.

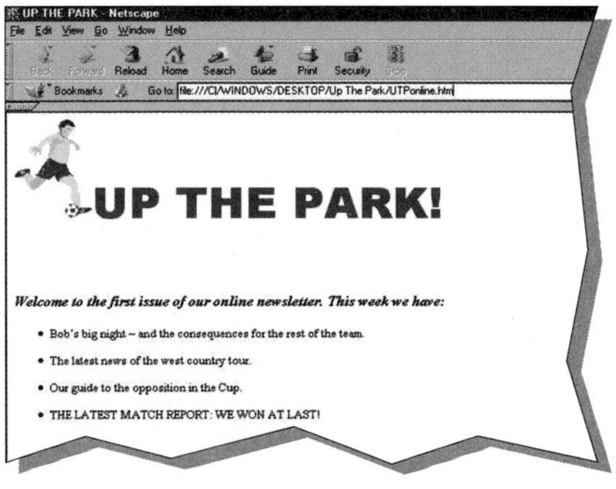

Introducing Word 2000

The latest version of Microsoft's word processing program, Word 2000, combines useful new features with an improved and intelligent set of menus and commands.

If you've just bought a new PC that includes a bundle of software, you might find that you have Word 2000 – and not Word 97 – installed on your hard disk. Likewise, if you're currently looking to buy a word processor, you might find that Word 97 is no longer being offered for sale, and that Word 2000 is the available version.

Fortunately, Word 2000 is only a slight overhaul of the Word 97 program. Microsoft has made a few tweaks and improvements here and there, but the basic program is just as easy to learn and use as its predecessor.

There are a number of well thought-out, time-saving features in Word 2000. These, plus the enhancements to the way you interact with the program, make the new version much more user-friendly.

● Word 2000 basics

The great thing about Word 2000 is that most of its commands and buttons are identical to those of Word 97. This makes it very easy to learn if you're upgrading from Word 97. It also means that all the Word 97 exercises in *PCs made easy* will also work with Word 2000. You will only find a few cases where the menu commands or toolbar buttons are in different places.

The most significant changes are based on ease of use. Just a handful of minor changes have been made to the look of Word 2000, and if you're familiar with the previous version, you won't get lost. The most obvious change is that the two toolbars of Word 97 have been replaced with a single toolbar in Word 2000 but all the toolbar buttons are still available. This saves space and makes more room for your document.

The menus also look and work differently, adapting automatically to the way you work. They are set up to show a subset of Word 97's commands but can expand to show the full set if you need them. The menus also change to reflect the commands you use most often.

WORD 2000

Word 2000 has most of Word 97's commands, so whichever program you use, future Word exercises in *PCs made easy* will work in both programs.
Where there are any differences, we'll highlight the Word 2000 method with this type of box.

● Smarter saving

Word 2000's Save and Open dialog boxes have had a useful facelift, too. A column of buttons lets you quickly find the locations that you use most often when saving or opening your files. This is a very useful feature that is almost certain to save you a great deal of time which would have previously been spent searching through folders.

A brief tour around Word 2000

Here we take a look at some of the new features supplied with the latest version of Microsoft's handy word processing program and show you how they work.

1 Click on the Start button, select Programs from the menu and then click on the Microsoft Word option.

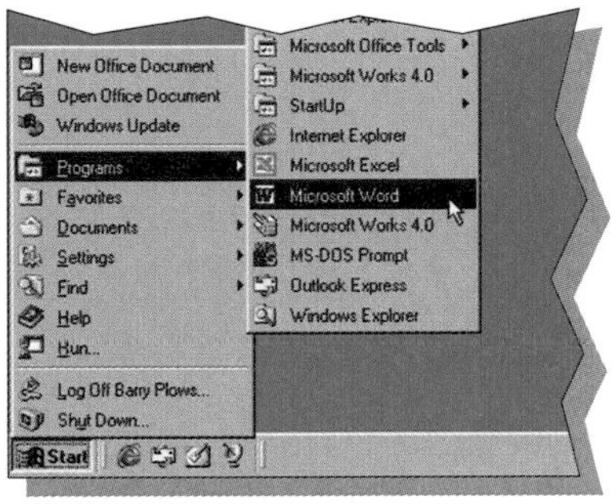

2 When the Word 2000 window opens, you'll immediately notice a few changes. For instance, fewer buttons are shown, as the two toolbars of Word 97 have been squeezed into a single line along the top to maximize the amount of space for your document.

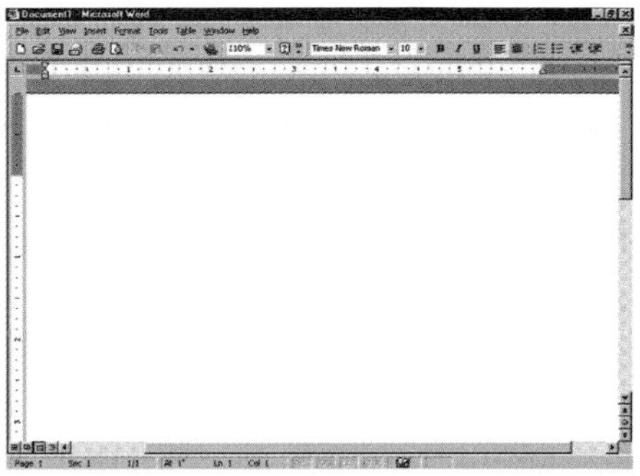

3 You can still get access to all the usual toolbar buttons if you need them, however. To do this, click on the More Buttons arrow on the far right of the toolbar. The other buttons that are available will appear in a pop-up panel.

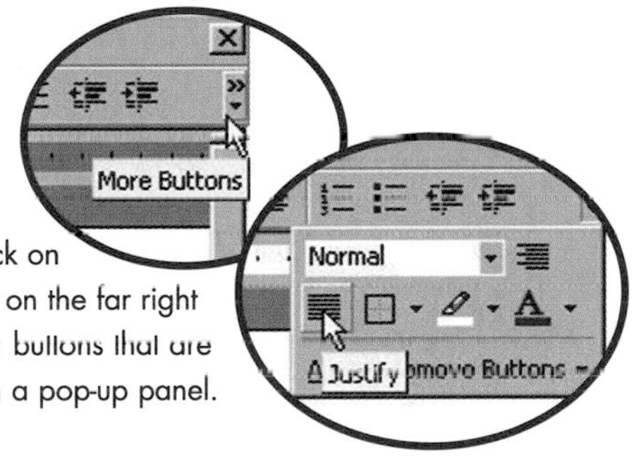

4 Word 2000's menus work in a different way: click on the Format menu and you'll see that it is a lot shorter than Word 97's Format menu, with fewer commands listed. There's also a downward-pointing arrow at the bottom of the menu.

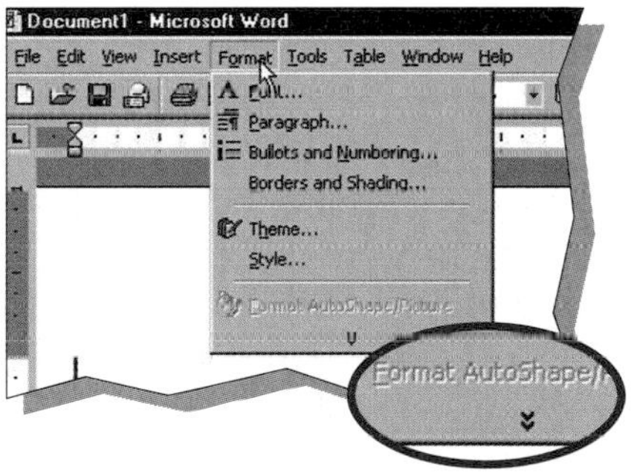

5 Click on this arrow and the menu will expand to reveal extra commands. Word 2000 conceals the less frequently used commands, allowing you to concentrate on the most commonly used ones.

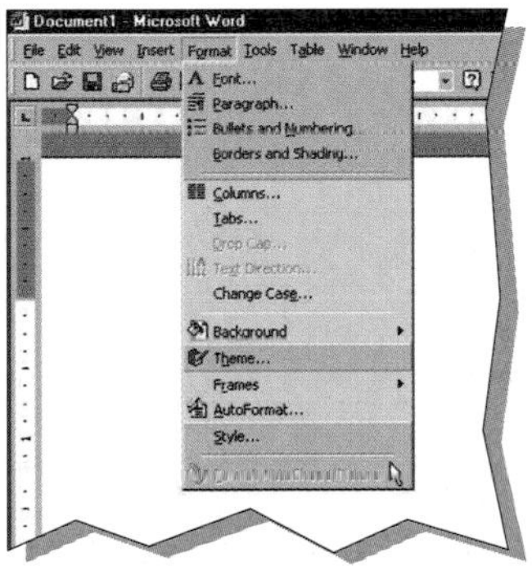

6 The mouse pointer also has added capabilities. Double-click anywhere on the blank page and the pointer turns into an insertion mark (inset) and Word 2000 lets you start typing here. This is a very useful time-saver.

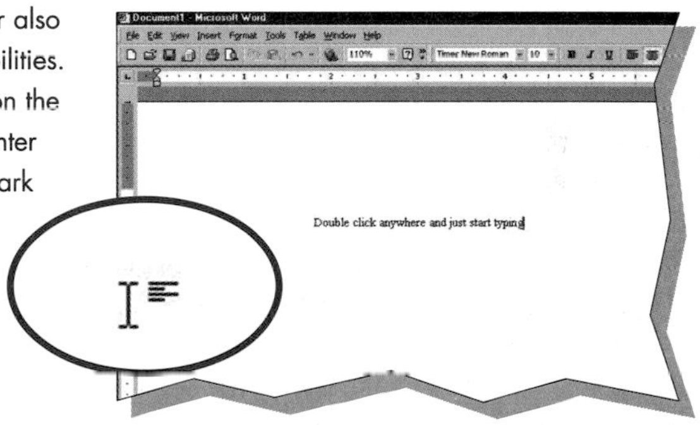

7 When you save or open documents, a column of buttons provides quick access to many different locations, including a History list of the folders you have most recently used, and a single click button to get to the My Documents folder.

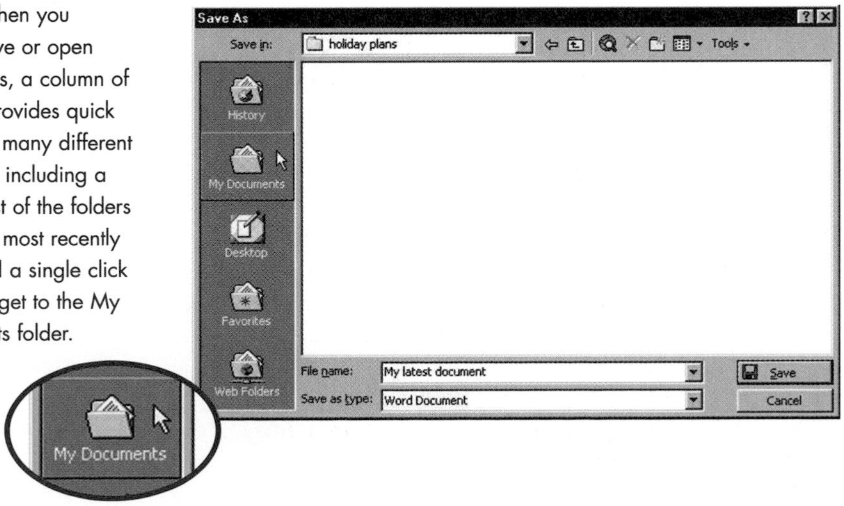

MASTERING MENUS

If you wait for a few moments after opening a menu, Word 2000 automatically expands the menu for you. This is to ensure that you don't accidentally miss important commands temporarily hidden from view.

Once you have used a command that was previously hidden, Word 2000 will show it in the shortened menu. In this way, the menus are constantly updated so that they reflect the commands you use most often, while hiding the commands that you rarely use.

Introducing Excel functions

In order to benefit from Excel's full potential, it's worth getting to know about some of its more powerful tools.

WHAT IT MEANS

FUNCTIONS

Functions are efficient ways of specifying complex calculations but with much shorter Excel commands. For example, working out a loan repayment – from the interest rate, loan amount and loan period – requires a long and tricky calculation. Using Excel's built-in payment function cuts down the formula for the calculation to a few words and characters.

We've already seen how to carry out mathematical calculations using some of Excel's formulae (see Stage 1, pages 52-53). Most of these examples involved using the basic arithmetic symbols for addition (+), subtraction (-), multiplication (*) and division (/).

However, Excel also includes a range of more powerful operators, which make it possible to carry out even more useful and complicated formulae. These operators are known as **functions**.

In fact, we've already encountered some examples of Excel functions. For instance, we saw how to add up a column of figures by using the AutoSum button in the standard toolbar (see Stage 1, pages 60-61). As its name suggests, the AutoSum function automates the process of adding up a list of figures. To do so, it uses a function called SUM. If you look at a cell where you've used AutoSum, you will find that it contains a formula that looks something like =SUM(B2:B5).

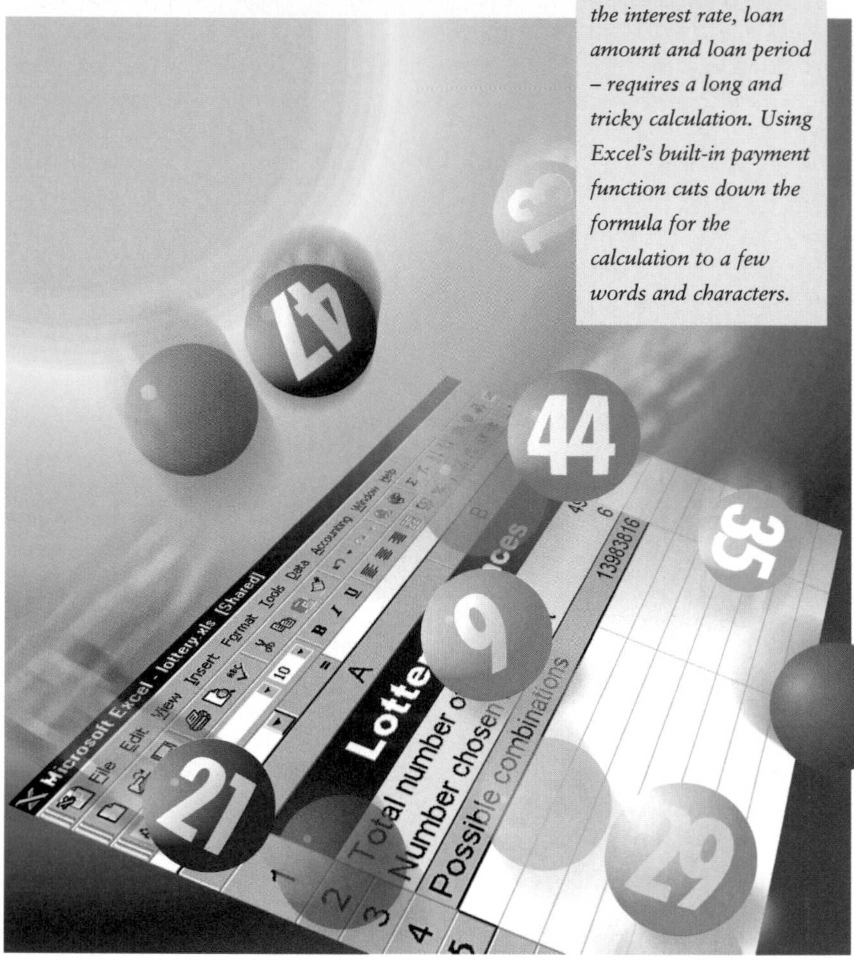

● How functions work

Like most other functions, SUM cannot produce a result without being given further instructions. The information it needs is contained in a pair of brackets that follow the name of the function (cell references B2:B5 as shown, right). Each information item used by a function is called an argument and can be a cell reference, a number or even text.

As this suggests, functions deal with much more than just arithmetic. For example, there is a function called PMT, which works out loan repayments, and a function called MONTH to convert a number from 1 to 12 into a month. Excel organizes its functions into nine groups: Financial; Date & Time; Math & Trig; Statistical; Lookup & Reference; Database; Text; Logical; and Information. Each group contains a number of functions related to that topic. For example, PMT is in the Financial group and MONTH is under Date & Time.

● Using functions

You can include any function in the formulae you create in the Formula Bar. All you have to do is click the Paste Function button in the standard toolbar (it looks like a letter f with a small x beside it). This opens a window that lets you select the function you want. If this function requires arguments, Excel will prompt you to type them in or select the cells where they are held.

Opposite, we look at an example of how to use a very simple function in order to calculate the odds against winning a lottery draw. On pages 48-49, we will look at some other useful Excel functions.

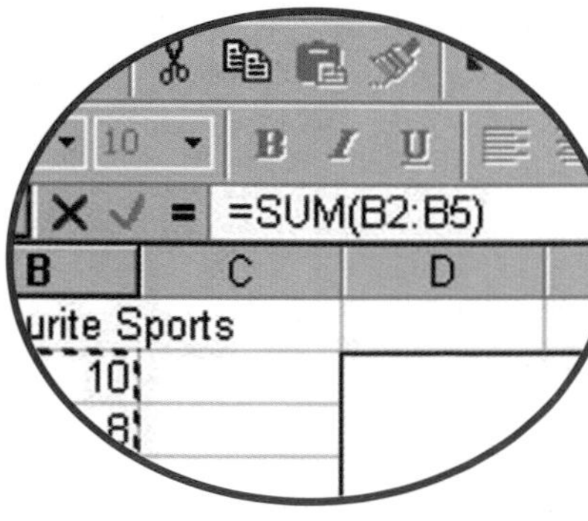

If you've used Excel's SUM function, you will already have explored the basic principles needed to use many of Excel's more powerful commands.

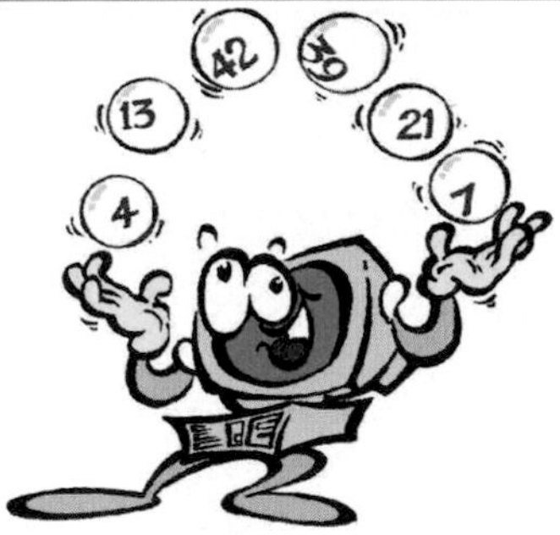

How to apply a function

In this exercise, we use Excel's powerful COMBIN function to work out the odds involved in a lottery draw.

1 In this example, based on the UK National Lottery, we want to calculate the number of possible combinations – in other words, the odds against winning. Start by typing in the text headings shown here.

2 Now type in the number of balls in the draw (49) and the number drawn out (6). (You can type in different numbers to suit other lotteries.) Then click on the cell where you want to put the number of possible combinations.

3 We are going to use a function, so press the Paste Function button on the standard toolbar.

PC TIPS

The COMBIN function can work out many other questions about combinations. For example, imagine that an ice-cream stall has five basic flavours. How many different desserts can be made using just three of the flavours? By typing =COMBIN (5,3) you get an instant answer: there are 10 different possibilities.

4 In the dialog box that appears, click on Math & Trig in the Function category list and then select the COMBIN option in the Function name list. The text below tells us that the COMBIN function works out the number of possible combinations, which is just what we want. Click OK.

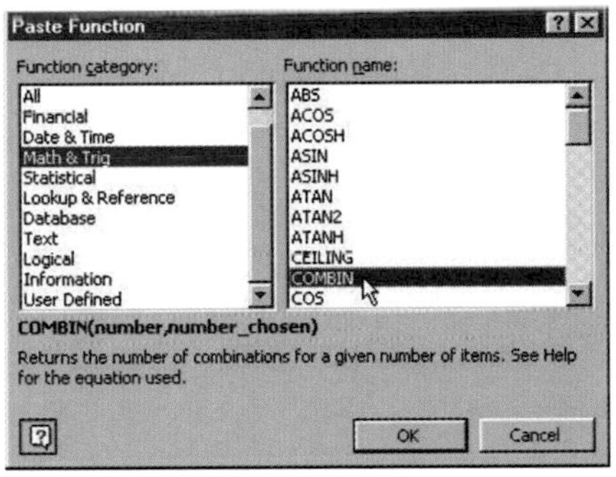

5 Excel now brings up a floating window just under the formula bar (right). Click on it and drag it down a little (below right) so that you can see the information you've already typed into the worksheet. The COMBIN function has appeared in the cell where we want our answer.

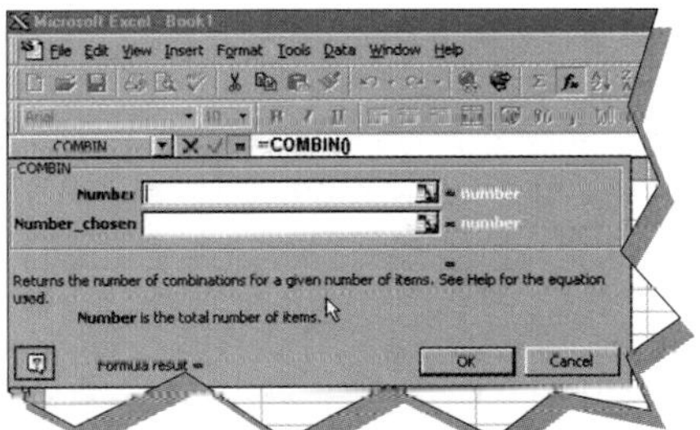

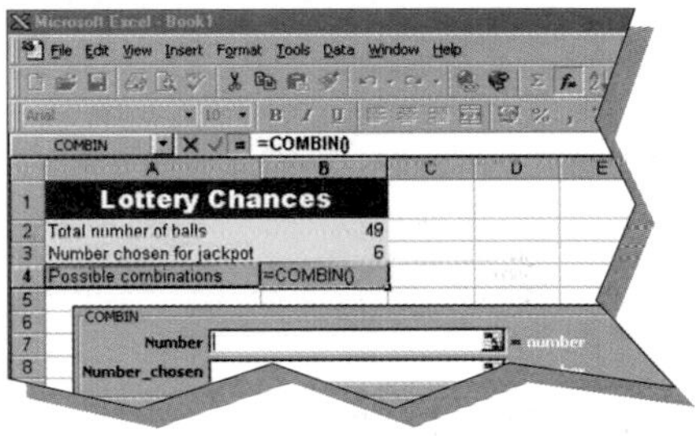

6 The window allows us to enter the two arguments that COMBIN uses: Number and Number_chosen. Click on cell B2 (which holds the total number of balls) and you'll see B2 appear in the floating window's first box. It also appears after COMBIN in the cell that will display the answer.

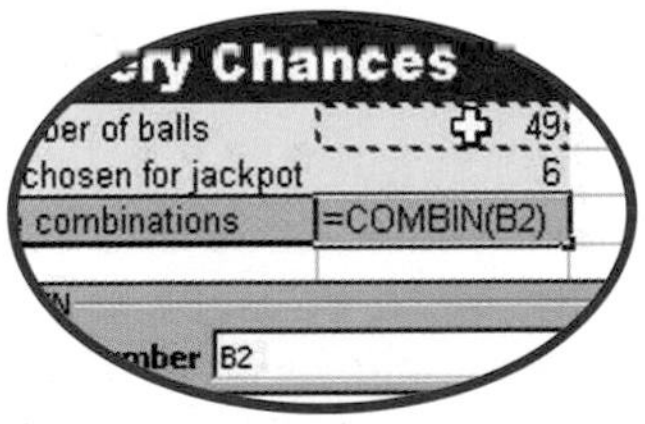

7 Now click on the Number_chosen box in the floating window (top right). The flashing vertical cursor appears there. Click on cell B3, which holds the number chosen (right) and press the floating window's OK button.

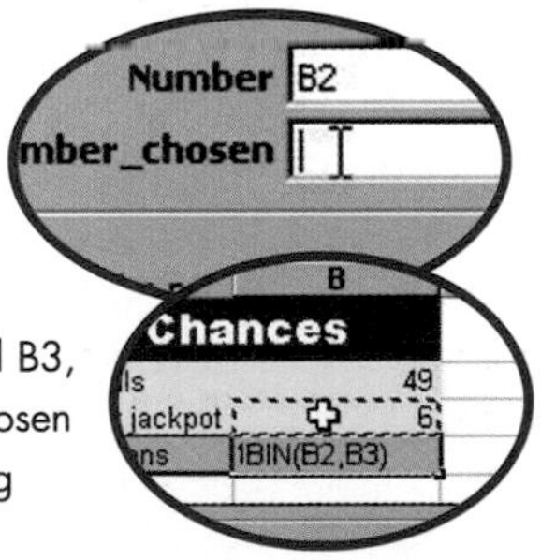

8 In less than a second, Excel works out the total number of possible combinations of six balls chosen from 49 and displays the result – almost 14 million. That means the chance that any single lottery entry will win is nearly 14 million to 1.

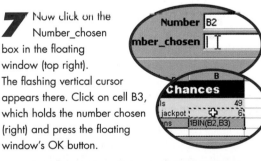

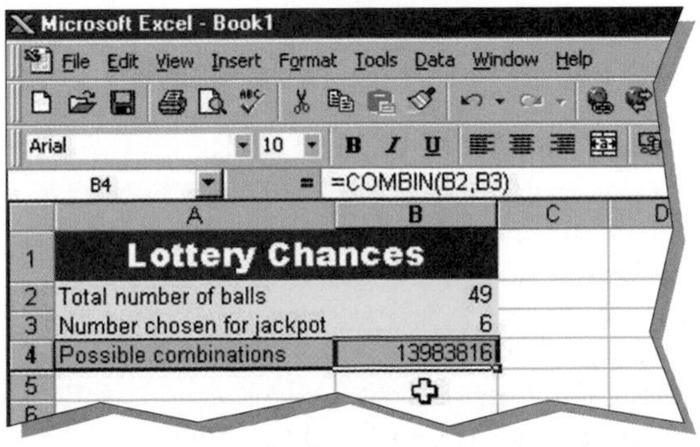

SHORTCUTS

If you've switched off Excel's Formula Bar, you won't be able to see the formulae in the worksheet cells very easily. Select a cell and press [Ctrl]+['] and you'll instantly be able to see the formula that it contains.

Eight essential Excel functions

The best way to gain confidence with Excel's functions is to use them. Here's our guide to some functions that will prove handy time and again, plus tips on where to get further information.

We explored an Excel function properly for the first time on page 47, where we used COMBIN. This is just one of the functions available for carrying out complex calculations, but most are only occasionally useful, and many people rely on the same number of functions over and over again. As you grow more confident you can try more advanced functions, using Excel's Help files to find out how they work. In the meantime, here's our selection of eight of the handiest functions to get you started.

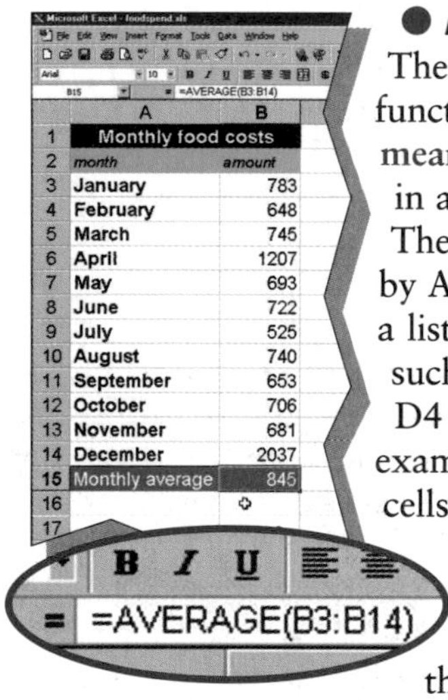

Microsoft Excel - foodspend.xls
=AVERAGE(B3:B14)
Monthly food costs
month amount
January 783
February 648
March 745
April 1207
May 693
June 722
July 525
August 740
September 653
October 706
November 681
December 2037
Monthly average 845
=AVERAGE(B3:B14)

● AVERAGE

The AVERAGE function calculates the mean of the numbers in a group of cells. The arguments used by AVERAGE can be a list of cell references, such as A1, B2, C3, D4 or, as in this example, the range of cells B3:B14, which will calculate the average of the numbers in all the cells between B3 and B14. You can also type numbers in directly as arguments – for instance, you could use the formula AVERAGE(2,5,11) to find the average of 2, 5 and 11.

● ROUND

The ROUND function limits the calculation's answer to a set number of digits in cases where it might result in unwanted decimal places. Here, for example, we've used ROUND to ensure that a financial calculation results in a whole number of pence. The ROUND function needs two arguments: the number you want to round up or down and the maximum number of decimal places you want. You can also use ROUND to produce a whole-number answer by setting the number of digits to zero.

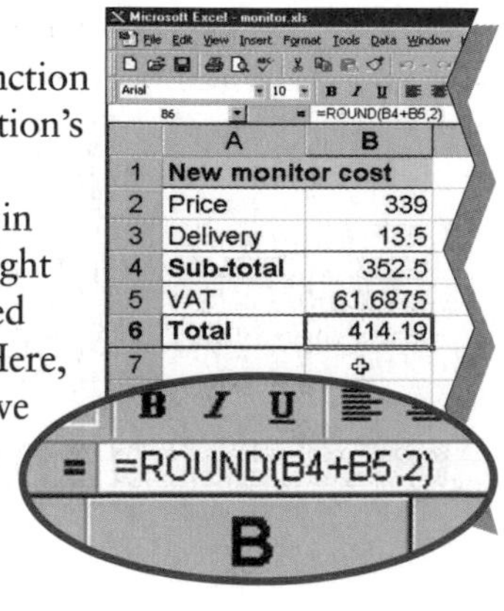

● CONCATENATE

Despite its long name, the CONCATENATE function does a simple job – taking chunks of text and joining them together to make one long line of text. The example overleaf shows a common use for CONCATENATE: joining first and last names together to make a full name. The first name is stored in cell B2,

WHAT IT MEANS

MEAN

There are several ways to calculate an average. The one most often used is called the mean. A mean is worked out by adding up a group of numbers and dividing the result by the number of entries in the group. For example, the mean of 2, 5 and 11 is 2+5+11 (=18) divided by 3, which equals 6.

which is used as the first argument. Cell C2 is used as the third argument. In the example (right), we've added a space inside the quotation marks between the two text entries. Excel treats this space as the second argument, placing it between the two names 'Peter' and 'West' so they don't collide.

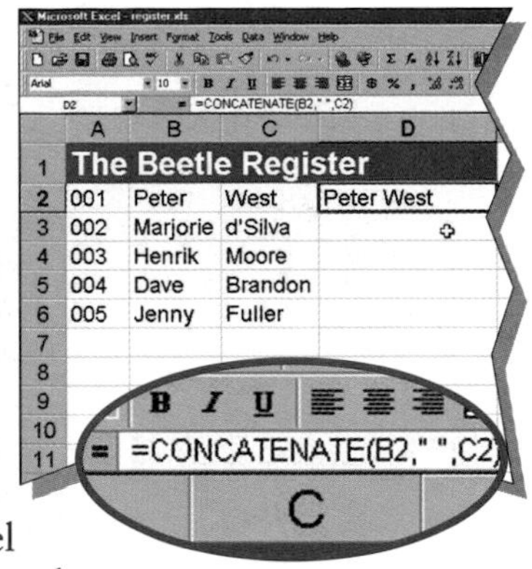

● LOWER

LOWER is a text function that converts all the upper case (capital) letters in text into lower case (small) letters. It requires only one argument – the text to be converted or a reference to the cell that contains that text. The formula in our example ensures that text is consistent, converting 'WHITE' to 'white'. LOWER is a handy way of ensuring that lower case letters are used if the caps key is accidentally set.

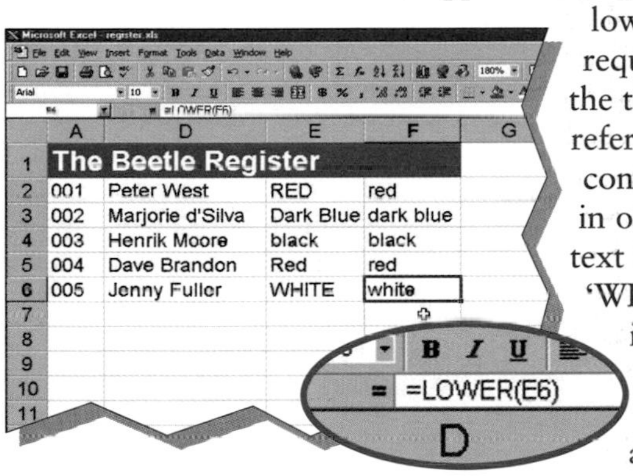

● TODAY

This function generates a number that represents the current date. The day, month and year are taken from your PC's internal clock, so if this is set incorrectly, the result of using TODAY will be wrong. You can apply formatting to the cell in order to control the way in which the date is displayed.

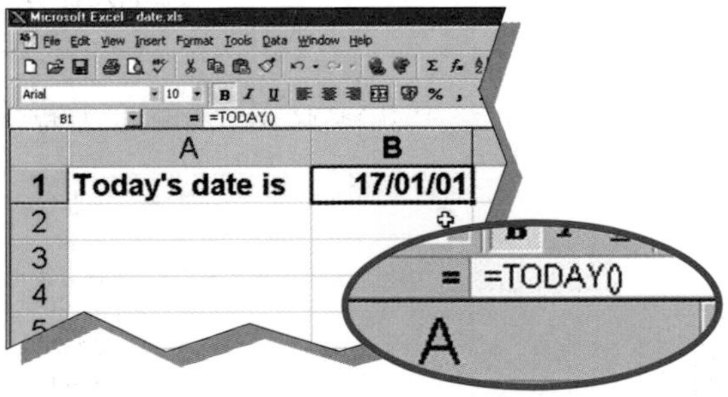

● SUMIF

The SUMIF function adds up the contents of a group of cells – but only if they meet certain, specified conditions. In the example top right, there are two columns of information – items of expenditure and their cost. We have used SUMIF to pick out all the cells that relate to expenditure on food and then to add them up. In the formula, the first argument after SUMIF tells Excel where to look for the condition. The second argument shows what to check for, and the third tells Excel where to find the numbers that it has to add up.

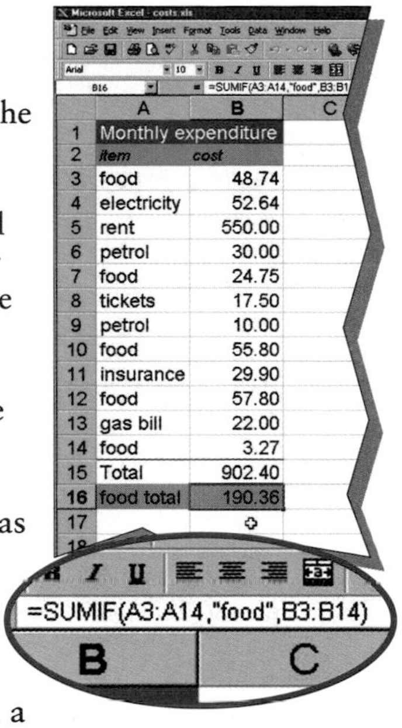

● MAX

MAX finds the largest number in a group of cells. Its arguments can be a list of cell references such as A1, B2, C3, D4 or it can be a range of cells, as in this example (left) where the largest number in the cells between B2 and B14 is calculated.

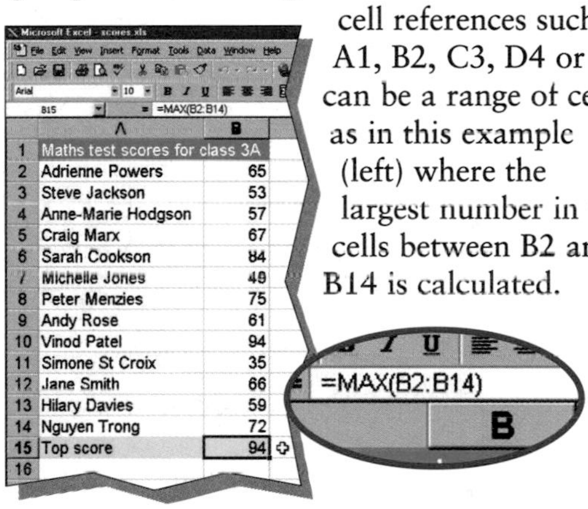

● PMT

The PMT function calculates the cost of loan repayments over a number of set periods at a fixed interest rate. It requires three basic arguments: the interest rate; the number of periods of the loan and its present value.

However, as this is a very powerful function, you can add other arguments, for example, to cater for interest-only loans. In this example, we've used the PMT function to show the monthly repayments for a five-year loan of £9,000. The first argument (E4%/12) shows that the monthly percentage rate of interest is held in cell E4. The second and third arguments show where the number of repayments and the amount of the loan appear in the table.

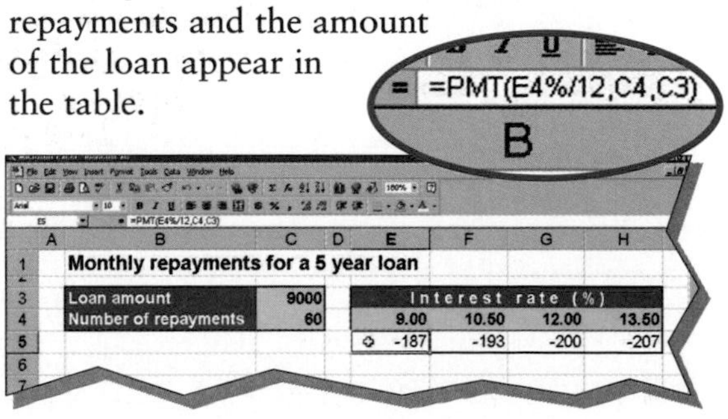

PC TIPS

Find out about functions

Excel's Help files include explanations and descriptions of how to use all the functions. For example, to get information about the PMT function, choose Contents and Index from the Help menu. Select the Index tab in the Help Topics menu. Next, find the PMT worksheet function in the list and then click on the Display button.

Customizing your toolbars

As you become more expert, why not take advantage of the opportunity to set up Excel to suit the way you work?

The two standard toolbars in Excel look very much like the two in Word. This is because all Windows programs – Microsoft products in particular – try to use as many common toolbars and buttons as possible in order to make learning and using software easier.

Not only are Excel toolbars similar to Word's, but you can also change them in the same way. We have already seen how to customize Word's toolbars (see pages 30-33), so let's do the same thing in Excel.

● What you can alter

The main reasons for customizing the Excel toolbars are the same as for Word: to save screen space, to allow commonly used commands to be accessed with a single mouse click, and generally to make the program work in a way that specifically suits you. If, for example, you find you are using a particular option frequently and it's not on the toolbar, you can create a button for it and put it on a toolbar of your choice. You can even create a completely new custom toolbar to replace the existing two.

The two main Excel toolbars are called Standard and Formatting. As in Word, you can access other, more specific toolbars from the Toolbars option on the View menu, or by pressing certain buttons on the Standard and Formatting toolbars.

The Standard toolbar commands are very similar to Word's, with buttons to Open and Save, Cut, Paste and Print. Options specific to Excel include AutoSum, Sorting and the Chart Wizard. The Formatting toolbar, below the Standard toolbar, is also similar to Word's. From here, the typeface size and type can be changed and text can be made bold, underlined or italicized. There are also some formatting options that are particular to Excel. Opposite, we show you how to alter the buttons on either toolbar.

PC TIPS

Undoing changes

If you make a mistake when customizing toolbars, such as deleting a useful button by mistake, or adding too many unnecessary new ones, don't worry. You can easily return any toolbar to its original state and simply start again.

To do this, click on View to see the menu, click on Toolbars, and select Customize from the menu. This will show you a list of all the toolbars. Select the one you want to return to its original state, and click the Reset button. The toolbar will then be returned to the state it was in when Excel was first installed.

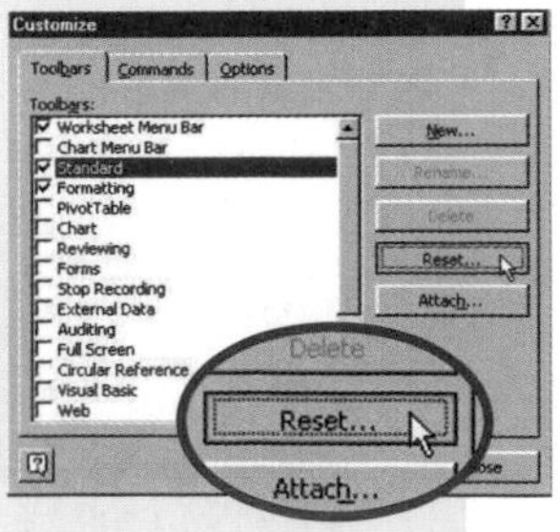

Altering the standard toolbars

You can customize the existing toolbars by removing or adding buttons. We'll practise on the Standard toolbar – the one under the menu bar.

1 One button that is seldom used by most users is the Drawing button, so we'll remove it for the purposes of this example. Hold down the [Alt] key and drag the Drawing button away from the toolbar with the mouse. You will see a small image of the button move with the mouse pointer; release the mouse button over any part of the worksheet and the Drawing button will disappear from its usual position on the toolbar.

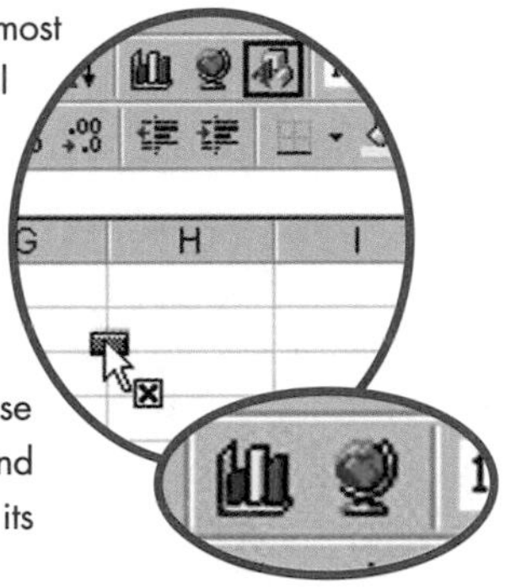

2 A useful button to add is Cycle Font Color. This one-click command lets you change the colour of any text in the worksheet easily and quickly. To add a new button (or to replace one you have previously deleted), go to the View menu and choose Customize from the Toolbars sub-menu.

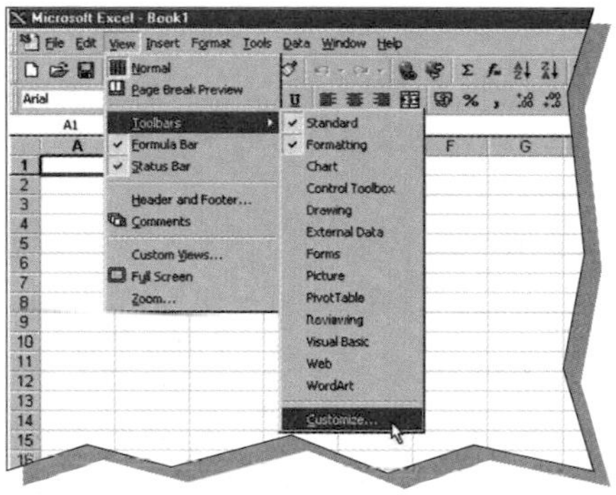

3 Under the Toolbars tab, click on Standard in the Toolbars list. Then select the Commands tab. This will bring up the Commands available.

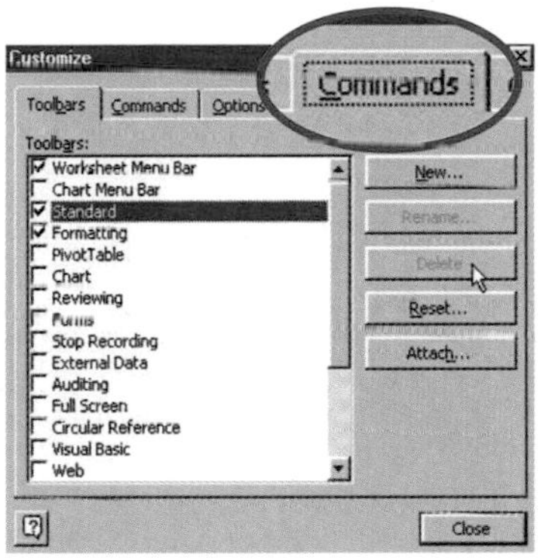

4 First select Format from the Categories menu on the left. Then scroll down the list of the Commands and their buttons on the right until you find the one that you want to insert – in this case, the Cycle Font Color button.

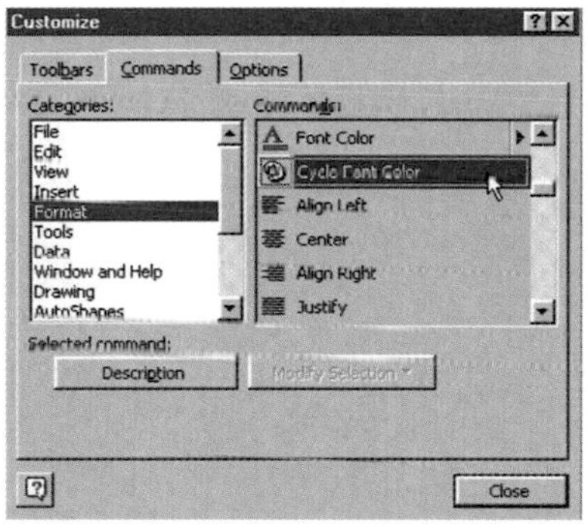

5 Click on the button and drag it to the toolbar. A black vertical line will appear on the toolbar to indicate where the button is going to appear.

6 You can also move a button from one toolbar to another, using the [Alt] key as in Step 1. Hold down the [Alt] key and click on the Cycle Font Color button you have just placed on the Standard toolbar. Drag it to the Formatting toolbar. Excel knows that you want to move the button rather than delete it, so when you release the mouse button the button automatically moves to its new position.

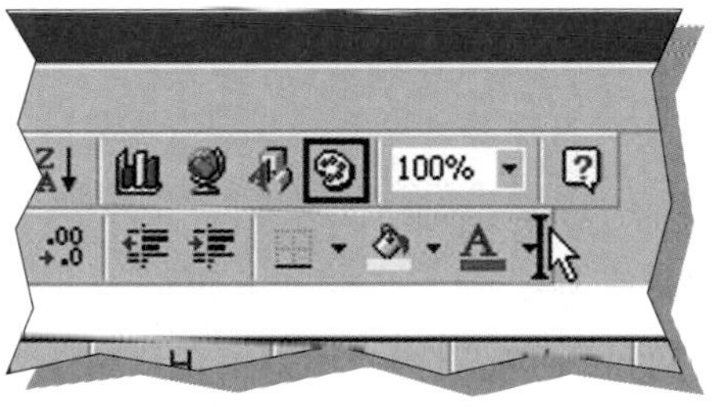

CUSTOM TOOLBARS

You can create your own specialized toolbar by clicking the New button in the Toolbars section of the Customize dialog box and giving it a name of your choice.

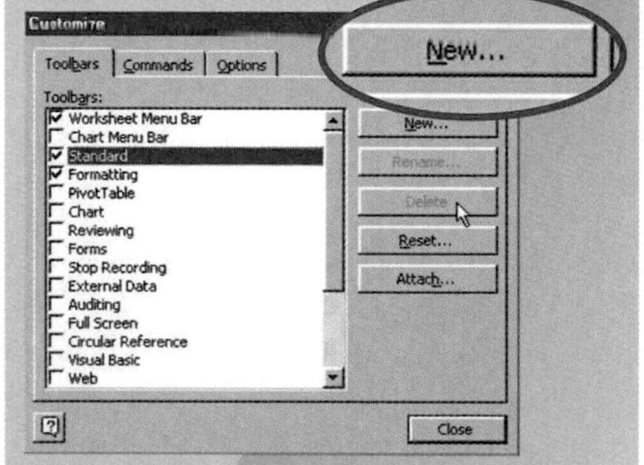

On the other hand, you might want to delete a toolbar you have created and now no longer need. In the Customize dialog box, click the Toolbars tab. Select the toolbar you want to delete and press the Delete button. Note: you can only delete new toolbars that you have created; the Excel toolbars can only be altered, but not deleted.

PC TIPS

A handy option available from the Toolbar window (under View) is the ability to enlarge the buttons on your toolbar. This makes it easier to press the buttons – especially for children or the sight-impaired. The default toolbars have too many buttons for them all to be enlarged, but if you've removed some buttons (see Step 1), there might then be enough space to do so. Select the Options tab from the Customize dialog box and check the Large icons tick box. To reverse the process, simply untick the box.

7 If you rarely use a toolbar, you might not want it on screen. You cannot delete Excel's toolbars, but you can remove them from view. There are several ways to do this, but the easiest is to untick its name in the list on the Toolbars menu under View.

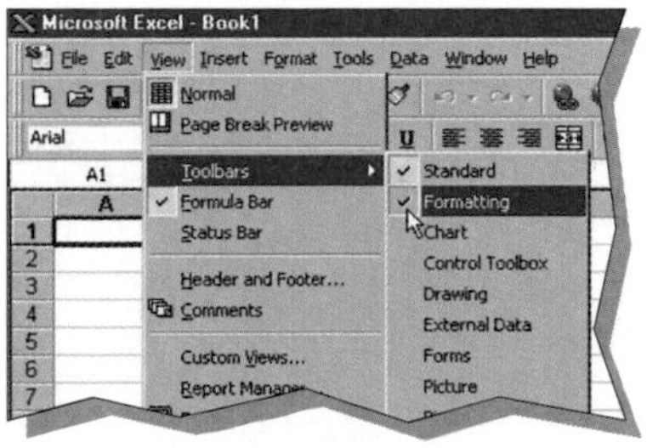

Working with dates and times

Excel's number-crunching abilities are only part of its power. You can also perform useful calculations on date and time information to solve complicated problems effectively.

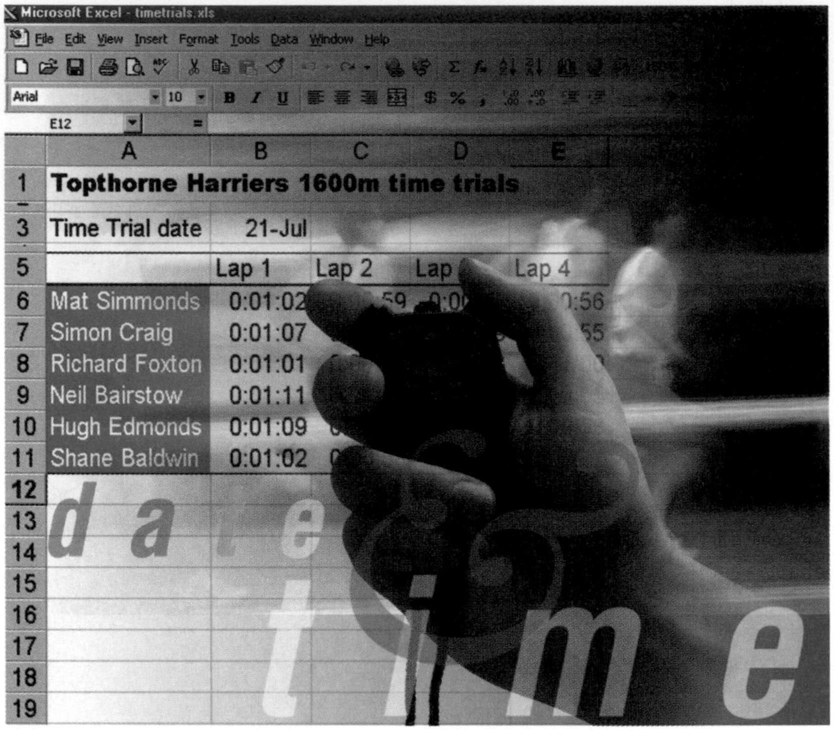

Sometimes date or time calculations can be confusing, but Excel lets you race through them.

Most of the calculations you do with Excel concern normal numbers: totting up the family food budget, keeping track of your motoring bills and so on. But Excel can also help with other types of calculations. Using maths to work on dates and times is one of the easiest ways to get more out of the program.

A saving grace

If you have a savings account that requires 90 days' notice of withdrawals, for example, it would be useful to be able to subtract 90 days from the date when you need the money without the need to reach for the calendar and count off the days one by one. With Excel, you can type in the date you want to make the withdrawal and simply subtract 90 days from it. Excel knows how many days there are in each month and will give you the right answer almost at once.

Excel can do this because, behind the scenes, it stores all dates as numbers. Whenever you type in a date – 01/01/2002, for example – Excel converts the date to a code number (37257 in this case) which it keeps hidden from view. As a clue to the fact that Excel thinks of the date as a number, notice how the date aligns to the right of a cell, like a number, but unlike text.

Once the date is converted to a number, you can use it in calculations. Subtracting 90 from the date you typed in will tell you when you can give notice of withdrawals. Excel subtracts 90 from 37257, and converts the answer – 37167 – back into a date, 03/10/2001.

Times and numbers

It's not only date information that Excel secretly converts into a number; times get the same treatment. Try typing 10:25 into cell A1 of a blank spreadsheet and you'll see that Excel lines it up to the right of the cell – just like a date or number. Now type 4:37 into cell A2 and =A1+A2 into cell A3. When you press the [Enter] key, you'll see that Excel has added the two times and shows 15:02.

Counting days on a calendar is awkward enough but calculations involving hours, minutes and seconds, even with a calculator, are hard. Opposite we'll see how easy it is to do date and time calculations using Excel.

PC TIPS

You can tell Excel how you want your date and time information displayed. Highlight the cells and select the Cells command from the Format menu. In the dialog box that appears, select the Number tab and then click on one of the Date or Time categories. The list of Types on the right of the dialog box changes to show you a preview of the formats. Simply choose the one you want and press the OK button.

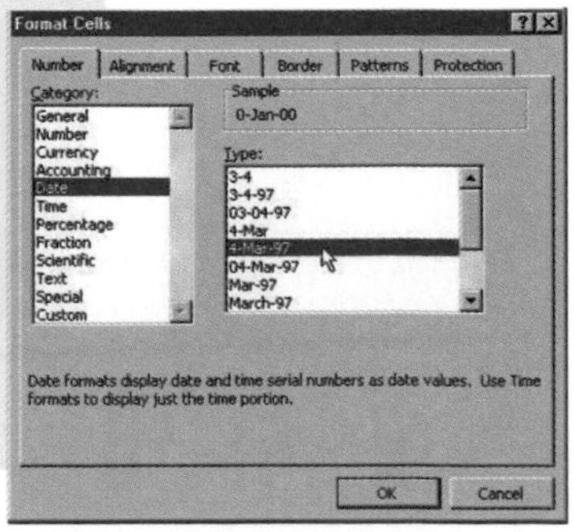

Date and time calculations

In this exercise we show you how to use date and time information in a formula and how to combine it with Excel's other powerful functions.

1 For our example we'll do some date and time calculations on a results sheet for an imaginary school athletics team. Here we've started with a record of the date of the 1600 metres time trial and added four lap times for six athletes. Note that the figures are entered as hours:minutes:seconds.

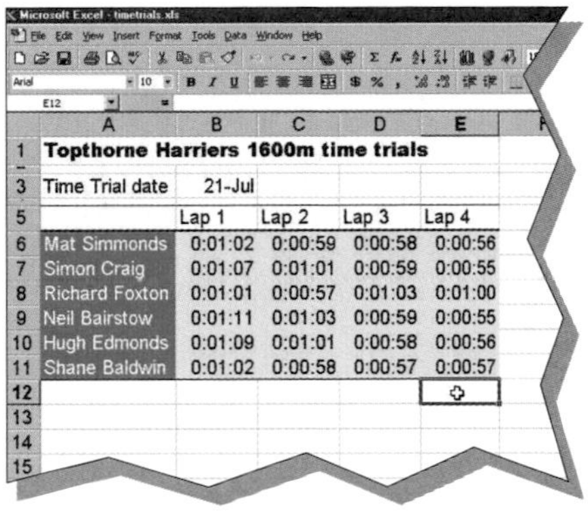

2 Type in an extra heading for the overall 1600m time and in cell F6, double-click on the AutoSum button to get Excel to add the times in the cells on the left.

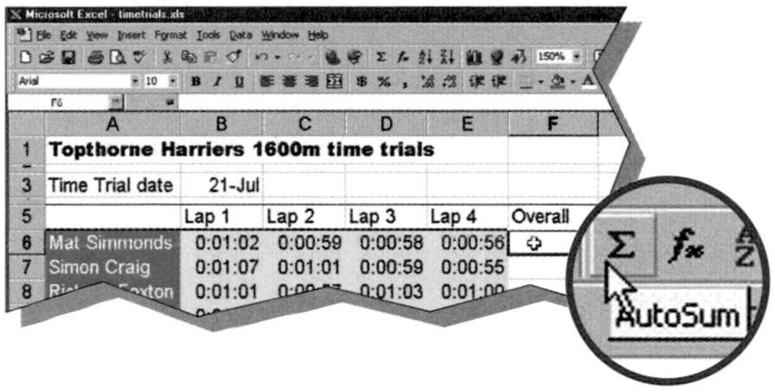

3 You'll see the overall time appear, displayed in the same time format. Add formulae for each of the other five athletes.

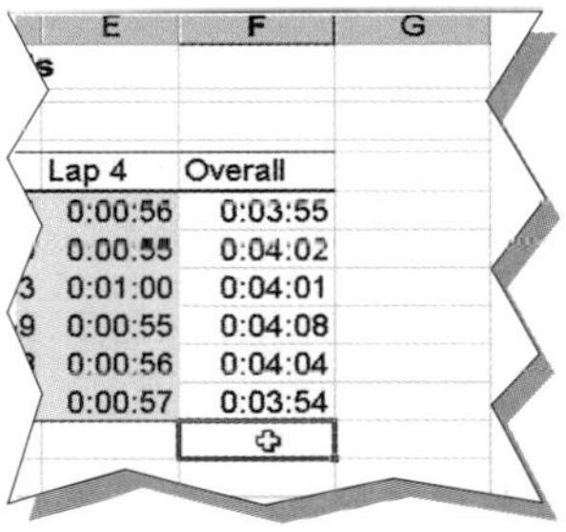

4 We'll also use some of Excel's functions to save more manual effort. Add an extra row to the table for the best lap time of all the athletes.

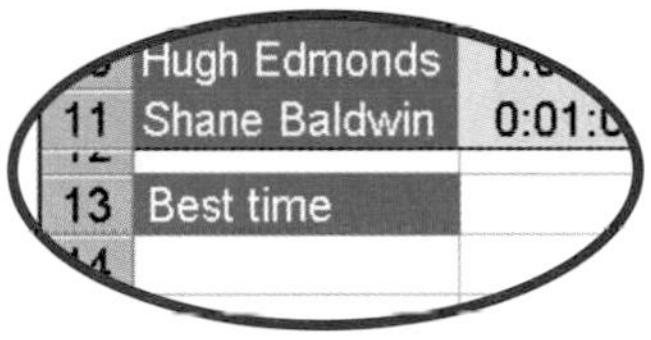

5 Into the next cell type =MIN(B6:E11) and press the [Enter] key. Excel uses the MINIMUM function to look through the table of times and displays the lowest (or minimum) time it finds.

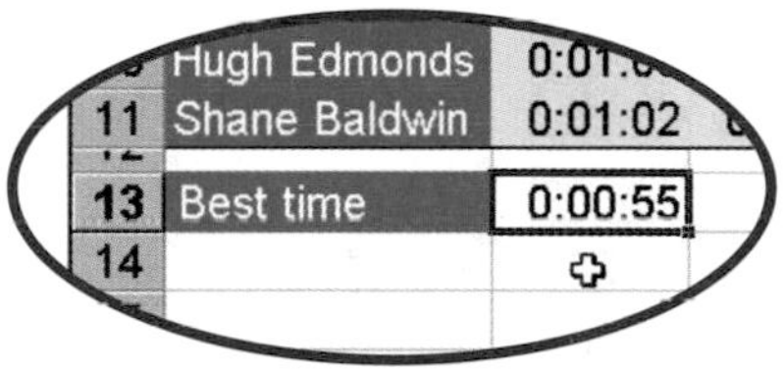

WORKING OUT TOTAL TIMES

When working out time calculations, be aware that Excel normally uses a 24-hour clock and rounds down to the nearest day. This is fine if you want to work out what time it will be 11 and a quarter hours after 3:30pm. Just type in 15:30 (3:30pm on a 24-hour clock) and add 11:15. Excel will tell you the answer is 2:45 (or 2:45am) the following day, which is correct. On the other hand, if you want to add 11 and a quarter hours to 15 and a half hours and get the total time elapsed, you need to change the format of the cells (see PC Tips box, opposite) to display it in the 37:30:55 option. The sample below shows the answer, which is 26:45:00.

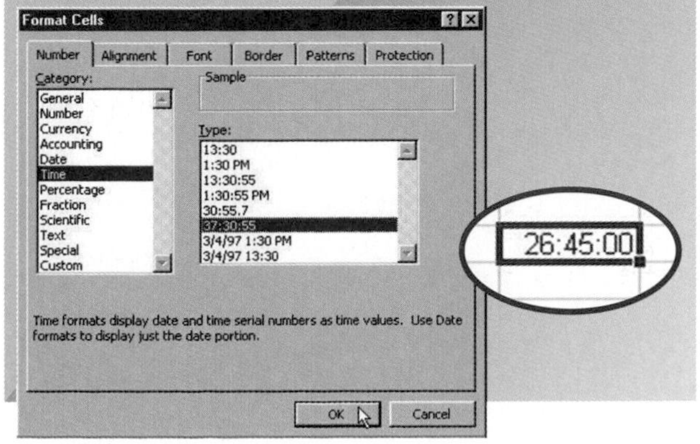

6 Add two more lines: one for the average lap time of all the runners and another one for the slowest lap time. Use =AVERAGE(B6:E11) and =MAX(B6:E11) to calculate the figures.

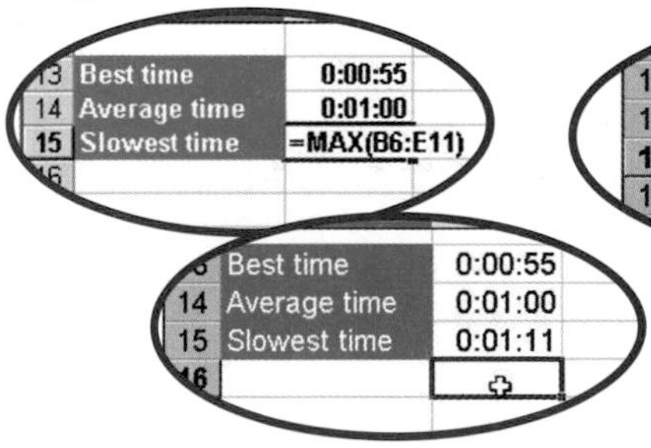

7 We can also carry out a simple calculation on the date of our time trial. Add a line at the bottom of the table for the date of the next meeting, as we show below.

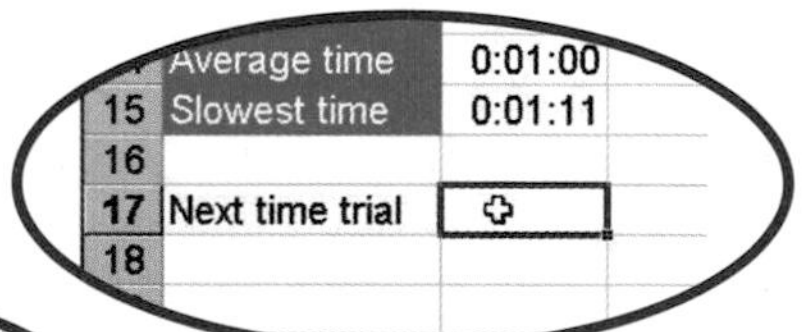

8 We want Excel to work out the date four weeks hence: in cell B17, type =B3+28 (note: B3 is the date we entered in Step 1). Press the [Enter] key and the next date will then appear.

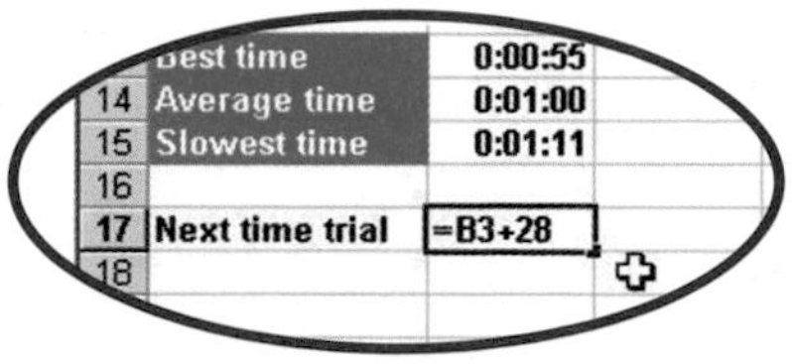

Recording your first Excel macro

You'll often need to repeat the same sequence of commands in Excel to carry out your regular tasks. So why not save time and effort by using macros to teach Excel to do those jobs for you?

Imagine how much time and effort you would save if you could automate everyday chores, such as cooking meals, vacuum-cleaning or doing the laundry. The same could also be said of repetitive tasks in Excel. Wouldn't it be great if you could apply a regularly required piece of formatting, add a frequently used formula or create your favourite type of chart with a single click of the mouse button or a keyboard shortcut?

The good news is that there is a way you can teach Excel to do the jobs you have to perform often – by creating a macro. Once Excel knows what to do, it will do it for you automatically, at the click of a mouse, time after time.

● What is a macro?

A macro is a saved sequence of actions linked together to perform a particular task. The easiest way to create a macro is to record one. All you have to do is start up Excel's built-in Macro Recorder and show it the sequence of actions in the job you want it to remember.

The Macro Recorder memorizes these actions in much the same way as a person watching you cook might write down a list of the steps you perform to prepare a dish. You only have to run through the steps once and Excel will record the exact sequence and be ready to repeat it whenever you want.

● Name that macro

When you record a macro, Excel asks you to name it and gives you the option of typing in a brief description of what it does. It's wise to choose a meaningful name that you'll be able to remember in the future and to take advantage of the opportunity to provide the description in case, in a few months time, you forget the purpose of your macro.

Excel also gives you the chance to set up a keyboard shortcut for your macro. If you do this, you'll be able to run your macro just by pressing the [Ctrl] key and another key simultaneously. Be careful which key you choose, though, because Excel already uses several keys as shortcuts for various standard menu options.

However, you can still run your macro, even if you decide not to set up a keyboard shortcut. All you have to do is select the Macros option from the Tools menu to view the Macros dialog box. This will give you access to all the macros you have recorded. Then it's just a matter of highlighting the macro you want to use and clicking on the Run button to play it.

Opposite, we show you how to apply several formatting commands with a single action. And over the next few pages, we'll show you how to create even more powerful macros.

PC TIPS

Excel provides reference information about how to record, edit and run macros. The best place to start is by looking under macros in Excel's help index. You can also visit Microsoft's Web site (www.microsoft.com) and search for 'macro tips' for a list of helpful pages.

Recording an Excel macro

Here we use a macro to apply labour-intensive cell formatting. Like any macro, once recorded, it can be used with any Excel workbook you start in the future.

1 We've already learnt how to apply formatting to a cell by using the buttons on Excel's Formatting toolbar (see Stage 1, pages 56-57). Here we've changed the font, the font size and colour, the cell background colour and made the text bold. However, this process has taken several clicks of the mouse to do it.

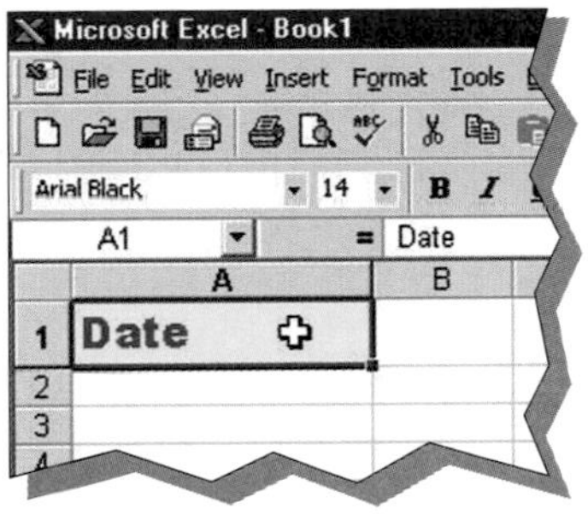

2 It would be much more convenient to use a simple keyboard shortcut to apply this formatting regularly. Let's use Excel's Macro Recorder to record the steps we use to apply the formatting. Select Macro from the Tools menu and choose Record New Macro from the sub-menu that appears.

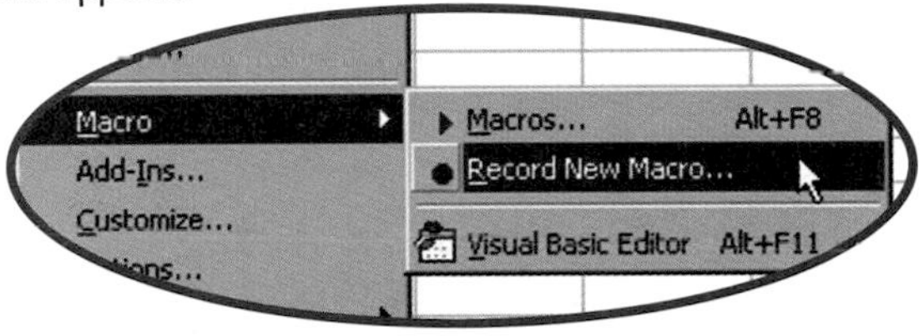

PC TIPS

Sometimes you might find it useful to stop a macro while it is running – perhaps because you started it accidentally or because you have applied it to the wrong cell. All you need to do to stop a macro before it completes its actions is press the [Esc] key.

3 Next, fill in some details about your macro. Type a meaningful name into the Macro name text box. Then type a description of what the macro does into the Description text box. It's important to do both of these so that you can check what the macro is used for in the future.

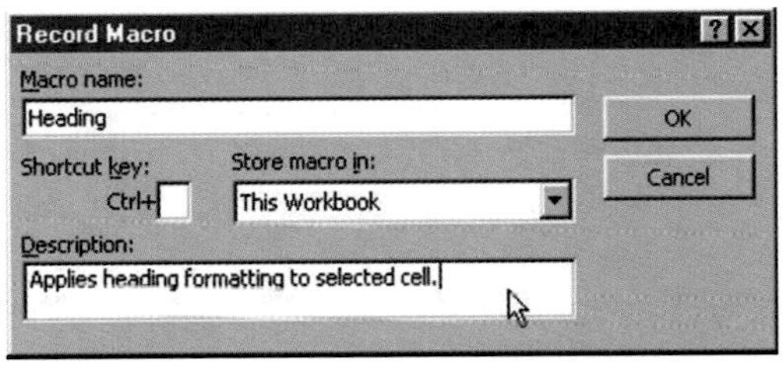

4 Now you need to decide what keyboard shortcut you want to use to run the macro. Be careful to choose a key that isn't already used for something else, such as a shortcut for a command on one of Excel's menus or for another macro you might have recorded earlier. We've typed an [m] into the Shortcut key box. Press the OK button.

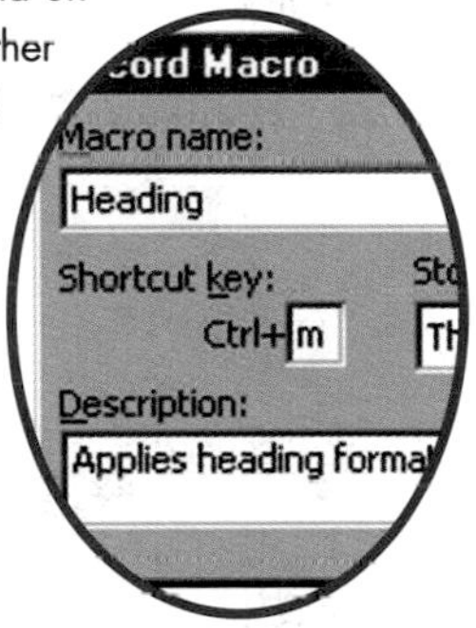

5 Excel starts the Macro Recorder and displays this small toolbar. From now on, every action you perform is recorded as a part of your macro.

6 Now work through the steps you would usually take to apply the formatting you want to the selected cell. Use any of Excel's cell formatting commands: colour, font size, bold, italics and so on.

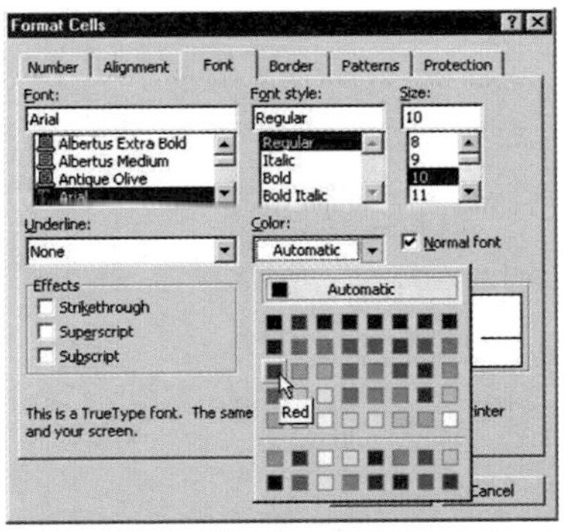

7 Notice how the status bar at the bottom of the Excel window reminds you that the Macro Recorder is recording.

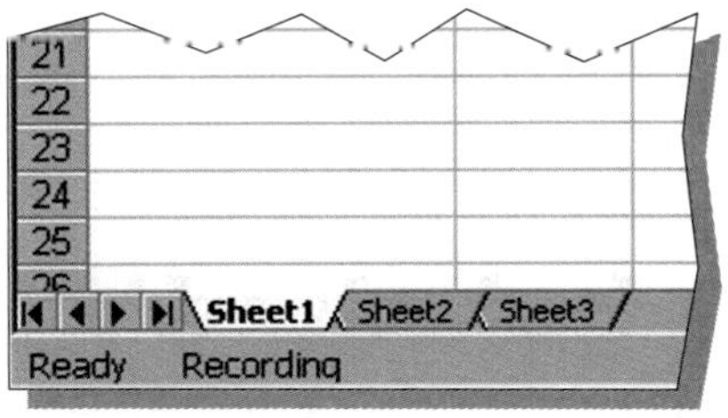

8 When you have completed all the steps, click on the Stop Recording button on the Macro Recorder toolbar (it's the button marked with a small, dark blue square).

9 The quickest way to run your macro is to highlight the cells you want to format and press [Ctrl]+[m] together. Here we've selected two cells and added the formatting to both at once.

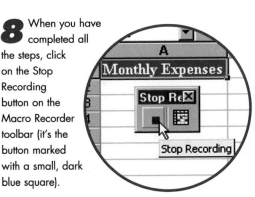

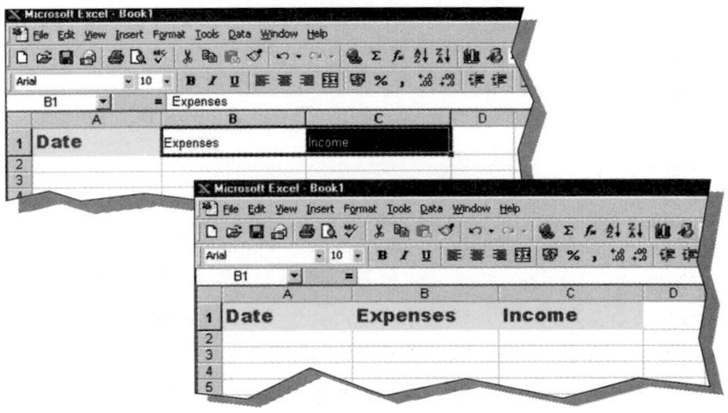

Macros and cell referencing

Your Excel macros may need to refer to particular cells in your spreadsheets. Here's a way to avoid any confusion between absolute and relative cell referencing.

Both absolute and relative cell references can be used to send data exactly where you want to send it – automatically.

We've already seen how to use macros to get Excel to perform frequently repeated tasks (see pages 54-55). The process starts with you recording the individual steps that make up the task. You can then save them as a macro, giving it a name as well as a keyboard shortcut, which allows you to play it back whenever required.

Recording and playing macros in Excel uses almost exactly the same process as in most Office programs. However, there is one important difference – the extra complication of the choice between absolute and relative cell addressing (see Stage 3, pages 62-63).

● Absolute and relative referencing

Absolute and relative cell referencing are the two ways you can tell Excel which cell you want it to work on. If you think of another type of addressing, street directions for example, you can quickly see the difference. A direction such as, 'Go to the police station and the hospital is directly opposite', is an absolute address: no matter where you are it works – as long as you know how to find the police station! However, 'Turn left and then take the second turning on the right to reach the hospital', is a relative address – it works only from your current position. If you try it from other locations it is useless.

Just as each set of directions has its place, so Excel's absolute and relative cell addressing allow you to create formulae and macros that are right for the task in hand.

● The right choice

It's important to be certain which sort of cell referencing you want to use, or you could end up with some unexpected results. For example, suppose cell B2 is selected and you record a macro that refers to cell A1 with relative, instead of absolute, addressing. When you play the macro it will refer to the wrong cell, not the one that you intended.

Excel's Macro Recorder toolbar includes a button that you can use to tell Excel whether you want to work with absolute or relative cell referencing. On the next page, we'll show you how you can use this to help record similar macros for moving cell data – one to move the data to an absolute position in the worksheet, and another to move the data up by a row and left by a column.

PC TIPS

Setting cell references

To record a macro with absolute cell references, make sure that the Relative Reference button in the Macro Recorder toolbar is *not* pressed in (below).

To record a macro with relative cell references, make sure this button *is* pressed in (below).

If you wish, you can also switch between absolute and relative references while recording your macro. This will allow you to take advantage of both types of addressing in one macro.

Recording relative and absolute macros

The first of these two exercises sets up a macro that copies data to a cell at a point near to the one you are working on. The second creates a macro which always sends data to a particular point on the worksheet.

1 Start with a new worksheet and type a single word, 'Balance', into cell B2. We'll move this word around our worksheet to demonstrate how to use macros with relative and absolute cell referencing.

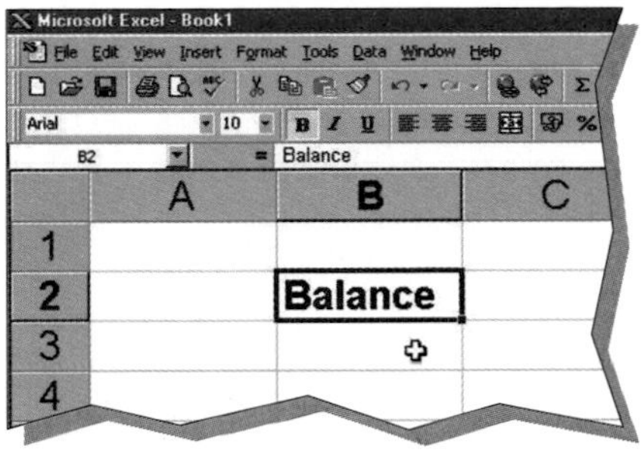

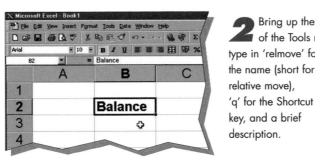

2 Bring up the Record Macro dialog box through the Macro section of the Tools menu (see pages 54-55). When the box appears, type in 'relmove' for the name (short for relative move), 'q' for the Shortcut key, and a brief description.

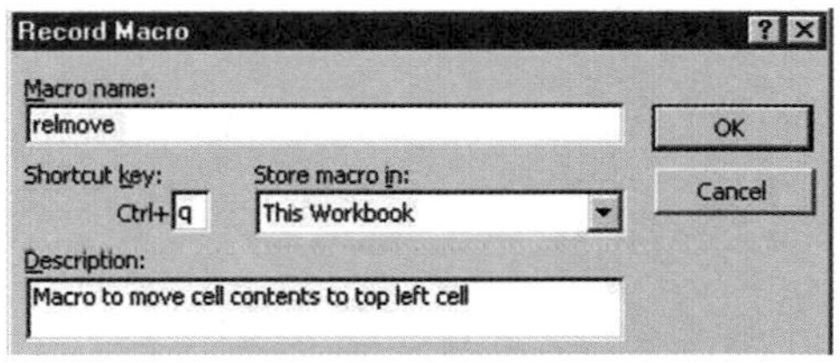

3 The Macro toolbar appears. Press the Relative Reference button and then press [Ctrl]+[X] to cut the cell contents from cell B2.

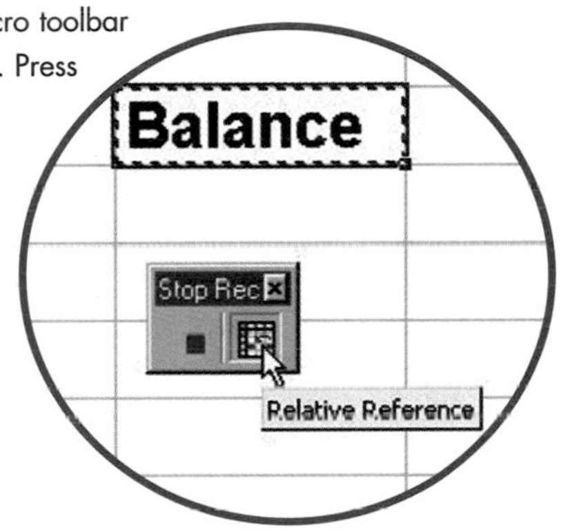

4 Click on cell A1 and press [Ctrl]+[V] to paste the cell contents. Then press the Stop Recording button.

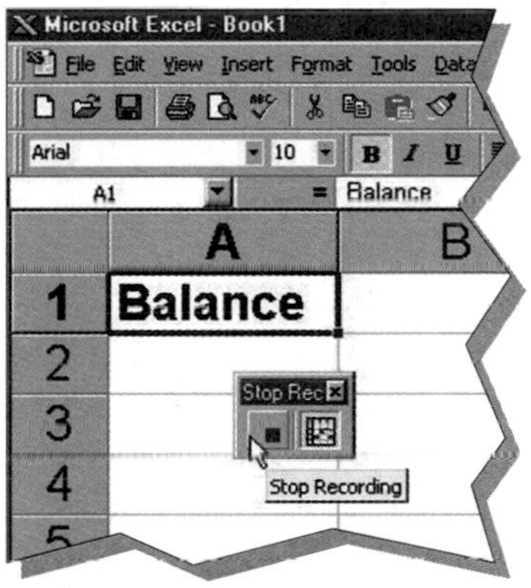

PC TIPS

Sharing Macros

Macros are usually just saved for use with the worksheet where they are recorded. If you record a very useful macro you can use it in other worksheets. Just select Personal Macro Workbook from the Store macro in the Record Macro dialog box.

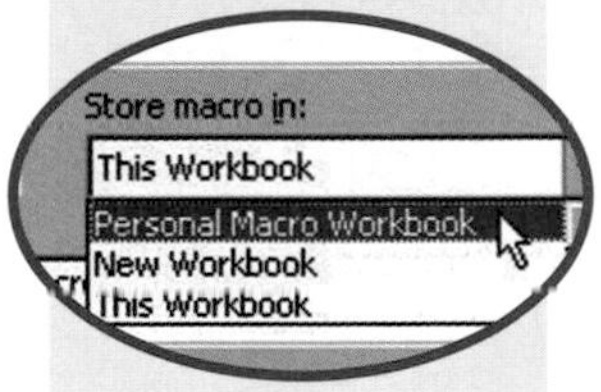

1 We'll repeat the process – with a difference: move 'Balance' back to cell B2 and bring up the Record Macro dialog box. Name the macro 'absmove' (for absolute move), type 'n' into the Shortcut key, then type in a new description.

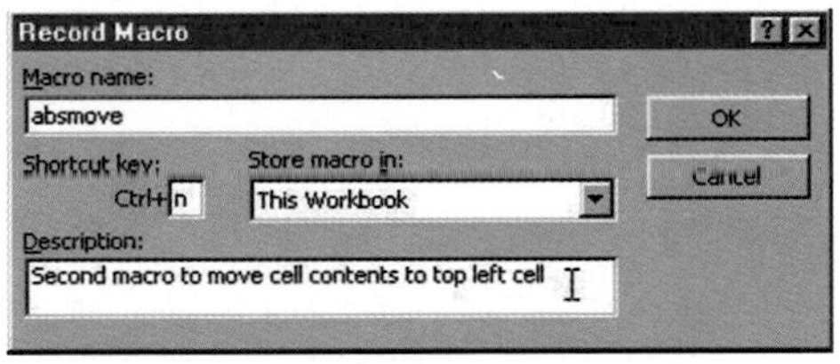

2 Press the Relative Reference button again to turn it off. Then press [Ctrl]+[X] to cut the cell contents from cell B2, click on cell A1 and press [Ctrl]+[V] to paste 'Balance' again. Then press the Stop Recording button.

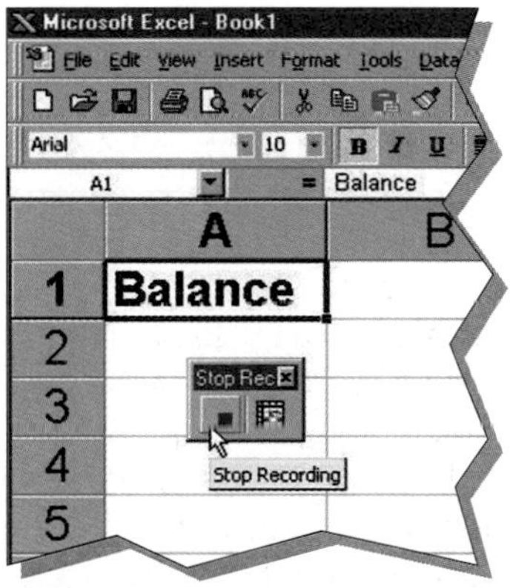

3 Delete the contents of all the cells in the worksheet and type 'Income' into cell C3. Press [Ctrl]+[q] while C3 is the current cell. This is the shortcut for 'relmove'. You'll see that instead of being copied to the top-left cell (A1), 'Income' is copied to B2 – one cell up and to the left of its original place – exactly the same relative position as the move you made in Steps 3 and 4 (above).

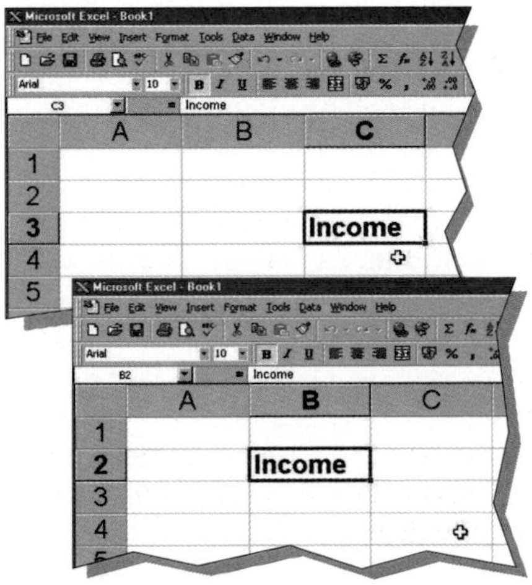

4 Repeat Step 3 (left), but this time press [Ctrl]+[n], the shortcut for 'absmove'. You'll see that 'Income' is copied to the top left cell. That's because this macro uses an absolute cell reference to A1. No matter where the current cell is in your worksheet, pressing [Ctrl]+[n] will always copy it to cell A1.

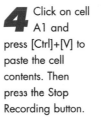

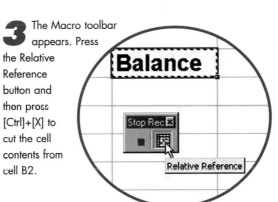

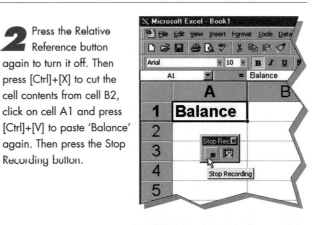

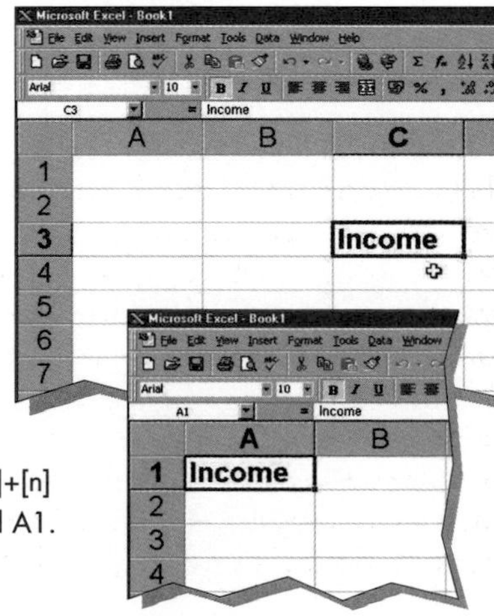

Tips for recording and playing macros

Once you have created a macro, you can allocate a button for it on the toolbar.

Experienced Excel users employ many clever little tricks to make recording and playing macros much easier. Here are some expert tips to help you master macros.

We covered how to record and play macros on pages 54-55 and explained how to avoid confusion between absolute and relative cell referencing on pages 56-57. This time, we want to give you some ideas that will help you to record and play macros more efficiently. We also include some tips on how to avoid the usual pitfalls you might encounter. Most of the advice is pure common sense and involves planning what you want to do in advance.

● Rehearse the steps of your macro
Once you've decided that you need to record a macro, the best thing to do is plan out all the steps that will make it up. It's a good idea to list the sequence of steps on paper. Then, practise doing them a couple of times without starting the Macro Recorder so that you're confident you know all the steps by heart. You should then be able to record your macro perfectly on the first attempt.

● Work round mouse actions you can't record
Excel's Macro Recorder can't record all the mouse movements and clicks you make. The computer will beep to warn you if this happens while you are recording a macro. Don't worry, though, because you can use the keyboard's cursor keys to do many of the mouse actions that aren't recognized by the Macro Recorder. So, if you hear a beep, try the action again using the keyboard.

● Save before you play a new macro
Once you've recorded and saved a new macro, don't rush into playing it straightaway, because you can't use the Undo command to reverse the effects of a macro. Instead, save your worksheet and then play your macro to see if it behaves as you intended. This way is much safer because, if things go wrong, you can close the worksheet without saving the changes the macro has made and you will be able to open it up again.

Once you are happy with the macro, you can add a button for it to Excel's toolbar. This gives you one-click access to the macros. We show you how to do this opposite.

● Keep the Macro Toolbar out of the way
If you're recording a long, complex macro, it can be easier if you move the Macro Recorder Toolbar right out of your way so that you can see everything clearly. This won't affect the macro at all. Simply click on the Macro Recorder Toolbar and drag and drop it where you like.

PC TIPS

Why use a macro?

Before you record a macro, ask yourself if you really need one. Excel often includes tools to help simplify various tasks. Check first that there isn't a menu option, toolbar button or Wizard that does what you're looking for. Check this under Wizards in Excel's Help window.

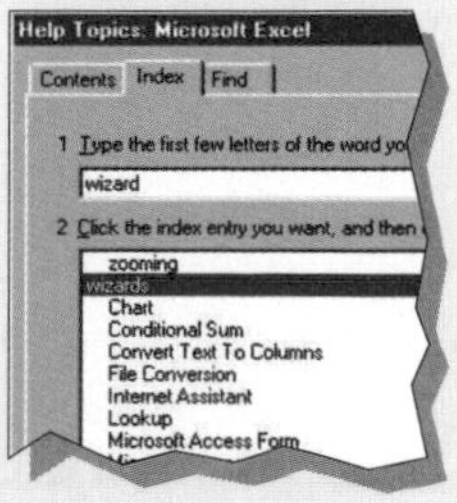

Adding a macro toolbar button

For quicker access to a useful macro, why not add a button to your Excel toolbar? Here's how to add and customize a button for any of your macros.

1 Start Excel and open the worksheet that you used to create your macros (see pages 56-57). Bring up the Customize dialog box by selecting Customize from the Tools menu.

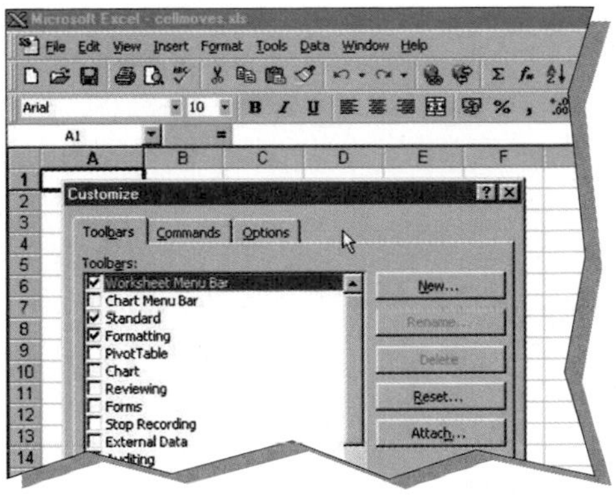

2 Click on the Commands tab and scroll down the Categories list until you see the Macros entry. Click on it and you'll see the list of Commands on the right change.

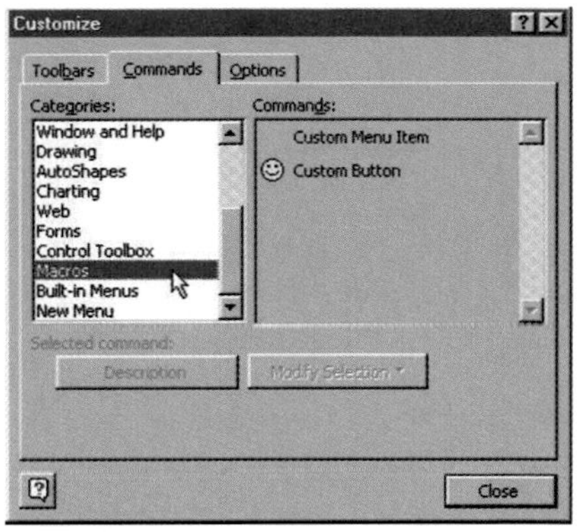

3 Click on the Custom Button command and drag it onto one of Excel's toolbars (right). You'll see a vertical bar appear; release the mouse button when this bar is in the right place. Your button will appear as a smiling face (far right).

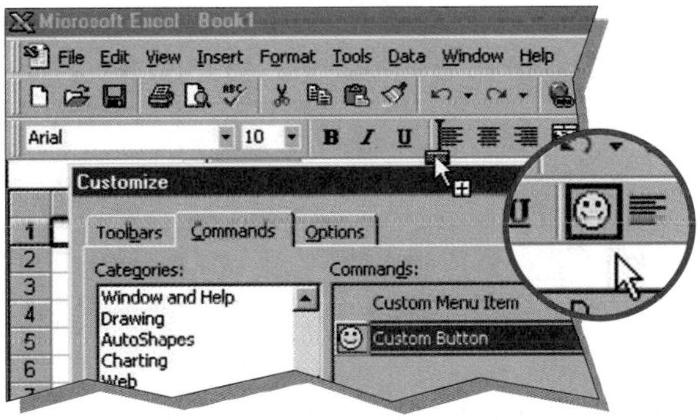

4 Right-click on your new button. In the Name section of the menu that appears, enter a description of what it does (this appears when the mouse passes over your new button).

5 Now click on the Assign Macro command from the same menu. When the dialog box pops up (right), click on the absmove macro and press the OK button. Don't close the Customize dialog box.

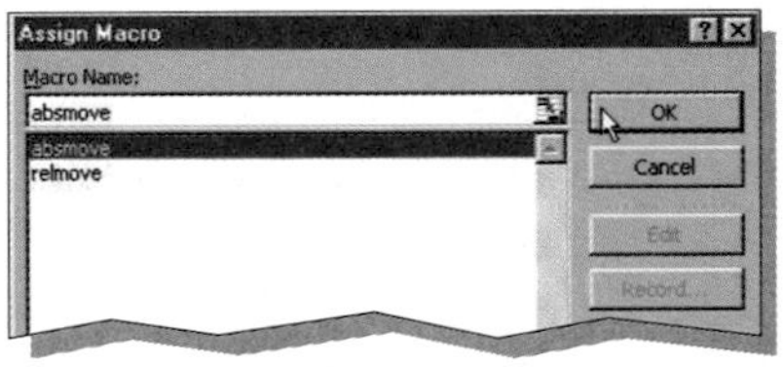

6 Let's change our button icon to one that suits our macro. Right-click on the button to bring up the menu and then select the Edit Button Image command.

7 The Button Editor is like a tiny paint program – you can edit the button image dot by dot. Press the Clear button to remove the smiling face.

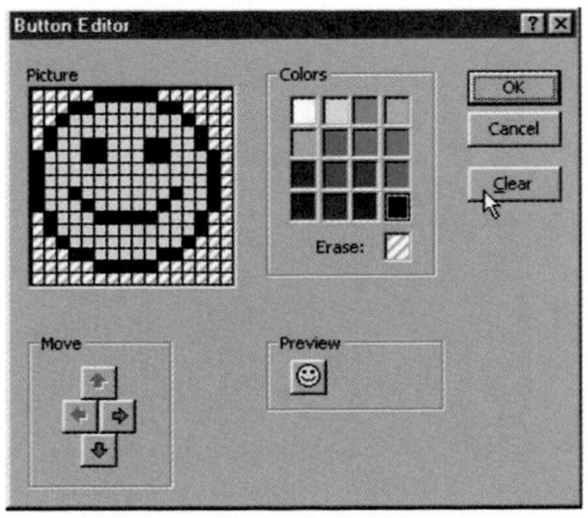

8 Paint your image by clicking on a colour and then clicking on the dots. We've gone for an image that visually explains the button's function.

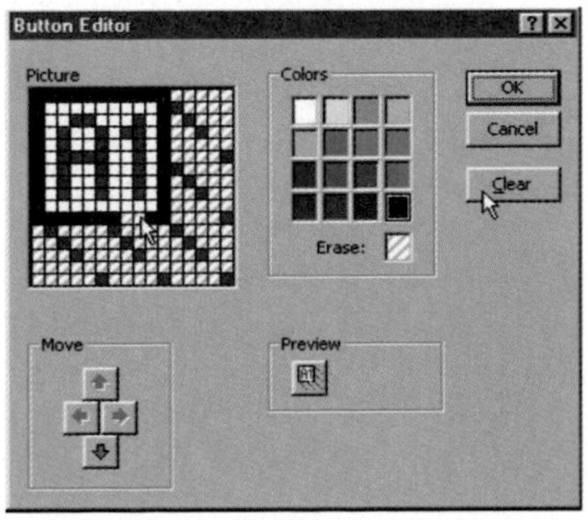

9 When you've finished your image, press the OK button and close the Customize dialog box. Your personalized button and its label will now work just like any of Excel's normal buttons (inset).

Adding a background

You can liven up even the least interesting set of figures in a worksheet by adding an appropriate picture to the background.

Excel's formatting tools, which include typefaces, font sizes and cell background colours, are invaluable in making worksheet information stand out (see Stage 1, pages 56-57).

We've also seen that adding a picture to the chart's bars or segments produces a much more original and interesting look (see Stage 3, pages 66-67). To help lift even the most flat and boring worksheet, you can go even further and add a background picture to the entire worksheet.

● Background information

A background picture works rather like the wallpaper you can add to the Windows Desktop (see Stage 2, pages 10-13). The picture you choose lies behind the information in the worksheet, just as Windows wallpaper lies behind the icons on the Desktop.

Not all worksheets actually merit a picture background: accountants are unlikely to add a picture to an annual budget, for example. However, Excel's grid-based structure makes it perfect for less formal documents, such as an athletics results sheet (see page 53). Many worksheets with a relatively low level of information in their cells present an ideal opportunity for a picture background.

Adding a picture as a background to a worksheet is easy; the most difficult aspect is choosing the right kind of picture. In order to be able to read the text and numbers in your worksheet clearly, you need to make sure that the colours in the picture contrast with the colour of your text.

Busy and very colourful pictures can often prove difficult to work with. If the picture you want to use makes the information in the worksheet difficult to read, you have several options. The first is to choose text colours and typefaces that will aid legibility, such as heavy, bold typefaces. You can also try using a graphics program such as PHOTO-PAINT that will decrease the brightness and/or contrast of the picture.

Finally, try adding background colours to those cells that contain information. The picture will still show through, but adding a cell colour obscures the cell's background and ensures the text in the cell is legible.

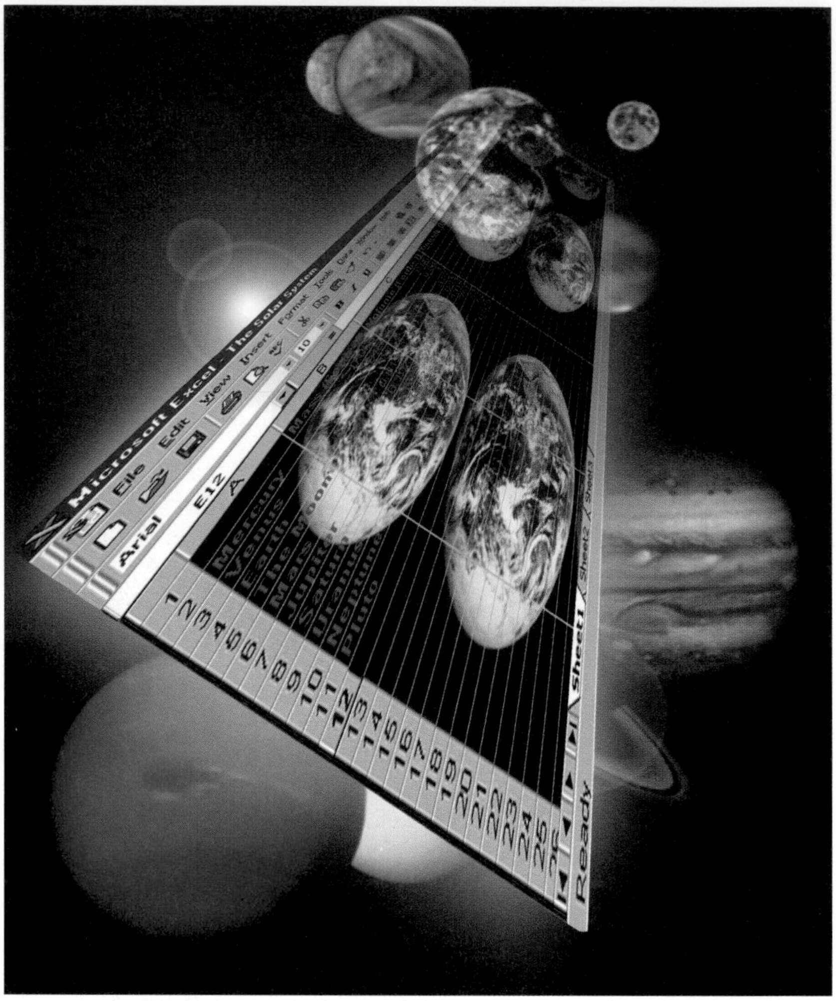

It's easy to give an extra dimension to your Excel worksheets by adding a picture to the background. We show you how to explore the options on the next page.

TILING PICTURES

Background pictures in Excel are tiled. That means that pictures are repeated horizontally and vertically to fill the worksheet – just like tiles on a bathroom wall. Some pictures work better than others when tiled; in particular, you'll probably want to avoid distracting edges where tiles meet. To avoid the unattractive sight of poorly matched tile edges, look carefully for pictures that tile seamlessly so that the join between them is completely invisible.

Adding a picture background

Picture backgrounds can be used to enhance any type of Excel document.

1 Here's a worksheet containing homework about the solar system. We could give some of the cells background colours, but instead we'll experiment with a space theme to spice up the worksheet's appearance.

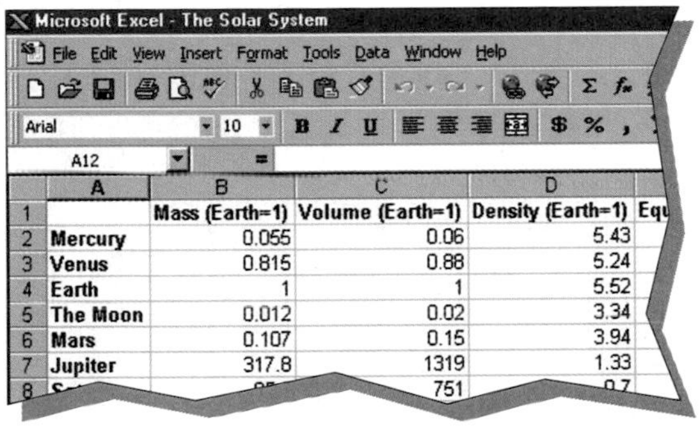

2 Click on the Format menu, select Sheet and click on the Background option in the sub-menu.

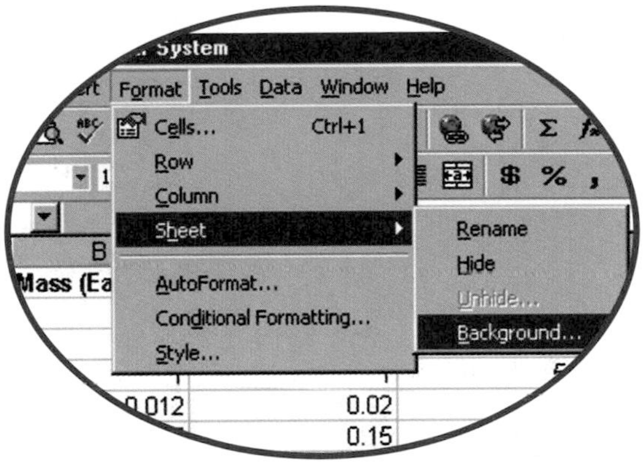

PC TIPS

Finding a background

When adding a picture background, try out the free clip art images supplied on your software CD-ROMs. If you have the CorelDRAW or Microsoft Office CD-ROM, you'll have several thousand pictures to try.

3 This will open the Sheet Background dialog box so that you can choose the picture you want to use. Locate the picture (we've used a clip art picture from a CD-ROM) and then click on the Open button.

4 Here's the worksheet with the Earth background – notice how it's tiled to fill the entire space of the worksheet. The problem is that it's almost impossible to read the information in the worksheet's cells because it's in black text in unfilled cells.

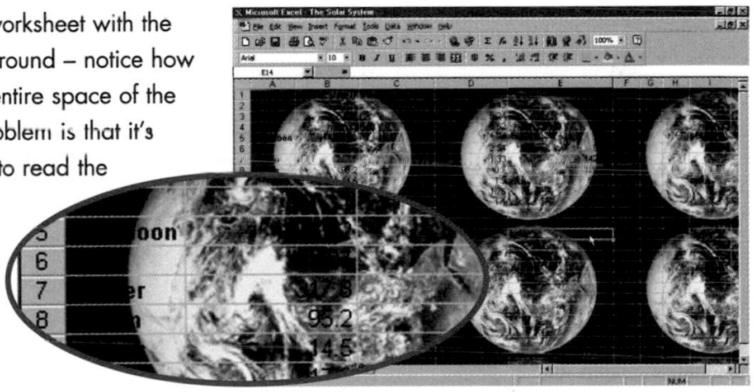

5 To solve this problem, we've tried changing the colour of the text to magenta. It helps, but the text is still hard to read in places.

6 Try experimenting with different backgrounds to optimize legibility. Remove the current background by selecting Delete Background from the Sheet sub-menu.

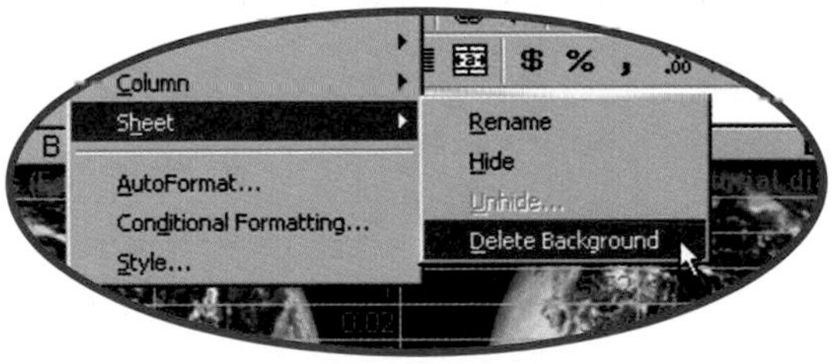

7 Now open the Sheet Background dialog box, as in Step 2, and look through some other pictures. This time, before pressing the Open button, click the Preview button to see what each picture looks like.

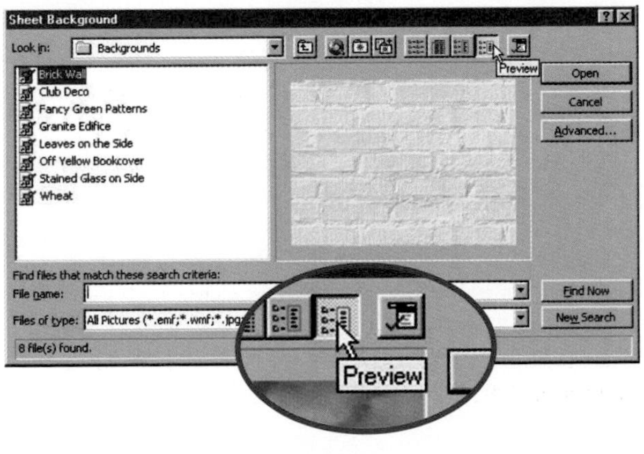

8 This granite picture is better as it has less contrast than the previous image. By changing the text to bold bright yellow, it becomes easily legible.

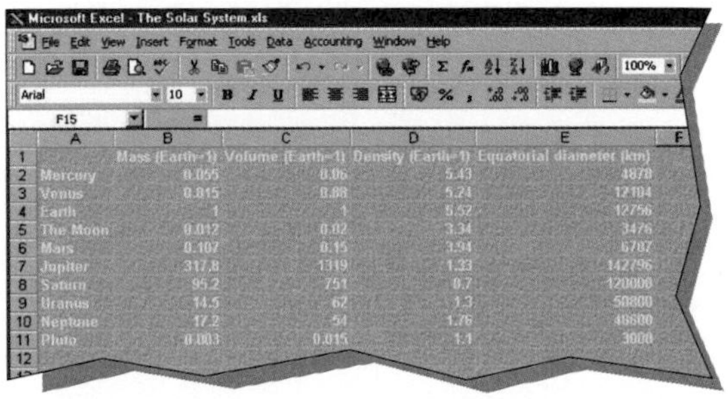

Simple cell naming

Excel's cell references, such as A1, B6 and ZZ193, can be hard to remember. Avoid taxing your memory by giving these cells recognizable names.

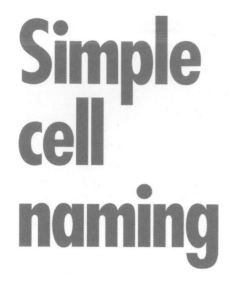

Using names in cells as part of a formula can make worksheets easier for people to use both at home and at work.

Almost everything you do with Excel involves working with cells in worksheets. Up until now we have always talked about cells in terms of their alpha-numeric references, or co-ordinates. For example, A1 is the top left cell of a worksheet. Though alpha-numeric cell references are convenient to start with, they aren't very user friendly.

A few days or weeks after you've created a worksheet stuffed full of cell references, it can be hard to remember which cells hold which bits of information. For example, to work out exactly what's going on with the formula =(C1/D4)*G2 you need to look back at each of the cells mentioned to see exactly what information they represent. A formula, such as =(Distance/FuelEconomy)*PetrolCost would be much more useful. Fortunately, Excel is as adept at working with names as it is with cell references. All you need to do is give your cells relevant names.

● Naming names

Cell names can be as obvious as you like, from 'JanExp' to 'January_Expenses'. Full-length names are easier to remember, but the shortened form is quicker to type (especially if typed into a lot of cells) and is almost as easy to understand.

There's an extra advantage to working with names rather than cell references. Anyone who needs to use your worksheet can understand it more quickly. This is of benefit to business users who share worksheet files with their colleagues over a network, but it can also help introduce worksheets to your family, who might find it difficult to work with algebraic formulae.

The only catch with naming is that it can take time to highlight and name all the important cells in your worksheet.

● Automatic naming

To save you lots of time and repetitive work, Excel provides a way of identifying cells automatically using information you've already typed in. For example, in many of our Excel exercises we've given the worksheet rows and columns labels such as 'Expenses' or 'Sales'. Excel can use these row and column labels to refer to all the cells in a rectangular area automatically.

Let's imagine that you have a worksheet with a table of months, January through to December, listed along the top; your expense items, such as Groceries, Bills and Savings, are down the left side; and your numbers are inside the worksheet to represent the amount spent on each item for each month.

Each cell of data automatically gets a special name, which is made up of the column label and the row label. If, for example, column D had the label 'January' and row 10 had the label 'Groceries,' then you are able to refer to cell D10 simply as 'January Groceries'.

PC TIPS

Cell names

Excel has rules about cell names. Names that you give to cells can be up to 255 characters long, but they cannot include spaces and must start with a letter or the underscore character (_). You can use letters, numbers, full stops (.) or underscores in the rest of the name. Note, however, that Excel is able to use spaces in names it makes automatically from labels, such as 'January Groceries', and you can use them in your formulae, as in =January Groceries/3.

Working with cell names and labels

To avoid confusion in the future when adding to, or otherwise altering, a worksheet, make the most of Excel's ability to create formulae using easy-to-understand cell names.

1 Here's a worksheet for recording monthly household expenses. Instead of using formulae with cell references to add up the monthly totals, we'll use names as an alternative.

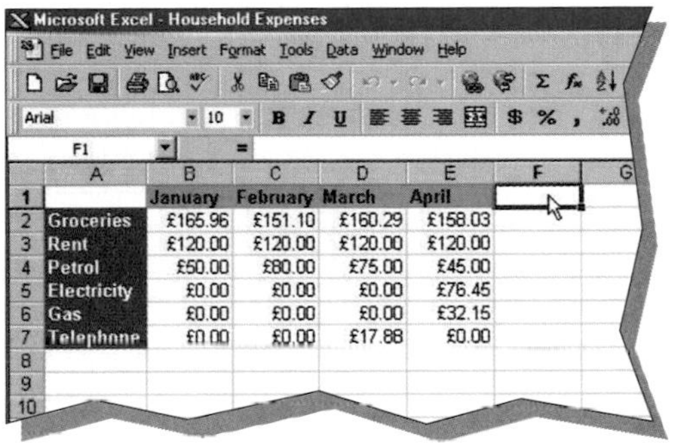

2 It would be time-consuming to name each of the 24 individual cells. Instead, let's take advantage of the fact that we've already typed labels for the rows (Groceries, Rent, Telephone and so forth) and columns (January to April). Highlight all the cells containing information and then select Name from the Insert menu. Choose Create from the sub-menu that appears.

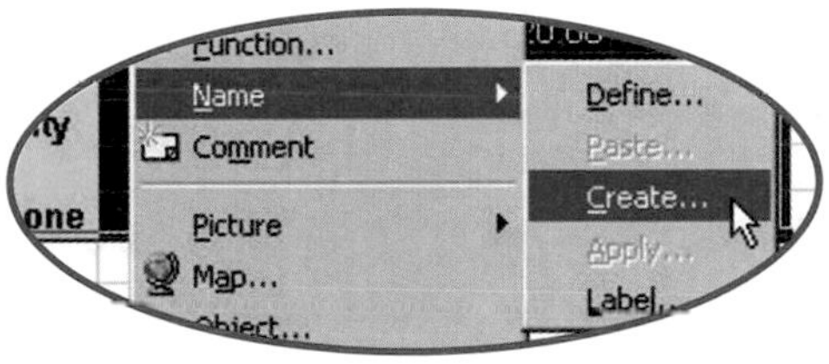

PC TIPS

Checking your cell names

For a reminder of which names refer to which cells, use the Define Name dialog box. To bring this up, click on the Insert menu, Name and then Define.

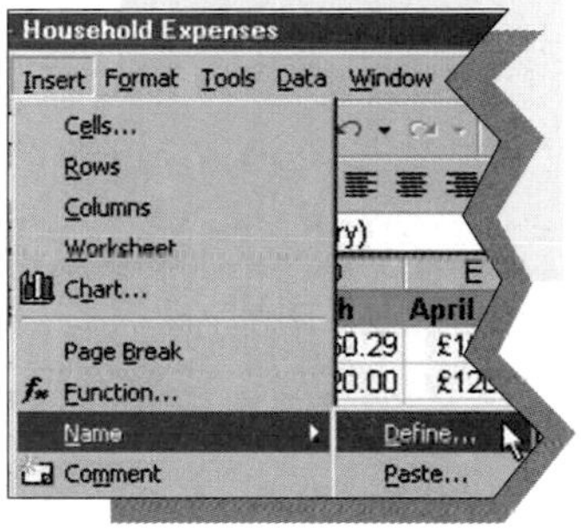

3 Now Excel will open the Create Names dialog box. Excel makes an educated guess at the names to use: if there aren't already ticks in the Top row and Left column boxes, click them to make ticks appear. This tells Excel to use the text in the top row and left column as names. Click on the OK button.

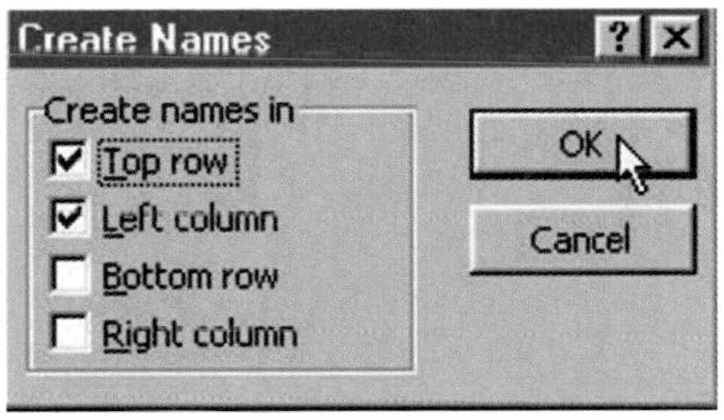

4 To add a total for the month of January, click on cell B8 and type =SUM(January), then press the [Enter] key. Repeat the process for cells C8, D8 and E8.

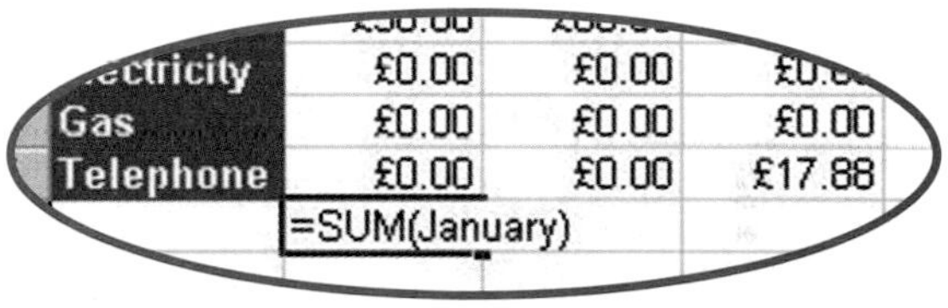

5 We'll name cell B8 manually: click on cell B8 and then click on the Name text box just to the left of the Formula Bar. Now type in a name (Jan_total) and press the [Enter] key.

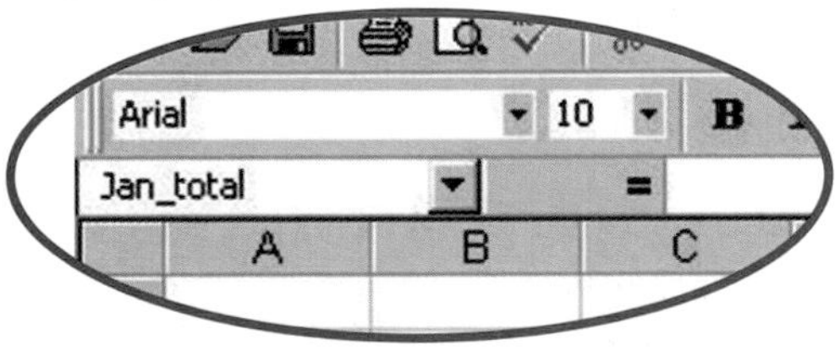

6 Repeat this exercise for the February, March and April totals (cells C8, D8 and E8) using the names Feb_total, Mar_total and Apr_total.

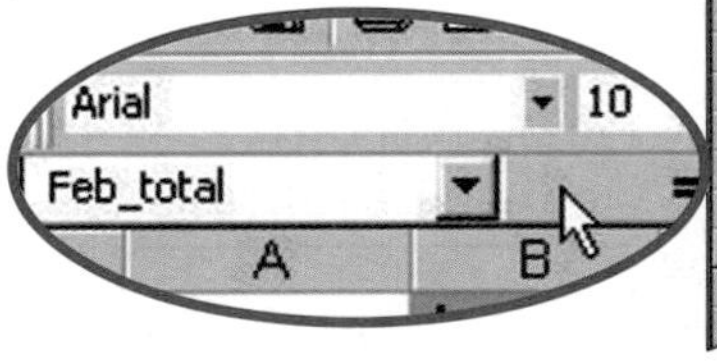

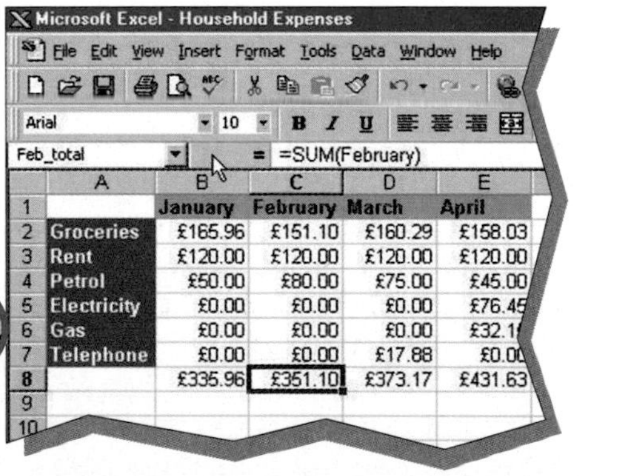

7 Now let's use cell F8 to add up a grand total for the four months. Click on the cell and type =SUM(Jan_total:Apr_total) – a much friendlier formula than its cell reference equivalent, =SUM(B8:E8).

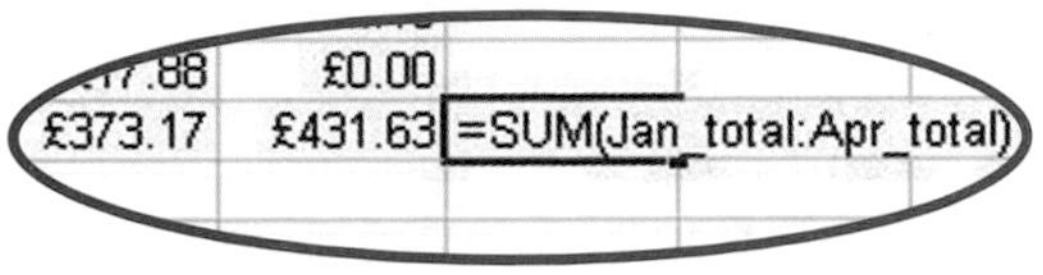

8 Press the [Enter] key and Excel will look up the cell names you entered in Steps 5 and 6, and work out the calculation just as it does with cell references.

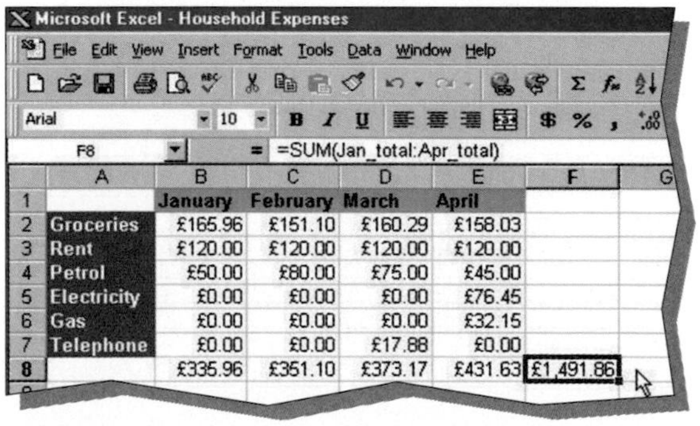

Introducing Excel 2000

Excel 2000 updates Excel 97 to give a new, more intelligent and user-friendly way of working. Here, we'll look at some of the changes to this popular program.

If you've recently bought a PC, you might find that it came with a copy of Microsoft Office 2000's suite of programs. This includes Word 2000's word processing program (see pages 44-45) in addition to Excel 2000.

Excel 2000 is an updated version of Microsoft's very popular Excel 97 program. Like its predecessor, it's an easy-to-use spreadsheet program. In fact, there are only minor differences between the two versions. Whatever you can do with Excel 97 can also be done with Excel 2000 because the core of both programs – the spreadsheet features, commands and calculation capabilities – are almost exactly the same. This means that the *PCs made easy* exercises set out in the Excel articles will work just as well with Excel 97 as they will with Excel 2000.

● Excel ease of use

Both programs can make light work of any home or business number-crunching task. Where Excel 2000 differs is primarily in the way it presents these features and commands. Microsoft has added some intelligence to the way that the menu and toolbar commands work, the basic principle being to highlight the options that you use most often.

This difference is most apparent in the program's menus. Whereas in Excel 97, the menus always list the same set of commands, in Excel 2000 the less-commonly used commands are hidden from view when you first click on a menu. However, there's a downward-pointing arrow at the bottom of the shortened menu: click on it and the full set of commands for the menu is revealed.

● Smarter file handling

Like Word 2000, Excel 2000 also includes easier-to-use Open and Save dialog boxes to make working with your spreadsheet files simpler and quicker. For instance, a single mouse click can take you to the folders that you have used most recently, or to your My Documents folder.

There is also a sprinkling of minor improvements throughout Excel 2000. For example, the Euro is now available as a currency option. Also Microsoft has made it easier to save spreadsheets in a Web page format, so you can post them on your Web site, if you have one.

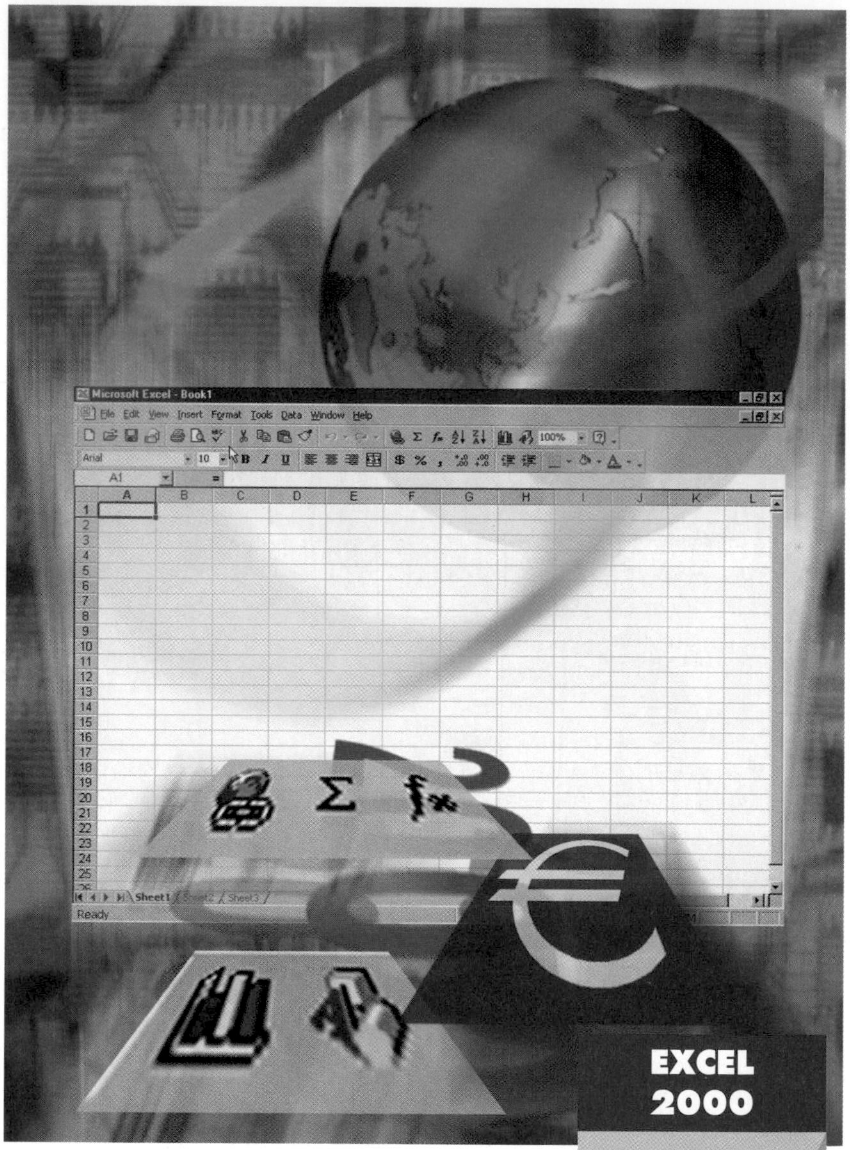

If you thought Excel 97 was smart, take a look at the updated Excel 2000. Its improvements will make working on spreadsheets easier.

EXCEL 2000

Excel 2000 has most of Excel 97's commands, so whichever program you use, future Excel exercises in *PCs made easy* will work in both programs. Where there are any differences, we'll highlight Excel 2000's method with this type of box.

A quick tour around Excel 2000

Excel 2000 brings the ubiquitous spreadsheet bang up to date. It has no problems dealing with new currency symbols and makes it easy for you to present your spreadsheets on the Web.

1 Click on the Start button, select Programs and then click on the Microsoft Excel program option. Note: Excel 2000 has a slightly different icon from that of Excel 97.

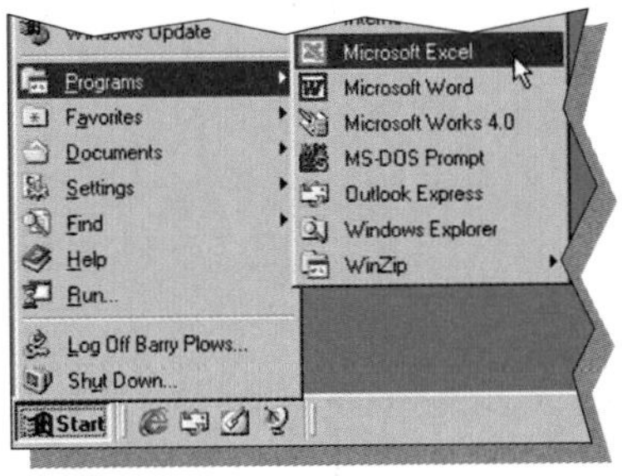

2 Unlike Word 2000, which combines the two toolbars of Word 97 into a single line (see pages 44-45), Excel 2000 keeps the two toolbars separate.

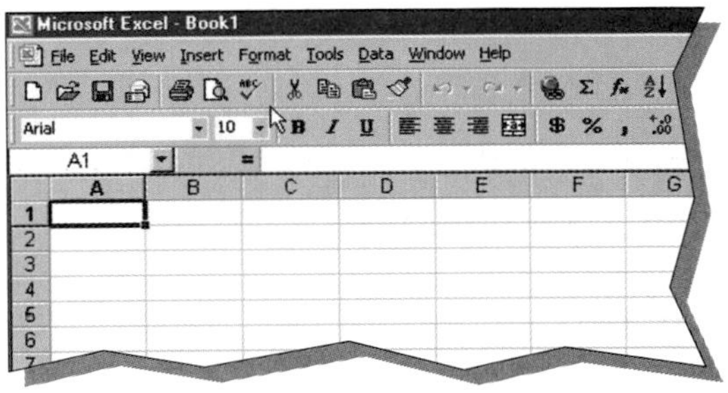

3 If you want to maximize the area available for your spreadsheet, you can drag the toolbars onto the same line, making the More Buttons icon appear, as in Word 2000.

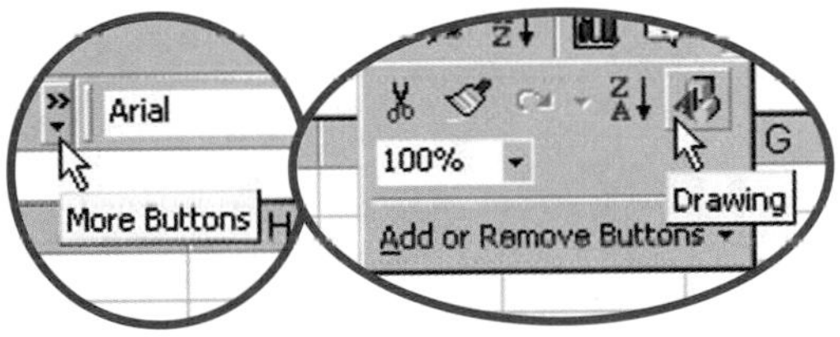

4 Excel 2000 also has shortened menus. These menus have downward-pointing arrows that you click on to reveal the full set of commands. This allows you to concentrate on the commands you use most often.

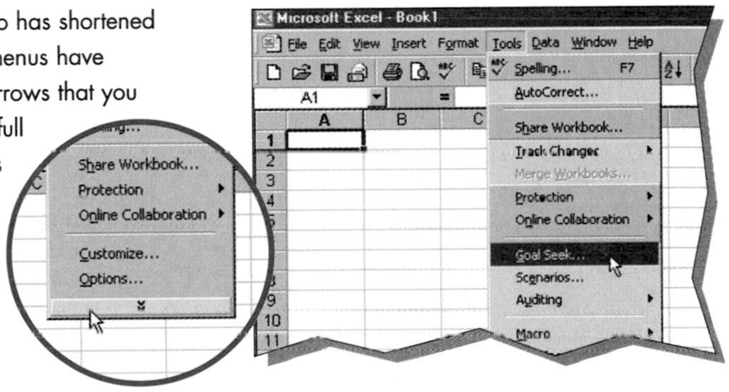

5 In keeping with new developments in international currencies, Excel 2000 now includes the Euro as an option in the Format Cells dialog box.

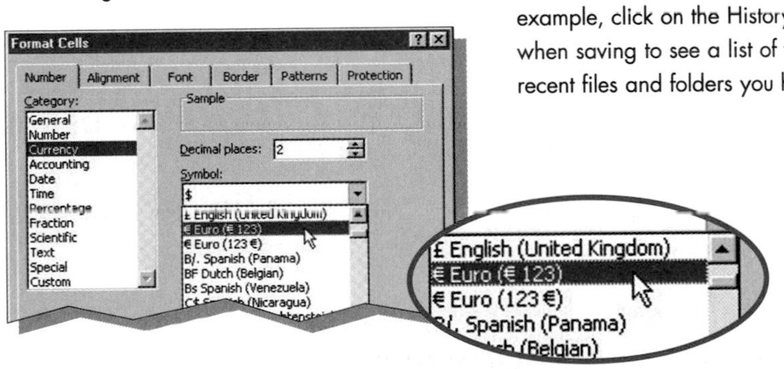

6 When you save or open documents, the dialog boxes have a column of buttons to provide quick access to many useful locations. For example, click on the History button when saving to see a list of the most recent files and folders you have used.

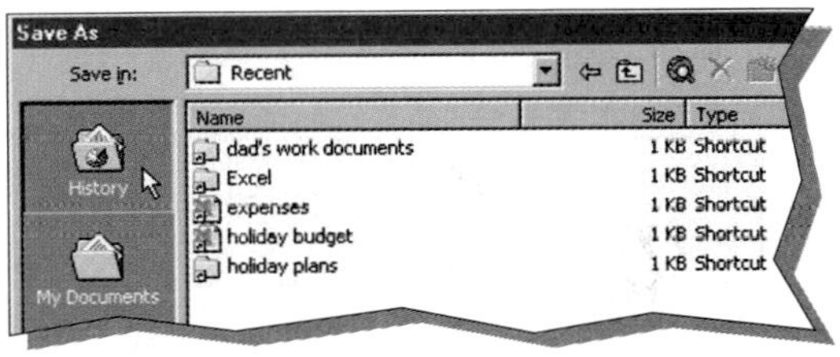

7 If you have a Web site and want to include your spreadsheets on it, you can do so by utilising the easy-to-use Save as Web Page command in the File menu. You can use the Web Page Preview command to check them before saving.

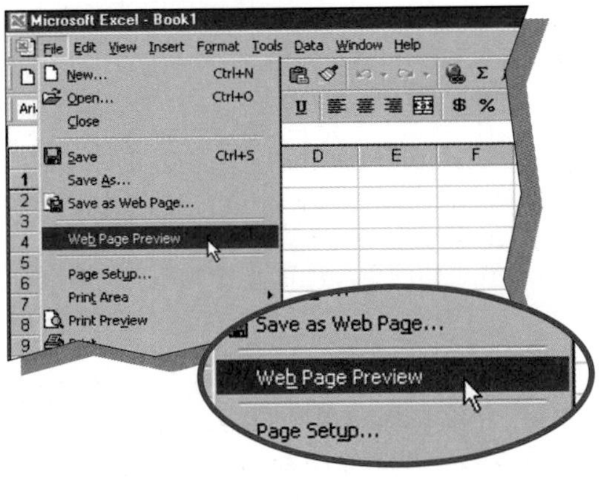

PC TIPS

Expanding menus

Look closely at the fully expanded Excel 2000 menus and you can see that little has changed between Excel 97 (below left) and Excel 2000 (below right). In fact, over all the menus, there is only a handful of new commands and some slightly different command locations.

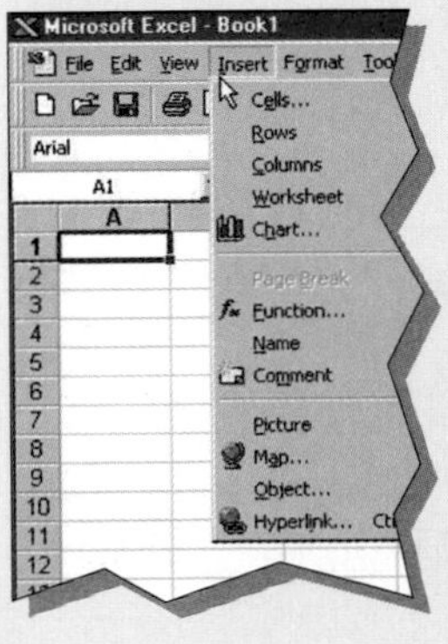

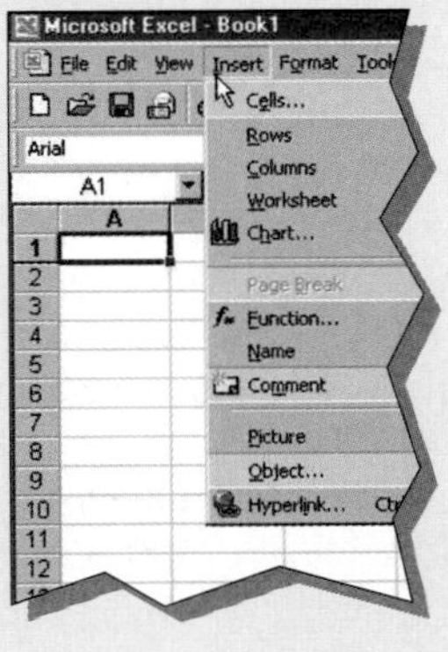

Lining up and spacing objects

Placing objects in a perfectly straight line with exactly the right amount of space between them can be infuriatingly difficult if you are forced to rely on your own judgement. But CorelDRAW can help you get things exactly right.

Creating a repetitive pattern or a picture consisting of identical elements – such as a row of terraced houses – is simple in CorelDRAW. All you have to do to produce a series of duplicated images is to use the Copy and Paste functions. However, if you need to line up a series of images accurately or space them out evenly, this can be a tricky, time-consuming job.

Fortunately, CorelDRAW can do this for you as well, thanks to the Align and Distribute function. This will ensure that any objects you select line up exactly in relation to one another and appear precisely where you want them. CorelDRAW also has a useful built-in grid to guide you in positioning them.

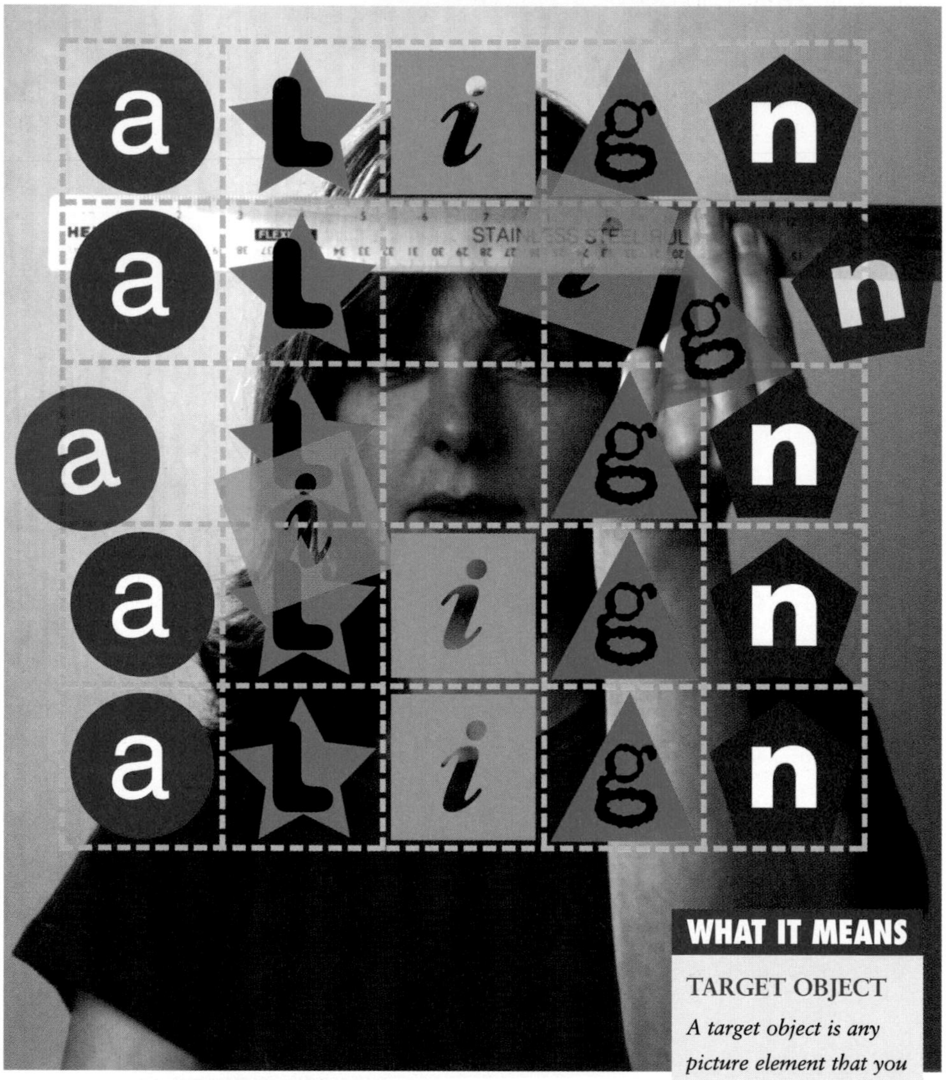

● Aligning objects

Using the Align options, you can choose to line up images horizontally or vertically. You also have the choice of aligning them along whichever 'edge' you specify. For example, if you create a row of houses, you will want them all to line up at their base, but a row of stalactites would look better aligned at the top.

You can even align objects from the centre. This might not seem very useful, but, as we show on page 68, you can use this option to place a series of objects on top of one another. We show how to use it to produce a pattern of concentric circles looking like an archery target. In our example, the circles end up on top of the largest circle in descending order of size, thus producing the target effect.

Finally, instead of aligning objects against a common edge, you can choose to line them up against a specified image or target object. This is useful when you want to organize elements that have an irregular shape and size.

● Distributing objects

The spacing between objects is controlled by the Distribute options, which allow you to space elements evenly within a designated area or around a specified image.

Although you might not need this option as often as Align, it can still be very useful. Lots of picture elements are based on a series of repeated objects with regular spacing between them, such as the garden fence design used as an example on page 69.

WHAT IT MEANS

TARGET OBJECT

A target object is any picture element that you specify as the reference point for positioning other objects. It will be set automatically if you select several shapes together (by pressing the [Shift] key while you click on them). The target object is the last one that you select.

To space the fence posts, you only have to position the extreme left- and right-hand ones exactly. The remaining posts can then be evenly distributed in between. By choosing the target object and distribution carefully, you can create a design where elements are spaced at equal distances from any image – a task which would be very awkward and time-consuming by hand.

● Flexible controls

The Align and Distribute function is available either from the Arrange menu or directly from the Property bar after more than one object has been selected with the Pick Tool. The controls for both functions also include Preview buttons, which allow you to see what a design looks like before you decide to save it, and a Reset in case you don't like the result. This is particularly useful when positioning a large number of objects, as the results can sometimes be difficult to predict. As both tools are easy to experiment with, Preview means that you can try out various options without ruining your previous picture.

Follow the examples on the next two pages and then try out some of your own ideas. Soon you will have mastered how to space objects with precision – and you will wonder how designers ever coped without CorelDRAW's Align and Distribute functions.

● Positioning on a grid

CorelDRAW also offers handy shortcuts. In the examples discussed above, the reference points used for alignment and distribution are all elements of the drawing. But you can just as easily position objects by reference to a point on the screen. To help you with positioning, CorelDRAW can display an imaginary grid on screen (see Using the Grid, below). Instead of having to place objects precisely, you can set them to Snap To Grid, which means they will automatically align themselves with whichever grid point is nearest when you let go of them.

Using the Grid

CorelDRAW can provide you with a grid of regularly spaced lines to give you a visual reference for positioning objects on the page.

1 One very simple way to position objects on a page is to use the rulers at the top and left-hand side of the screen. However, to ensure that objects line up accurately in relation to one another, it is better to use CorelDRAW's grid.

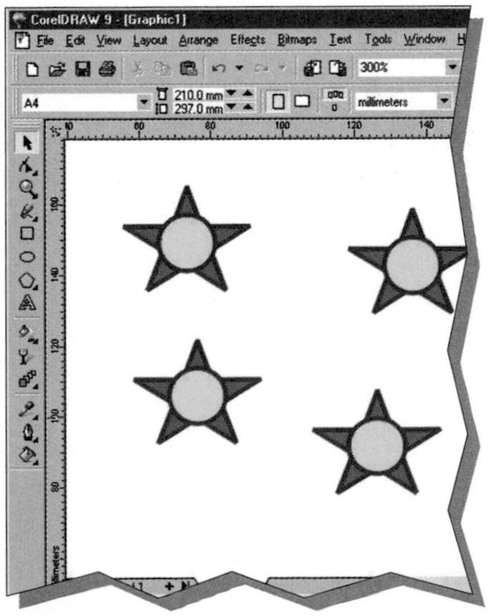

2 Click on View and choose Grid from the drop-down menu. A grid of grey lines will then appear on screen. This will help you to see how each element lines up on the page.

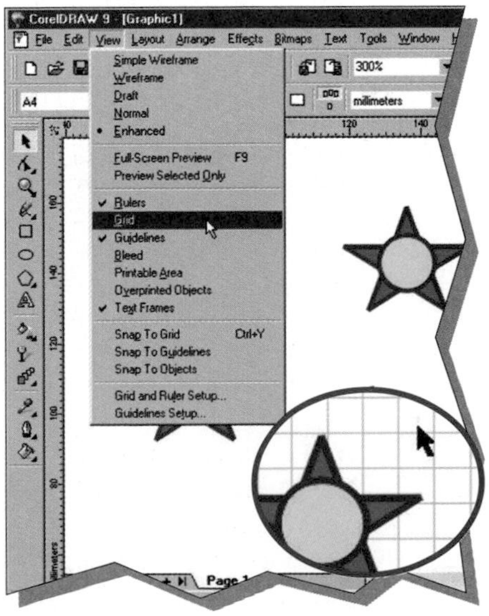

3 To help you position the objects accurately over the grid, click on the Snap To Grid button.

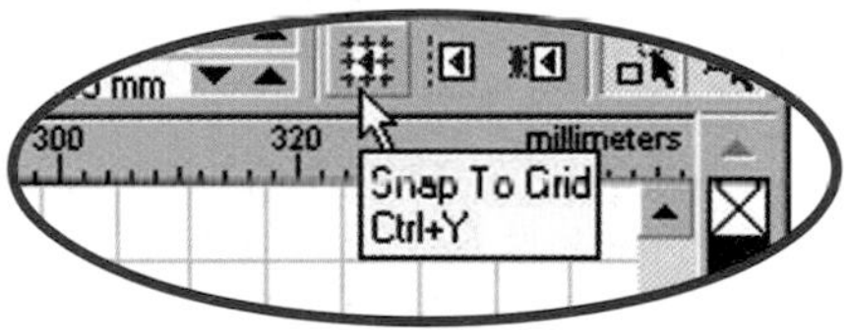

4 Now, whenever you move an object with the Pick Tool, the normally invisible box around it will automatically 'click' into place over the nearest intersection of the lines. Here, we are using this to align the four stars exactly.

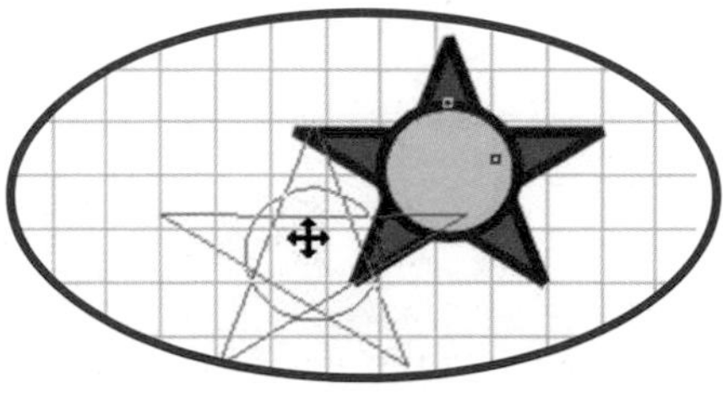

Experiments with alignment

Although alignment is often used to position objects in a straight line (see opposite), it allows you to do much more. Here we see how to place six circles on top of one another.

1 Start by drawing half a dozen circles, each slightly smaller than the one before. Fill each circle with a different colour so that you will be able to see what happens when they overlap (see Stage 2, page 71). For now, exact placement doesn't matter.

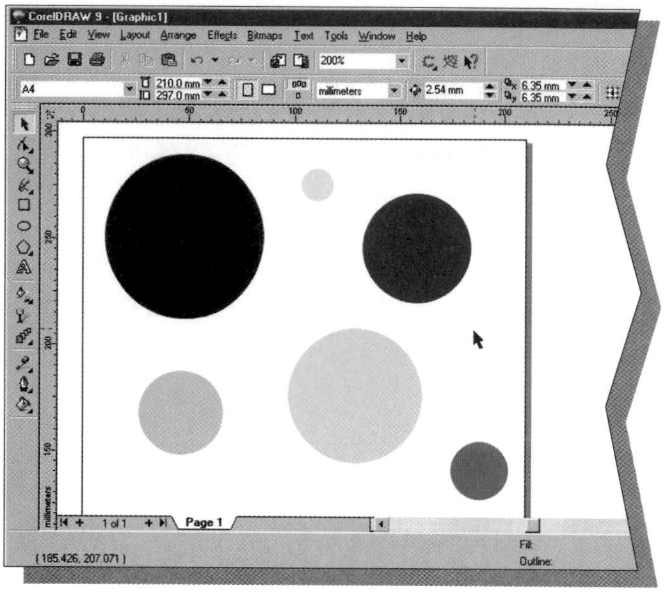

2 Select the Pick Tool from the toolbox and drag it across an area that completely encompasses the circles on your page. You'll see a single set of selection handles appear around your shapes (below). If any shape is left outside this area, try again.

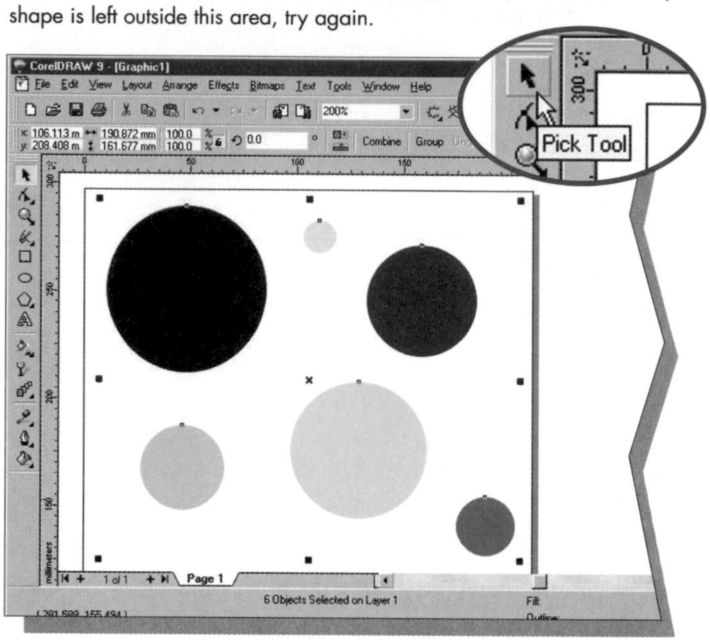

3 Click on the Arrange menu and then select Align and Distribute from the drop-down menu.

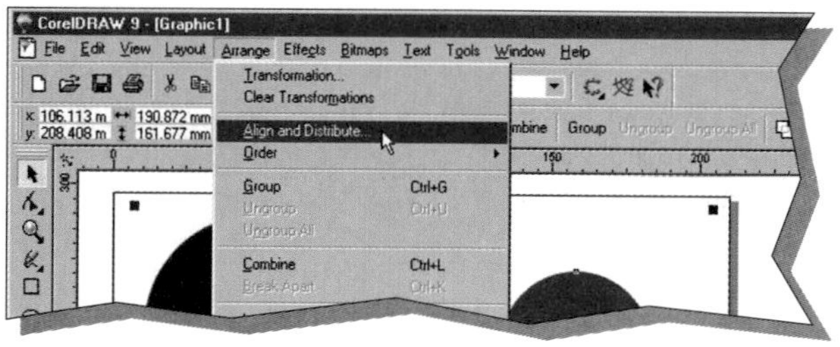

SHORTCUTS

CorelDRAW offers a number of time-saving keyboard commands. You can quickly bring up the Align and Distribute dialog box by pressing the [Ctrl] and [A] keys at the same time.

4 The dialog box that pops up has two tabs. Select the Align tab and then the Center option for both horizontal alignment (at the top of the dialog box) and vertical alignment (on the left of the dialog box). Click the Preview button.

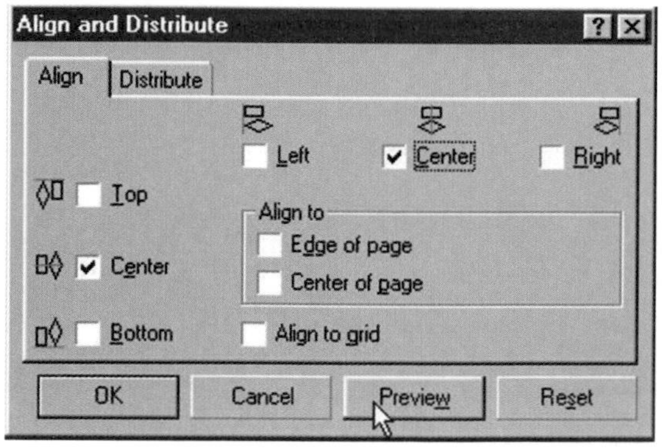

5 You'll see that all the circles move on top of each other. They are arranged with the largest at the back and the smallest at the front because that is the order you drew them in Step 1. All the circles are aligned perfectly, in a way that would be very time-consuming and almost impossible to do so well by hand and eye. Press OK to keep this arrangement.

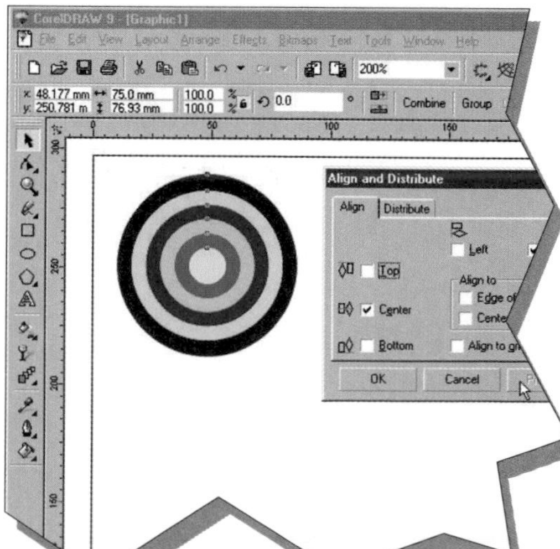

CorelDRAW™

Using Distribution

In this example, we will use Alignment and Distribution to create a regularly spaced picket fence to use as a logo.

1 Start by drawing a single fence post. We've used a simple rectangle and then put a spike on top by adding an extra node to this edge (see Stage 3, page 73).

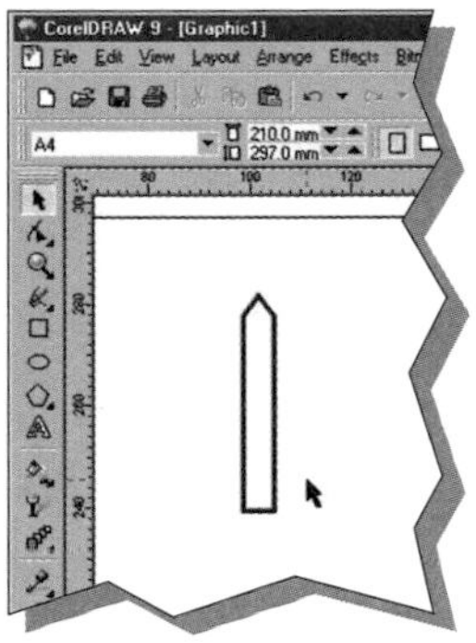

2 Copy and paste the fence post several times, and then position the posts very roughly at the top right of the page.

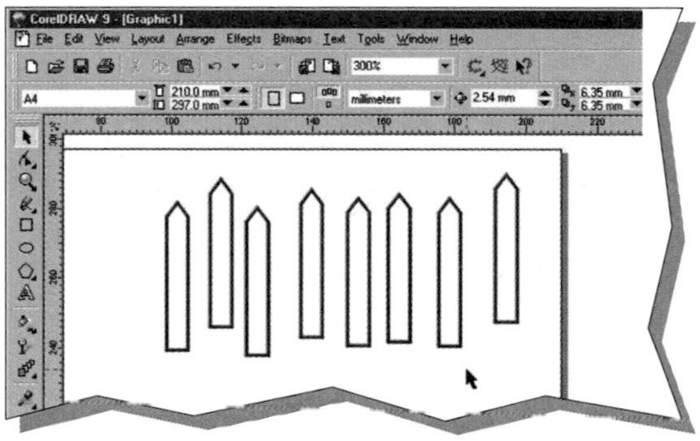

3 First we need to line up the posts. Follow Step 3 on the previous page to bring up the Align and Distribute dialog box, and select the Align tab. This time, tick the Bottom option from the vertical alignments on the left. Then press OK.

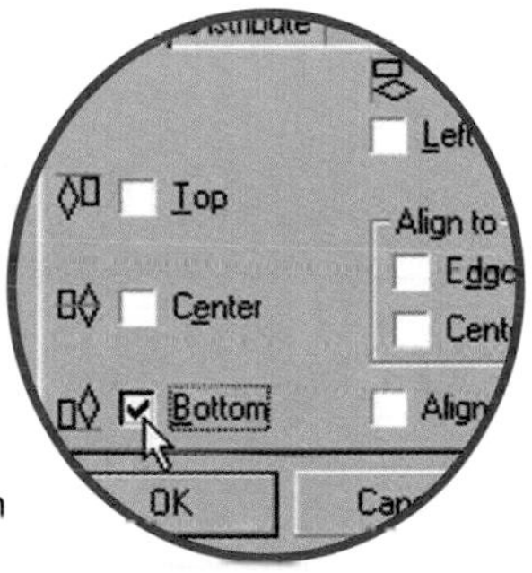

4 This has moved the posts so that they now all line up at the bottom, but the horizontal spacing is still variable.

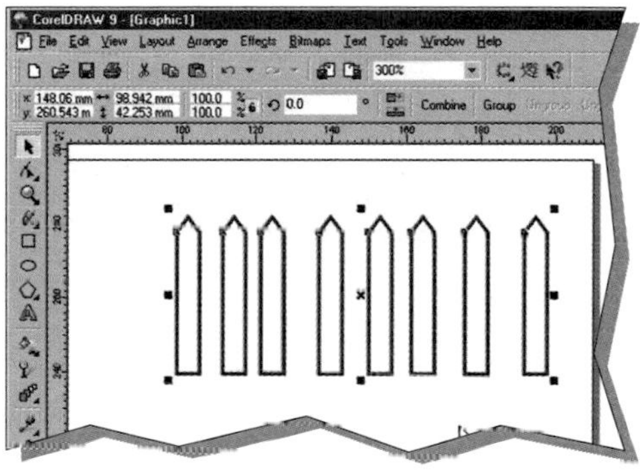

5 Bring up the Align and Distribute dialog box once more, and this time click on the Distribute tab.

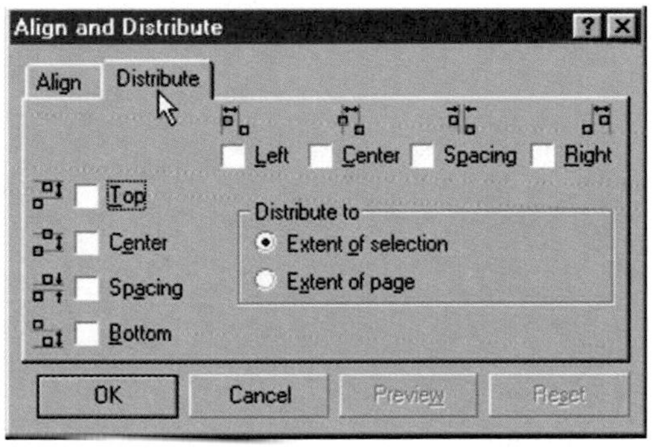

6 The top line of options controls the objects' horizontal distribution. Select the Center option. The setting below (Extent of selection) means that the objects will be spaced evenly between the two outermost objects. Leave this alone and press the OK button.

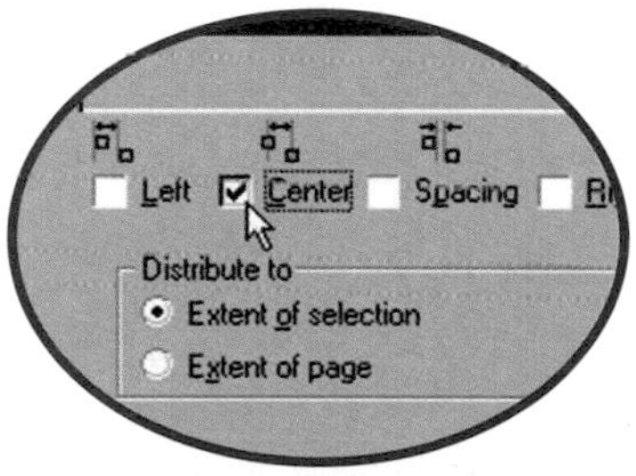

7 You'll now see that CorelDRAW has moved the fence posts so that they are equally spaced. Once again, a few simple mouse clicks have saved an awful lot of trial-and-error positioning.

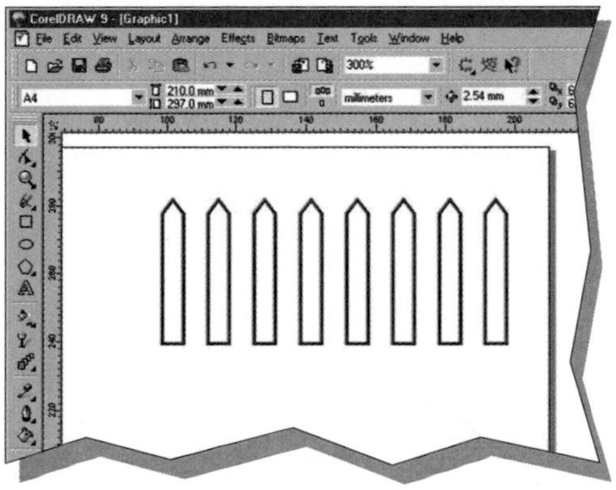

8 Finally, we've added two rails as horizontal rectangles behind the posts (for how to set an image behind another, see Stage 2, page 71) and some text to finish off our logo.

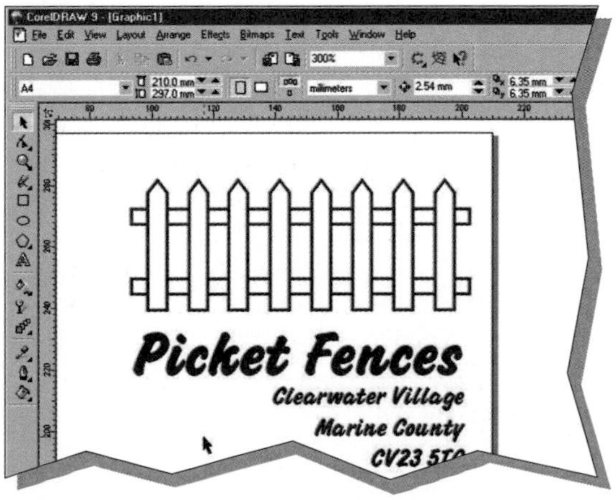

PC TIPS

Once you have finished aligning and distributing your collection of objects, you will need to protect them to avoid accidentally changing the arrangement.

Usually you will want to move the image as a whole, so group them after you've positioned them. To do this, press [Ctrl]+[G] while the items are still selected. This shortcut groups the items so that you can move them together (see Stage 2, pages 80-81).

Managing and layering complex images

You can make detailed pictures easier to handle by using layers to separate objects.

Images created in CorelDRAW are made up of numerous individual objects. The more complex the image, the greater the number of objects involved. This in itself isn't a problem, but moving and working with an image made up of a large number of objects can be awkward.

Even if the objects are grouped together, it can still be difficult to pick out a particular object for editing. To help avoid this problem, CorelDRAW has a tool called Object Manager which opens a new window next to your drawing and displays the hierarchical structure (showing you what is in front of what) of all the objects in your current document. One of the important ways that Object Manager helps is by allowing you to put objects into separate layers.

● Working in layers

Rather than attempting to work on all the different objects at any one time, you can assign related objects to their own layer. This makes it far easier to work on a particular aspect of the picture. For example, imagine a picture of someone standing outside a house up in the hills. All the objects that make up the land and sky could form the background layer, all the objects that make up the house could go to another layer and the person out in front might form a third layer.

As a practical example, imagine that you created an architect's diagram, complete with plumbing and wiring plans. By layering the wiring details separately from the plumbing plans, you can then work on one without disturbing the other.

If you want, you can also hide layers while you're not working on them. This temporarily removes objects that might otherwise get in the way.

Another advantage of using layers is that you can make sweeping changes to all the objects within a layer simultaneously. For instance, you can change the colours across the board, or swap layers between documents (allowing you to re-use a favourite background, for example, on other pictures).

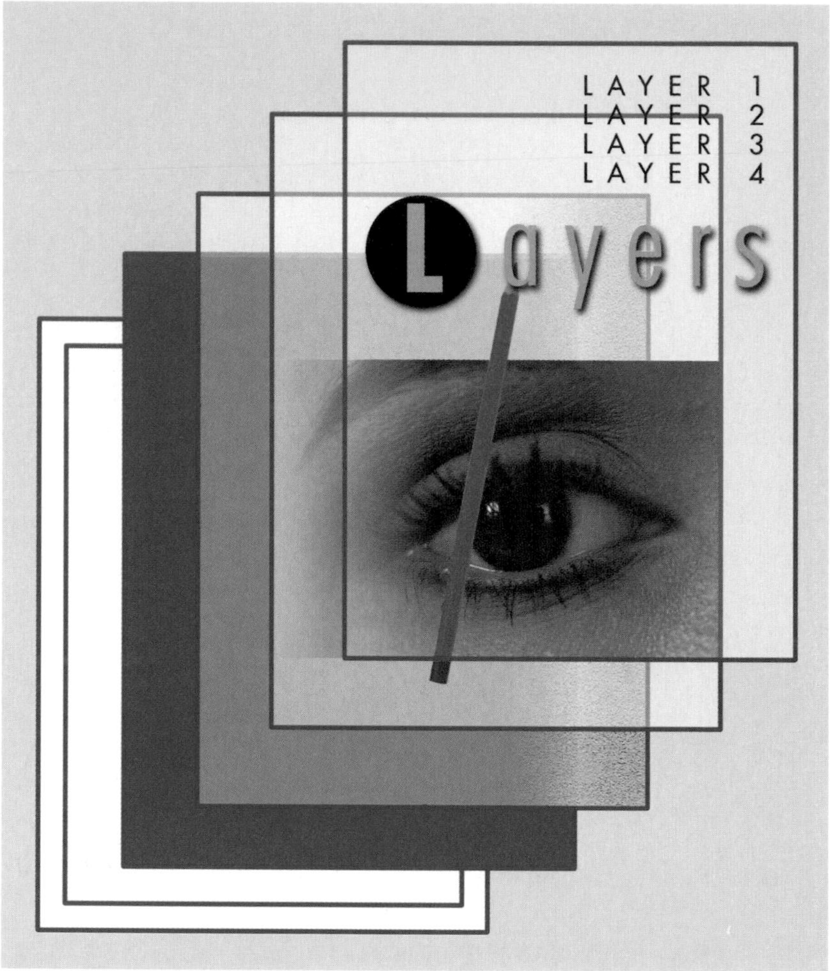

When a picture is split into layers, it's easier to move the component parts of the image.

WHAT IT MEANS

LAYERS

To help organize the components of a picture you can place various elements in a number of different layers. For example, the sun, clouds and sky in a landscape might comprise the background layer; some hills and a few distant trees another layer; a house another; and a person mowing the front lawn, yet another. The overall effect is a bit like grouping, except that you can move each component of a layer around independently.

● List editing

Even if you have assigned numerous layers, however, you might still have the problem of working with scores of little objects that make up the whole image. Object Manager allows you to select and edit an individual object by clicking on its listing rather than on the object itself. This means that you don't have to root around with the magnifying glass, ungroup a grouped image, or try to keep your hand steady as you click on one of two objects a few millimetres apart.

Object Manager also comes in handy when cutting and pasting. It is much easier to deal with object names contained in the Object Manager list than to fiddle around with the actual objects themselves, when you run the risk of accidentally moving or altering them instead of simply selecting them.

Object Manager lists a number of attributes for each object, so quite often you won't even have to look at the whole image to tell which object is which. A single icon indicates the type of object (curve, text, rectangle and so on) and its colour and thickness, while next to the icon a text description gives the style of its fill and the status of its outline.

Further uses for Object Manager include keeping account of additional pages if you are using more than one page when designing an image. These extra pages are displayed as icons at the top of the list, and moving objects between pages is done in the same way as moving objects between layers.

● Master layer

If working across many pages, you can make use of the Master layer to help organize your work. This extra layer is always present, whatever the number of pages, but with more than one page the master layer can be used to place the same information and objects on every page you are using.

For example, if you want some header or footer text to appear on each page (when creating a document in the style of a book, say), you can do so in the Master layer and instruct it to place the information on each page automatically.

Finally, Object Manager also works well with PowerClips. This powerful command allows you to place one object inside another. When the resultant image is viewed through Object Manager, the relationship between the two objects is far easier to see and, if necessary, to alter accordingly.

In fact, it's surprising how simple a complex image can become, and how easy it is to work on, when the component parts are listed in order in the Object Manager.

CorelDRAW™

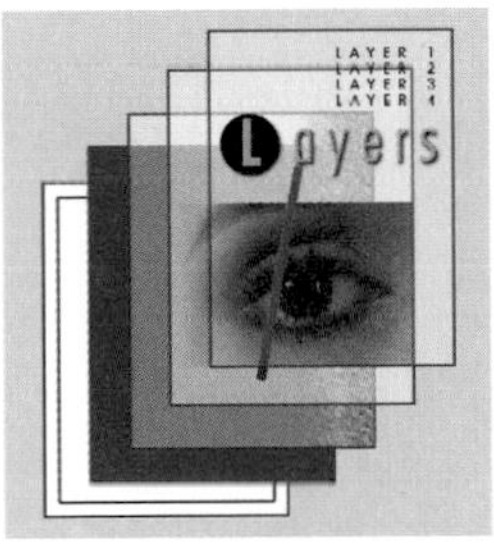

Introducing the Object Manager

Object Manager is at its most useful when you're working on complex illustrations, with hundreds of different elements, or a variety of layers. However, for this example, we're going to use a simple picture in order to demonstrate what Object Manager has to offer.

1 Load in a piece of clip art from the CorelDRAW CD-ROM. We've used NWAGE977.CDR, which you'll find in the Games folder, inside the Leisure folder. From the Tools menu choose Object Manager.

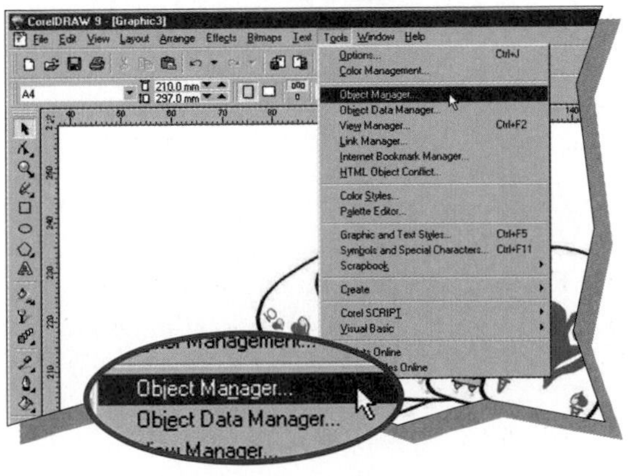

2 The work area will now have split into two parts, with your picture on the left and the Object Manager on the right. The Object Manager lists all the objects in the picture, along with text and icon descriptions of their style and shape.

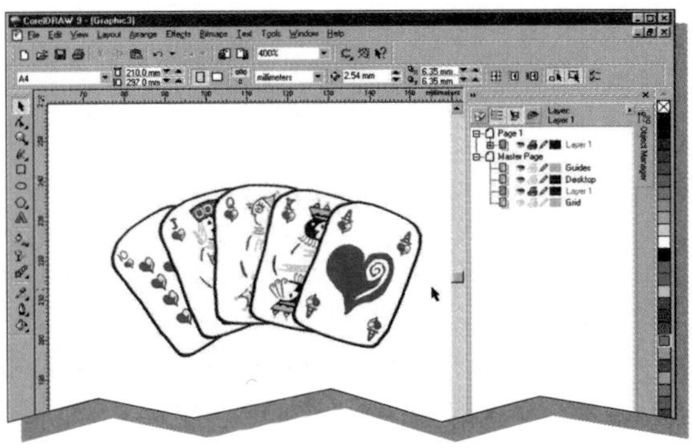

3 If there's no group shown under the Page 1 icon, click the small box with the cross (inset below) to expand the list.

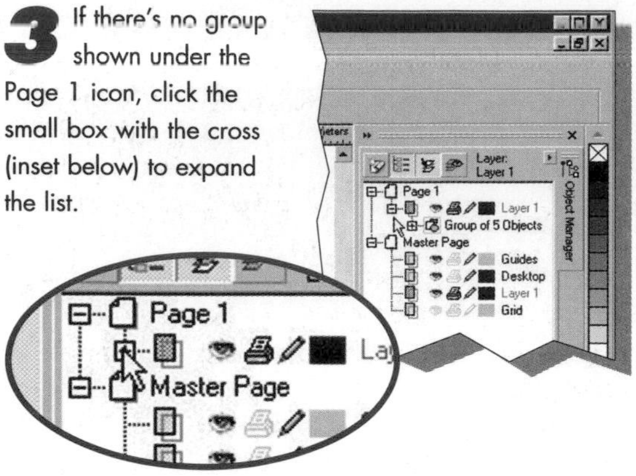

4 If you click on the picture in the work area, you'll see that the corresponding icon listing in Object Manager is highlighted. Click on the box next to the selected Group to see the full list of objects that make up the picture.

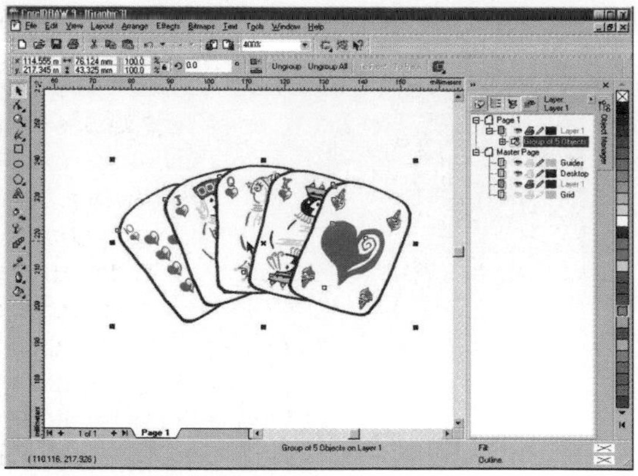

5 You can also select objects by clicking on their entry in the Object Manager list. If you click the Group of 16 Objects, for instance, the ace of hearts will be selected.

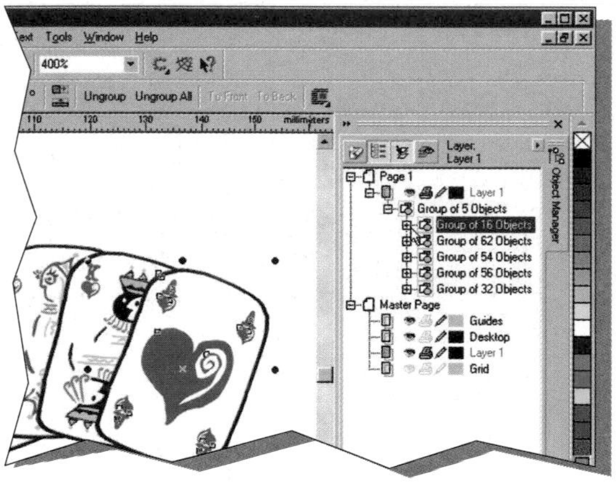

6 You can change the properties of objects using the Object Manager. Click the box next to the icon for the Group of 16 Objects and select the last red curve listed. Click another colour in the palette running down the right side of the dialog box to change the object's colour. Do this for the other red objects in the group.

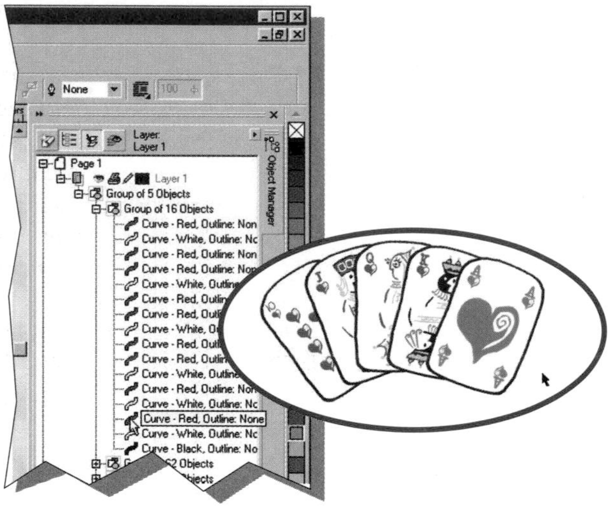

7 You can also delete items. Click on the first white curve in the ace group and press the [Delete] key. Repeat this for all except the last white curve.

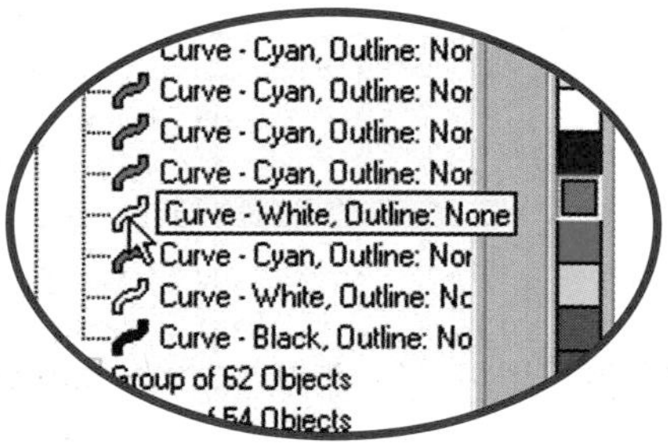

8 This deletes all of the fancy flourishes from the card (the final white curve is the card's white face, which we need to keep). Repeat the colouring and deleting process for other cards to see how easy it is to edit a picture without touching any of the unselected objects that you don't want altered.

LAYER ICONS

Each layer name in Object Manager has three icons next to it. These icons are handy controls that help to organize and maintain the objects in their own layer. The eye icon represents whether the layer is visible on screen; the printer icon shows whether the layer will appear in any printout; and the pencil icon indicates whether the objects in the layer can be altered or edited. To change the status of a layer, the icons can be toggled (switched on or off) by clicking on them. When an icon is dimmed, that layer will either not be visible on screen, or not print out or not be editable.

Using these three icons allows you to concentrate your attention on specific areas of the screen. You can hide the clutter of other objects as you work, for instance, by toggling the eye icon so they are not visible. The printer icon allows you to add non-printing comments by putting them in a layer where the printer icon has been toggled so the comments do not actually print out.

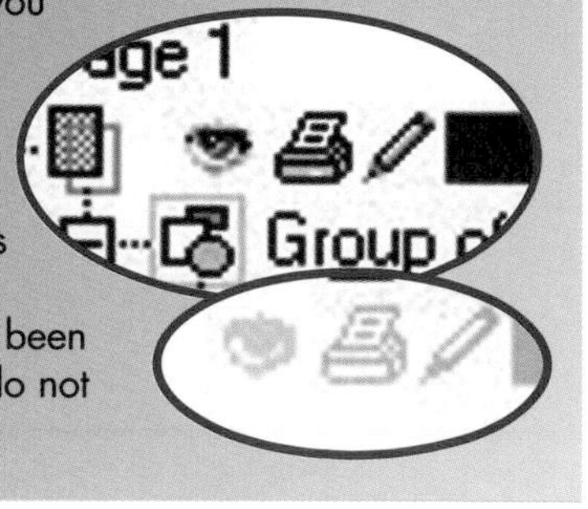

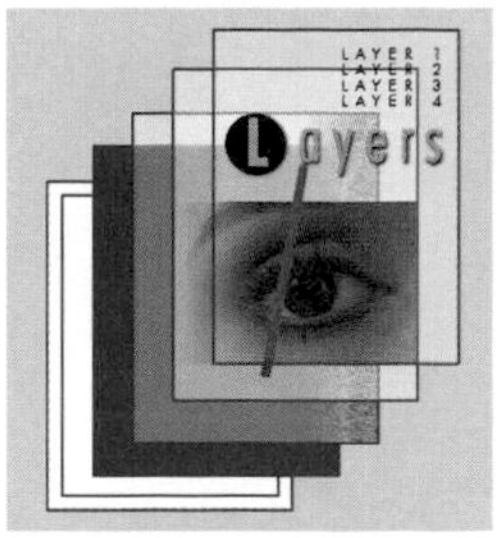

Working with layers

Use the previous page's example to create a card-game invitation.

1 At the moment all the objects are in the same layer, called Layer 1 in Object Manager. Rename the layer by right-clicking on it and choosing Rename. Call it something more meaningful – in our example we use 'Deck'.

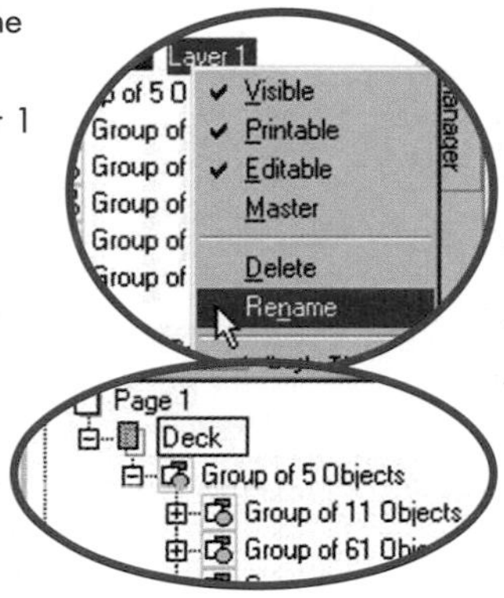

2 To create a new layer, click once on the New Layer button at the top of the Object Manager. Name it 'Queen'.

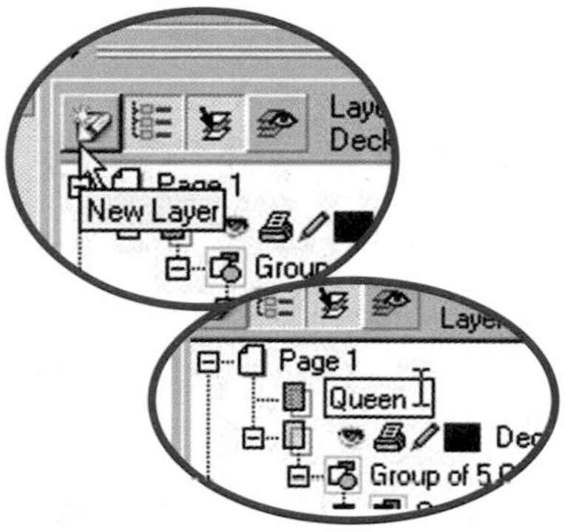

3 To move objects between layers, you drag them in the Object Manager. Before you can do this, however, you need to ungroup the cards. Click once on the picture in the drawing area and then click the Ungroup button.

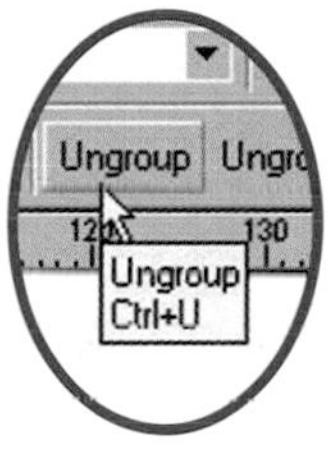

4 Now you can drag the Queen card group (Group of 53 objects) from the Deck layer on to the Queen layer you just created.

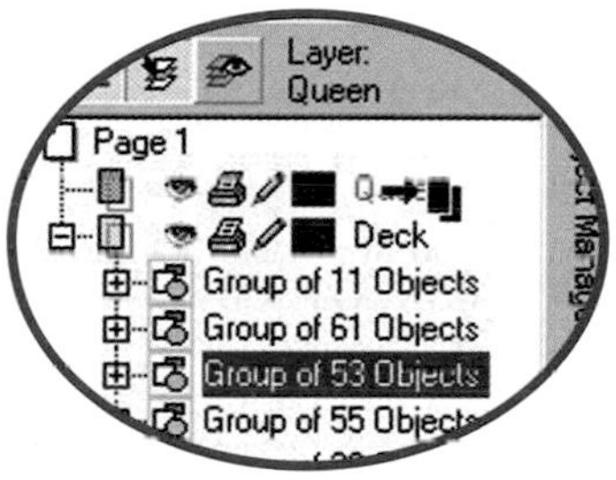

5 The Queen appears on top of the other cards because – as listed in the Object Manager – the Queen layer is on top of the Deck layer.

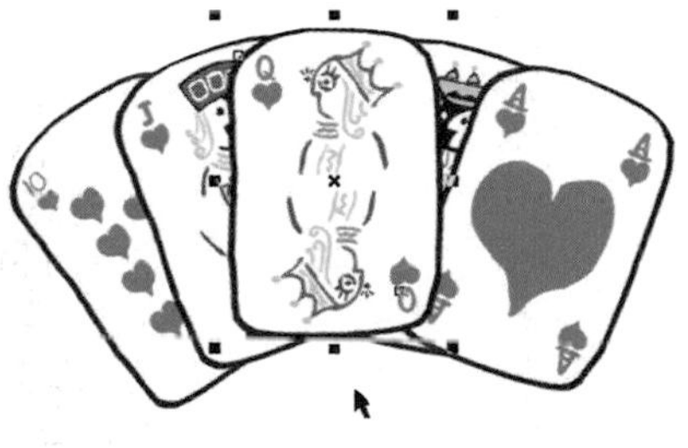

6 Try dragging the Deck layer so that it's above the Queen layer. You'll see that the objects in the deck layer now appear in front of those in the Queen layer.

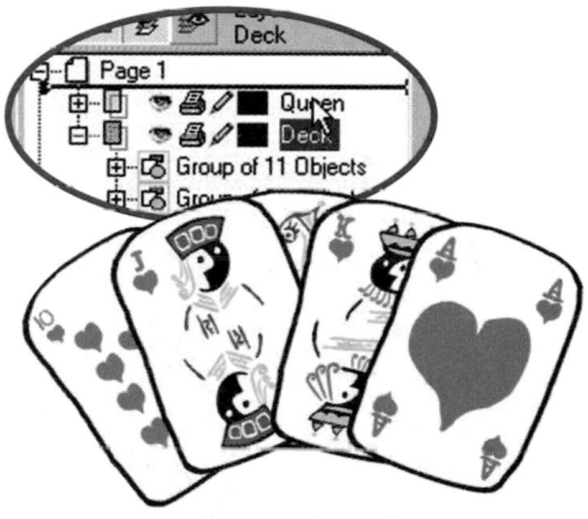

7 Using layers makes it easy to work with a particular part of the picture without disturbing others. There's no practical limit to the number of layers you can use or what you can use them for, so feel free to experiment. Here, for example, we've put the name of the event and the date on which it takes place into a new layer called 'Text' (inset below).

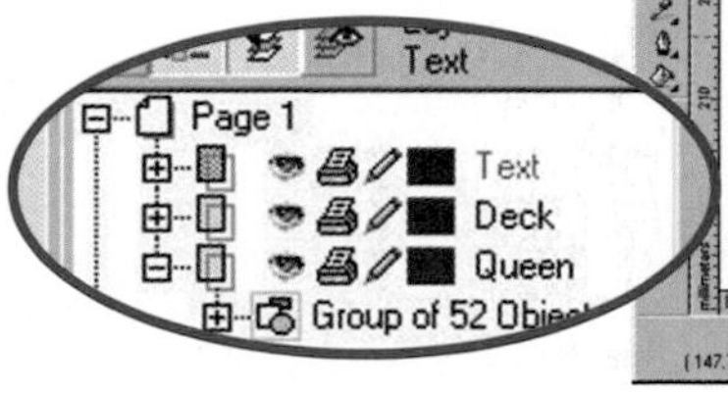

LAYER SAFETY

When working with multi-layered drawing objects, it is a good idea to save a copy in a safe place before doing any editing. If there is a catastrophe, you can always revert to your saved copy. Also, it can be useful to write down the main objects and layers in the image before editing begins. This will speed up your work and reduce the chance of mistakes being made.

File formats and picture quality

Choosing to save your images in different formats can have a tremendous effect on the quality of the picture and the size of the final file.

The Corel suite of programs provides a number of alternative ways in which to save your images. Each offers a different file size and quality of image; which one you choose depends on how and where you are going to use the image you are saving.

Whenever you save a file, the information in that file is stored. The structure of the stored data is called the format and you choose this when saving the file by selecting the three-letter extension.

● Three little letters

All formats have a unique three-character extension, which is automatically added to the end of any file created in that format. In Word it is usually .DOC and in Excel it is .XLS, for example. The extension tells Windows (and any program that needs to open the file) the kind of information that will be in the file and how it is written.

File formats are relevant to all types of document, whether they have been created in a word processor, a spreadsheet or a graphics package. However, picture formats tend to be more varied and more complicated than most. There are a couple of reasons for this.

First, some graphics formats are better than others for storing the high-quality files used in colour magazines. These files can be very large (over 30MB) and the choice of format can make a big difference to file size. Other graphics formats are useful when it's important to keep files very small. For example, the smaller the graphics used in Web pages, the faster they will download when you are browsing the Internet.

Some people choose to use certain formats purely because they are preferred by their graphics program. As we have seen (see Stage 3, page 76), in Corel PHOTO-PAINT it is CPT whereas Microsoft Paint prefers the BMP format. Typically, such formats allow you to use the widest possible range of features offered by the program but, as a result, they can end up being large and often can't be read by other programs. The CPT format of PHOTO-PAINT, for example, can rarely be opened by another program, which can be a problem if a file needs to be shared.

● Choosing a format

Fortunately, very few graphics programs are limited to saving files in their own unique formats; almost all allow you to use a number of common alternatives that enable you to swap pictures between programs.

It might not always be immediately obvious exactly what difference a particular file extension makes to the way an image finally appears. However, when comparing different file types 'under a microscope', the differences can be staggering.

In the panel below, we describe the most common alternatives, along with their advantages and disadvantages.

It's important to distinguish between two fundamental types of picture: vector-based images, such as CDR files created in CorelDRAW, which are made up of lots of different drawn shapes; and photographic images, such as BMP files, which are made up of tiny pixels. To transfer vector-based files between applications, it's often necessary to convert the format into a pixel-based one – a process you can't reverse. Consequently, for this, and other reasons, you might need to keep numerous copies of the same file in different formats to make editing easier.

Different image types

PHOTO-PAINT can save images in a huge range of formats, each of which has its own particular uses. Here we describe the five most commonly used file formats.

WHAT IT MEANS

LOSSY

There are effectively two different types of compression. The first squeezes the file into a small space for storage and unsqueezes it when you want to work on it. Examples include WinZip or LZW compression. The second type strips the picture of fine detail, radically reducing its file size at the same time as compressing it. The stripped information is irrecoverable, which can cause a (sometimes shocking) loss of quality, described as being 'lossy'.

● BMP

BMP (Bitmapped) is a very popular file format as it is Windows' default format for pictures. It is often used as background wallpaper for the Windows Desktop, for example.

Any other good graphics program will also be able to work with BMPs, but not Web browsers: you can't view a BMP image on the Web. While unwieldy in their uncompressed state, BMP files do compress well.

● CPT

This is the default Corel PHOTO-PAINT file format. It is similar to the Windows BMP format, but includes additional PHOTO-PAINT information, such as printer settings and tool preferences.

This format is very useful when working exclusively in PHOTO-PAINT, but few paint programs recognize the file type. Therefore, you may have to save your file in an alternative format if you want to transfer it to another program or upload it to the Internet; do keep the original as a master version.

● JPG

The most common image format on the Internet, JPG is short for JPEG, which in turn stands for Joint Photographic Experts Group.

The format is popular because it creates small-sized files while still being able to offer up to 16.7 million colours. This is ideal when you are using the Internet or when you are trying to squeeze as many pictures onto a floppy disk as possible.

When saving pictures in JPG format, you can choose the amount of lossy compression you want. If you choose a low setting, you can achieve quite good compression without the loss in picture quality becoming too noticeable. At extreme compression settings, the image becomes noticeably 'blocky'.

● GIF

Like JPG pictures, GIF (Graphics Interchange Format) pictures are viewable in Web browsers, and since the Internet has become so popular in recent years, so the GIF format has become important for graphics users. However, it has one main weakness: where all the other graphics formats covered here can store photo-realistic pictures containing millions of colours, the GIF format stores a maximum of 256 colours.

When saving a picture in GIF format, the program simplifies the colours used. However, the file size of GIFs is very small indeed – and without being lossy either.

● TIF

The TIF (Tagged Image File) format is very popular among professional graphics users. Almost all graphics programs allow you to save in this format. It can store images with millions of colours, and includes LZW compression (see below), which provides a means of reducing file sizes without any reduction in image quality. TIFs, however, can be rather large, even when compressed.

LZW COMPRESSION

One of the highest quality compression techniques was invented in 1977 by Jacob Ziv and Abraham Lempel, two mathematicians. It was later refined in 1984 by Terry Welch. Therefore, LZW stands for Lempel-Ziv-Welch. Compression can be used on both text and image files and works by detecting repetitive sequences of information in the original file. For example, if you save a text file with the word 'the' in it 42 times, then LZW stores the word 'the' only once and notes that the other instances of it are identical to the first, removing the need to save the same piece of data in 42 places.

How formats affect quality

Save a colour image in different formats using PHOTO-PAINT.

1 Start with a bright image that contains lots of contrasting colours. We've chosen a photograph of fruit, which shows many different hues and shades.

2 We'll want to try some format changes, but first you must save the picture as a CPT file so that you can come back to the original image for comparison.

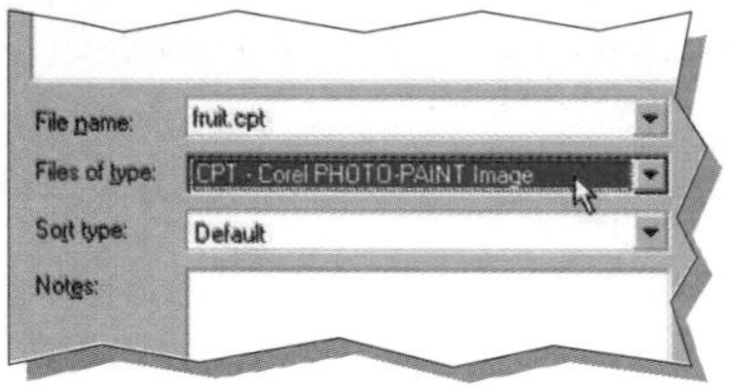

3 To save the image in GIF format, first convert it into a 256-colour picture: click on the Image menu, then the Mode option and then select the Paletted (8-bit) option.

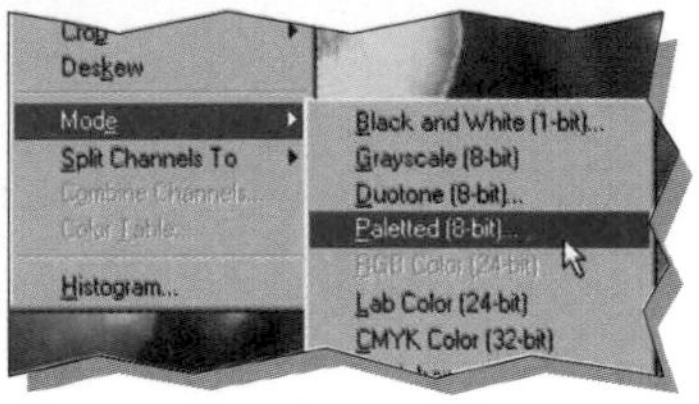

4 PHOTO-PAINT lets you to choose the type of palette; select Optimized from the drop-down Palette listing. PHOTO-PAINT now analyses all the colours in the picture and chooses 256 that can best represent the colours in the original. A preview image will appear on the right of the screen. At first it doesn't look too bad. Click on OK.

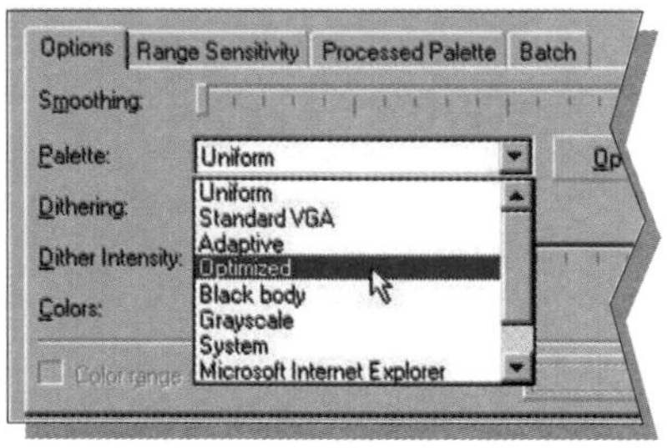

5 When the conversion process is complete, you'll see the image flicker and change. As you can see from our before (left) and after (right) examples, the effect is noticeable.

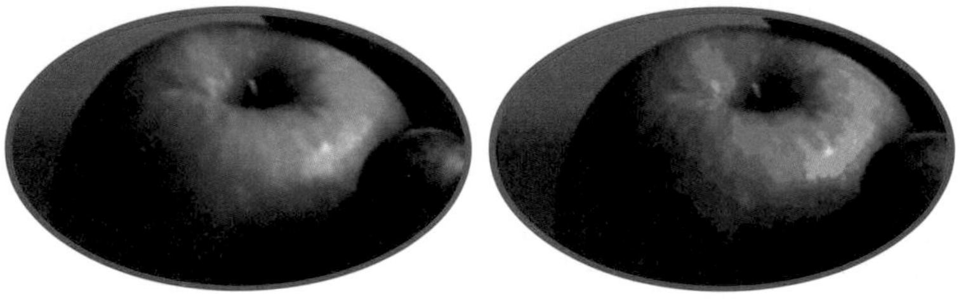

6 Select Save As from the File menu and in the Files of type box choose GIF - CompuServe Bitmap from the drop-down list of formats. PHOTO-PAINT automatically changes the file extension to .GIF. Save the picture into the same folder as the original (Step 2). Click OK in the dialog box (right).

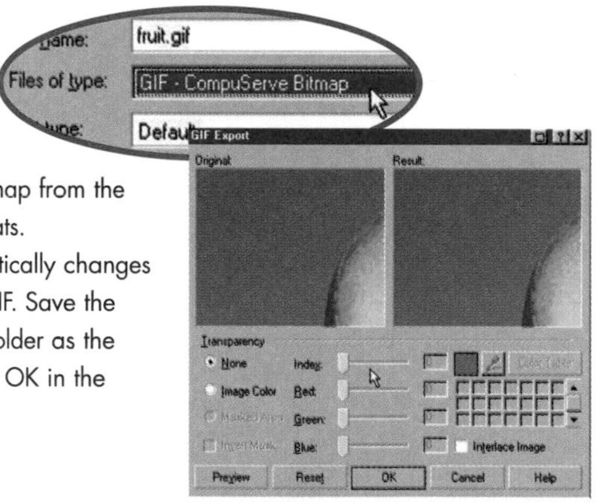

7 Now open the original CPT file again and select Save As from the File menu. This time when the dialog box appears, select JPG - JPEG Bitmaps from the list of file formats. Click the Save button.

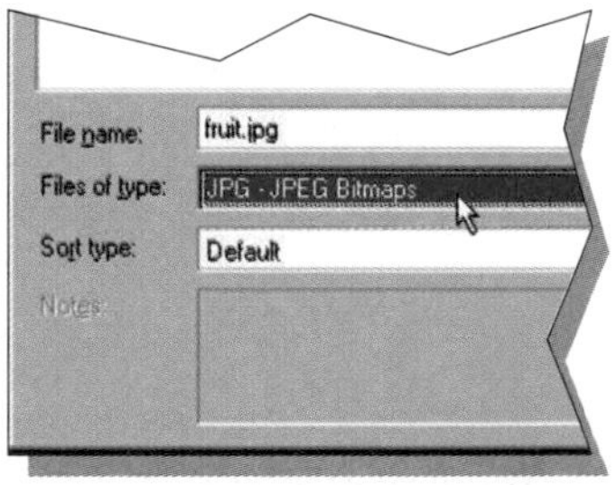

DISPLAY COLOURS

When following this exercise, make sure that Windows is set to display the maximum number of colours. If you are running Windows in just 256 colours, you won't be able to see the true difference between the full-colour image you start with and the result you get after decreasing the colours to 256 to make a GIF file. To check the number of colours Windows is using, open the Display Properties dialog box (see Stage 2, pages 12-13) and look at the Settings tab. The Color palette setting should be 24-bit color or 32-bit color.

8 PHOTO-PAINT lets you set the amount of compression: drag the Compression slider three-quarters of the way to the right. Press the OK button.

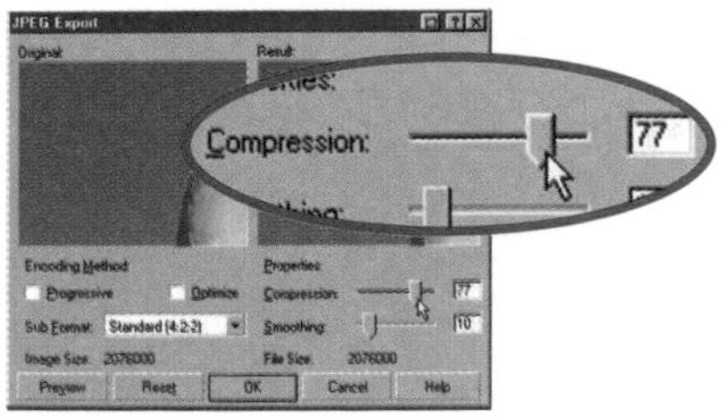

9 It doesn't look like the image has changed at all, but this is due to a peculiarity in the way that PHOTO-PAINT works. Close the image and open it again (make sure to open the JPG version you just saved). You'll now see that the lossy compression has caused small blocks to appear in the image.

How formats affect file size

We'll now try some of the other file formats. Although these don't affect the quality of the image, they can have a marked impact on the size of your files.

1 Open the original CPT file you created on page 76 and, without changing anything, choose Save As from the File menu. This time, select the TIF - TIFF Bitmap format; as you do, you'll notice that the Compression type box changes, allowing you to choose from two options. Make sure that the Uncompressed option is selected and click the Save button. Note: you won't see any change in the picture, because the TIF format is not lossy.

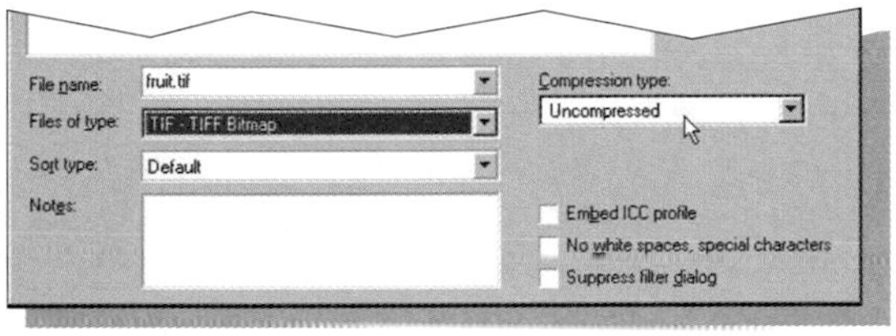

2 Now save the picture as a TIF again, but select the LZW Compression option from the Compression type box. Give it a slightly different name (we've chosen fruitlzw.tif), so that it doesn't overwrite the TIF you saved in Step 1.

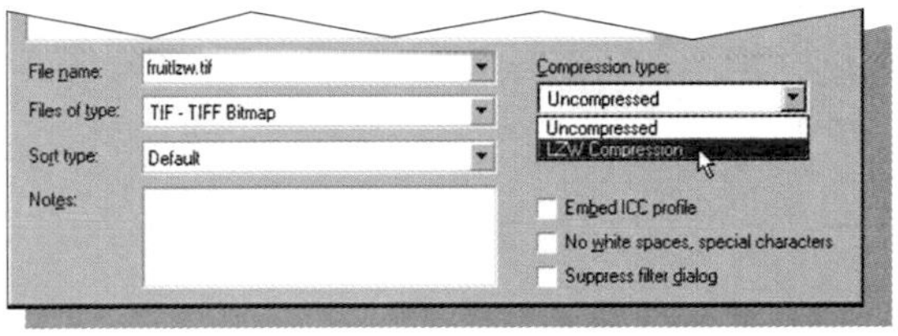

3 Save the file yet again, but this time select the BMP - Windows Bitmap file format (there are no compression options for this format) before you press the Save button.

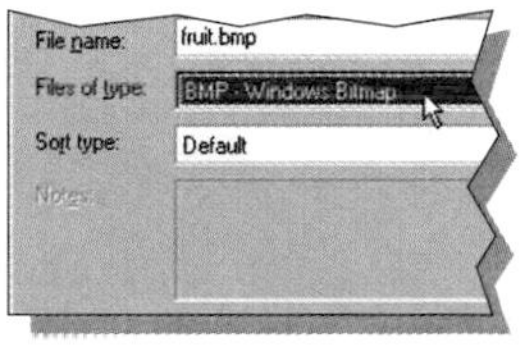

4 Close the PHOTO-PAINT window and open the folder that contains the files you have saved in these exercises. You can see your picture files listed. We want to see the sizes of the files, so select the Details command from the folder's View menu.

5 You can now see the files listed, with one file per row. Click on the Size column heading button twice and the list will be sorted in descending order of size. You can see that at the top is the uncompressed TIF file, with the BMP file fractionally smaller. Then comes the LZW compressed TIF and the original CPT file, around 40 per cent smaller. Then come the lossy files: first the GIF, which is around a quarter of the size of the CPT file. Much smaller, however, is the JPG file – around one tenth the size of the GIF and a massive 99 per cent reduction in file size from the original CPT file.

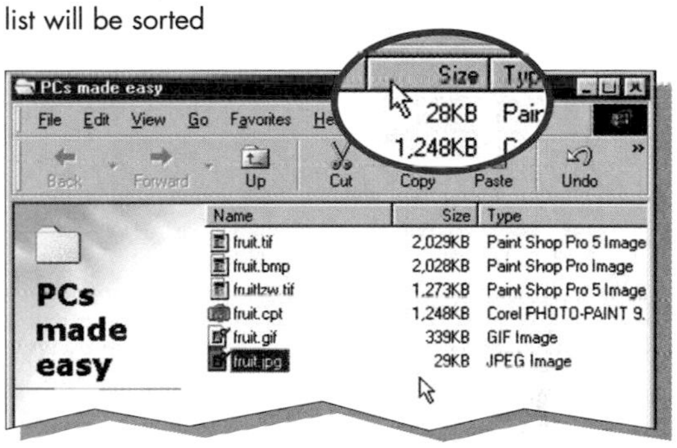

Which type of compression?

As you can see from the exercise above, it's the lossy or 256-colour file formats that create the smallest file sizes. This is especially important if you're creating pictures for your Web site (see Stage 3, pages 154-157): you'll have to save pictures in either GIF or JPG. The question is, which is better? For photographic pictures, the JPG format will provide better images. The colour loss isn't so obvious and with lower Compression settings – between 10 and 50 – you'll still get reasonable image quality. Repeat Steps 7, 8 and 9 on the opposite page, with different settings to get a feel for how far to push the compression before it gets too obvious (far left).

However, for some types of picture, the JPG format creates ugly and distracting effects and the GIF format may well prove more useful. For example, the simple four-colour logo (left) has a noticeable distortion along the edges when saved as a JPG (inset left).

When the same original picture is saved in GIF format, there is no effect at all; the limited number of colours in the original image ensures that there's no loss of quality when converted to 256 colours. In general, where the original image has lots of subtle tones and shadows blending into each other, the JPG format works well, but where the image is made up of solid and continuous areas in a few colours, the GIF format is better.

Using Artistic Text

Special effects with text can be highly effective. Use your artistic judgement when experimenting with these effects and explore how you can attract more attention to your work.

CorelDRAW has a wide range of graphic options and special effects – and things are no different when it comes to text. We've already seen how to use Artistic Text to create special characters (see Stage 3, pages 70-73) but you can also combine text with other objects to make even more effective designs. Here, we show how to exploit Artistic Text and turn a few words into an effective logo.

Artistic Text is most useful for applications such as logos or headlines, where you just want to add a single line or two of text. Once the words are placed on the screen, you can then add any of the standard CorelDRAW effects to create unusual and unique styles, which have great impact. Large blocks of text containing several sentences are best entered using **Paragraph Text** instead (see pages 80-81). Typically, such text needs only simple formatting – bold, italics, and so on, rather than special effects.

● Click here to begin

Artistic Text is created by selecting the Text Tool and single-clicking anywhere on the CorelDRAW page. A flashing cursor will then appear on the page, indicating that you can begin typing. As we have already seen, the main benefit of Artistic Text is that text is treated like a series of drawn objects that can be manipulated, rather than simply edited as you would with a word processor.

You have the choice of tweaking individual letters or adding overall effects to whole words. You can choose any of CorelDRAW's standard graphic effects but most often you'll probably want to add a special type of fill to the text or to give it some depth and an illusion of 3D modelling.

● For my next trick ...

Another very useful ability of Artistic Text is that you can use it to fit text into a shaped area. By simply clicking on the edge of an object, you can cause the text to run around its outline as you type. This effect can be further refined so that the text appears to go around the inside of the object or at a specified horizontal or vertical distance away from it. You can even make the object itself invisible after you have typed the text so that the text itself looks as if it is defining a shape.

We touch on all these aspects of Artistic Text in the following exercise, in which we create a logo for a local football team's badge.

WHAT IT MEANS

PARAGRAPH TEXT

Paragraph Text is the alternative to Artistic Text. It is also created using the Text Tool, but instead of just clicking on the page to type in your text, you must drag a rectangular text box for the Paragraph Text to appear inside. Once this is done, it behaves much like a word processor and you can use standard word-processing commands to set aspects such as line spacing, alignment and simple text formatting.

Creating a badge with Artistic Text

In this exercise we'll be using Artistic Text to jazz up a badge design for the local football team. You'll see how text can be made to follow a shaped path and how it can have any of the standard CorelDRAW effects applied to it.

1 First we need to create a badge with a picture on it. We'll do this using an ordinary circle and a piece of clip art of a football. Draw the circle using the Ellipse Tool, holding down the [Ctrl] key to make sure a perfect circle is created. Fill in the circle with a solid colour.

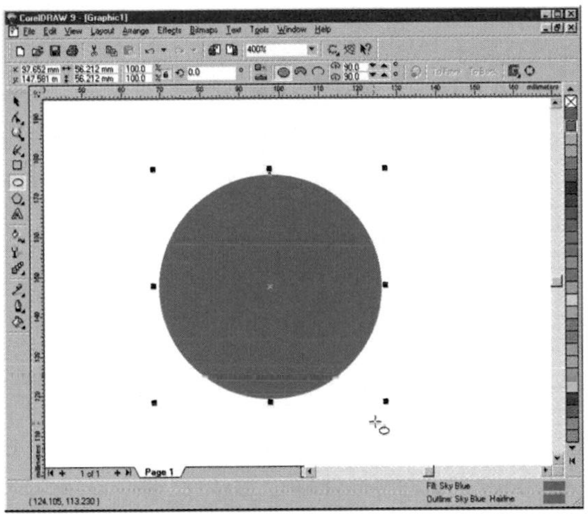

2 Now import a football from the CorelDRAW clip art CD-ROM (see Stage 2, page 75). We've used Sball123.cdr from the Collection/Sports/Soccer folder. You might have to shrink it from its original size to fit the badge.

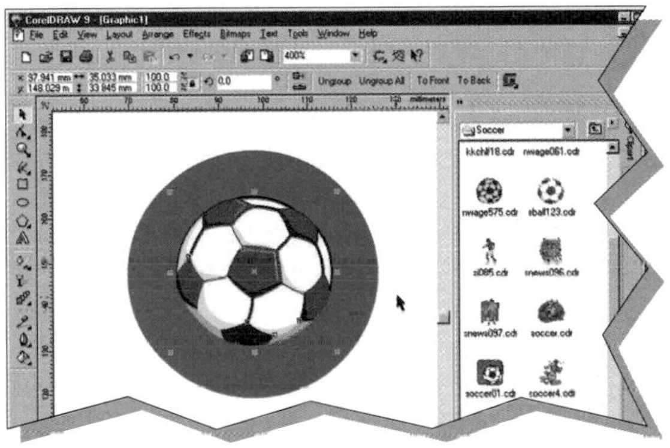

3 Running text around a path works only with simple objects, rather than grouped ones like the football clip art. To circumvent this problem, draw an unfilled circle around the football as a guide for the text. We'll make the circle invisible later.

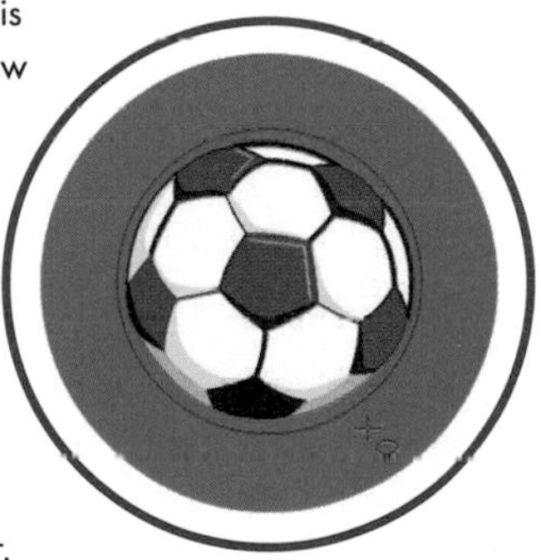

4 Now choose the Text Tool from the toolbar on the left. Move the cursor onto the edge of the new circle and you will see the cursor change to a small 'A' over a curved line (right).

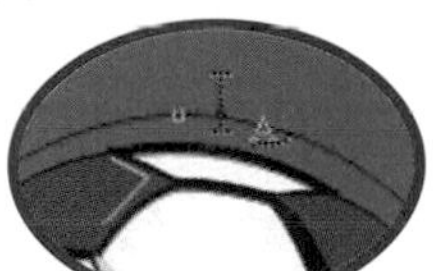

Click the left mouse button and type in your text. You'll find that it follows a path running round the outside of the circle around the football (right).

5 You can change the way the text follows the path by using the drop-down list boxes on the Property bar. For example, try changing the Distance from Path setting to move the text away from the circle outline.

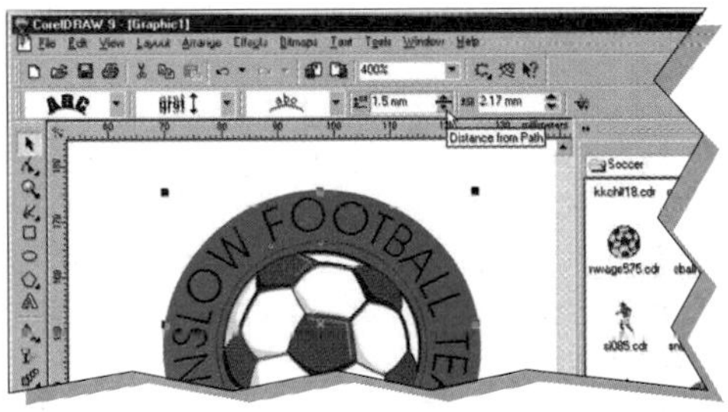

6 Now hide the guide circle. Right-click on the outline and choose Properties from the pop-up menu (inset). Choose the Outline tab of the Object Properties dialog box (below) and click the button in the top right-hand corner. Click the Apply button to turn off the outline.

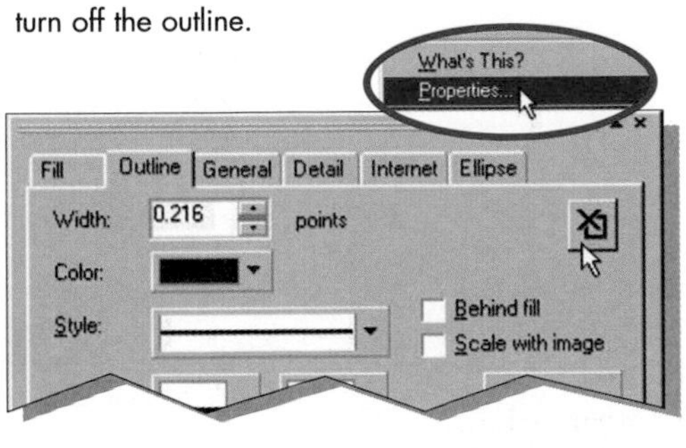

7 The circle is not filled, so it will disappear, leaving the text in place.

8 To finish off, you can put in some more Artistic Text at the bottom of the badge and then add a special effect. From the Effects menu, choose Add Perspective and pull the two bottom corners of the text box outwards, to give a distorted effect to your text.

Flowing text

Here we show how the Paragraph Text commands can make your documents more eye-catching by running the text around pictures and shapes.

We've seen how text can be fitted around shapes using Artistic Text (see pages 78-79). This works by allowing you to convert text into an object and then to manipulate it in various ways. However, it has a drawback: once converted, you can no longer deal with the words as text. This means that if, for example, you notice a spelling error after conversion, you can't amend it. You might even have to start again from scratch.

Paragraph Text, on the other hand, lets you manipulate the shape of a block of text, while still allowing you to edit and format it in the usual way – with bold, italics and different typefaces, for instance. If you want to make things a bit more interesting, you can also make the formatted text flow around, inside and between objects, creating eye-catching designs in the process.

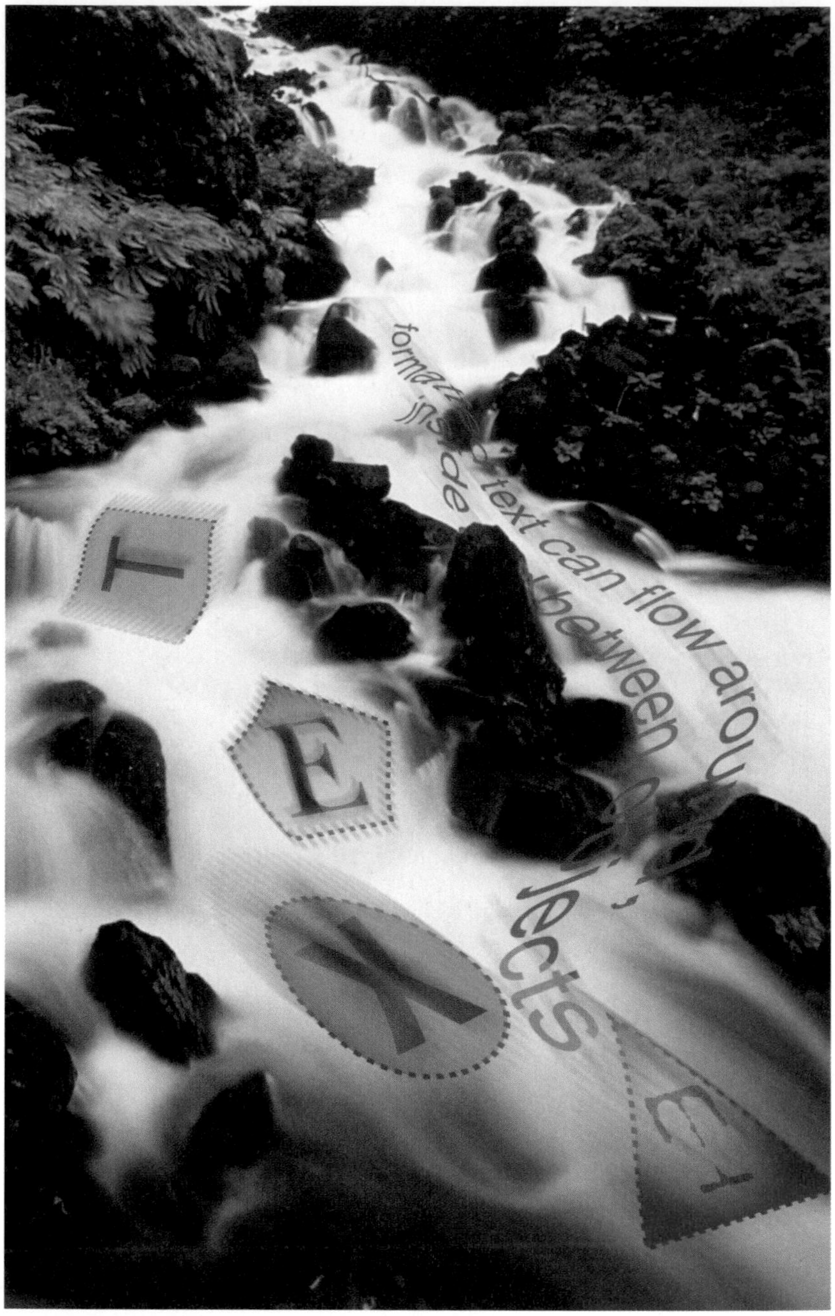

● Wrapping blocks of text

You can make text run around either the outside or the inside of an object. To run text around an object, you simply apply the Wrap paragraph text command. This works for an object of any shape, including those you have drawn yourself. To confine text inside an object, you can adjust the Envelope of the object (see Stage 3, pages 70-73). You have the choice of a number of preset envelopes, or you can draw your own – both are freely editable. Alternatively, you can fit text within an existing object by clicking the Text Tool on an object when the pointer changes to a box with 'AB' inside.

When wrapping text around irregular objects (such as the elephant shown opposite), there are two approaches. CorelDRAW normally wraps text so that it follows the object's outline. However, for some irregular shapes this can make the text harder to read, as it wraps around every nook and cranny. In such cases, add an extra regular shape – such as a circle or a rectangle – to use for the text wrap. You can then hide it by removing its outline so that it is completely transparent.

PARAGRAPH OR ARTISTIC?

Although both are created using the same tool, there is a significant difference between Artistic Text and Paragraph Text. Artistic Text is used for single words and short sentences – the letters themselves are expected to be worked with as individual objects – while Paragraph Text is used for longer strings of text. As a general rule, text that is more than one sentence long is best entered into CorelDRAW as Paragraph Text, and any short phrases or titles as Artistic Text.

Flowing text into a poster

Here we create a poster for a white elephant sale, featuring a picture of an elephant with words running behind it.

1 First, we want a central object to be the basis of the document. The text for our poster will come later. Draw your own central object, or insert some clip art. Here we've used Elephanc.cdr – from Collection\Animals\Wild – which we've coloured white.

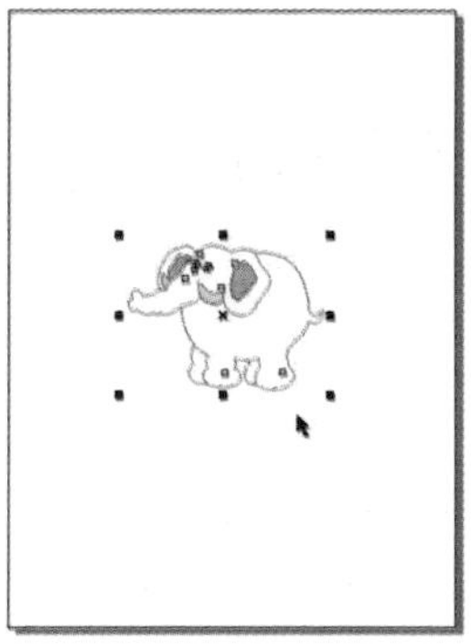

2 Although paragraph text will flow around an object of any shape, it usually looks better with a uniform outline. Draw a circle around the elephant and then make its outline invisible. Do this by right-clicking on the circle, selecting Properties from the menu, then clicking on the Remove Outline button in the top right-hand corner under the Outline tab and clicking Apply.

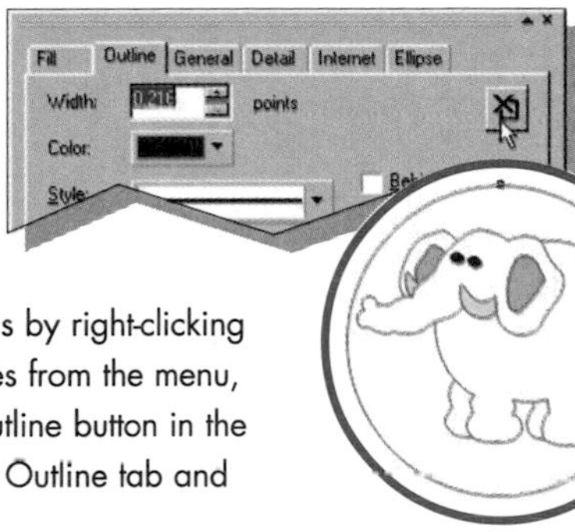

3 Click on the General tab of the dialog box. Then click on the Wrap paragraph text check box. Click Apply again.

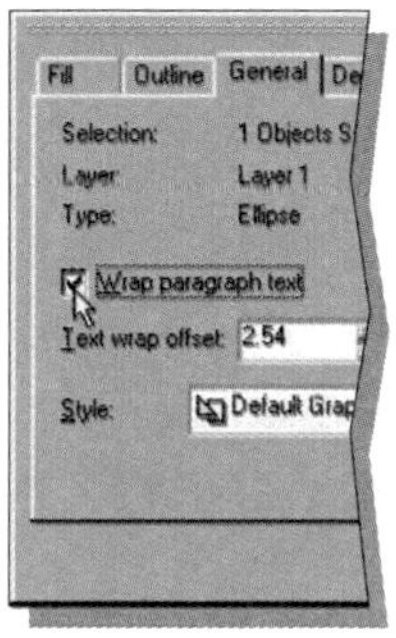

PC TIPS

Text offset

More often than not when adding flowing text effects, you will want to make sure that the text itself is not too close to the object; both the text and the object have more impact if they are clearly separated. You can easily change the amount of space between flowing text and the shape it is next to. Use the shape's Object Properties dialog box (see Step 2), choose the General tab and increase the value in the Text wrap offset box (below).

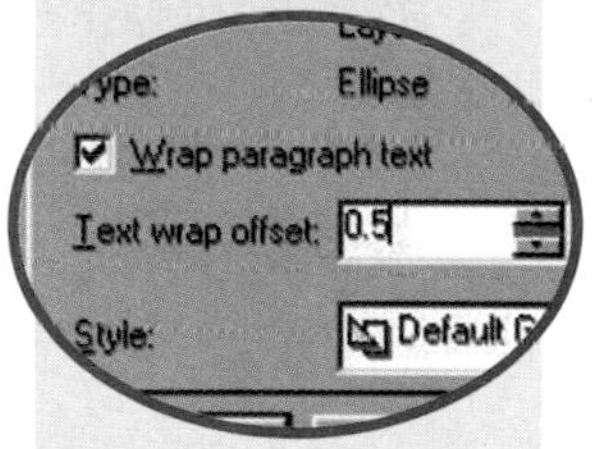

4 We now need to add some text. Select the Text Tool and, holding down the left mouse button, draw a text box that covers the circle with at least a centimetre to spare on all sides. Type in the words, copying and pasting when you run out of inspiration. We have made the text a light grey colour and used a fairly small font size to make sure it doesn't overshadow the picture.

5 This looks reasonably good, but we can improve it by changing the shape of the text box. Select the Paragraph Text box and then choose the Interactive Envelope Tool. You can now move each of the box's handles to a new position. Click the Property Bar's Add Preset button and then the diamond shape.

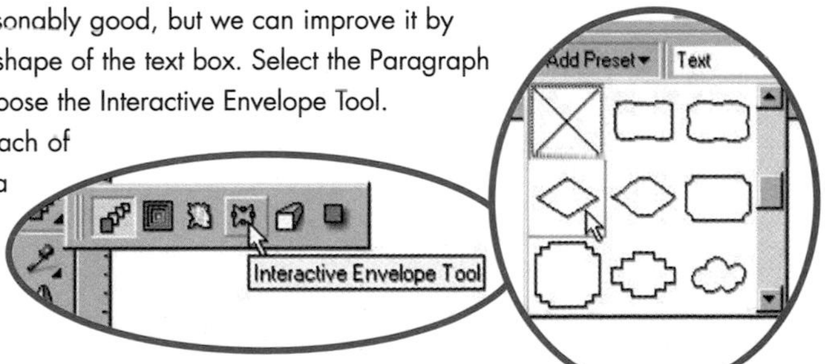

6 The text box changes shape, and the text inside it reflows to follow its new shape. Make the diamond shape fill the full height and width of the page by dragging the four handles.

7 Finally, create a series of triangles in each of the poster's corners and fit text into them. To draw a triangle use the Bezier Tool to define the three corners of the object. When you've finished, fill in each of the triangles with a bright colour.

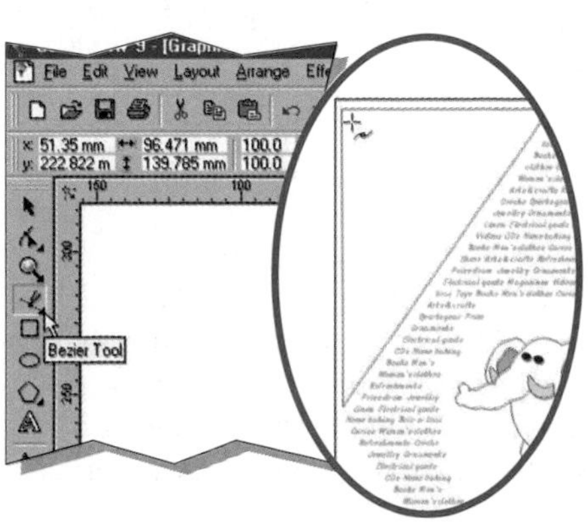

8 Select the Text Tool. Click on the edge of a triangle when the cursor becomes a box with the letters 'AB' in it. Type in the text so that it appears only in the triangle. Repeat with all four triangles to produce the finished poster.

Getting fast results with Artistic Media

CorelDRAW's powerful Artistic Media features make complicated artistic techniques a matter of simply clicking or dragging to apply them to your pictures.

With constant development for almost 10 years, CorelDRAW has added more instant art techniques with each new version. The idea is to make computer art so easy that anyone who can use a mouse can get quick art results.

If you're finding that CorelDRAW's standard collection of square, circle and line shapes isn't inspiring, try the Artistic Media effects. This collection of strokes combines shapes and special effects to create fantastic results – all in a few seconds.

● Pen mightier than the mouse

One of the most useful tricks that you can achieve with the Artistic Media tool is to simulate calligraphy with the mouse. The nib on a real pen draws lines of different widths depending on the direction of its travel: horizontal lines are thinner than vertical lines, for example.

With CorelDRAW, you can get your mouse to emulate this effect if you choose the right Artistic Media option. This is great for creating simple Web graphics where you want to produce a hand-drawn effect. If you have a pressure-sensitive drawing tablet you can get interactive control over the thickness. By pressing harder with the stylus on the tablet, you can draw thicker lines in your drawing.

● Using images as strokes

Even without a drawing tablet, you can create 'hand-written' text in a variety of calligraphic styles. You can also use the typefaces installed on your computer as the basis for stroke effects. This is perfect if you want to jazz up some text on a poster or leaflet, but none of the typefaces on your computer is suitable on its own. Strokes aren't merely for jazzing up text – they work just as well with any type of line in your drawing. In fact, they can give a new lease of life to the simple rectangle, ellipse and polygon tools in CorelDRAW's toolbox. Often, when you know the basic shape you want but you're stuck for ideas about how to make it interesting, one of the ready-made strokes will suggest an approach that you wouldn't otherwise have considered.

CorelDRAW's strokes are very versatile. At their simplest, they're just black and white curved shapes which you can apply to another line. This results in a new shape that has the basic outline of the stroke but has been stretched and distorted to run from the start of the original line to the end of the line. As CorelDRAW treats all shapes as lines, you can apply these strokes to circles and polygons.

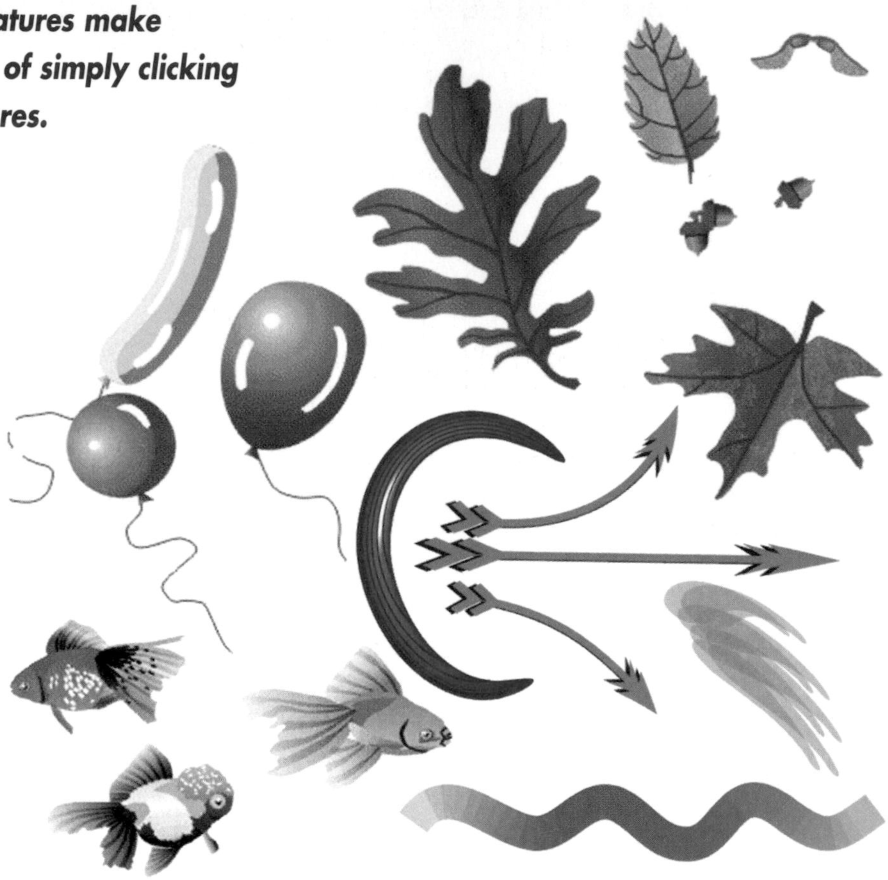

Personalize your documents by using the art tools CorelDRAW makes available to you.

WHAT IT MEANS

STROKES

These are ready-made designs that can be applied along any path. You can apply strokes to a shape's outline or a line already in your drawing. You can also draw strokes directly with the mouse.

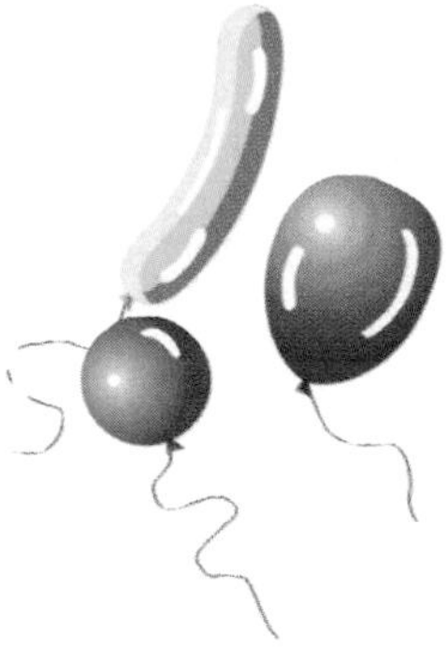

For more drastic changes, there's a wide selection of coloured strokes, ranging from abstract patterns and rainbow effects, through to arrangements of leaves and animals. By applying these designs or image strokes, you can completely change the look of your original line or shape. Your original line is hidden from view by CorelDRAW, so it's impossible for people to see how easily you achieved the dramatic effects.

● Fast results and instant ideas

CorelDRAW's Artistic Media strokes can achieve results way out of proportion to the time you put into using them. Once you've got the hang of how they work, they're a powerful adjunct to CorelDRAW's regular drawing tools. Even if you just want to dabble, they're a great source of inspiration.

DIY STROKES

CorelDRAW's ready-made strokes are .CMX files and they are shown in the Artistic Media docker (display panel). The program lets you save any part of your own drawings as a .CMX file, so you can make strokes of your own. Use the Files of type box in the Save Drawing dialog box and select the 'CMX – Corel Presentation Exchange' option. By using the Browse button on the Artistic Media docker, you can also select your own strokes.

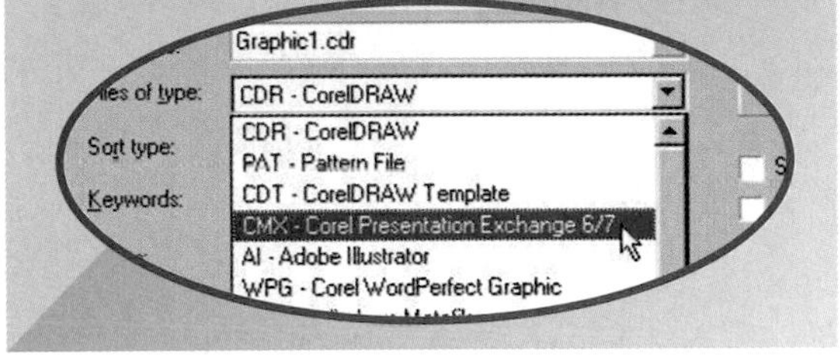

Artistic Media basics

It doesn't take much experimentation to learn the ins and outs of the Artistic Media commands – and the results are really worth while.

THE BASIC IDEA behind the Artistic Media strokes is to apply a ready-made shape, image or set of images to a line. This line can be the outline of a shape in your drawing or a curved or straight line that you draw on the page. Many of the strokes can completely change the look of the line – often in ways that seem difficult to predict – so it pays to experiment a little before using these techniques in your drawings.

1 Open up a new CorelDRAW document. Select Artistic Media from the Effects menu to see the strokes available in the bottom part of the docker (the display panel, shown right and inset below).

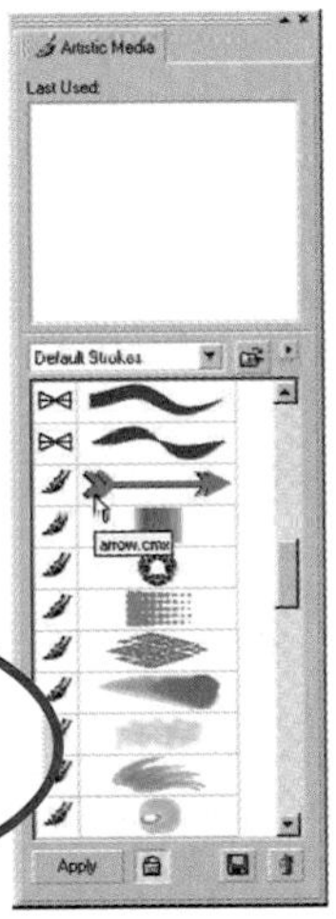

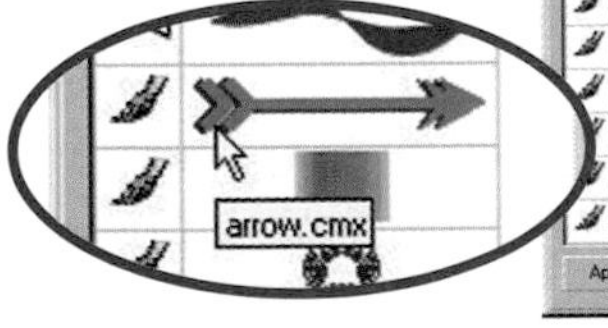

2 Use the Freehand Tool to draw a straight line on a blank page. While it's still selected, click one of the strokes in the docker and CorelDRAW immediately applies the stroke to the line you have drawn.

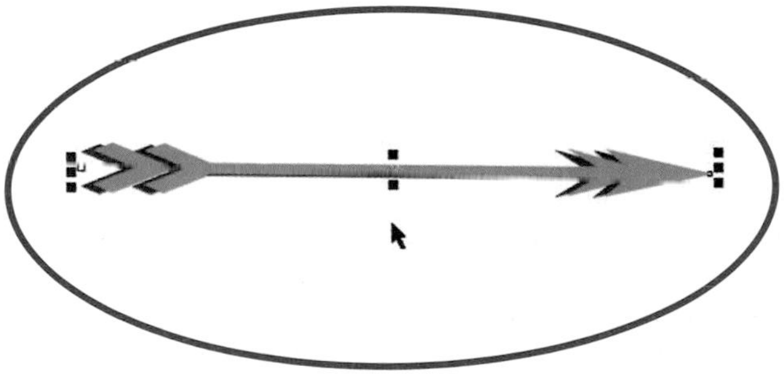

3 If you do the same with a curved line, CorelDRAW just applies the stroke along the path of the curve. Try this with several of the other ready-made strokes to see how they work. The effects are frequently amazing for very little effort.

4 Some strokes use your lines only as a rough basis for their position. Scroll down the list to see Object Sprayer strokes. These work like PHOTO-PAINT's Image Sprayer tool: several objects are sprinkled around the path of your line. There are many types of object, including leaves, fish and seagulls. We have used pebbles here.

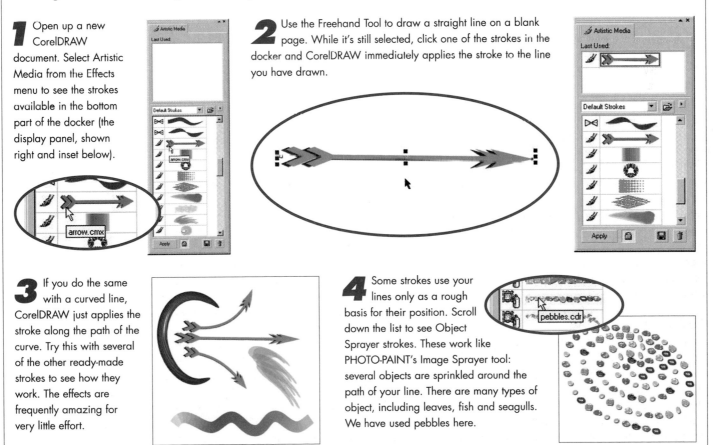

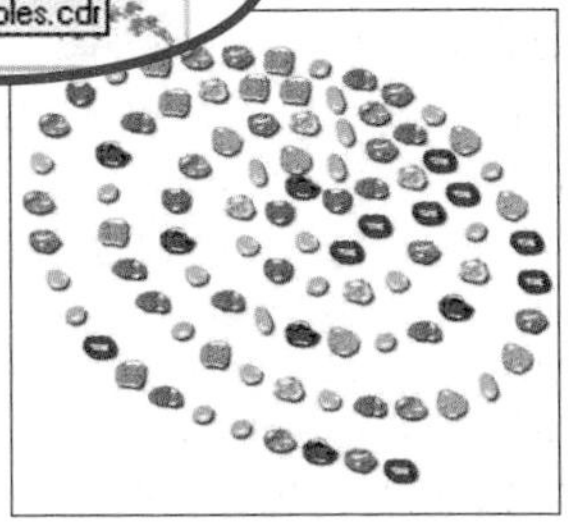

Drawing your own letters

CorelDRAW brings the power of the pen to your mouse by adding hand-drawn calligraphic effects to your lettering.

1 When you start CorelDRAW, the Artistic Media Tool is normally hidden from view. Click on the Freehand Tool in the toolbox to see the full range of line drawing options and select the Artistic Media Tool from the pop-up options.

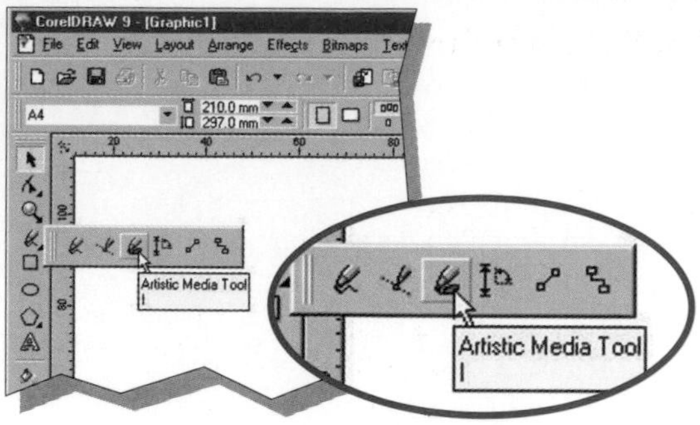

2 The Property Bar changes to show the relevant settings and options for this tool. To imitate hand-written text, first click on the Calligraphic button.

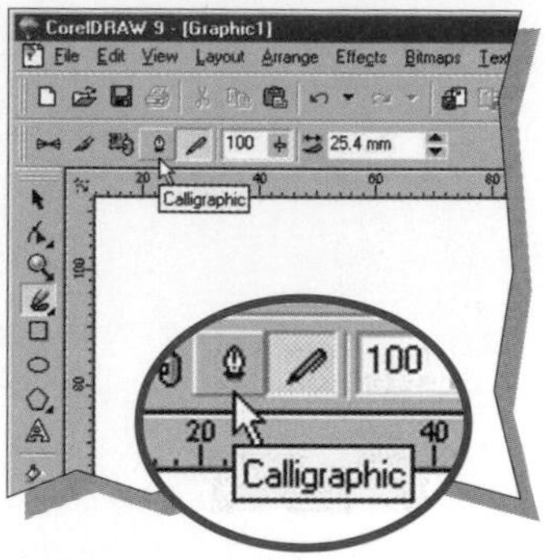

3 The mouse pointer changes to a pen shape when it's over the drawing area. Draw a letter shape to see how the tool works. You can write in joined-up style – as you'd write on paper – but it's best to start by creating a letter with distinct strokes, like the three strokes in this 'H'. Note that the vertical strokes in this letter are very thick, but the not-quite-horizontal centre stroke varies in thickness from left to right.

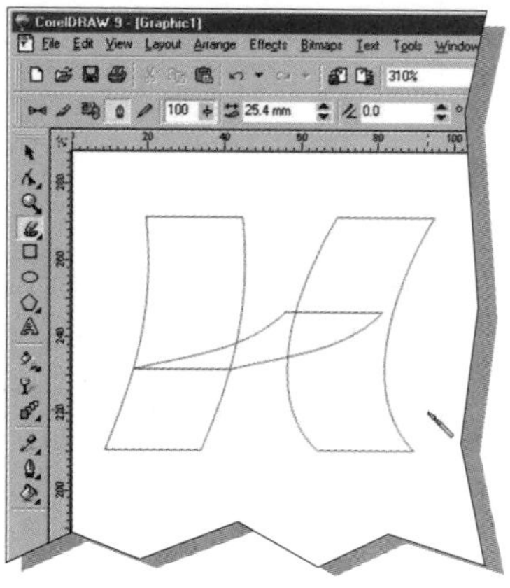

4 To apply solid colour to the strokes, click on the black square in the colour palette to see the letter more clearly. Although the letter looks like a solid shape, your three lines are still underneath. Drag one of the strokes to the side and CorelDRAW moves the one you originally drew. Release the mouse button and the stroke shape reappears.

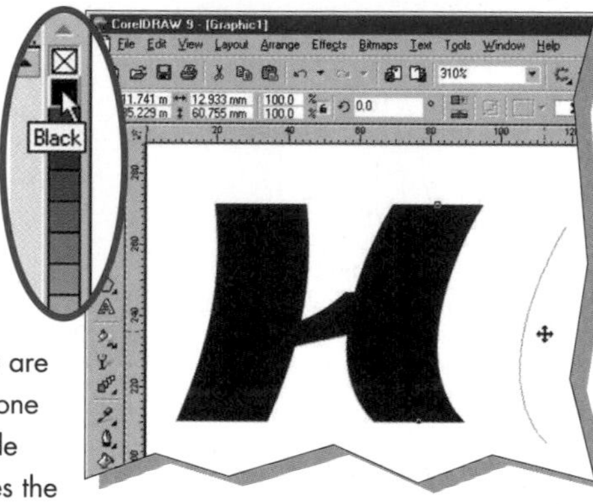

5 This makes it very easy to redraw the letter with different calligraphic settings. Select one of your strokes and reduce the figure in the Artistic Media Tool Width box on the Property Bar.

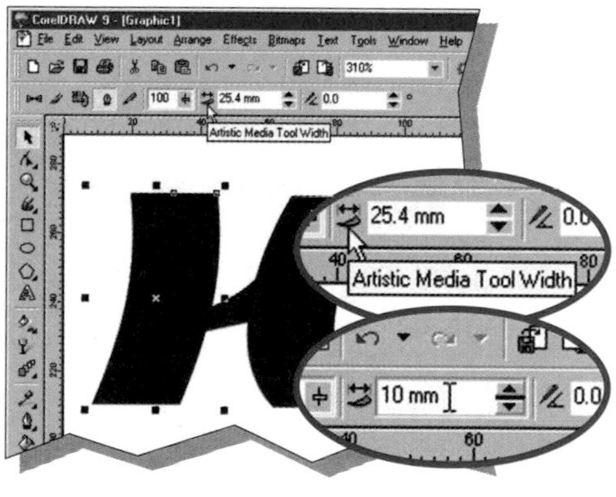

6 When you press the [Enter] key, the line is redrawn with the new setting. Repeat the same process for each of the strokes in your letter. In this version, the vertical strokes don't dominate so much.

7 Experiment until you have a stroke thickness you're happy with, then write the rest of the letters for your text in the same way.

8 There's no end to the variations you can get. You can try different angles for the calligraphic nib – even after you've written your text. Just select all the strokes and type a new angle into the Calligraphic Angle box on the Property Bar (inset). Press [Enter] and CorelDRAW adjusts all the strokes accordingly.

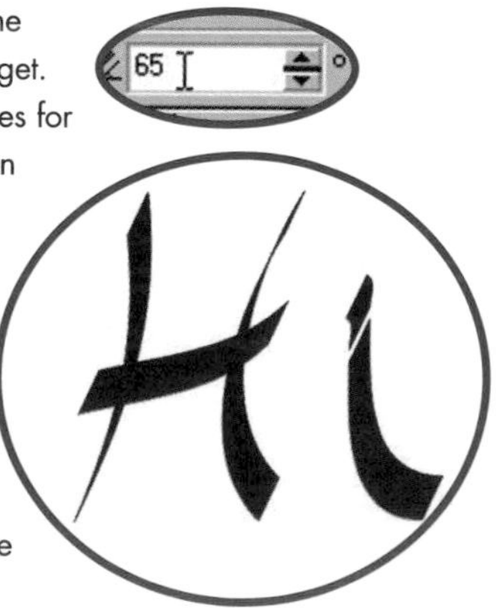

PC TIPS

Smooth lettering

If you want to write an 'i' or 'j', you might find it awkward to make the shape and place the dot in alignment over the downstroke. They can, in fact, be drawn with one stroke. The letter is drawn as a single stroke and a small rectangle is drawn to intersect it near the top. The rectangle is then changed to match the page's background colour.

Changing shapes into strokes

If you are looking for inspiration, use Artistic Media effects to turn CorelDRAW's standard shapes into something completely different.

1 Here's a CorelDRAW business card design. All it needs is a finishing touch – something to represent the nature of the business.

2 There's plenty of gardening and plant clip art to choose from, but if used too often, clip art loses its impact. Instead, draw a circle on the blank area of the card and then select Artistic Media from the Effects menu.

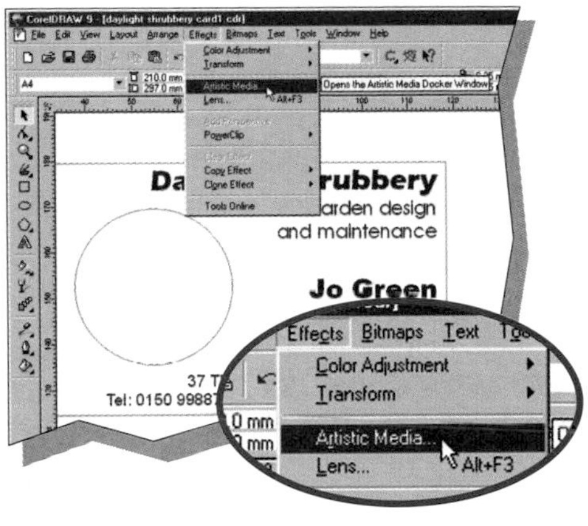

3 The Artistic Media docker opens on the right of the window. Select the circle, scroll down the list of Strokes and click on the a1.cmx stroke.

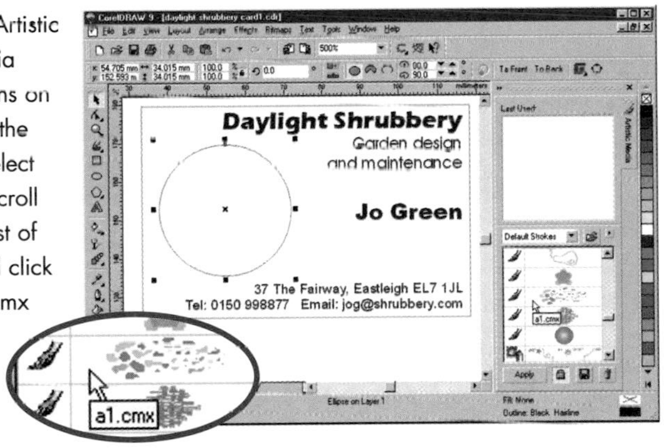

4 The original single circle outline is redrawn with a reddish-brown stroke running clockwise from the top. It is thick to start with but thins out as it goes around the circle.

5 There are three shades in the stroke. Click a dark green colour in the palette.

6 Draw another, smaller circle inside the first and repeat the process, choosing another shade of green. Note how the stroke's 'paint' is concentrated at the top right of the circle. This happens because CorelDRAW creates a circle as a curved line that starts at the top and runs clockwise back to the top – the a1.cmx stroke is wider at the start and narrower at the end.

7 It's easy to change this by rotating the inner circle. Select it, then type a new figure into the Angle of Rotation box on the Property Bar. Try 180 degrees. Press the [Enter] key to see how the paint is redistributed.

8 Repeat the process for more circles in other shades, rotating them as necessary. Eventually, with just a few circles, you have a smart-looking abstract design that would have been hard to imagine and even harder to achieve by using the regular drawing tools.

PC TIPS

Stroking text

If you don't want to draw every stroke of every letter of text in your drawing (as on the previous page), you might find it useful to stroke the text with one of the Artistic Media Tools presets. To do this, place some Artistic Text (see pages 78-79) in your drawing and then convert it to curves using the Property Bar button. Then,

bring up the Artistic Media docker and click on any of the black-and-white shapes at the top of the stroke list shown in the docker. The text is immediately redrawn with strokes around the outline of the letter shapes.

Outline

If you don't like the result, just try another stroke until you get an effect you're happy with.

CorelTEXTURE

Hidden away in the depths of the CorelDRAW package is the useful and fun utility CorelTEXTURE. This allows you to create all sorts of patterns and give the illusion of depth to your work.

If you selected the Typical option when you installed CorelDRAW, some of CorelDRAW's most useful programs are left uninstalled. One program which is especially good for creating new and original graphics is CorelTEXTURE.

As the name suggests, CorelTEXTURE is used to create custom textures, which can then be exported and used in any other CorelDRAW package – and in many other software packages as well.

● Plumbing the depths

In computer art software, a texture is any pattern which gives the illusion of depth. Textures are often computer-generated abstract designs but many patterns are based on real objects. Textures that give the illusion of wood, marble or metal, for example, are commonly available.

For instance, if you draw an image of a table, you could use a texture image of wood to paste over the Corel objects that make up its shape. A simple poster heading could be made much more arresting by making it look as though it is carved into solid marble.

Using textures as patterns to 'colour in' existing objects gives a more realistic look, rather than using plain colours (even with subtle shading). Suppose you are drawing a tree; simply colouring its trunk brown will give a flat and simplistic effect, compared to filling it with a texture that looks like tree bark. Textures are particularly useful when creating images for Web sites, where a texture can 'lift' a shape above the flat background of a Web page.

Like most Corel programs, CorelTEXTURE has a powerful Wizard which enables you to create your own textures from scratch. You are taken through what amounts to a multiple-choice quiz asking you to specify what type of texture you want to create. Start the process by deciding which of five built-in textures you wish to use as a base – marble, wood, granite, a logo or clouds. (You can also use bitmaps you have created yourself, perhaps in Corel PHOTO-PAINT.) You can then mould the basic texture by choosing a colour scheme and specifying which light and shading options you would like applied.

● Scratching the surface

Whether you use the Wizard or build them from scratch, CorelTEXTURE patterns are created in stages. In each case you start with a blank surface, upon which you begin to define colour, depth and lighting. These attributes can be edited after the texture has been created and you can fiddle with the controls to fine-tune them to what you want.

The four main texture attributes that you can alter are described opposite. Experiment with the effects and once you are happy with the settings of each one, you can save your texture. Then you can start to use it in your other graphics.

INSTALLING ADD-ONS

Like other graphics utilities supplied with CorelDRAW, CorelTEXTURE must be installed manually. Insert the original CorelDRAW disc into your CD-ROM drive and start the Setup program. Then, use the Add New Components option to choose just the CorelTEXTURE program from the installation options.

Using textures creatively can enhance plain objects by bringing them to life with depth, colour and light.

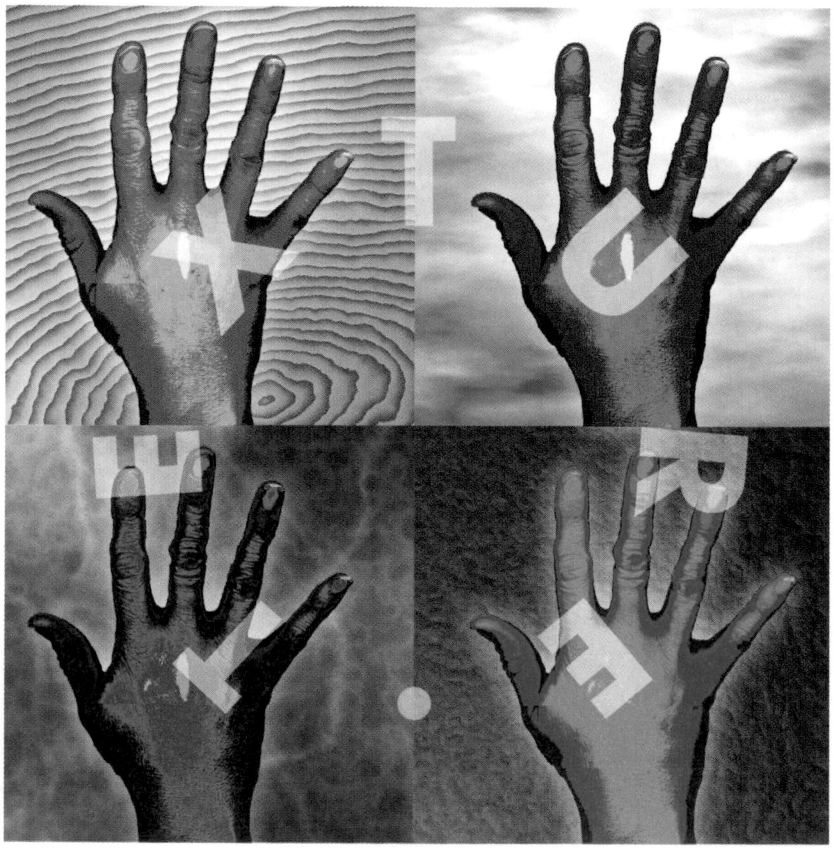

The four texture attributes

Controlling the attributes of a basic texture lets you modify it to suit your every need.

Topography
You can define the contours of the texture of your pattern – whether it is bumpy or smooth, rippled or wavy, for example. Setting the type and number of these surface features not only changes the physical nature of the texture but also alters how it looks when a light source shines on it, creating longer or shorter shadows and shapes.

Shader layers
The shader layers alter the basic colours of the graphic. Most textures have more than one shader layer – often three or four. Each layer is semi-transparent and is used to define the colour and detail of a different surface component. So, for example, you might have one layer for the underlying colour of the base texture, another for the colour of any pattern that runs across it (such as the veins in Marble), another for any spots or bumps, and so forth. The colours used are defined via a palette bar.

Lighting
A texture can have up to three different light sources pointed at it, which can have a big effect on the way it appears when finally rendered – you might have created a lovely crimson metallic effect on one portion of your texture but, if it's cast in shadow then nobody is going to see it. You can move each of the light sources to any position above the texture and also alter the values of shading and highlights for each individual source.

Edges
If you are creating a texture to fill a large object, you might find that it is too small to cover the whole area. Although the texture can be tiled easily, this can still be a problem as the result can look untidy if the edges of the texture don't fit together well. Fortunately, one of CorelTEXTURE's toolbar buttons will instantly convert your texture into one that tiles seamlessly. This makes it easy to create repeating patterns.

PC TIPS

Textures in CorelDraw

Most of the programs in the CorelDRAW suite can make use of textures – either in their raw format or once they have been converted to bitmaps. Both CorelDRAW and PHOTO-PAINT are designed to work with a number of existing textures that are supplied with them – and so work particularly well with new ones created in CorelTEXTURE. Once you convert textures to bitmaps, you can use them in other programs, such as Microsoft Word and Windows itself.

The five basic textures

These examples are based on CorelTEXTURE's five built-in designs, with the attributes modified as shown.

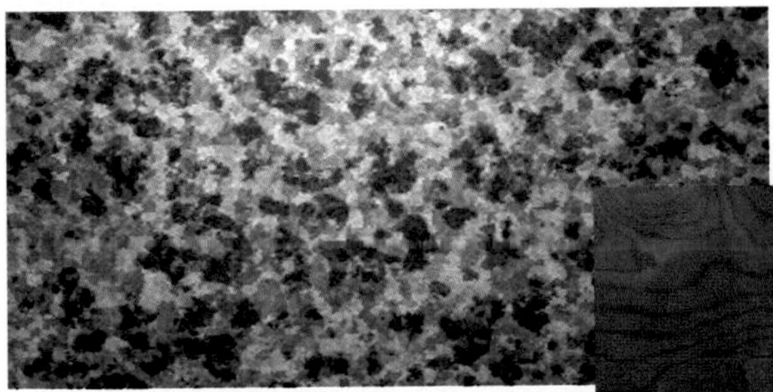

This Granite design has a blue-azure colour scheme and one light source.

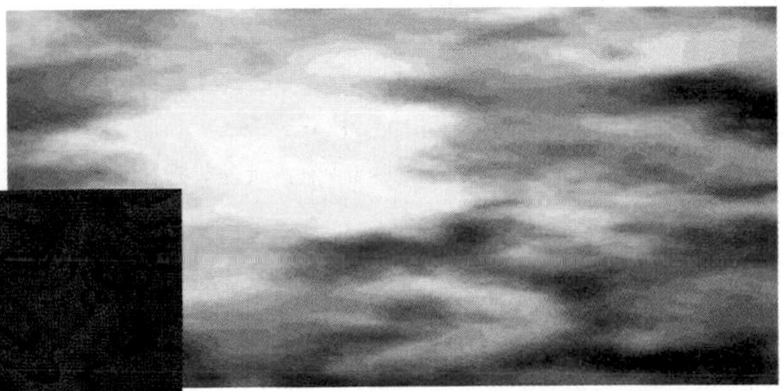

If you're tired of Microsoft clouds, create your own sunset with CorelTEXTURE's Clouds design.

It's easy to create your own customized version of a texture. This one is a red lacquer effect based on Wood, using the redwood curl option to produce an attractive high-grain finish.

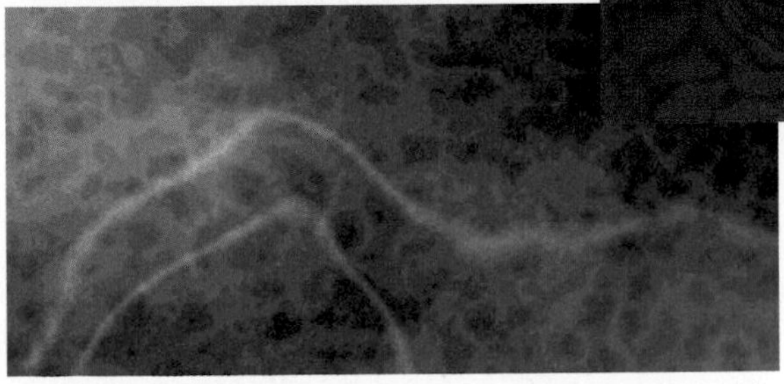

This slice of CorelTexture's Marble design has complex veining and subtle depth.

With the Logo option you can use any picture to create a relief image for your background.

Using the Texture Wizard

For this exercise we'll use the Texture Wizard to create a pine veneer effect. We'll make the edges bevelled so that the texture will look like wood blocks when tiled.

1 To start the Wizard, select New from the File menu and choose Texture Wizard from the list of options that appears. Click the New button when you are ready to begin. There'll be a page of text introduction, which you can skip by pressing the Next button. Then you're ready to begin.

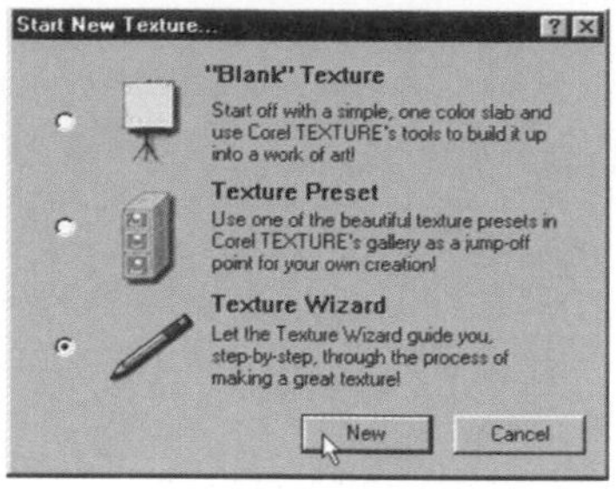

2 The first thing you have to decide is what size your texture is going to be and what resolution to use. Keep to the defaults and press Next.

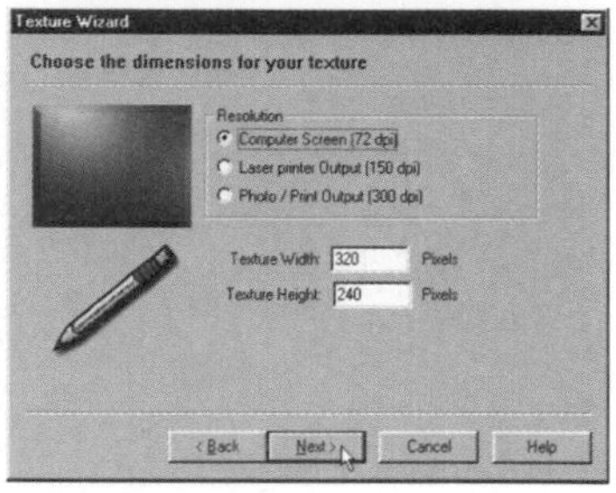

3 Your first design decision entails choosing which of the five basic textures you want to use as a basis for your work. We're after a wood effect, so click the Wood option.

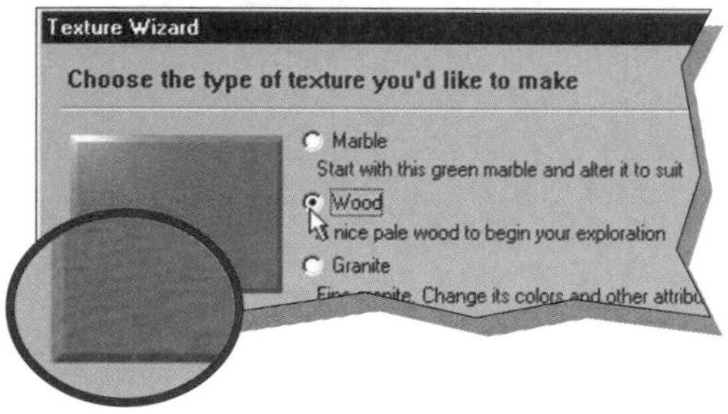

4 Now you can choose the basic colour scheme for your texture. You can preview each option just by clicking on its Radio button. The Maple option is the closest to what we want, so select that. Now you can choose how smooth the surface is – CorelTEXTURE calls this 'turbulence' – on the wood effect. Click on each option in turn to see which effect you like best. We've gone for A Little More.

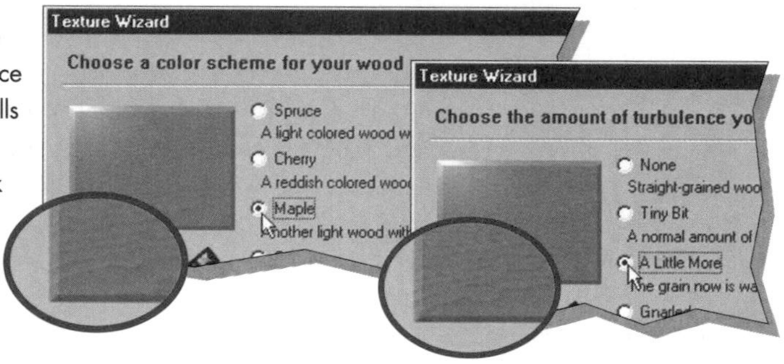

5 On the next screen you can select the cut of wood. (Imagine that the texture is based on a huge block of wood and the actual texture we use is just a slice of this.) Again, just choose the option you like best and press Next.

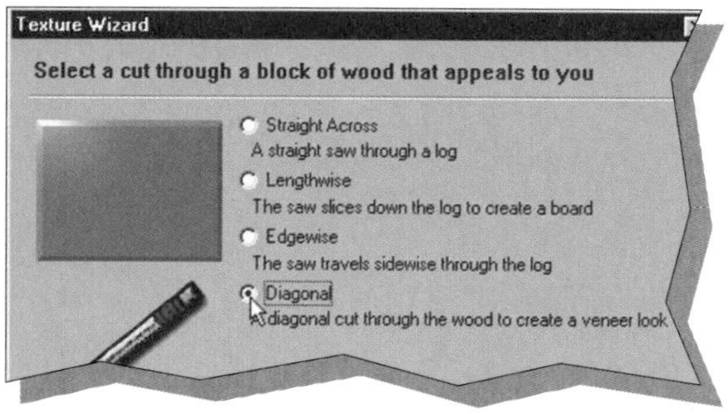

6 You might have noticed that the wood effect looks a little dark. You can change this now, by selecting from the choice of options. We've chosen Fat Light.

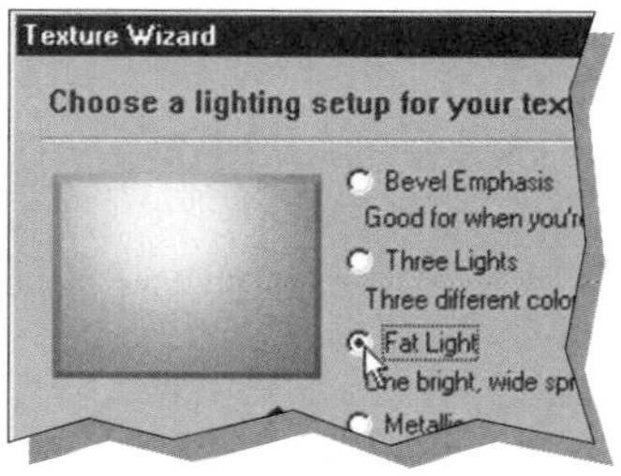

7 The next decision is very important as it defines how effective your texture looks when tiled. If you think sections will fit together seamlessly, choose the Flat option. Otherwise, select the Beveled or Rounded options so that breaks between sections look intentional, rather than a mistake. Then click on the Finish button.

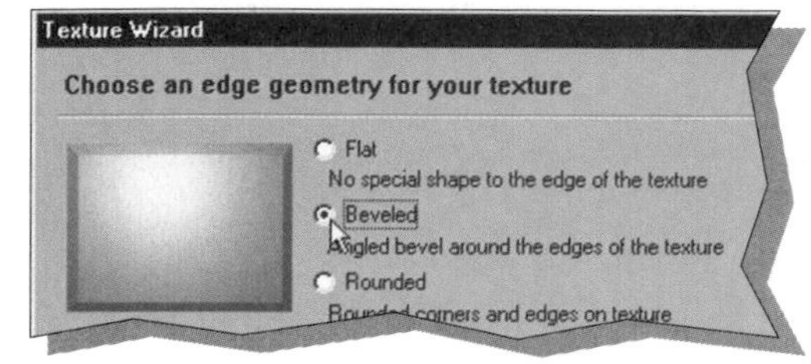

8 Your texture will appear in its own window with the Shader Layer window on its right. Use the Save command from the File menu to save the texture to your hard disk so you can use it in a picture or edit it later.

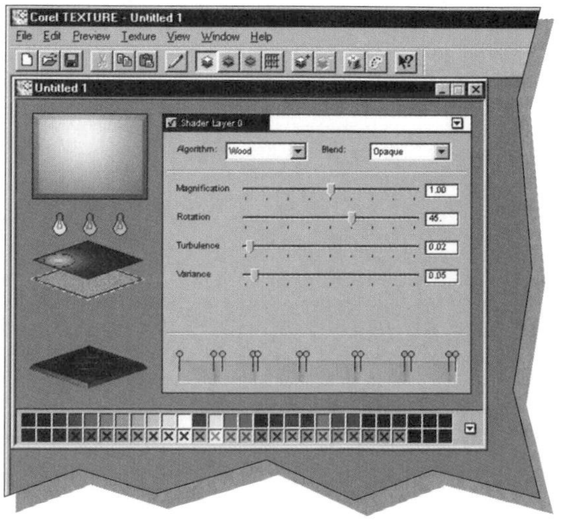

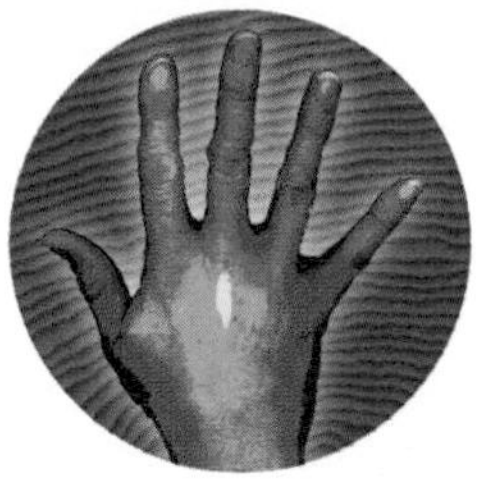

Fine-tuning and using a texture

Here we edit the texture we created on page 92. We'll refine its colour and lighting effects and then convert it into a bitmap format for use in a CorelDRAW picture.

1 Start with your texture from the previous exercise. Click on the bottom layer in the diagram under your texture (inset, below).

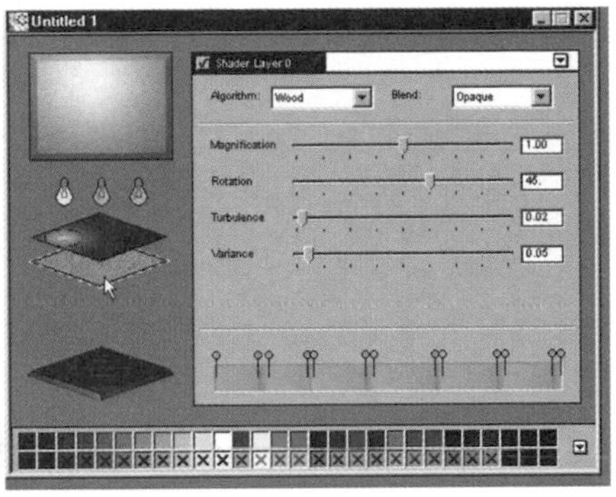

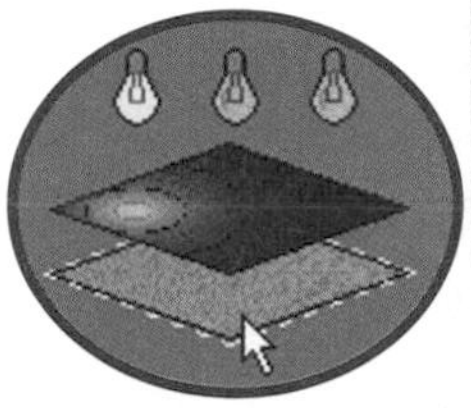

2 The Shader Layer window on the right changes to display the properties of this layer. The layer palette at the bottom of the Shader Layer window shows the colours in use (denoted by round-topped 'pins'), as if it were a slice through the texture. Add a new colour into the mix by selecting one from the colour palette and dragging it onto the left of the layer palette.

3 You'll notice an immediate change in the texture. To alter the background colour more drastically, drag the original pins further to the right of the layer palette. If you don't like the effect, simply reload the original saved texture.

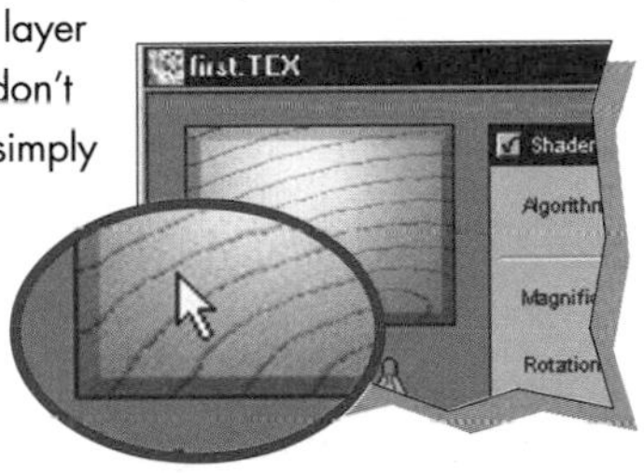

4 Another change to make is the light source. Click on the picture of the light bulbs, just below the texture preview. Move the position of the light source by dragging and dropping the pin in the diagram on the right. As you do so, note the difference this makes to the preview.

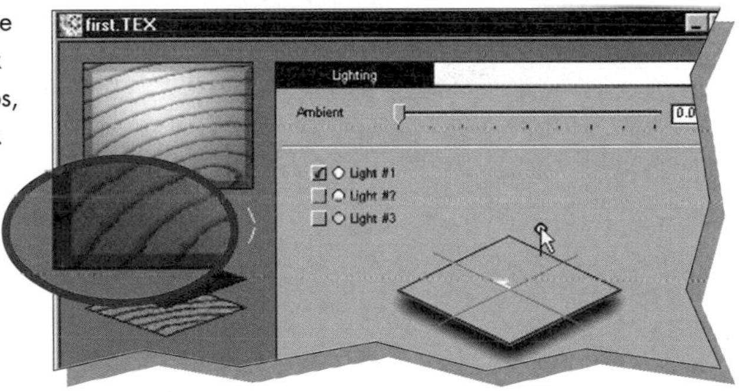

5 You can alter the intensity of the light source by moving the Highlights slider to the left or right. The Ambient slider sets the amount of overall brightness, while the Shading slider sets the length of shadows created by surface details.

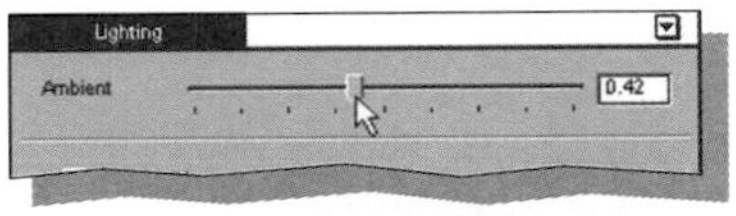

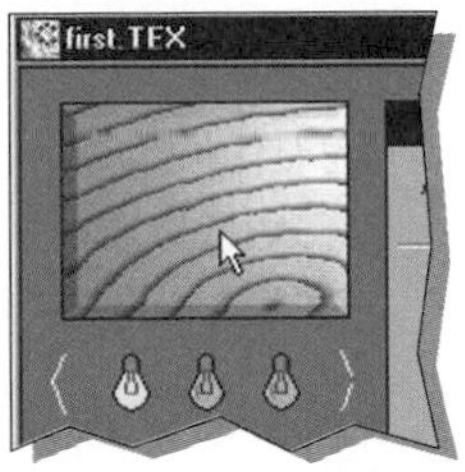

6 When you're happy with the look of your texture select Render To File from the Texture menu. CorelTEXTURE will use the popular BMP file format. Give your texture a name and press the Save button. The rendering will take a few seconds, depending on the speed of your computer, but when it's finished, the texture is ready to use in another program.

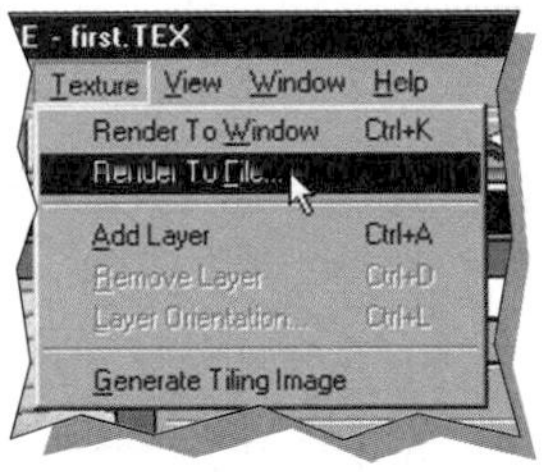

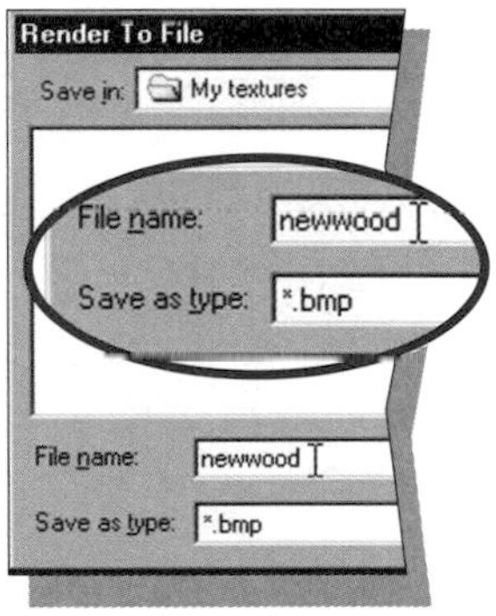

7 Start CorelDRAW and draw a simple object, such as a circle. Right-click on it and select Properties from the pop-up menu.

8 In the dialog box, click on the Fill tab and then the Pattern button (the third from the left in the row of six). To choose your own bitmap, click the Bitmap option and press the Edit button.

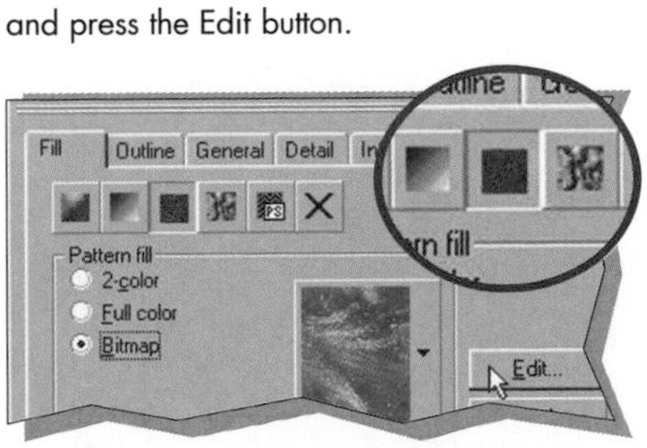

9 From the Pattern Fill dialog box, click the Load button – this allows you to find and select the bitmap texture you saved in Step 6. Press OK and then Apply. When you return to your CorelDRAW graphic, it will be filled with your texture (below right).

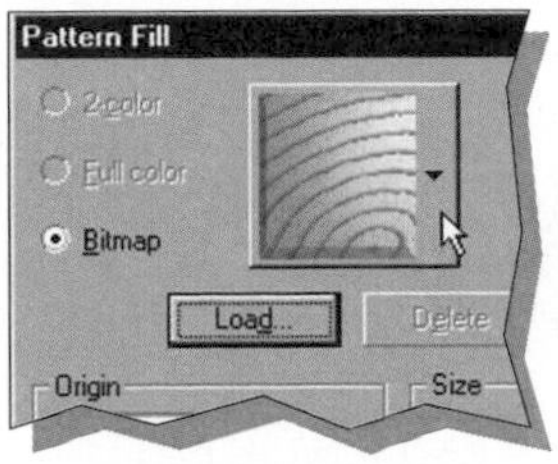

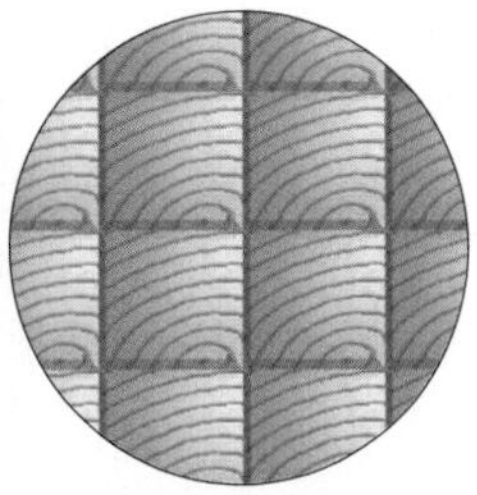

Hardware

The floppy disk

At well over 10 years of age, floppy disks are among the oldest computer accessories. Even today, however, they're very important, so it's useful to learn how they work, what they do and how to maintain them.

Ironically, today's so-called floppy disk is anything but flexible, but its name, derived from the days of the very early disks which were floppy, has stuck.

Like the hard disk inside your PC, floppy disks are a means of storing information. While they hold much less than a hard disk, they have the advantages of being small, cheap and easily portable. Typically, you can use them to store small files and documents so that you can move them easily from computer to computer and from office to home and back. Or they can be used to back up your original files in case any are lost or accidentally deleted. While 'floppies' have been overtaken by newer technology, which can store many more and much bigger files, they're such a quick and simple technology that they're unlikely to become obsolete for quite a while.

● Formatting your floppy

Floppy disks work by recording digital information onto a thin disk of magnetic material divided into concentric 'tracks' and segments known as 'sectors'. Because the magnetic disk itself is highly sensitive, it is encased in a fabric liner and further protected by a plastic case.

Before you can use floppy disks, you may have to format them (see page 98). Some floppies are sold pre-formatted and can be used immediately.

Modern floppy disks come in a standard size of $3^{1/2}$ inches wide and in two standard varieties of storage capacity: 720KB (or 0.72MB) and 1.44MB. These sizes refer to the capacity of the disk after you have formatted them, so don't be surprised if you see them sold as 1MB and 2MB floppy disks. A 1MB unformatted disk

WHAT IT MEANS

FORMAT

A blank disk must be formatted before use. This process divides the disk into areas that your programs can use to store information. Think of these areas as a series of invisible circular 'lanes' on the disk's surface. The magnetic sensor in the floppy disk drive follows these lanes to write and read computer data.

has a capacity of 720KB after formatting, while a 2MB floppy has a storage capacity of 1.44MB after formatting. A 1,000-word Microsoft Word file is about 15KB in size, so a 1.44MB floppy disk could store almost a hundred documents of this sort of size.

● Limitations of floppies

While floppies are ideal for copying or backing up smaller files and are eminently transportable and easy to swap between different machines, they are not able to deal with the size of modern software. A popular set of business programs, such as Microsoft Office, for example, can easily be 300MB in size, which would take up hundreds of standard floppy disks. Other programs are even larger.

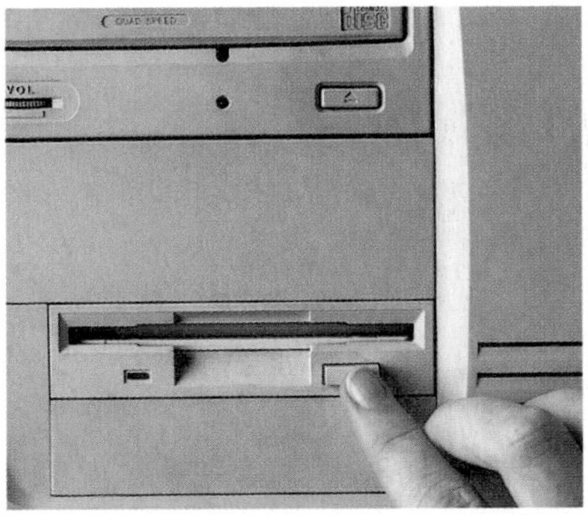

After using the floppy, eject it from the PC and store it carefully. Don't leave it next to an electrical appliance, as this can easily corrupt the data stored on the floppy.

That's why almost all software companies now deliver their programs on CD-ROM discs, which hold up to 650MB of data.

CHECKPOINT ✔

TAKING CARE OF FLOPPIES

If you don't take care of them, floppies can be damaged or have their data corrupted. Follow these guidelines:

✔ The casing of the floppy protects the disk inside, but you must be careful not to open the metal shutter and touch the surface of the disk. As with a CD-ROM, you can scratch the surface, damaging the data.

✔ Be careful when storing floppies, as a strong magnetic source can corrupt the data. Most electrical devices produce a magnetic field, so be sure not to leave floppies on a hi-fi or near your speakers, for example.

✔ Never store disks at a temperature below 10°C (50°F) or above 60°C (140°F) or, once again, you risk losing data.

✔ Floppies are not designed for long-term storage. They can become corrupted if files are kept on them for more than a couple of years.

Inside a floppy disk

Here's a visual guide to the parts that make up a standard floppy disk.

Protective cartridge
The plastic case is the main way of protecting the magnetic disk.
Read/write slot
The slot through which your PC reads information from the magnetic disk.
Metal shutter
This slides back when you put the floppy into your PC.
Write-protect tab and label
You can stop changes being made to the contents of the floppy by write-protecting, or 'locking', the disk.
Magnetic disk
This is where information is stored on the floppy.
Drive centre
Your PC uses this to spin the magnetic disk so that it can read the disk contents.
Fabric liner
An extra layer of protection for the material on the magnetic disk.

Checking space available on a floppy

Due to their limited storage capacity, it is always useful to know how much space you have left on your floppy disks. You can check this easily using Windows.

1 Double-click the My Computer icon on the Desktop to open the My Computer window. One of the icons in the window represents the floppy disk drive (A:). If you double-click on the icon when there isn't a disk in the floppy disk drive, an error message will appear, informing you that 'the device is not ready'.

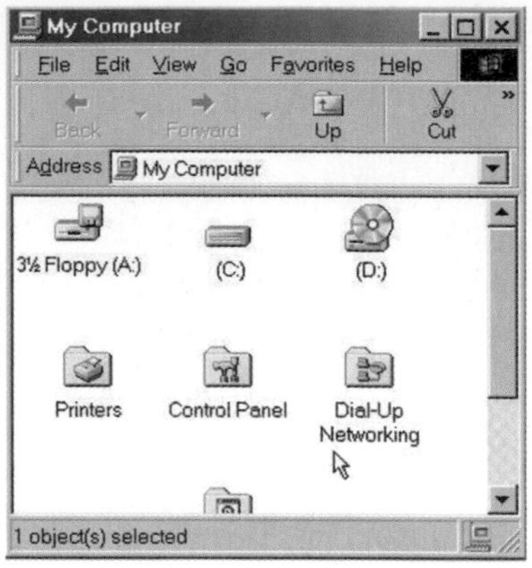

2 Insert the floppy disk in your disk drive, with the metal shutter end going in first and the label side facing upwards. Move the pointer over the 3½ Floppy (A:) icon and select it with a single click. Now open the File menu and select Properties.

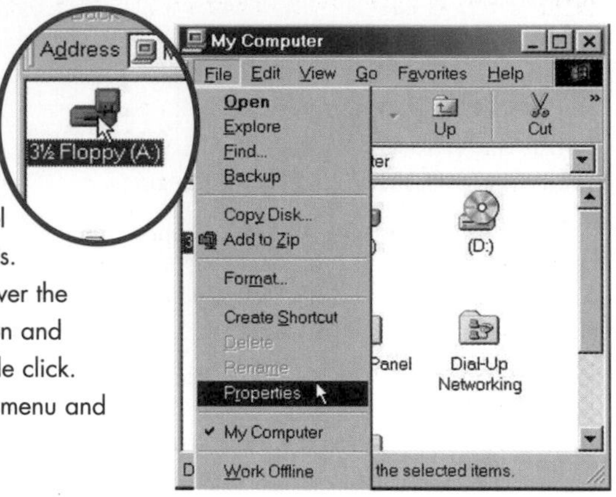

3 The screen that pops up will tell you how much space is left on your floppy, how much is used up and what the total capacity is. There is also a pie chart to help you see how full it is. The pink area is free space and the blue area is space occupied by your files.

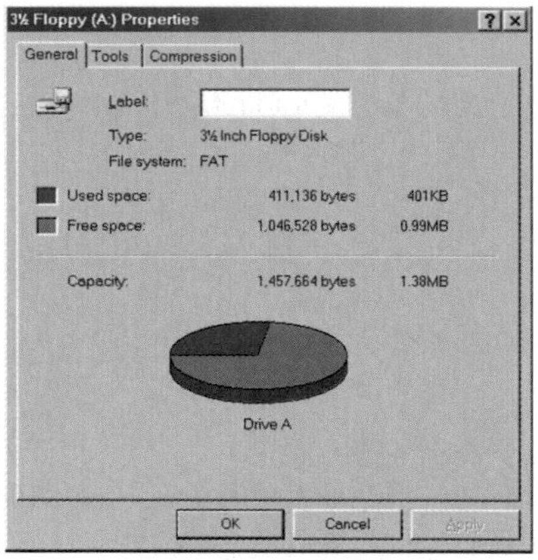

4 To show how this information changes according to the data you put on your floppy, copy a new file to it. Choose a file from your hard disk, say a Word or an Excel document, select Send To from the File menu, and then choose 3½ Floppy (A) from the sub-menu that appears.

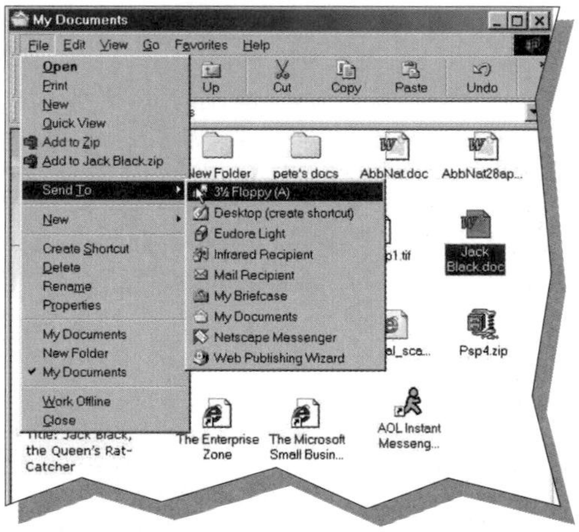

5 A window now pops up, telling you that the file you have chosen is being copied to the floppy disk in the A: drive.

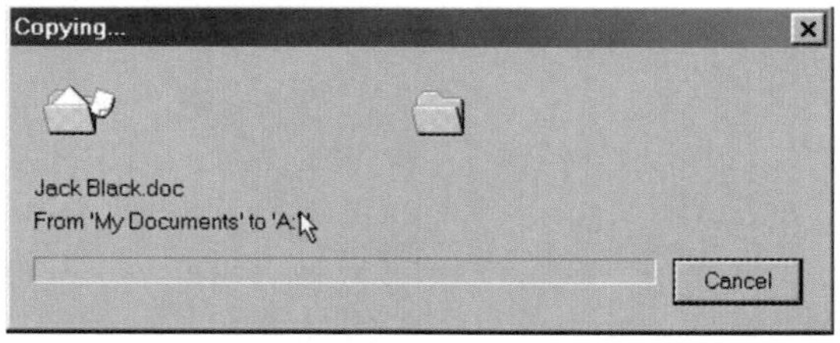

6 When this is done, check the space on the disk again by selecting File, then Properties. You'll see that the blue area of the pie chart has increased, indicating that more space is occupied and the pink area has shrunk, showing there is less free space.

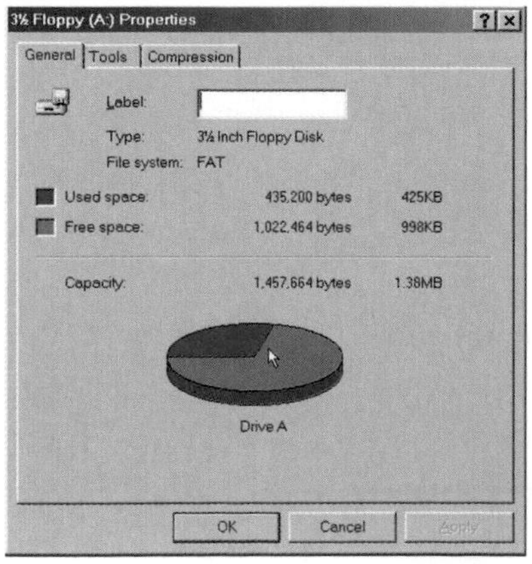

PC TIPS

Write-protected data

When trying to copy a file to a floppy, don't worry if you are told: 'Cannot create or replace [your file]: The disk is write-protected'. This means Windows has identified that the disk is protected from having files added or erased. It is called 'write-protect' because you can't write to the disk or take data off it, but can read from it. You can choose whether or not to write-protect a disk by moving the small square tab on the corner of the disk to open the hole, often shown by a 'locked' symbol (inset). Always write-protect a disk containing important data.

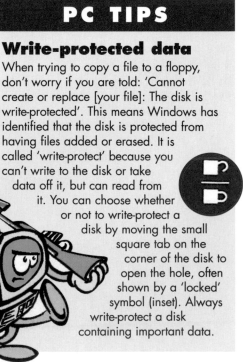

Formatting a floppy disk

In order for a new floppy disk to work on your PC, it will need to be formatted. You may also want to format a disk that is full of old files. As formatting automatically wipes all data from a disk, this is often quicker and easier than deleting large numbers of individual files.

1 Insert a floppy into the disk drive. For this example, use one containing files you don't mind losing. Make sure the write-protect tab is closed (see PC Tips box, opposite). Open the My Computer window and click on the floppy disk drive icon.

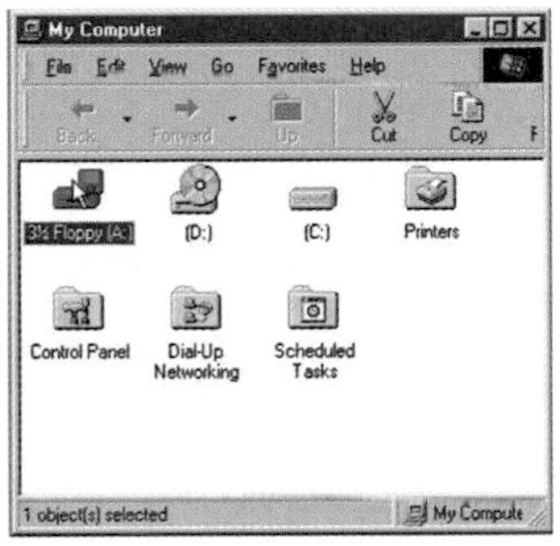

2 Go to the File menu and choose the Format option. You can also access the same option by right-clicking on the floppy disk icon and selecting from the menu that appears.

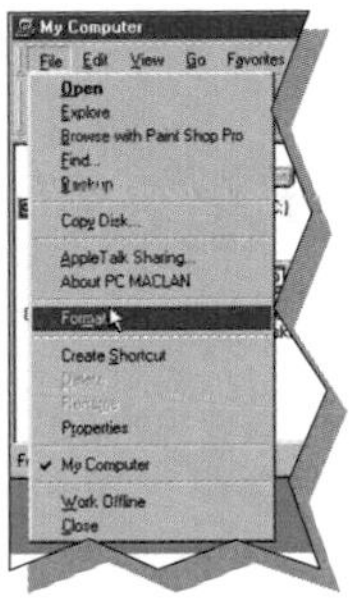

3 A new window opens, offering several options. The first of these is the capacity of your floppy. Choose 1.44MB or 720KB, according to the disk you are formatting. If you aren't sure of its size, select 1.44MB. If the disk turns out to be smaller, Windows will tell you and format it to the highest possible capacity.

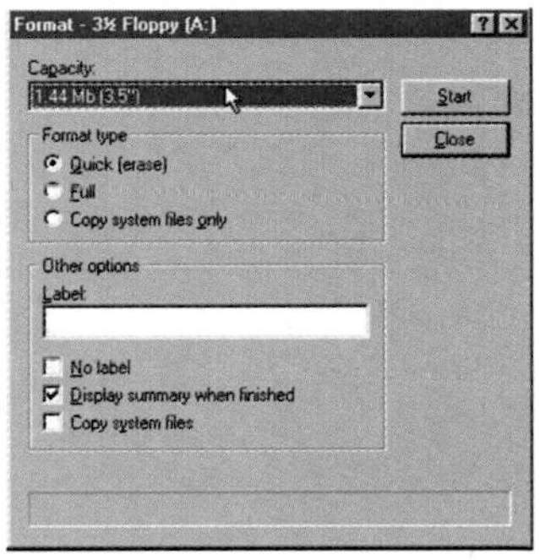

4 Now choose the format type – quick or full (ignore the Copy system files only option). A full format is used for disks that have never been formatted before, or for disks that have been used on a computer other than a PC. As the disk is already formatted, select a quick format which, as Windows indicates, is better described as an erase.

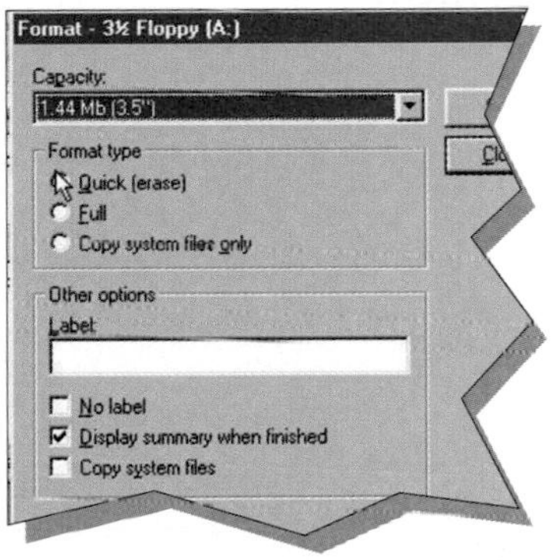

5 Other options are mostly concerned with giving the disk an identity. Just as writing a name on the label on the disk helps you to remember what is on it, you can also give the floppy a 'name' by typing it into the Label text box. This name will appear in the 'Properties' window and when opening and saving files to the disk. If you don't want to give the disk a name, click in the No label box. If you don't need a summary of the format's success when it's finished, click on the Display summary when finished box to make the tick disappear.

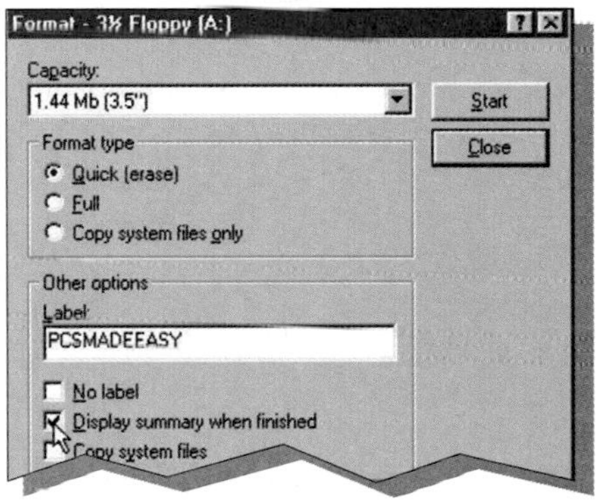

ALERT!

Be careful when formatting! Whether you choose a quick format or a full one, it will wipe all the data from your disk. You will not be able to retrieve any files lost in this way, so always write-protect a disk with important data on it. If in doubt, you can copy the floppy's contents to your hard disk until you are sure you no longer need the files.

6 When you've selected all the options you want, click on Start and Windows will begin to format your disk. A full format may take some time, but the dialog box that appears tells you what is going on. A quick format should be much shorter, though, as most of the work has already been done.

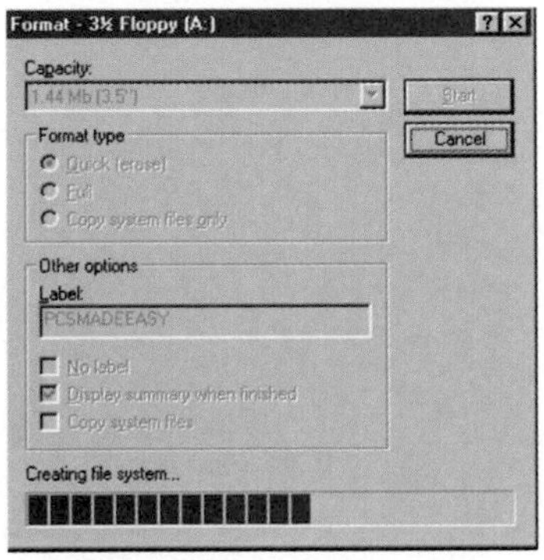

7 When the formatting is finished, return to the My Computer window and click on the floppy disk drive icon. From the File menu, choose Properties and you'll see that the pie chart is entirely pink, indicating that the whole disk is free.

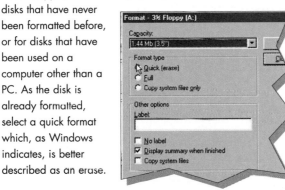

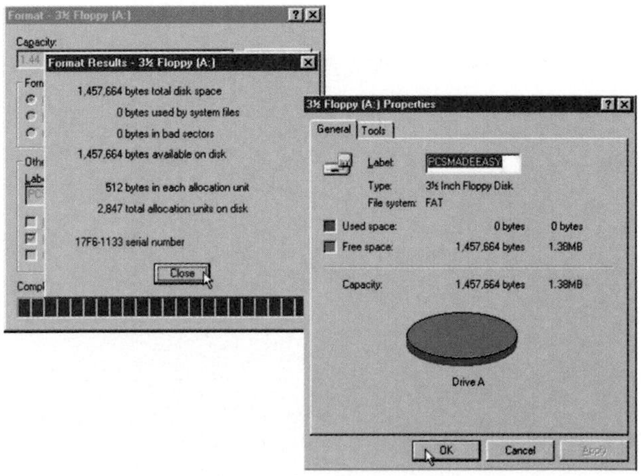

Introducing DVD

DVD is the latest step in CD technology. It combines the functions of a CD-ROM, an audio CD and a video recorder in one disc.

The same size and shape as a normal CD-ROM, the Digital Versatile Disc (DVD) is the latest generation of CD technology. Utilizing both sides of the disc, a DVD can store up to 17 gigabytes (17,000MB) of digital information – this works out at about 26 times the storage capacity offered by a standard CD-ROM.

For the PC user, this means being able to get bigger and better Multimedia applications, massive reference works, games with video, sound and graphics (the likes of which haven't been experienced before) and, in time, recording systems offering almost unlimited storage.

With a picture quality three times better than that of a VHS tape, DVD also revolutionizes the way we watch movies at home. But this is only part of the story. DVD's phenomenal storage capacity allows movie studios to include alternative scenes or multiple storylines, letting the viewer choose which version of a film to watch.

Although each double-sided DVD disc is the size of an ordinary CD-ROM, it holds 17GB. That's around 26 times as much data.

An upgrade kit like this one from Creative Labs could enable your computer to play DVD discs. The computer card is a special piece of hardware that decodes the signal from the DVD drive.

The DVD's secret lies in its use of a blue laser to read information, as opposed to the red one found in a CD-ROM drive. The blue laser has a tighter beam and produces a smaller dot on the surface of the CD. This means that more dots (bits of data) can be placed on a DVD than on a conventional CD-ROM.

And, just in case you were worried, you don't even have to throw away your old audio CDs and CD-ROM collections. DVD drives can play audio CDs and computer CD-ROMs just as easily as the new DVD discs.

● How to get DVD today

You can enjoy the benefits of DVD today, either by buying a DVD computer or by upgrading your current computer. A computer with a DVD-ROM drive instead of a normal CD-ROM drive will cost an extra £50-£100 or so. If your computer already has a CD-ROM drive, you can get a dealer to replace it with a DVD-ROM drive for £100-150.

If you buy a DVD player, it can be connected directly to your TV, just like a video recorder. There are also extra connections for the sound signal, and these can be connected to your hi-fi. (You'll also get surround sound if you have a compatible home audio system.)

● The first of the few

Even though DVD has quickly become very popular, the format has not been without its teething troubles. The main problem is that film studios have used the introduction of DVD as a way of reinforcing international movie markets. So, while a Hollywood blockbuster will be released first in the US, it will only appear in Europe six months later. This is enforced in DVD through 'territory codes' (see Movies and territory codes, right), which ensure that movies and software released in one area are not compatible with hardware sold in another territory.

● Regions to be cheerful

For DVD users in Region 2 (the UK), this can be a problem although availability is improving month by month. Be aware that if you purchase a DVD overseas, it might not work on your PC. However, some DVD drives have a special feature that lets you configure your drive for Region 1 or Region 2. There are often special settings, a switch on the unit or a button on the remote, that allow you to change between regions whenever you like rather than having to configure the drive again completely.

MOVIES AND TERRITORY CODES

For many years the big film studios have maintained a staggered release schedule across the world, launching a film in the US and then opening it in Europe around six months later. DVD allows the film studios to cement the boundaries between these markets in the following way.

The UK is in Region 2 – along with the rest of Europe, South Africa and Japan. This means that DVD disks bought in Japan will work on UK DVD systems, but the on-screen instructions might be in Japanese, even if the film has an English soundtrack.

America is Region 1 and it is illegal to sell US discs in the UK, although individuals are free to import them and play them on a US system or DVD upgrade set to Region 1.

To find out more about DVD news, developments and releases, try visiting: www.dvdreview.com

What DVD can do for you

Computers

A game that comes on four CD-ROMs, or a clip art collection provided on 10 CD-ROMs, can be supplied on a single DVD disk. This format will make a big impact by allowing more gameplay and more sound, video and programs.

As they become more affordable, DVD-RAM drives will offer PC users almost unlimited removable storage.

Music

DVD-Audio provides better-than-CD sound quality, combined with multi-channel surround sound.

Movies

A DVD recorder that looks like an audio CD player will replace your VHS video recorder. Although video has the edge on availability and price, the future belongs to DVD. What will finally win is DVD's impressive combination of features, with the quality of picture and sound heading the list. DVD also offers extra features, including one that allows you to go straight to a favourite scene, as well as a choice of languages and commentaries by the director. Finally, DVDs are far easier to store than VHS videos.

This DVD-ROM drive from Toshiba will fit into the same space in your computer case now occupied by the CD-ROM drive. Toshiba also produces DVD-RAM drives, which, like hard disk drives, can be written to and thus used for data storage.

Message modems

All modems allow computers to talk to each other over telephone lines, but some also combine the capabilities of an answering machine and a hands-free speakerphone.

A modern modem, such as the Self Memory 2000 from Olitec, can not only deal with your surfing and email but also answers the phone and takes messages.

Modems allow computers to communicate with one another over telephone lines – to swap emails or browse the World Wide Web, for example.

In addition to this, most modern modems can also act as fax machines, cutting out the tiresome steps of printing your fax, then having to wrestle with the fax machine to send it. Any faxes received can be displayed on the screen and then printed out, a factor which greatly increases your computer's potential as an all-round communications centre. But better still, an increasing number of modems are now able to deal with voice messages. Such models are called message modems.

● Constant communications

By adding a message modem to your PC, you get all the capabilities of a normal modem plus a built-in answering machine and fax store.

Some conventional modems come with special programs which give them similar capabilities, allowing storage of voice messages and faxes on the computer's hard disk. The problem with these modems is that the PC must be switched on the whole time so that the software can answer incoming phone calls and record them. This means the system is constantly consuming power and that you live with a non-stop hum from the computer's power supply.

A message modem, by contrast, has extra circuits and features that handle all incoming communications without the need to store data on the computer's hard disk. This means that the modem works whether or not your computer is switched on, though to read the faxes, you will need to switch the computer back on.

Of course, to be able to do its job while your computer is switched off, a message modem can't be dependent on the computer for its power supply. For this reason, you won't find any internal message modems. They are all external units, with their own power supply and their own control panel appearing on the casing.

The most important extra in a message modem is a large helping of computer memory. All modems have some memory, but it's usually only sufficient for storing a handful of settings. This extra memory is used for storing incoming voice and fax messages. The exact amount of information that a message modem can store depends on the amount of memory built in. Memory of 2MB, for example, gives enough space to store around 20 minutes of voice messages or up to 50 faxed pages.

● How it works

To be able to store calls from people who telephone you, the message modem must first convert sound into computer data. Likewise, to replay the messages, the message modem must convert the stored data back into sound. You then hear this through the modem's built-in speaker.

Many message modems can also work as hands-free speakerphones. This means that you can use your PC to dial a telephone number and then all you need to do is ensure that you talk near the modem. A microphone built into the message modem picks up your voice and transmits it to the person at the other end of the phone line, while you hear that person's voice from the modem's speaker.

Message modems can be installed as easily as normal modems (see Stage 1, pages 138-141). The answerphone features are controlled by extra buttons on the modem itself. Faxes that have been received while the computer has been switched off can be viewed and printed once the computer is switched back on.

Some modems offer extra voice features, but fall short of full message modem capability. For example, some use their built-in memory to hold email messages only. You can program these devices to contact your ISP and collect your email messages when your PC is switched off.

WHAT IT MEANS

FLASH MEMORY

All modems have a small amount of memory that contains tiny, but vitally important, software used to control the modem. In many modems this memory is permanent but some modems use 'flash memory' which can be overwritten, allowing you to upgrade the software from floppy disk or via the Internet.

● Upgrading modem software

As with any modem, it's wise to buy with a view to the future. Many models are designed so that they can be upgraded by changing the modem control software. For example, some modem manufacturers have offered updates to make the modem work faster. Such upgradable modems are provided with flash memory and are less likely to go out of date.

In these cases, the modem manufacturer provides a program so that all you have to do to update the control software is run it on your PC. The program will then communicate with the modem and replace the old software stored in its flash memory chips with new software which can be downloaded either from the manufacturer's Internet site or direct-dial bulletin board.

Although the manufacturer's software updates can help improve your modem beyond its initial capabilities, they can only go so far. Don't expect even a flash memory modem to keep up with future changes indefinitely.

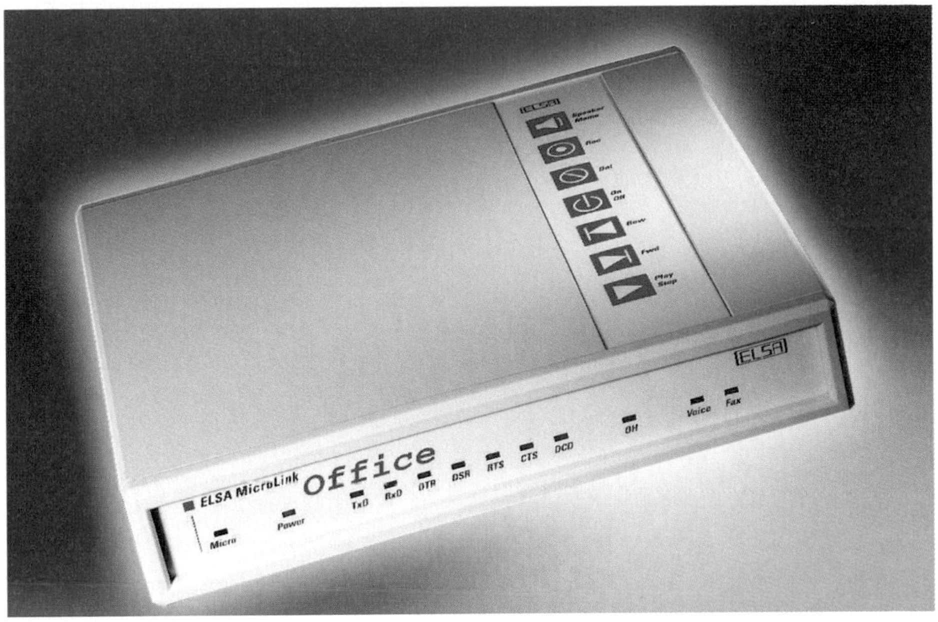

With the ELSA Microlink Office, you can connect headphones or a handset to listen to your stored messages.

AUTO-ANSWER ALERT

While you might well want your modem to answer voice telephone calls automatically, you need to think through the consequences of letting your modem auto-answer calls from other computers. It can be a very bad idea. On the one hand, if you travel with a portable or notebook computer, being able to dial up and connect to a desktop computer at home to pick up files and information can, of course, be very useful. On the other hand, there is a risk: if someone else dials your telephone number, they might be able to gain access to your important files. Even home computer users need to be alert to this possibility.

To protect against this risk, you should read the manuals for your modem and also those for any communications software (such as fax programs) that you use. Programs that allow you to dial in and both see and use your computer's hard disk are known as remote access programs. If you need to use this type of software, check the manuals for the sections that deal with security aspects. Passwords, for instance, can make it much harder for someone to break into your PC, and extra layers of security – such as getting the modem to hang up and then dial you back – make it even tougher.

Videophones

With some easy-to-install technology, you can speak 'face-to-face' with people all over the world.

The notion of a device that allows you to see someone at the same time as you speak to them – the videophone – has been around for over 50 years. And, for a long time, it was firmly in the realm of science-fiction fantasy. But now it's a cheap and easy reality for anyone with a PC and an Internet connection. In fact, the hardware itself has become so cheap and so widespread that many PC makers will supply everything you need as part of a new system. Even if you are adding to your existing setup, your outlay will be under £100.

● Who needs it?

Videoconferencing, as such hardware is known, has widespread and obvious advantages. In business, it can save time and money by allowing home-workers or colleagues and collaborators to communicate face-to-face without travelling. For large meetings, where many people might be present in the same room, highly sophisticated and expensive equipment is needed. But if you just need a chat with the boss on a one-to-one basis, then nothing more is required than the kind of home hardware set-up we are looking at here – and it is mainly in the home environment that cheap video-conferencing is really taking off.

WHAT IT MEANS

USB

The Universal Serial Bus (USB) (see pages 114-115) is a recent innovation in connecting computers and devices such as modems, mice and video cameras. It's fast and can link up to 127 devices in a daisy-chain arrangement. Eventually, it will replace the serial and parallel ports of today's computers. The best aspect of USB is that you do not have to turn off your computer when you want to attach or disconnect a USB device.

A videophone not only makes communication more fun, it also makes it much more likely that you will understand exactly what people are talking about.

● What you need

The basis of home videoconferencing software is the Web cam. These small cameras – some so tiny you can literally fit them in a shirt pocket – supply the video images you see on Web cam sites, where a camera is pointed at something of interest and you can check out what's happening at any time by logging on to the Web site.

There is a wide range of Web cam manufacturers, including Logitech, Philips and Kodak. Some models resemble a large golf ball, while others have a squarer design. Whatever it looks like, the camera will be supplied with some sort of base that allows you to position it in a convenient place – typically, on top of your monitor so that it is pointing straight at you while you work. Alternatively, you can place it just about anywhere you want to capture the images that you wish to transmit. The most popular way of connecting a camera to your PC is via the USB socket, although if your PC is old and doesn't have one of these you can connect your camera via the parallel port instead. The advantages of a USB connection are that it is easy to use (you simply slot it in) and the fact that it does not take up a parallel connection that you might need for another device, such as a printer.

The other vital element of the package is the software supplied. What you get varies slightly from manufacturer to manufacturer, but typically you will have videoconferencing software, such as Microsoft NetMeeting, to allow you one-to-one connections with other users; video-mail software, which enables you to send moving images with sound via your email package; and even a simple graphics package to allow you to touch up still images before you send them. In addition,

CHECKPOINT ✔

VIDEOPHONE ESSENTIALS

You'll need the following equipment and software to get the best from a camera:

✔ A video camera with the right type of connection socket for your computer (make sure you check your computer before buying the camera).

✔ A computer with a spare port to accept the signal from the camera.

✔ A modem for connection to other videophone users.

✔ A microphone so that your callers can hear you.

✔ A sound card and speakers so that you can hear your callers.

✔ Videophone software (probably included with the camera).

the package might also install a number of popular audio and video plug-ins if it does not find them on your computer.

● Image quality

A Web camera will not produce particularly high resolution images; there is too much data to be transmitted so images are best displayed at a lower resolution, having been compressed by software.

You lose some detail and usually the image will look jerky, which takes a bit of getting used to.

To keep things manageable, the image size is relatively small compared to your screen area; around 15 per cent of the screen area is typical. Having said all this, for such cheap hardware the quality you get is surprisingly satisfying.

Sending emails with still-picture attachments or vmails (video mails) with moving images and sound are likely to be two very popular ways of using a Web camera. If you want to use it for videoconferencing or chat, then you have two possible methods of connection.

The first of these is by direct dial-up, where you call the number of another videophone user; their system must, of course, be set up and they must be ready for your call. The second, which you might use if you want to chat to a variety of people, is to use an Internet connection to log on to a service such as CU-SeeMe.

CONTACT POINTS

Logitech QuickCam
Logitech
www.logitech.com
Price: £59:99*

*UK price

Installing a Logitech QuickCam

Installing a camera from the QuickCam range is easy: you simply plug the USB lead into the PC's socket. First, however, you need to install some software from the supplied CD-ROM.

1 Put the CD-ROM in your drive. From the main menu select Install QuickCam Software.

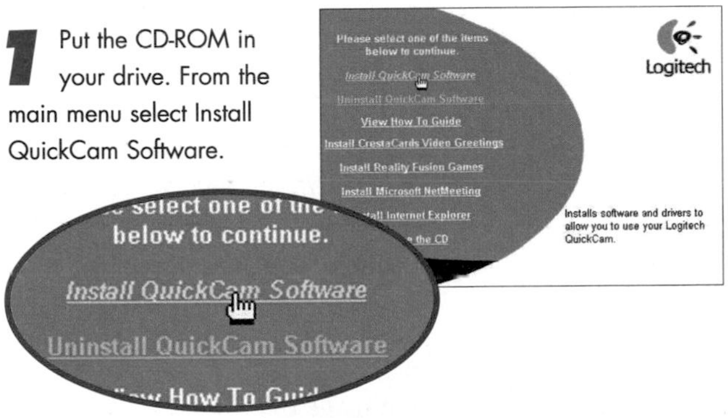

2 Follow the Installation Wizard instructions. Then plug in your camera to the USB port when the appropriate screen appears.

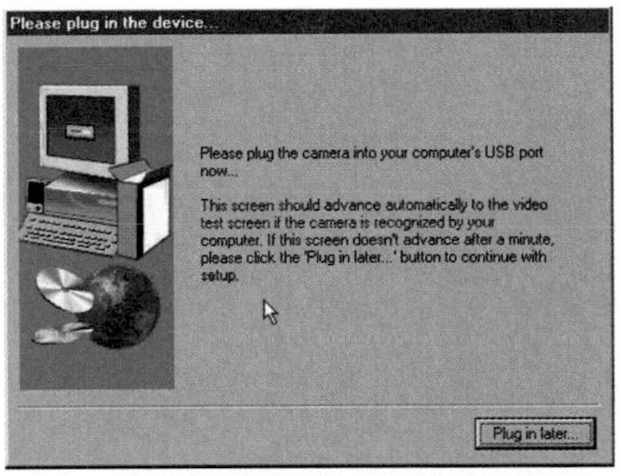

3 You can hold the camera in your hand or set it up on its stand. An image of whatever it is pointing at will appear in the on-screen window. If the quality is not quite right, click the Adjust Image button to calibrate.

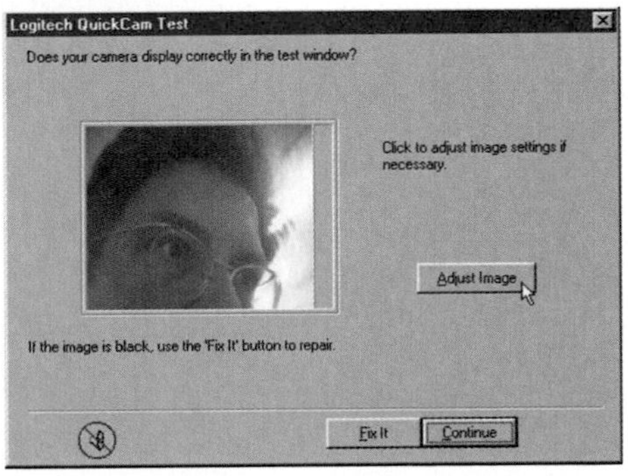

4 Click the Device Settings tab on the next screen. Now you can alter the slider bars for each setting, checking the image until you are happy with the quality. Now you're ready to go!

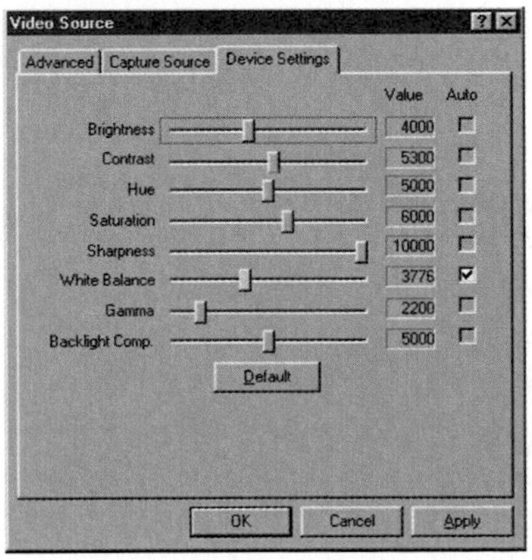

Label printers

If you find it tricky to print labels on your regular printer, take a look at label printers. These are custom built for the purpose. Using one might save you wasting both labels and time.

With a label printer you can print labels for everything from personalized stickers for private or business use (above) to your video tape collection (below).

Your computer is well equipped to print labels with Word. Despite this, label printing – especially short runs – can still be problematic. There are several reasons for this. First, you need to remove the plain paper from your printer and replace it with special label pages. Second, you need to make sure your software knows how to use these labels. Finally, you may need several trial runs to get alignment of the text on the labels exactly right. This is because most desktop printers are designed to print a certain size of document, typically large pages such as A4. The variables in the printing process don't usually matter too much: an A4 page may slip a millimetre or so as it goes through the printer without causing problems. That's because exact alignment from one page to the next is rarely required when printing whole A4 pages. But, when printing labels, small deviations can be disastrous. This is due to the fact that around 20-30 self-adhesive labels are supplied on A4 backing sheets. If there is even a tiny mismatch between the size of each label and the size that your software thinks it is, the error then builds up as successive labels are printed down the page. When this happens, text on the labels towards the bottom of the page might end up partly on the next label, so you'll have to start again.

● Wasting labels

There's also the problem of wastage when you are printing just a couple of labels at a time, in which case you'll be left with a sheet missing the first few labels. The next time you want to print some labels, trying to get your software to ignore these blanks and start on the first label is difficult and time-consuming. You can minimize wastage by turning the page upside-down and starting again, but you'll probably still have some wastage.

Using your regular printer is only feasible if you're doing a long print run of, say, more than 30 labels. If all you want is one label to stick on an envelope, the chances are that all the work involved is just too much hassle and it would be far simpler to handwrite it.

● The solution

For the home user, the answer is a label printer that can print labels without wastage and frustrating fiddling to get the settings right. These purpose-built machines are desktop printers that use a continuous roll of labels. They don't print on plain paper and they can't print on A4, so they cannot replace your existing printer. However, they're extremely handy for labels that need to be printed one at a time, such as stickers for envelopes, floppies, files and video tapes, and for printing handy index cards.

Another use for a label printer is to create name badges, particularly for conferences and exhibitions, or just for a party. Label printers at the higher end of the price range can print one label every three seconds, so you needn't worry about waiting for long runs to finish.

One of the other advantages of label printers over ordinary printers is that they use a special thermal printing process. The text is printed by heating the label paper. This means that there is no ink to smudge, should the label get wet. Another bonus is that there's no need for ribbons, inks or toner cartridges. Thermal printing isn't ideal for all printing, but for labels it works well.

The SLP 200 label printer from Seiko Instruments can print labels up to 54mm wide. Blank labels are stored in the cassette above the main body of the printer.

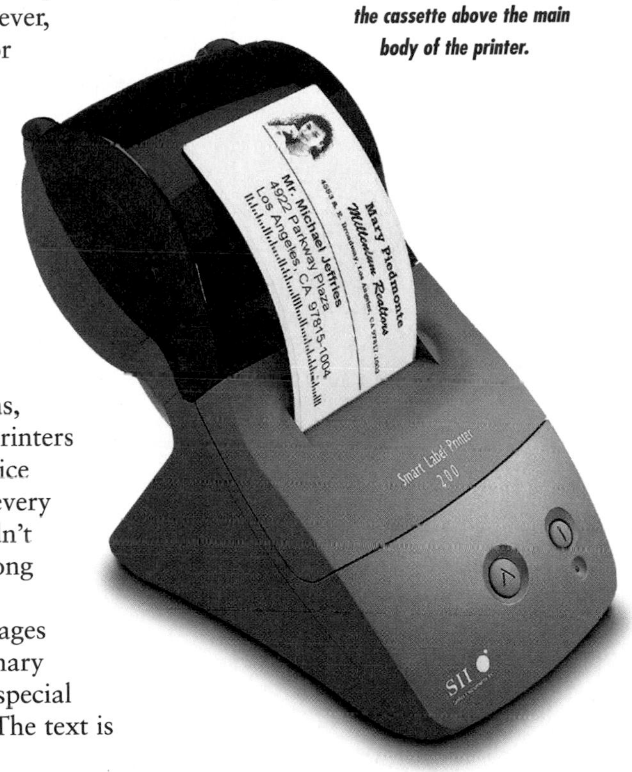

● Special software

Modern label printers have software that lets you perform a number of special functions. As well as printing whichever typefaces and graphics your software can create, a good label printer will also be able to print barcodes. This is extremely useful if you have a company with a barcode-based stock-control system. And, as you can print the postcode of outgoing letters in barcode form, this can make a big difference to how fast your mail gets to its destination.

The Seiko range of label printers comes with a contacts program, which allows you to record name and address information from any other piece of software you may have on your computer. You can even print addresses directly from a PalmPilot handheld computer.

Buying a label printer

The most popular type of label printer is made by Seiko (UK tel: 01628 770 988). There are three SLP (Smart Label Printers) products in the Seiko range. The basic model, the SLP 100 (around £110), is suitable for simple text and graphics, but is fairly slow, taking some eight seconds to print each label. It has a print resolution of 203 dots per inch (dpi), which doesn't match a desktop printer's minimum 300dpi, but is still very respectable. Certainly, this low resolution is adequate for envelopes, floppy disk, video labels and so on.

The next level up is the SLP 200 (approximately £185), which takes around the same time to print labels, and at the same 203dpi resolution. But, its labels are substantially wider than the SLP 100, and thus a better bet for jazzier labels or those with graphics. At the top end is the SLP 240, (around £220), which prints labels up to 54mm wide, but at more than twice the speed of the other two models.

Seiko isn't the only company making label printers, but it does seem to be the one most keen on targeting the home computer user and the small/home office market. All three models are network compatible, and so can be shared by a number of users. They also have USB connections, which means you can simply plug them into your computer and get them to work immediately.

If you find it difficult to track down a label printer, your local computer store should be able to help out by ordering one for you.

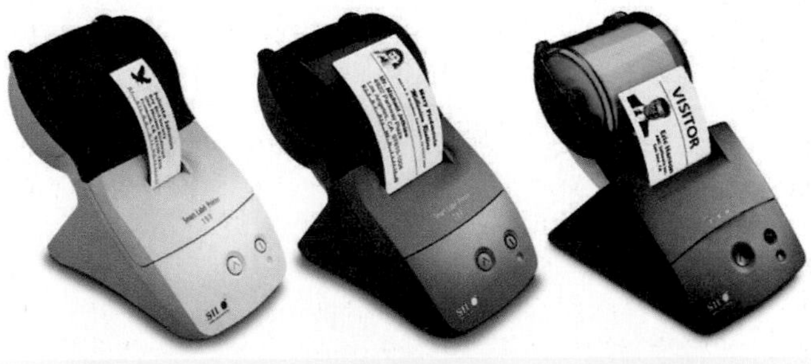

Three models in the Seiko range of Smart Label Printers are the SLP 100 (left), the SLP 200 (centre) and the SLP 240 (right), which is the top of the SLP range.

Hand-held computers

Once available only to science-fiction characters, the hand-held computer is now a practical reality for anyone who needs to compute on the move. Today's machines pack plenty of computing power into a box that will fit in your pocket.

Hand-held computers add power to your pocket as they not only organize your life, but can also connect you to the Web and allow you to carry huge amounts of information everywhere you go. They've certainly come a long way from their simple name and address – or databank – predecessors, and today's models offer the user real power on the move.

A hand-held computer is ideal for day-to-day use. Wherever you are, you can have instant access to contact details, an electronic notepad, a word processor, a spreadsheet or even games to liven up dull journeys.

● What's inside?

Most hand-held computers have a clamshell design where the protective case opens up to reveal an LCD screen and miniature QWERTY keyboard.

However, if you could look inside at the parts, you'd find some important differences from the computer on your desk. A few parts look the same, and at its heart the hand-held still has a processor and memory, although these use less power than a desktop PC's to maximize the battery life.

However, there's no hard disk or floppy disk inside a hand-held computer. It relies on the memory inside to store programs and your documents. Some memory – called ROM – is used to store the computer's built-in software permanently. For the data you create, the computer uses RAM. While the hand-held computer is switched off, a tiny amount of back-up battery power is used to store your data.

Of course, the normal computer monitor is replaced with the LCD display in a hand-held version. Most screens are quite small and black and white (or grey and green) instead of full colour. Like desktop computers, most hand-held computers can also have new hardware plugged into them, perhaps for extra memory (see pages 110-113). There's very little space inside, so these add-ons are much smaller. Most hand-helds use PC Cards for items such as modems.

For the ultimate in portable computers, Nokia has a mobile phone and modem in its Communicator 9110.

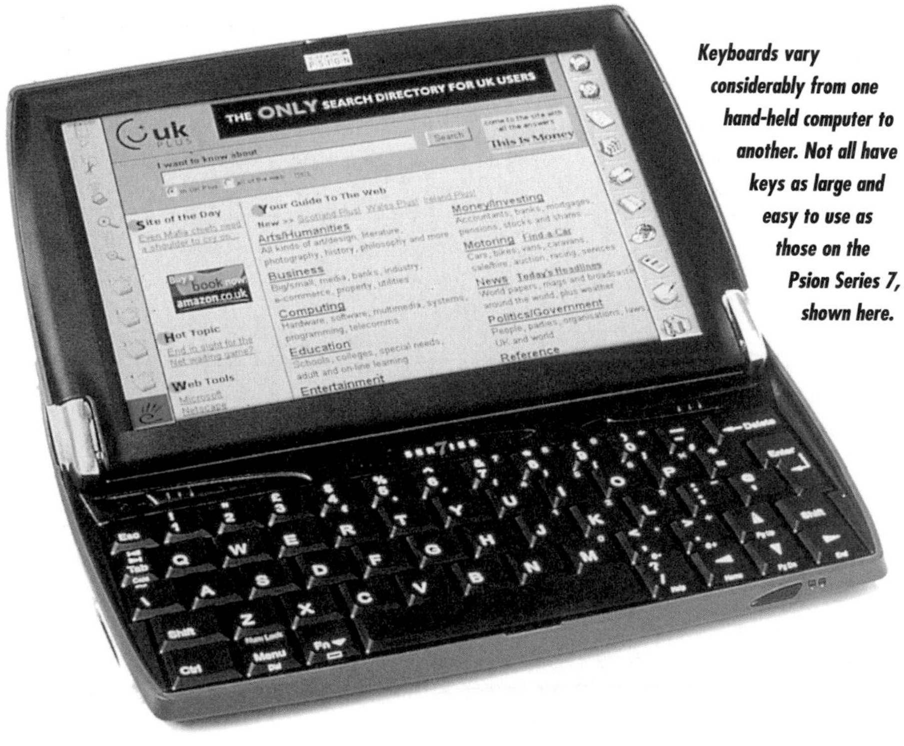

Keyboards vary considerably from one hand-held computer to another. Not all have keys as large and easy to use as those on the Psion Series 7, shown here.

WHAT IT MEANS

PC CARDS

A PC Card is a plug-in device for portable and hand-held computers. The PC Card is the same size as a credit card, but a lot thicker so it can contain electronic circuits. Some work like miniature hard disks, allowing you to store your documents and new software; others are used for modems.

● Different types

The pioneer company in hand-held computing is Psion. From its original 1980s personal organizer, which was styled like a fat calculator, it now offers a powerful blend of hardware, display and built-in software. Its Series 7 and Revo computers come with full software packages, which include many basic tasks, such as word processing and spreadsheets, plus personal organizers and contact books. There are also Web sites from which Psion owners can download lots of additional software.

● Windows on the move

Some hand-held computers have a cut-down version of Windows, called Windows CE or Pocket PC. These also include built-in versions of Word and Excel in addition to the personal organizer software. Windows CE computers are available from Hewlett-Packard, Casio, Philips, and other manufacturers. These hand-helds feature a PC Card slot for expansion and a pencil-like pointer to use with the touch screen.

CHECKPOINT ✔

BUYING A HAND-HELD COMPUTER

The most important factor when buying a hand-held computer is to decide what you are going to use it for. This will allow you to quiz your dealer for the answers to the following questions:

✔ **How much memory?**
The ROM and RAM determine how much room there is for the programs and your data – the more the better.

✔ **What software?**
Ask about the built-in software and the range of software that is available on the plug-in cards.

✔ **How much?**
Prices tend to vary a lot, so shop around for the best deal.

✔ **Upgradable?**
Can the computer be upgraded via PC Cards or via software from Web sites?

✔ **PC Connectable?**
How does the computer connect to your PC and do you need extra cables for this? For some, the lead is supplied; for others, it's in a kit costing £70!

The Nokia Communicator 9110 is a hand-held computer combined with a mobile phone and modem. This means that, in addition to making phone calls, you can send faxes and connect to the Web while on the move (though the high costs of surfing the Internet at mobile phone rates needs to be borne in mind).

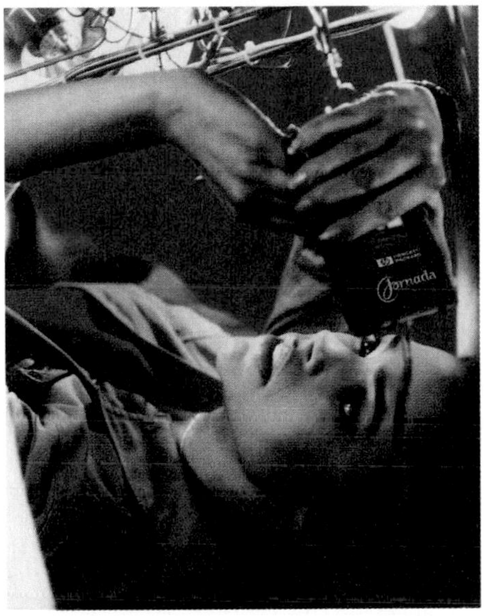

***The HP Journada is an extremely powerful hand-held computer – shown here in operation in the James Bond film* The World is Not Enough.**

The PalmPilot takes a completely different approach. While it offers the usual range of personal organizer software, there's no keyboard at all. You write everything straight on to the screen using the stylus. It doesn't actually recognize handwriting – that would require processing power that hand-held computers just don't have; instead it uses a system called Graffiti. You must learn the range of simple Graffiti symbols in order to input information into the PalmPilot.

Not all hand-held computers use keyboards. With the PalmPilot you write directly onto the screen.

● Living with a hand-held computer

The biggest stumbling block with hand-held computers is the keyboard. It's fine for entering short notes or contact details, but it is very cramped and you would struggle to write long letters. In general, hand-held computers are better thought of as mobile stores of information rather than full-blown computers.

Most hand-helds have two sets of batteries: standard AA-size batteries power the screen and most of the computer's systems. A lithium battery keeps your data safely stored in the computer while the machine is switched off and the main batteries are replaced.

However, for a safer back-up, invest in the necessary cables and software to link your hand-held computer to your desktop PC.

CONNECTING YOUR HAND-HELD COMPUTER TO A DESKTOP PC

Connecting a hand-held computer to your desktop computer is a simple process that can bring many benefits. It takes only a few minutes to link the cable between the two computers and install the special software on your desktop computer.

Once this is done, you can back up any important information stored in your hand-held and transfer files between the two machines. This means that you can write, edit or add to any document on your hand-held computer while on the move and then transfer it to your PC when you get home. If you have Internet access on your desktop computer, you can also use it to find and download new programs – first to your desktop computer and then to your hand-held computer.

Portable add-ons

There are accessories to help you work on the move and make the most of your portable PC. You can print out, fax or email without even plugging into a mains electricity supply.

When you're computing on the move, you want to travel as light as possible, but you still need to do most of the things you do at your desktop computer, such as accessing email and printing documents. Fortunately, there's a massive range of peripherals and add-ons for portable PCs – these are designed to help you to do all the things you need to while away from your desk.

The main reason for buying a notebook or hand-held computer is mobility: you can work in the kitchen at home, take the computer on holiday with you, or work on the train and be able to carry on writing that urgent report in Word or put together a business plan in Excel.

Almost all notebook and hand-held computers can carry out these tasks, but to get the most out of them, you might want to look at add-ons that help to augment the computer's capabilities. Few portable computers come supplied with everything you might need to cover all eventualities while you're out and about, but here is a selection of the most useful.

● The essentials

The most likely things you'll do are to print a document and use your email and fax. Many users of portable computers therefore see printers and modems as essential extras.

While there are many other add-ons you can buy, whether or not you consider them essential will depend almost entirely on the circumstances in which you use your computer. Here we take a look at some of the most popular categories of add-ons for portable computers.

● Keeping in touch

Communications devices – principally modems – are perhaps the most desirable and useful add-ons for mobile computer users. Adding a modem to your portable computer means that you can send and receive email, faxes and voice messages no matter where you are. You can also buy special communications devices that allow you to send email and faxes through a mobile phone. For business users, a network adaptor allows the computer to connect to an office network.

What you don't want for your portable computer, of course, is a modem the size of the one

you are quite happy to have on your desktop because it might well be almost as bulky as the portable computer itself. Fortunately, the large-scale adoption in recent years of the PCMCIA standard for credit card-sized devices, now more widely known as PC Cards, means that portable users are spoilt for choice when it comes to small, lightweight modems and communications peripherals.

Nearly all the major modem suppliers, such as US Robotics and Xircom, offer PC Card modems. Prices are generally somewhere around the £100 mark for a 56Kbps PCMCIA modem card.

● Advanced communications

For some of the more sophisticated communications features, such as an office network adaptor and/or an adaptor for your mobile phone, you'll pay rather more. For example, anything between £100 and £200 is not unusual, depending on the number of features involved.

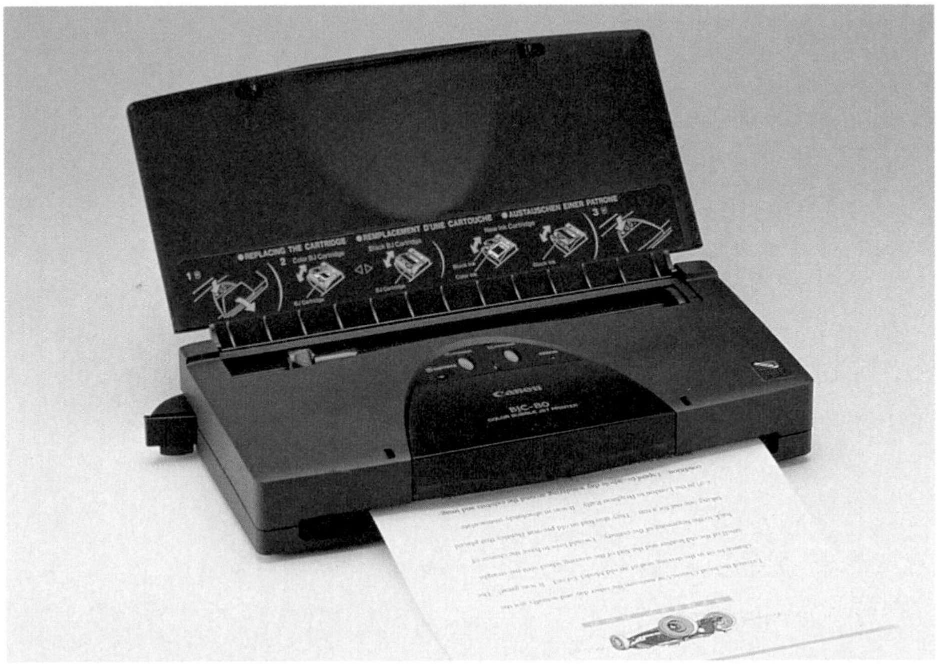

With this printer, the BJC-85 from Canon, you can travel anywhere and always have the ability to print high-quality documents, even in colour. Don't forget to take a supply of paper with you, though!

Note that to use a portable computer with a standard mobile phone, you'll also need a special connector cable that is often specific to a particular model of phone. Check the phone's manual for details.

One point to bear in mind if you're planning to travel abroad with a portable and modem is that phone sockets vary from country to country. Few things are more frustrating than finding that you cannot plug your modem into a waiting socket. You can easily get round this by taking a modem travel kit with you, which will allow you to plug into phone systems worldwide. Such kits cost around £50-£60.

● Printers

The paperless office remains only a dream and is likely to do so for the foreseeable future. Someone, somewhere is always going to expect a hard copy of a document or a paper fax rather than an email.

If you're out and about with your laptop, you might well be able to do

DIFFERENT PC CARD TYPES

There are three kinds of PC Cards: Type I, Type II and Type III. All have the same rectangular dimensions of 8.5cm by 5.5cm, but the thicknesses differ: 3.3mm for Type I, 5.5mm for Type II and 10.5mm for Type III.

The thicker PC Cards accommodate bigger components, including miniature hard disks. Portable computers usually have two PC Card slots into which these devices simply slide. Once they are fitted, and any special software is installed, the cards work in exactly the same way as any other internal component of the computer.

Most portable computers offer a choice of one Type III slot, or two Type II slots (Type I is rarely seen nowadays).

A Type III slot will accept a Type II card, but not vice versa. Most current PC Card modems and related devices are Type II.

Wireless communication

A Psion handheld is designed for portability and ease of use on the move, so the last thing you want is a load of additional bits and pieces and wires tangling you up. Thanks to Psion's Travel Modem you can connect to the Internet and check email with no such entanglements.

The 56K Travel Modem is an infra-red device: just position it by your handheld and it automatically configures itself for your machine. However, you still need a phone line to connect to the Internet.

The Psion Travel Modem is battery-powered, can be used in conjunction with a number of popular mobile phones, and is compatible with Psion Series 5MX and 7 and Revo handhelds. The Travel Modem costs around £130, including VAT.

any printing you need from offices or homes you visit. But if you know that you'll regularly need to print documents, you should consider buying yourself a portable printer.

These are surprisingly compact and lightweight, and typically use inkjet printing technology. As a result, you can switch from black and white to colour printing by simply swapping cartridges. They also give you the option of using special battery packs, so you are not reliant on having power sockets nearby.

A few printers even have special infra-red communications ports. Using a similar sort of signal to that of a TV's remote control, an infra-red port on a notebook computer can transmit the image of the page to the infra-red port on the printer. You don't need a cable at all.

The main attraction of these portable printers remains their small size. Canon's BJC-85, for example, weighs in at a mere 1.4kg (around 3.25lb) and is only 30cm wide by 16cm deep by 6cm high. With dimensions like that it doesn't really add too much bulk to what you have to carry around with you. Portable printers are available at a moderate price; for about £200 you can purchase such popular models as the Canon BJC-85 or the HP DeskJet 350.

● Power options

Power is always at a premium with a portable computer, no matter how good your batteries. Whenever possible, you should use an external power supply and conserve precious battery power for when it is really needed. Most portables are supplied with an AC/DC adaptor as standard but, as with modems, if you are travelling abroad you should invest in an international socket adaptor to make sure your power supply is compatible. A battery charger is also a very useful item and will cost around £75-£80; this might seem a lot until you consider that an extra battery could cost you over £100.

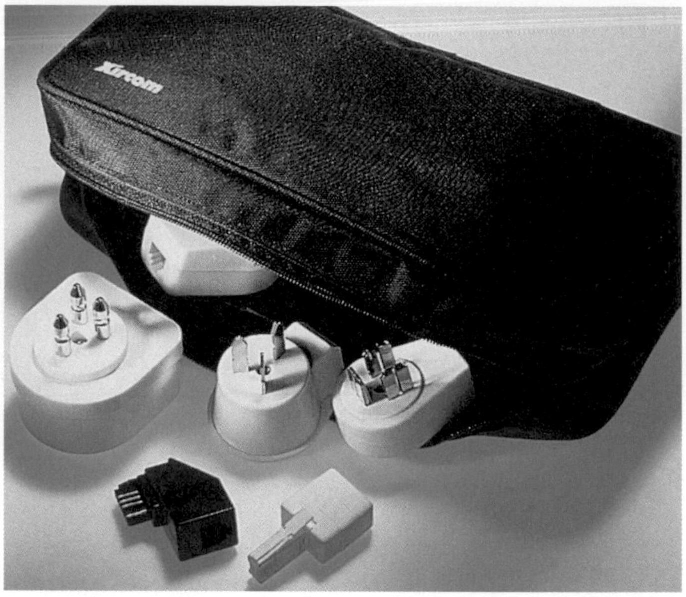

Xircom produce convenient international travel kits for your modem-equipped portable PC. These kits allow you to connect to electrical sockets and phone systems worldwide.

● Storage

Because hard disk drives, CD-ROM drives and floppy drives are all heavy components that take up a relatively large amount of space, notebook computers rarely have all the storage options of desktop machines, or the large hard disk capacities. Storage space is therefore always an issue for users of portable computers.

With smaller portable PCs – sometimes called 'sub-notebooks' – you might have only a hard disk built into the case. On larger portables, you will find a CD-ROM drive or a floppy disk drive as standard, in addition to the hard drive. On some models the CD-ROM drive is interchangeable with a floppy disk drive: you simply swap the units around, depending on which one you need to use.

Whatever configuration you have, you will probably want to have some means of transferring files, other than by email. Perhaps the best option is an external Zip drive (see Stage 3, pages 98-99). Zip drives are quite small and light, while the disks have a capacity of up to 250MB – the equivalent of more than 175 standard

ADDING A KEYBOARD AND MOUSE

One of the compromises you must make when you buy a notebook computer is the size of the keyboard – a notebook computer usually manages with around 80-90 keys instead of the full desktop complement of 102 keys.

The keys are also slightly smaller and don't travel quite as far when you press them. If you miss the typing action or the numeric keypad of a full-size computer keyboard, add one using the keyboard socket. Just plug a keyboard into the socket located at the rear of the notebook – no extra software is needed.

If you use your notebook mainly at home and very rarely on the move, the £10-£20 invested in a desktop keyboard could certainly be worthwhile.

You can also add a conventional mouse to your notebook computer to replace the trackball or finger pad. Adding it is as easy as plugging a mouse into a desktop computer and, at around £15, it's another low-cost and effective add-on. Your notebook computer's manual will give you guidance on the presence of external keyboard and mouse sockets and any special fitting instructions.

If your portable computer doesn't have a CD-ROM drive fitted, you can plug a special portable CD-ROM drive into the PCMCIA slot.

For safety, an adaptor is inserted into the floppy disk drive of a portable computer so the steel cable can then be locked to a convenient fixture.

floppy disks. Zip drives are increasingly common in homes and offices and are fitted as standard on some desktop computers, so there is a very good chance that you will be able to swap data with most users. External Zip drives cost around £100, while the cartridges are around £10 each. If you don't have a CD-ROM drive built into your notebook and find that you need one, you can get an external lightweight CD-ROM or CD-RW drive, specifically designed for use with portables, for around £100-£250. These drives are slimline, weigh around 0.5kg (1lb) and connect to your computer via the PC Card slot (a few cheaper versions connect via the parallel port, which is much slower). If you are a serious computer user and need massive extra storage options, consider an external hard drive. Rather than a conventional hard disk, look for PC card disks when travelling. A 2GB PC card hard disk costs around £300-350, but you can get cheaper smaller capacity cards.

● Security

Computer theft is on the increase and portables are a prime target. Vigilance is the best safeguard against theft so, if possible, never let your portable out of your sight. Clearly, though, there will be occasions when you are using your computer in one location and will not be able to oversee it without a break. Some portable computers have a built-in security retention slot which allows you to attach one end of a lockable steel cable to the computer and the other to an immovable object, such as a heavy table or filing cabinet. These devices are simple and relatively cheap at around £40. If you don't have a security slot, there are plenty of alternative systems available, many of which work on similar lines, such as those that lock into the computer's floppy disk slot.

● Portable comfort

When you're actually on the move, you'll want something that provides comfort for you and protection for the computer. There is a vast range of portable carrying cases available. These start at prices around £20-£30.

At the bottom end of the price range there are some perfectly acceptable padded cases. You can get something a little more spacious, possibly with a rigid shell, for around £60-£70. An alternative to this, and at a similar price, is a case that offers extra protection in the form of a pressurized air bag which surrounds the computer.

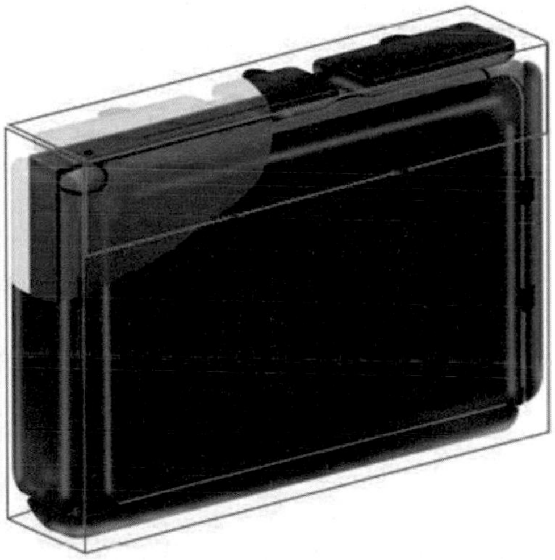

If your portable computer is in a case protected with pressurized air, it is theoretically protected in drops of up to 2 metres. The engineering used to create the case is based on the way a racing car chassis absorbs energy to protect the driver in the event of a crash.

If your portable PC doesn't have a floppy drive, get a special anchor plate to allow use of a security cable.

An inexpensive case (below) might be fine, but it won't offer much protection or extra storage space.

SITES TO @ VISIT

The Internet is a good way to check the market place for portable computer products:

Canon
www.canon.co.uk
Xircom
www.xircom.com
Codi carrying cases
www.codi-inc.com
SecuPlus security
www.secuplus.co.za

For useful information about everything on the PC market, try:
Computer Users Home Page
www.cuhp.co.uk

Universal Serial Bus

Thanks to Universal Serial Buses (USBs), you can plug new hardware into your PC and use it right away without first having to install driver software or restart your computer.

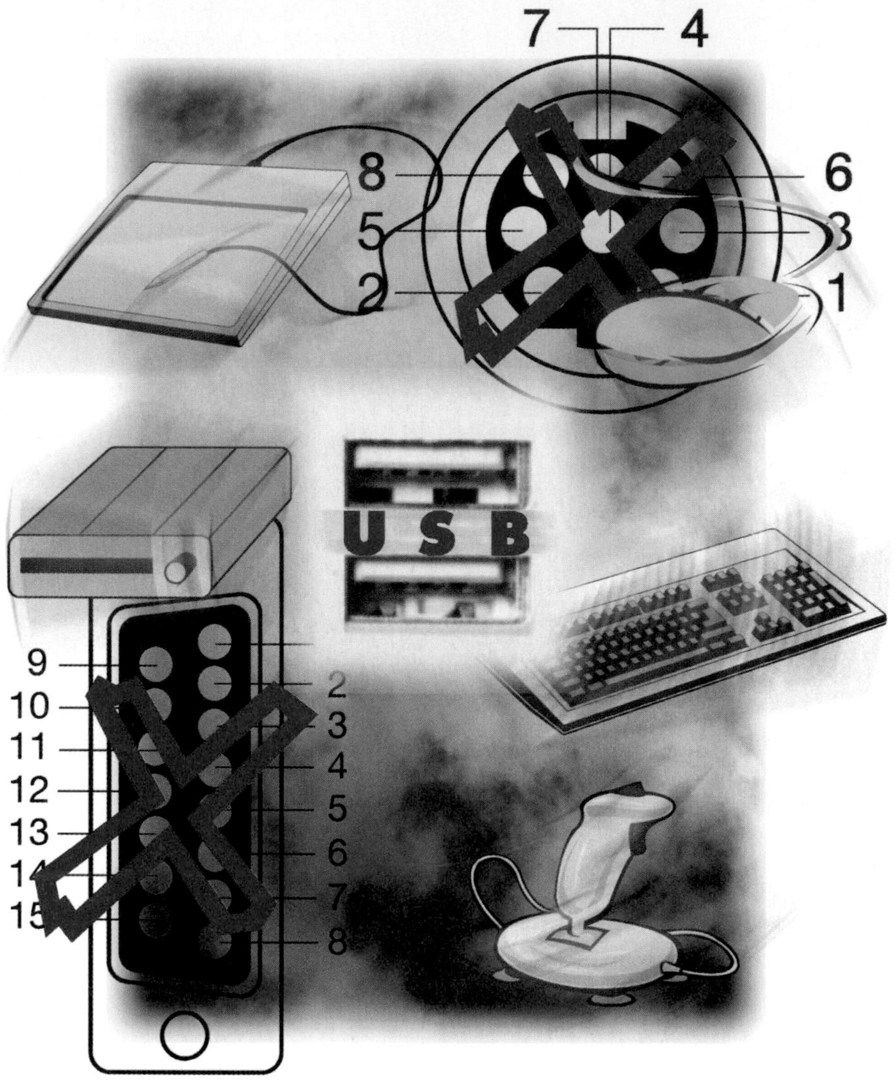

Throughout the Hardware sections, we've seen how the process of adding a new piece of hardware via your parallel or serial ports has often required you to turn your computer off before you can plug in the new device. The Universal Serial Bus (USB) has changed all that: it's a way of connecting devices together which is now the standard for computers and associated hardware or peripherals.

● USB vs parallel and serial ports

The modern PC has many ports of different shapes and sizes: parallel, serial, a PS/2 socket for the keyboard and often another PS/2 port for the mouse. Usually, you simply plug a device into its own socket, but if all your ports are in use, you might have to unplug something you are currently using to connect a new device.

To simplify matters, computer manufacturers adopted the USB standard, and now supply USB versions for almost every type of external hardware. It features on printers, modems, joysticks, mice, keyboards, digital cameras, scanners, digital speakers, floppy and tape drives and many other devices.

The Universal Serial Bus (USB) does away with a confusing and complex array of ports on your PC. USB sockets can accommodate all types of peripherals.

USB UPGRADE

If you have an older PC and so have no USB ports, do not despair. You can buy expansion cards that simply slot into your existing computer to provide the connection. A two-port USB card costs around £25, while a four-port card is around £10 more.

● USB benefits

One of the greatest features of USB is that the devices don't each require a port of their own on the back of the PC. So you can plug a USB monitor into the USB port of the PC and then plug in a modem, say, into the USB port of the monitor.

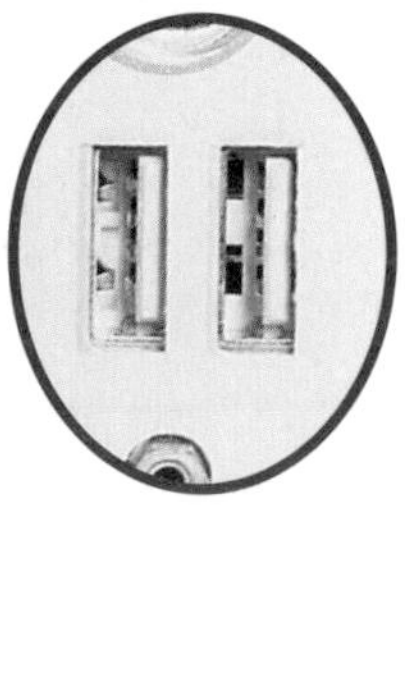

If you can see sockets like this on your computer, it's ready for USB computing. You need only an operating system with USB support and some USB devices.

USB technology makes the day-to-day use of your PC more convenient, too. The USB port is robust enough to cope easily with the various new devices you might want to add, even while the system is up and running. You can plug and unplug devices as you please, without having to switch off and on again or without having to restart. The changes to your setup will be recognized immediately.

All you have to do is just plug in this high-quality video camera from Logitech into your USB socket and it's ready to work immediately.

● High-capacity port

The USB port is a modest-looking piece of equipment. One device, typically the monitor or the keyboard, plugs directly into the USB port on the back of the PC. This device can work as a hub – connecting the other devices to the PC. A maximum of 127 extra devices can be connected to one PC via USB, each one with up to 5m of cabling between them!

In data transfer terms the USB port is a real flyer. This means that printers will receive their data faster. The overall time needed to print out your documents should be significantly less. The same applies to USB scanners, which also take less time to send the scanned information to the computer. In addition, the technology is fast enough to offer simple networking possibilities. For devices that need even more speed, another, faster, connectivity standard, called FireWire, complements USB.

WHAT IT MEANS

FIREWIRE

Even faster and newer than USB is a connection standard called FireWire (sometimes called IEEE1394 or iLink). This is designed for peripherals that must transfer a lot of information very quickly, such as digital camcorders and DVD players. Rather than being competition for the USB, the two complement each other. Some PCs have both, with certain products more suited for low-cost USB connectors, and others for the more expensive FireWire.

● Built-in power

Just as handy for the individual home computer user is the USB designer's inclusion of a 5V power supply within the connector. This means that the USB cable can also supply the power to many USB add-ons – they no longer need their own mains adaptor. This helps to minimize the number of cables that snake across and under your desktop. Also, printers, scanners and other USB devices can be further away from the computer itself, which helps to reduce clutter around your keyboard and screen.

There is no catch. USB brings the Plug and Play principle used for internal devices to externals, but

If you have a USB socket on your computer, think about replacing worn-out peripherals with USB-compatible ones, such as this mouse from Genius.

rather more efficiently. There were a few teething problems with Plug and Play (largely ironed out now), which led to a revised buzz phrase being applied to USB – 'True Plug and Play'. However, the USB technology is now extremely reliable.

● USB and Windows

For USB to work, it requires the close collaboration of Windows itself. USB support was added to Windows 95 in CD-ROMs pressed after October 1996 but is now, of course, an integral part of Windows. USB is intended to do away with the need for driver disks and setup programs. Ultimately, all software required by extra hardware will be included in Windows and will be both loaded and unloaded automatically, as required. In the first few years of USB, however, new and innovative add-ons will still include a disk containing drivers. Even so, the installation procedures for both hardware and software have been made a great deal more simple than they used to be.

What has made the USB such a winner is the support it has gained from the computer 'giants'. Everyone who's anyone pushed it as a common standard: Microsoft, Intel, Compaq, IBM, NEC, Northern Telecom and Apple. With these companies behind it, and with new PCs now including the port as a matter of course, it really couldn't fail to be a success.

● Where are USB devices?

USB peripherals of every kind are now available. Any PC bought today features the USB port as standard. In fact, if you bought your computer from 1997 onwards, it probably already has USB ports.

The inclusion of USB ports on a computer can be especially beneficial where two or more devices share the parallel port with conflicting demands as to which device has precedence, as in the case of an external Zip drive and a scanner.

You should consider buying USB add-ons instead of the older, soon to be outdated, parallel or serial devices. That way, you'll have a head start as hardware in the future will definitely be based on the USB standard.

USB PRODUCTS OUT NOW

All manner of USB products are available. Much touted as a technology for Multimedia fans and gamers, USB already boasts a wide variety of joysticks and game controllers from all manufacturers. This will be good news if you've ever struggled with the settings of a games device – possibly the most fiendishly tricky of all computer peripherals to install.

There are USB digital speaker systems and digital cameras, and Compaq have released a flat screen monitor that works as a USB hub. Of course, the simpler devices – mice and keyboards – are also available. And, if you want to link two or more PCs, consider using USB hubs for the job.

Home Learning & Leisure

Maths fun

The value of early learning software depends on its success in persuading young children that learning can be fun. Here's how to make maths enjoyable.

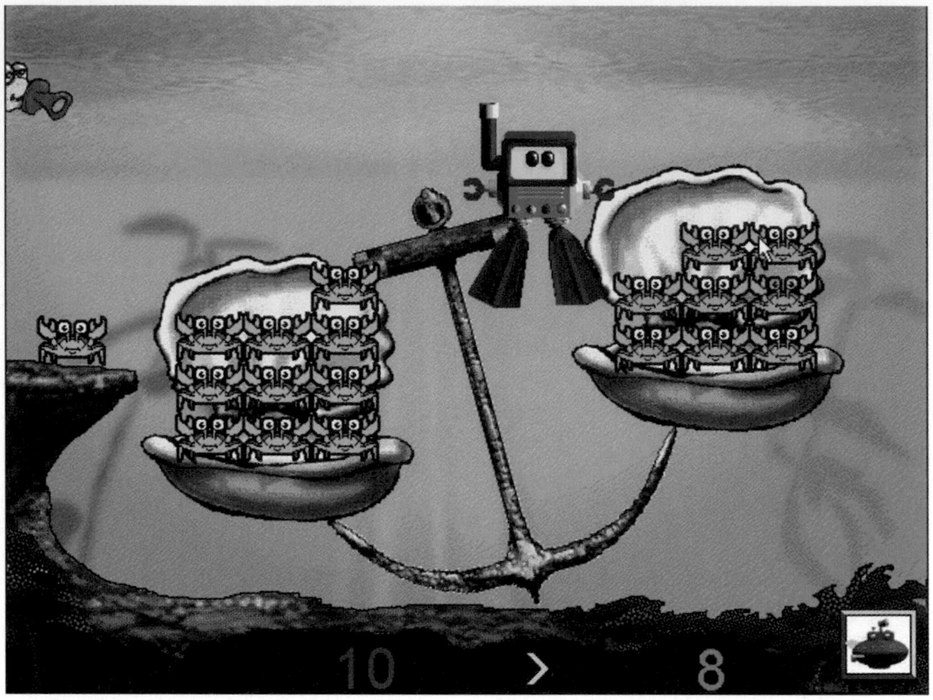

Maths Ace Junior ***is a counting game that also develops notions of equality and difference. Bit Bot the robot will help you rearrange the crabs in the clamshells to mirror the 'greater than' or 'less than' figures at the bottom of the screen.***

Children delight in acquiring new skills as much as they do in playing, although adults might find it hard to remember that this is the case. If you can combine learning and playing with a subject like maths (usually the least popular school topic) you are well on the way to giving your kids an enjoyable head start in education.

● Undersea sums

Maths Ace Junior, from Focus Multimedia, takes us down to the undersea world of Bit Bot, a cute robotic character who takes us on a Maths Voyage in his submarine. With his digital voice and graphic restlessness, Bit Bot is an engaging guide, and the 4–9 year olds that this program is aimed at will warm to him at once. Bit Bot's sub-aqua world is similarly engaging and full of bright colours and friendly fish.

Bit Bot's aim is to introduce the user to 15 different mathematical concepts, covering topics such as shape recognition, addition, subtraction, multiplication, telling the time and so on. The player kicks off inside the submarine. You move your pointer around to click on objects which reveal a mathematical game you can play. Bit Bot is always present to give encouragement, with his cheery, 'Ahoy matey, let's look for sunken treasure' way of speaking.

The games themselves are simple but good fun – and they'll certainly get the mathematical message across to the target audience. Each one has four levels of difficulty to test the child with each time it is played. Balance the Anchor is a good example of the way these games work. The anchor is the middle of a pair of scales; using skills of addition and subtraction, your child has to move the crabs from one shell to another to make the scales tilt correctly. Bit Bot himself is on hand – right in the middle of the scales – to give encouragement.

There are lots of things about *Maths Ace Junior* that will make it a useful program for the early learner. It's colourful and jaunty, genuinely good fun to play and learn, and the variety of games and levels means that children will keep getting more out of it over an extended period of time. See www.focusmultimedia.co.uk for more on this and other CD-ROMs.

● Back to school

Nursery School, from Europress, is a series comprising three separate CD-ROMs, one each for ages 2–3, 3–4 and 4–5. All three share the same approach and the same author, and all three are accompanied by an invaluable printed Parent's Guide. This booklet outlines some of the major developments taking place in the child at the given age, suggests activities the parent can devise to enhance learning, and gives detailed advice on how the child should use the CD software. The software itself works on the 'show and play' principle, first demonstrating how a particular task is done, and then providing a play activity for the child.

● Friendly pictures

All three CDs take place in a suitably warm and friendly rural landscape that will feel familiar to all children who have seen picture books: watercolour-style graphics create a world of gently rolling hills, calm blue seas, soft fluffy clouds and eternal sunshine. A jaunty tune plays as a cartoon car rolls onto the screen, containing Wally Wimbush, the cute bear (with a Somerset accent) who is the guide to each program. Your mouse cursor is transformed into a magic wand and then all you have to do is touch a cloud or an object to play a game.

While the *Nursery School* series covers the whole range of early learning activities, maths and maths-related ones inevitably feature

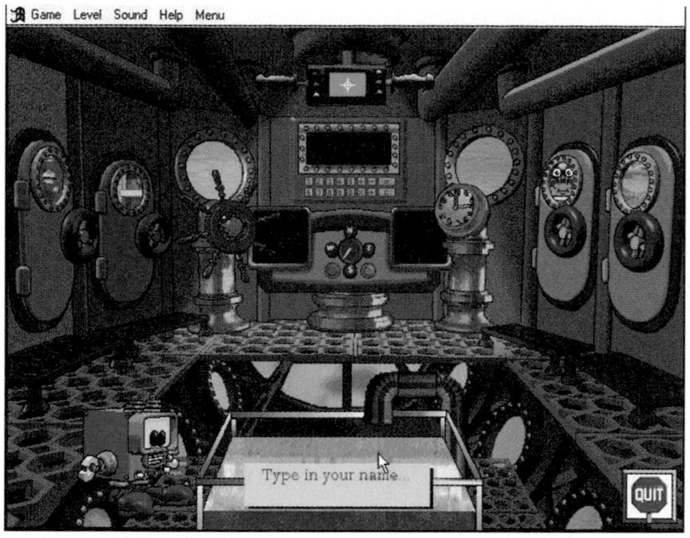

Type in your name on the home screen of **Maths Ace Junior** *and click on a nautical object to play one of the 15 games available. Games can be saved so that you can go back to them, while the program has four levels of difficulty to extend the challenge.*

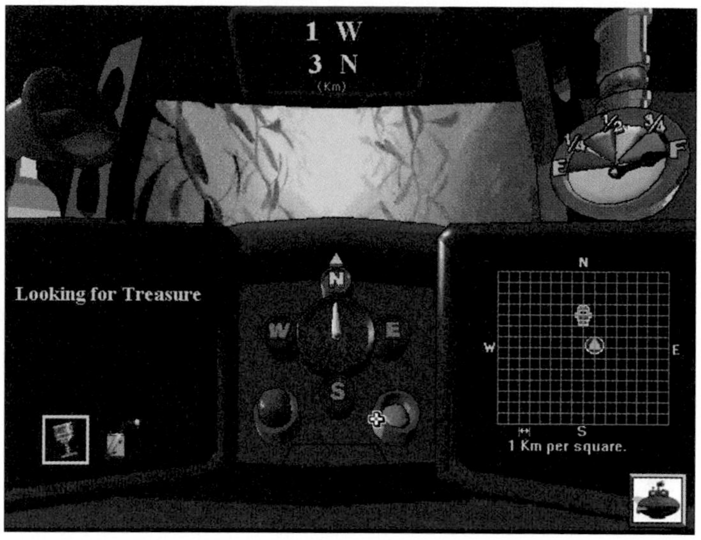

Maths Ace Junior *does not forget that maths has to be applied to the real world. This game teaches counting – but in the context of buying desirable objects in a shop. As ever, the robotic Bit Bot is on hand to help and encourage.*

quite heavily. In the CD-ROM for children aged 2–3 years old, games concentrate on shape-recognition, sorting objects and some very simple counting. Here, as throughout the series, much emphasis is laid on rhymes and jingles, which both the child and the parent can join in with to reinforce the lessons.

● Increasing the challenge

As the CDs advance in age range the games get more sophisticated and the activities more demanding. Now, for example, the child might have to count as many as ten glittering coins into a magic sack. Each CD in the series can be used individually. However, since *Nursery School* has been conceived as a whole there is an obvious advantage to starting your child on the first one. You can find the Europress Web site at www.europress.co.uk. Whichever route you take, your kids will have fun – and improve their maths.

Here, in this **Nursery School** *program for children aged 2-3 years old, is a game that involves fishing for the faces of friends hidden in the trees. The program gives plenty of audio-visual help to the younger learner.*

DOWNLOADING MATHS

As with any category of software, you can generally find some useful shareware or freeware on the Internet. One of the richest sites for children's educational software is tukids, found at http://www.tukids.tucows.com. This is the child's version of the popular tucows site. As with all the software available from tucows, the educational games here are given a 'cow-rating', depending on the popularity of downloads – five cows means it's very popular. Since most of the games are relatively quick to download, you have nothing to lose by checking them out. ArithmeTick-Tack-Toe is a fairly typical game – a version of noughts and crosses in which you have to answer a maths question correctly before you can put down your O or X. It's quite a simple idea, but it works, and is entertainingly accompanied by encouragements and congratulations in a suitably upbeat voice, such as 'Excellent!' and 'Way to go!'

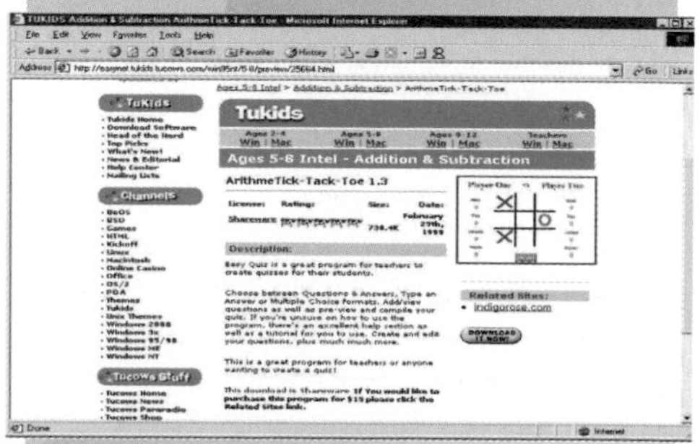

Biology revision aids

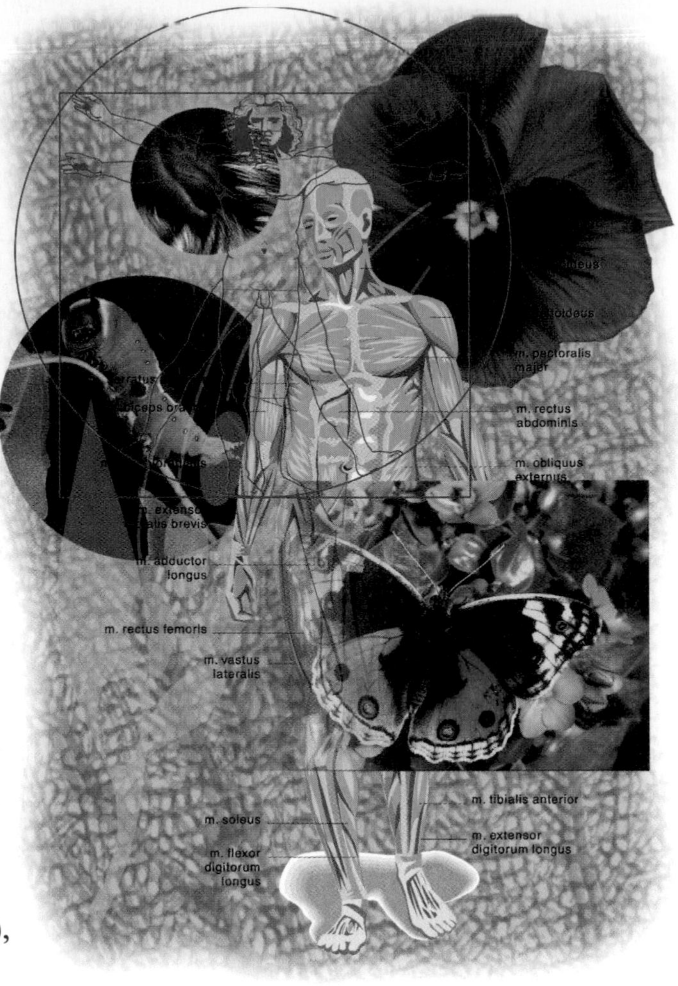

Even the most reluctant GCSE student will be encouraged in their biology studies if they use a Multimedia CD-ROM written by either Dorling Kindersley or GSP.

The onset of exams is always a stressful time, but with Multimedia revision aids the student can relax more and practise in a familiar environment at his or her own pace.

There are some excellent Multimedia revision aids available and GCSE biology is no exception. We've looked at other revision aid titles in *PCs made easy* (see Stage 1, pages 116-117), so you won't be surprised to learn that there's a wide choice of products available.

What's slightly different with biology, though, is that as a science, it can be approached on its own or together with chemistry and physics. This is reflected in the products we look at here: one is a single-topic CD, while the other is part of a set. This is a little unusual, but it's actually quite convenient. Obviously, your choice will depend on what subjects you're studying. *GCSE Biology*, from Dorling Kindersley, is everything you would expect from this publisher. It's solidly thought out, easy to follow and well presented. In common with other titles in the DK multimedia range (now published by GSP), it's test-based, offering more than 1,000 questions, written by practising teachers. The program can be customized to the student's particular exam board and it spans the entire biology syllabus at GCSE Key Stage 4 (14–16 year olds). The program is broken down into modules, with the main headings as follows: Processes of Life, Reproduction and Inheritance, Ecology and Diet and Digestion.

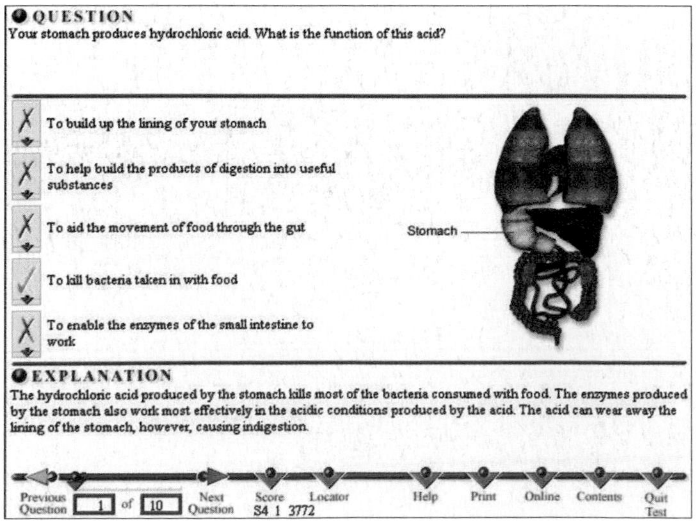

QUESTION
Your stomach produces hydrochloric acid. What is the function of this acid?
To build up the lining of your stomach
To help build the products of digestion into useful substances
To aid the movement of food through the gut
To kill bacteria taken in with food
To enable the enzymes of the small intestine to work
Stomach
EXPLANATION
The hydrochloric acid produced by the stomach kills most of the bacteria consumed with food. The enzymes produced by the stomach also work most effectively in the acidic conditions produced by the acid. The acid can wear away the lining of the stomach, however, causing indigestion.
Previous Question
1 of 10
Next Question
Score S4 1 3772
Locator
Help
Print
Online
Contents
Quit Test

The multiple choice interface in Dorling Kindersley's GCSE Biology is clear and colourful. Once you have answered a question correctly, it gives you more detailed information about it.

● A question of choice

There's a clever slider bar at each level so that you can specify how many questions you want to answer on any given subject, up to the given total. This provides you with complete control over the bias of the tests, so you can concentrate on any chosen area.

That said, it's not necessarily a good idea to work through all the questions on any one subject systematically, as a lot of them might depend on the same, or very similar, labelled diagrams.

Whatever approach you take, it's probably always wise to leave a few questions unanswered in any category, so that you can give yourself a complete, all-round test at the end of your revision. You can easily keep track of what you've done via the Progress section of the Main menu, which also allows you to complete any unfinished tests.

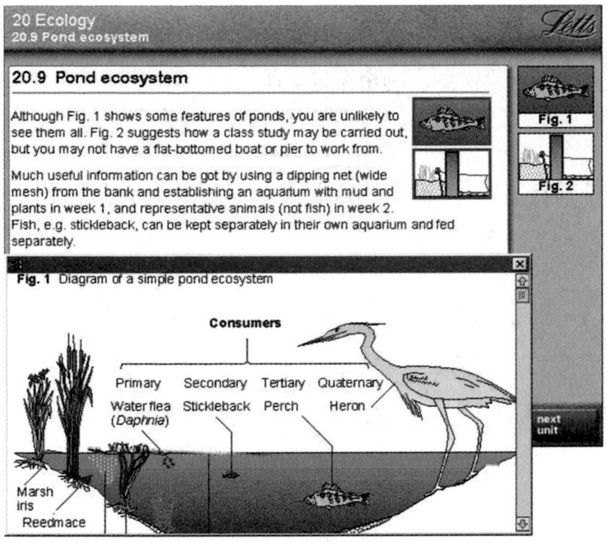

A representative revision course screen from the Letts Revision CD (left). Topics are presented with text and small graphics. Click on the graphics and you get a more detailed labelled diagram.

You've done your revision and taken the progress test – and here are the results (below). They're not too good, but the Letts Revision software points you to the areas you need to revise to improve your results.

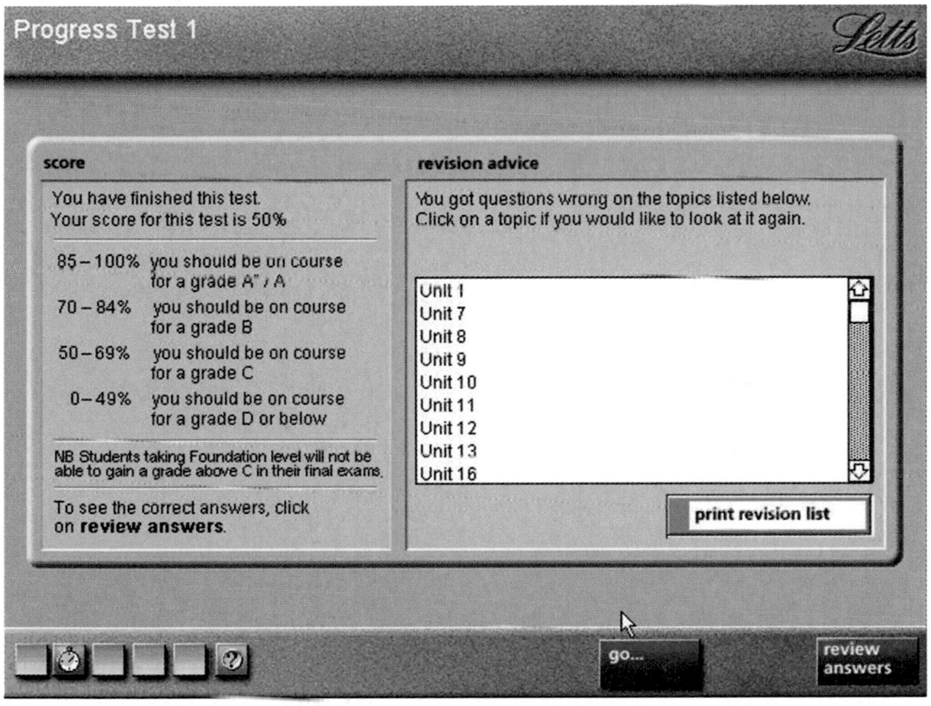

● Multiple choice

The questions themselves are multiple choice and once you get the answer right, the program offers a clear and comprehensive explanation of it. So, even if it takes you several stabs at getting the right answer, you do eventually succeed.

There are over 800 attractive graphics, enlivened by the occasional 3D animation. A score is kept throughout, which also provides handy analysis of your strengths and weaknesses. The program has a useful logging-on procedure, whereby you have to identify yourself and give a password, allowing more than one person to use the software to revise for the same exam. Crucially, this ensures that one student's progress isn't confused with another's.

● Exam success

Letts Revise for GCSE Biology, like the DK program, is aimed at Key Stage 4 students and it, too, is customizable, depending on which GCSE syllabus you are taking. Thereafter, the program takes a slightly different tack, being relentlessly goal-driven – the goal, of course, is to pass the GCSE exam with a good grade.

Everything here is geared to exam success. So when you log in for the first time you have to give the current date and the date of your first exam, the number of subjects you are taking and the total amount of time per week you are going to devote to revision. It is, of course, best to be honest with yourself here and not exaggerate your good intentions.

If, however, you don't really have a very good idea of how to go about the whole business of revision then this program, and its companions in the series, will supply a wealth of practical and valuable tips. You'll find out, for example, what the optimum amount of revision in any given session should be, how to go about acquiring an overview of the subject and how often you need to test yourself as the exams draw nearer.

The core of the software, however, is made up of the revision course and the progress tests. Based on the syllabus you selected when logging in, the software gives a thorough and well-illustrated presentation of everything you need to pass your Biology GCSE. Topics are presented with a text explanation in the main window and one or two diagrams to the right; click on these to get more detailed information. There are animations, where appropriate, to liven things up, while the text explanations are models of lucidity.

● How did you do?

When you've done your revision, you move to the Test Your Progress section. These timed tests cover every angle of the syllabus in a variety of question styles. If you haven't mastered a topic you will soon be found out – and given every chance to repeat the revision modules again.

If you use either of these packages properly, you really have no excuse for not doing well in the exams, especially as packages are updated to take account of syllabus changes.

CONTACT POINTS

Dorling Kindersley GCSE Biology
GSP
Price: £19.99*
Letts Revise for GCSE Biology
GSP
Price: £19.99*
Tel: 01480 496 600

*UK prices

Ancient civilizations

With a host of excellent Multimedia titles, your computer can help to bring history to life and give you a deeper understanding of the development of civilization – from Ancient Egypt to the Roman Empire.

The visuals of Interactive Ideas' **Lost Civilizations** *are accompanied by audio commentaries. When complete, these appear as text so you can copy and paste them.*

One great advantage of Multimedia as a learning aid is its potential to bring its subject to life. Ancient history is a good example, as shown on a number of CD-ROMs through their use of interactive maps, time lines and animated reconstructions.

Nowadays, early history is an important subject area in schools, especially at primary level. But it holds a fascination for all ages.

● Voyage to the past

Ancient Lands and Civilizations is a wide-ranging collection from Interactive Ideas, which includes four programmes that focus on ancient civilizations. *Ancient Civilizations of the Mediterranean*, for example, is an ambitious title encompassing the Egyptians, Greeks, Romans, Etruscans, Phoenicians and Carthaginians on a single CD-ROM. It provides a comprehensive mix, covering the key races who played a part in the foundation of Western civilization. The idea behind the program is that you travel on a voyage of exploration, navigating by means of a map that shows each power base. For example, if you click on Greece, you'll be offered another map showing the major sites, plus social, economic and military information. You're not confined to travelling in a linear fashion either, as you can branch off on cross-referenced tangents.

Ancient Civilizations of the Mediterranean *is part of the four CD-ROMs in the* **Ancient Lands and Civilizations** *pack. On the left is a map of Ancient Greece from this CD-ROM.*

The CD-ROM helps to explain how civilizations interacted through trade, culture and war. A timeline explains how each one rose and fell in relation to the others and introduces key personalities such as Alexander the Great, Homer and Nero.

Three further CDs are included in the package. *Myths and Legends* concentrates on lost worlds such as Atlantis and Babylon. *Mythology* explores the stories from Greek and Latin myth that have had such a profound influence on Western thinking and art, while *Voyage in Egypt* allows you to wander through a recreation of ancient Egypt, learning all about everyday life.

● Lost Civilizations

Lost Civilizations is another collection from Interactive Ideas but it spreads its net even wider. It boasts analysis of eight historic sites from all over the world, including Pompeii, Easter Island, Troy, Tutankhamun's tomb and the burial site of the Terracotta Army. Each analysis follows roughly the same pattern, giving information on the origins of the site, its discovery and what it is like today.

The highlights are reconstructions, showing the sites in their heyday. They are quite small, so you can't walk around the whole of Pompeii, for example. However, they are very effective, not least because the colours are so bright and attractive. Hotspots

In Ancient Egyptians, from Granada Learning, a video pharaoh introduces a variety of topics, which are then broken down into simple, memorable explanations.

lead you to related information, most of it accompanied by audio commentary and sometimes video, as well. The commentaries are also presented in text form, so you can follow the story at your ease and then copy and paste the actual text elsewhere if you want to.

The depth of information and pictorial detail varies according to the site. Some are inevitably richer than others. The tomb of Tutankhamun, for example, is particularly striking because the remains themselves are so impressive.

● Learning through games

Another approach is demonstrated in *Ancient Egyptians*, from Granada Learning – an educational game created for the National Curriculum.

The CD-ROM takes a whistle-stop tour through Egyptian history and is based around an interface consisting of two walls of hieroglyphic symbols. Those on the left represent periods of history. The others represent the cast of characters: a priest, a farmer, a noble lady, the pharaoh and so on.

Clicking on the left symbols calls up a commentary, with the main points bulleted like revision notes. Clicking on the right symbols, however, is much more fun. They transform into video animations, who talk about day-to-day life in ancient Egypt. The subjects covered range from mummies to farming and are presented in the same, easy-to-follow bullet points. The heart of the game is a treasure hunt in which you try to free the soul of the dead pharaoh. You have to interact with the cast to find missing items, completing puzzles as you go. The game ends as the pharaoh becomes one with the gods. It's an interesting, well presented CD-ROM with an absorbing and different approach to this subject.

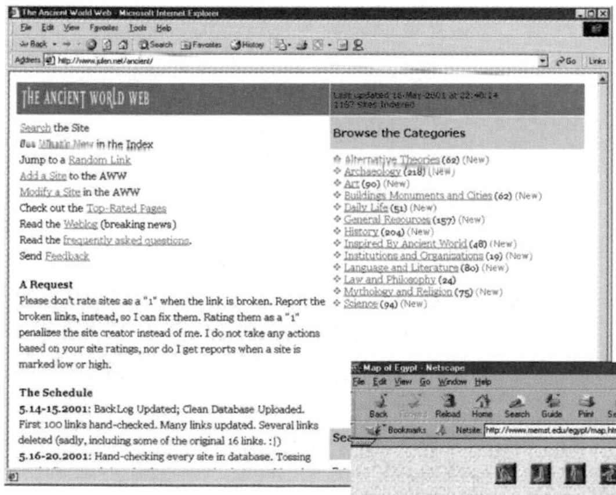

The Ancient World Web (AWW) on the Internet (above) has over 900 sites listed by category.

Many Web pages, like this one (right) on Egyptian sites (found via the AWW), use a Multimedia-style interface. Click on a site and you'll jump to relevant information and pictures.

CONTACT POINTS

Ancient Lands and Civilizations
Price: £29.99*
Lost Civilizations
Price: £34.99*
Interactive Ideas
Tel: 020 8805 1000
www.interactiveideas.com

Ancient Egyptians
Price: £57.50 for one copy,*
£11.75 each extra copy
Granada Learning
Tel: 0161 827 2927

*UK prices

SITES TO @ VISIT

There is a wealth of information available on the Internet. This might not be as slick as some of the commercial CD-ROMs, but the detail can be impressive. An excellent link to many sites is at the Ancient World Web.

Ancient World Web (AWW)
This is an example of a great site, maintained by a single individual for no commercial gain. Created and managed by Julia Hayden, it lists hundreds of sites by region and by subject. Most impressively, it gives a précis and critical appreciation of what each one has to offer:
www.julen.net/ancient/

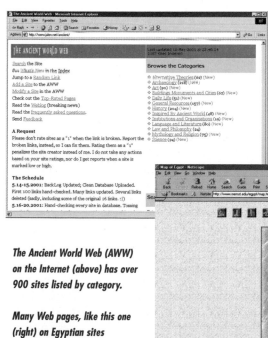

Manage your money

If your accounts are in a mess and you've lost track of what you've been spending, perhaps you need the help of money management software to help solve your financial problems.

Managing personal and household finances is a task we all have to do, but very few people enjoy it. Many of us are inefficient, putting things off, keeping relevant paperwork in all sorts of different places, not examining the state of our savings and investments and forgetting to pay bills. Financial management is important, and becomes even more so if you're running a small business.

● Financial management software

However, help is at hand in the shape of financial management software. Such software has been around since the dawn of computers and has been widely used in business for many years. Large companies need to know how much cash they've got, who is late paying their bills and how much VAT or tax is due in any given period. Managers need up-to-date reports on all aspects of the company finances so that they can make plans for the future. Until the 1980s, software that could do all this ran on large computers only, regularly maintained and updated by technical and financial experts.

With the arrival of affordable and powerful PCs, however, the kind of power that was once the privilege of big business is now available at home. Programs such as Quicken and Microsoft Money can really put you in control of your outgoings, income and savings.

They can give you instant reports on the state of your overall finances or on any given aspect, such as your mortgage or savings. With the increasing use of the Internet as a business tool, some types of financial management software will even let you connect via the Web to your bank, download your statement and then use it in the software.

Most personal finance programs are updated each year to reflect changes in taxation and fast-developing areas, such as online banking. However, the basic approach of the programs remains the same. The Microsoft Money series offers very similar functions to Intuit's Quicken range. At the core of the programs are very powerful accounting abilities.

● A good account of yourself

When you start using a financial management program you must enter all the financial details relating to the

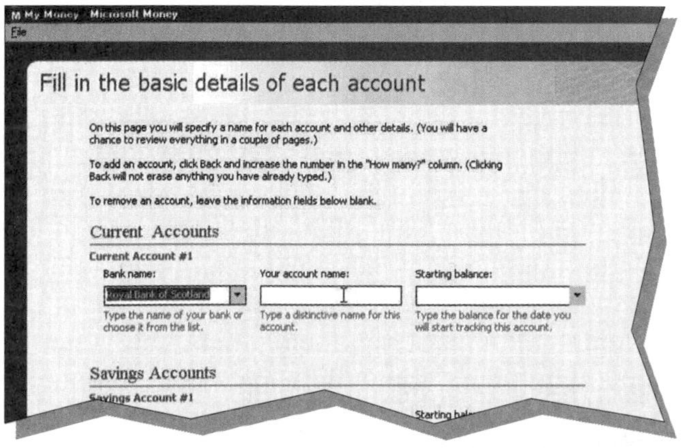

My Money - Microsoft Money
File
Fill in the basic details of each account
On this page you will specify a name for each account and other details. (You will have a chance to review everything in a couple of pages.)
To add an account, click Back and increase the number in the "How many?" column. (Clicking Back will not erase anything you have already typed.)
To remove an account, leave the information fields below blank.
Current Accounts
Current Account #1
Bank name:
Your account name:
Starting balance:
Royal Bank of Scotland
Type the name of your bank or choose it from the list.
Type a distinctive name for this account.
Type the balance for the date you will start tracking this account.
Savings Accounts
Savings Account #1

Microsoft Money takes you through the initial 30-minute process of setting up your accounts with voice-over Wizards.

Take most of the paper out of your paperwork – prepare your accounts by using a financial management program.

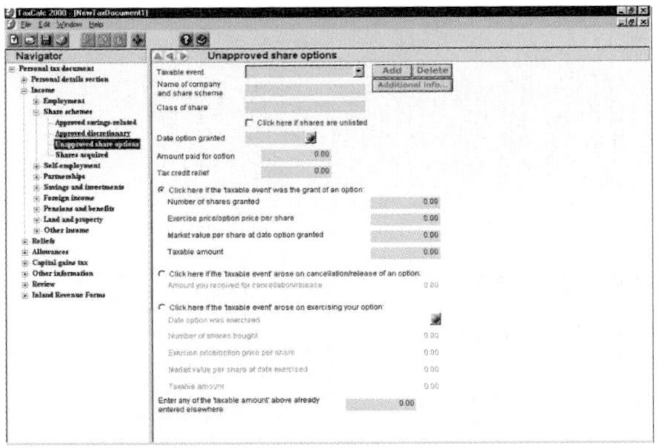

TaxCalc from Which Software makes filling in your tax return just about as easy as it's ever going to be, using a Windows Explorer-style navigation system to travel between different forms.

different categories of your expenditure and income. The more information you provide, the better.

In the characteristic Microsoft manner, a powerful Wizard helps you to set up various accounts, as needed. The type of account can be selected from a list covering pretty much everything you might need, including investments, house, loan, and so forth. Setting up your account is an easy process, although be aware that you must gather all the relevant documents, such as mortgage details and bank statements, so that you have the information to hand.

If you enter information about a recurring transaction – a monthly loan repayment, for example – Money automatically detects it as such, allowing you to enter it into the Bill Calendar, which will pop up with a reminder when payments fall due. And you can handle savings and investments just as easily as outgoings, setting up an account for different stock portfolios, for example. Money can even update your investment portfolios via its Internet connection.

● Setting goals

Another function most people will find useful is the lifetime planning. Tell Money where you want to end up and it will produce a plan based on the data you have entered.

Finally, and perhaps most importantly, Money has powerful reporting and charting facilities, which can help to give you a clear picture of where any given part, or all, of your finances stand.

You can create regular monthly reports showing where the money comes from and where it goes, or you can create specific reports and charts on, say, the performance of your investments and savings. It's this ability to produce a clear financial picture at the click of a button that really makes financial software worth the effort for the home user.

● Taxing times

One piece of financial management that comes round without fail every year is your annual tax return. With the introduction of Self Assessment, filling in your form correctly and sending it in on time are more important than ever. This can seem like an extremely daunting task.

This is when you need tax calculation software, such as TaxCalc, from Which Software. This program takes you through the entire process, starting with an 'interview' in which you fill in all the relevant details (so make sure you have these to hand) in the boxes. The software then works out your tax liability for you. There are also tips about how you can legitimately minimize liabilities.

The Inland Revenue accepts a print-out from TaxCalc as a valid document, thus saving you the task of filling in forms by hand, and making it much easier to complete it on time.

At work

Financial management software can help take the strain out of running a business.

IT'S ABSOLUTELY CRUCIAL to know where you stand with your finances if you are running a small business. This is because there are legal obligations to pay tax, National Insurance and VAT. Even the smallest business needs accurate, detailed financial data to plan for the future. No wonder that the introduction of the PC was accompanied by the introduction of accounting software. The popular Instant Accounting software from Sage reproduces the traditional book-keeping structure of sales, purchase and nominal ledgers but gives you a lot more besides. On the basis of information entered on sales and purchases, the software will calculate VAT and generate invoices and reports. Instant Accounting is suitable for small businesses of up to about 10 employees.

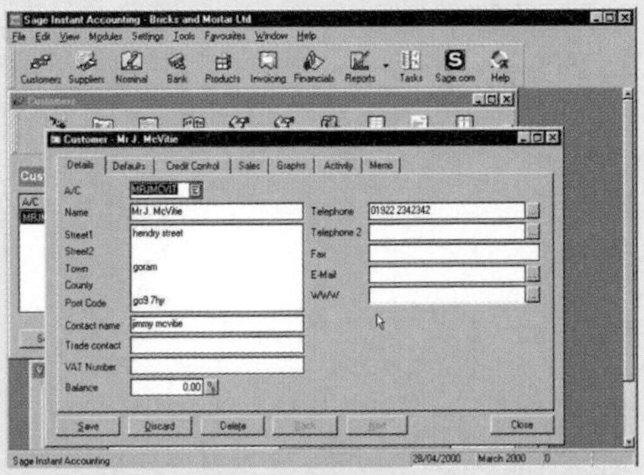

Instant Accounting requires little knowledge of accounting. Pop-up windows make things familiar and there's a plethora of Wizards to help you set up accounts.

CONTACT POINTS

Instant Accounting
Sage
Tel: 0800 447 777
Price: £149.00*

Money
Microsoft
Tel: 0870 601 0100
Price: £35*

Quicken
Intuit
Tel: 0800 585 058
Price: £29.95* (Regular)
or £49.95* (Deluxe)

TaxCalc
Which Software
Tel: 0800 920 140
Price: £24.99*

*UK prices

Formula 1 racing

Lightning-fast computers are used to monitor and enhance the speed and performance of racing cars, helping them become quicker than ever before.

The racing driver at the wheel is backed up by technicians watching screens that show all the readings from the car's telemetry.

The cars used in Formula 1 racing exhibit all the characteristics of modern high-technology: incredible speed, an inspired mix of analogue and digital systems and a hyper-streamlined shape. Each of these attributes is largely due to the modern Formula 1 car being designed, created – and even partly driven – by computer technology.

The computer's involvement in Formula 1 starts at the very beginning, when the car is conceived and designed. Because computers are now so powerful, and computer-aided design (CAD) so widely used, it is actually quite some time before a new design is able to be moved from the virtual drawing-board to the engineering shop.

● Co-ordinated by computer

A wide range of companies is responsible for creating components on a car, most notably the engine, suspension, brakes and tyres. The computer is particularly useful in co-ordinating this work, as high-speed data links and videoconferencing facilities enable companies to interact quickly and efficiently. Also, the team can have the latest versions of each component design instantly available. Perhaps the most important design work undertaken by the racing team is in the chassis and outer body shell. The design and testing are done on the computer, with a model tested in a wind tunnel when the final design has been all but approved.

Modern racing cars are among the highest of high-tech products and need sophisticated CAD systems to design each of their numerous components.

untutored eyes, even the tiniest detail can make a huge difference to a car's performance. For example, in 1998 the FIA (the body controlling motor racing) ordered that all Formula 1 cars should have a 10 per cent reduction in their width, from 200cm to 180cm. It doesn't seem much, but it had a massive effect on the airflow around the car, significantly altering its aerodynamics, and thus its speed.

● Aerodynamics

While building a chassis is a relatively simple task, due to the restrictions enforced by the FIA, the real skill comes in creating the body shell. Not only does it have to be as aerodynamic as possible, it also has to be the optimum shape for fast braking and helping with downforce and grip. The design of the body shell has to take these factors into account – and the best way to see the effect of these design changes is by simulating them on the computer, which speeds up the design process and keeps down costs.

All these different areas of design work take place concurrently, making a computer a necessity for organizing and centralizing the data. Nearly all the car's mechanical components are controlled by computer, enabling the pit crew to monitor the condition of the car by radio signal (known as telemetry), and respond to any damage or breakdown by preparing replacements in the pits and devising a new race strategy. Displays in the cockpit also inform the driver of any problems, so that appropriate action can be taken. The responsiveness of the car is also helped by the use of computers, with little of the actual driver interface controlled by cables or wires. This allows for quicker control of the mechanics.

In addition, the gears, brakes, and steering wheel are all controlled by electronics, allowing for relatively minuscule improvements which can result in a cumulative effect that is quite noticeable and significant.

● On track

Once the car gets out onto the race track, the computer's job is still far from finished. To fine-tune the various systems, the car is raced on a test circuit to monitor its performance in various conditions. Telemetry data is recorded from each of the computerized systems. The team can examine the performance of each component, from brakes to gears and optimize them for the coming race.

And, just as supercomputing has led to many improvements in desktop computer technology, the technology used in Formula 1 racing means that there will be eventual advances in safety, control and diagnostics for the everyday driver.

FORMULA 1 COMPUTERS

The actual types of computer used in Formula 1 vary according to the job in hand. PCs are widely employed during the design process, particularly by the smaller companies, but in general UNIX-based workstations are preferred because of the huge amounts of data involved. This is most obvious at the McLaren team, which is sponsored by SUN, a maker of such computers. These computers monitor the timing of cars and races, while others retrieve and correlate telemetry data. McLaren even use programs written in Sun's Java language to translate data transmitted during the race.

Computer manufacturers sponsor Formula 1 teams because the images of speed, precision and reliability support their marketing messages.

TRAINING ON GAMES

There is one other important way in which computers – and personal computers in particular – are used in Formula 1 racing. Many of the top drivers, including David Coulthard and former Grand Prix champion Jacques Villeneuve, have admitted to using computer games to practise and hone their racing skills. The simulation of choice is the Grand Prix series from Microprose, now on version 3. Over the years this has remained the top PC simulation, far ahead of its rivals in terms of accuracy and control. Jacques Villeneuve, in particular, found the game very useful, as he was able to use it during his first season to 'practise' on upcoming tracks that he had never raced on before.

You can find out more about the game – and how it is constantly updated to give new features mirroring the real world – at the official www.grandprixgames.com site, or at www.grandprix3.com, a very good unofficial site.

Star Trek games

***Star Trek* games were once scoffed at by PC gamers. In recent years, however, the TV and film series have become the basis of some excellent games, featuring popular genres.**

Star Trek has been a licensing bonanza for all sorts of products as it has evolved over the many years of its existence. For PC gamers the programme's fertility hasn't always been welcome; it resulted in a head-spinning plethora of average games in a variety of genres from a host of different publishers. Game-playing devotees of *Star Trek* just didn't know where to turn.

Now the situation has become much clearer, and the quality of the games somewhat better. Activision now owns most rights in the *Star Trek* licence, and so has the fullest catalogue and release schedule. But Interplay nevertheless retains some rights and has far from exhausted *Star Trek's* seemingly endless possibilities. The good news is that it means that there are plenty of *Star Trek* games out there, covering just about any game genre you could possibly hope for.

At last, the Star Trek games are beginning to match the exciting involvement of the original TV series and films.

CONQUEST ONLINE

Activision's *Star Trek: ConQuest Online* is a curious hybrid of PC and online gaming. You buy the CD and 'train' by playing against the computer's AI (artificial intelligence). Then you log on to www.conquestonline.com and take on all-comers. It's a kind of territorial domination strategy. There is also a card game, where you try to win areas controlled by other players. Collecting a given card – in the game these are called 'e-cards' – can gain you extra power or some other desirable quality. ConQuest Online takes place in a faithfully rendered *Star Trek* universe, but for some the gameplay can be slow or even confusing, so read the 80-page manual before logging on.

● Now Voyager

Activision's most recent title, released in late 2000, is *Star Trek Voyager: Elite Force*, the first game based on the *Star Trek Voyager* universe. It's a moderately violent, first-person shooter (with an 11+ rating), powered by the Quake III Arena game engine.

The *USS Voyager* has been mysteriously transported into a very dangerous 'null space'. Your job as a member of the Hazard Team is to defend the ship against invading aliens, infiltrate a Borg cube and then wipe out the enemy. You get nine weapons, each of which offers two firing modes, so there's plenty of variety in how you deal with the enemies. There's also a wide choice of game modes, with 40 single-player missions and 16 multi-player arenas. The whole thing is extremely faithful to its TV original in terms of graphics and characters – and you will certainly have a head start if you're familiar with the layout of the ship.

● Borg games

Activision's earlier release in 2000 was based on the Next Generation universe and was in the very different genre of real-time 3D strategy. In *Star Trek: Armada*, an almighty battle is looming involving the Federation, the Klingons, the Romulans and the Borg. Your job, of course, is to lead one side

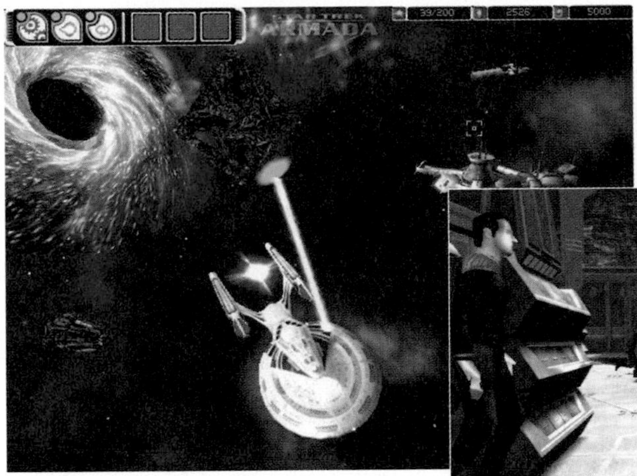

A colourful scene of action and mayhem from Star Trek: Armada (left), one of a range of titles from Activision.

In Star Trek: Hidden Evil (right), Data finds himself involved in thwarting the evil Romulan plot.

to victory. Each outfit presents its own tactical challenges, as does managing a fleet of 30 types of starships, not to mention a very well stocked armoury. As well as combat, the rules of the genre necessitate some planning and strategy, and you certainly won't get very far if you don't plot and build. There's a variety of game scenarios to try and if it all gets too much you can compete with up to eight players over a local network or on the Internet.

● Naughty Romulans

Late 1999 saw Activision produce *Star Trek: Hidden Evil*, this one in the action-adventure genre. You play the character Ensign Sovok, who finds himself at the heart of a dastardly Romulan plot. Taking your mission goals from your Tricorder and your orders from Captain Picard, you set off through a 3D world to explore, encounter and occasionally fight. There are plenty of other characters to communicate with and plenty of puzzles to solve. And when civilized conversation fails, you always have your trusty phaser and the handy Vulcan Nerve Pinch to fall back on.

Star Trek: Away Team is a squad-based strategy game featuring espionage, stealth tactics and new weaponry. You command an elite team whose members you have to nurture and assign to various tasks, ranging from hacking computers to destroying enemy units. In all, 18 different game worlds from the *Star Trek* universe are promised.

Star Trek: Bridge Commander is a space simulation set in the Star Trek Next Generation universe. From a detailed 3D bridge you will command a large starship, with strategic manoeuvrability, lots of firepower and configurable defence systems.

You play the part of Jean Luc Picard, commanding a skeleton crew of four, each with specialist know-how. Helmswoman Kiska handles all space flight, while the tactical officer has the full arsenal of the Enterprise's weapons at his disposal. A science officer and engineer provide extra backup – especially by using the shields if your defensive plans don't go quite right. However, if you find giving orders hard work, there's a mode which lets you do everything yourself.

● Online battles

Star Trek: New Worlds from Interplay, is very different. It is a real-time strategy game, set in the year 2292, in which you have to face up to challenges on distant worlds. You can play as good guys or bad guys, but if you choose the Federation you have to play by their rules and moral code. The Klingons have no such restrictions of course. There's a multitude of missions, each one with multiple objectives, so the gameplay is deep and long lasting.

Starfleet Command Volume II: Empires at War is based on a long-standing, turn-based board game, *Star Fleet Battles*, but has become an immense 3D real-time game on the PC. You'll be able to play it in single-player or multi-player mode, or even in what Interplay call the Dynaverse II – against potentially thousands of other players online.

Starfleet Command Volume II: Empires at War has over 100 spaceships and eight competing empires to explore.

Kiska takes command in Activision's Star Trek: Bridge Commander, a space simulation with 30 missions to play.

CONTACT POINTS

Star Trek: Hidden Evil
Price: £19.99*
Star Trek: Armada
Price: £19.99*
Star Trek: ConQuest Online
Price: £19.99*
Star Trek: Voyager Elite Force
Price: £39.99*
Star Trek: Away Team
Price: £29.99*
Star Trek: Bridge Commander**
Price: £29.99*
Activision, distributed by Centresoft
www.centresoft.co.uk
**(released November 2001)

Star Trek: New Worlds
Price: £19.99*
Starfleet Command Volume II: Empires at War
Price: £21.99*
Interplay
www.interplay-store.co.uk

*UK prices

Birds of Europe

Multimedia products can put some added fun into just about any subject, but you might be surprised to learn that one of the topics to which it is best suited is birdwatching.

If you want to identify a particular species of bird, the most obvious way to do so is to observe the animal's plumage and colouring, and then to look it up in a reference book. However, as any 'twitcher' (birdwatcher) will tell you, distinctive flight patterns and inherent calls are equally important means of identification. This is where the birdwatcher's CD-ROM beats a guidebook hands down.

By adding movement, sound and informative voice-overs to the standard fare of photographs, maps and illustrations, the Multimedia package can do all that a book can do – and much, much more. So, not surprisingly, there are several excellent and creatively produced ornithology CDs available, catering for every level of interest and age group.

● Virtual ornithology

At the budget end of the bird encyclopedia spectrum is Focus's *Birds of Europe* CD-ROM covering 310 species of birds. For each bird, there's a screenfull of information covering size, habitat, group, song, migration and appearance. For many of the species there are birdsong sound clips and there are also video clips for a few individual birds.

You can just browse your way through the alphabetical listing – by either English and Latin species names, or you can sort the birds according to size or group. Sorting by size helps you to narrow the field if you want to identify a bird you've spotted; you can then use the photo and appearance information to check other details. One click on the small photo brings up a larger image, making it easier to look for distinguishing features.

Use the bird selector screen and you can filter the 310 birds according to their habitat, choosing only to view woodland or urban birds, for example. If you already fancy yourself

If you spot something that seems unusual, you can identify it using the photos, size and habitat information and then check the colour-coded map of Europe to see if it's a year-round resident, a summer migrant, or a winter visitor.

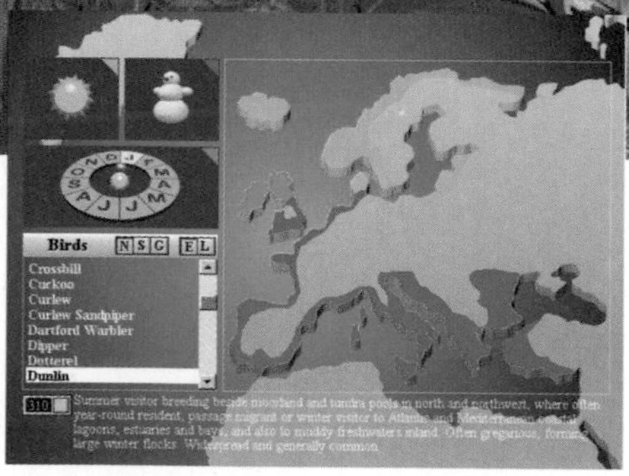

Birds of Europe includes recordings of birdsong and video clips of many birds at work, rest and play, in addition to a screen full of information for each species.

as a bird buff, you can try the quiz mode instead. The task is to choose one of five birds listed and then match the characteristics and the photo to your choice.

● Britain and Europe

The AA Interactive Encyclopaedia to Birds of Britain and Europe uses the idea of a bird sanctuary rather than a museum. The reserve houses an Ecology Room, an Avarium, an Information Room, a Games Room and a Hide. You are free to wander around these areas, clicking on anything that takes your fancy.

Again, if you prefer a more structured approach, or if you find the interface a little on the confusing side, you can select a list of topics and simply click on them to get the information that you want.

The core of the CD-ROM is the bird guide, which presents the 427 species of bird that breed in, or regularly inhabit, Britain and the rest of Europe. But the complete package will also help you to learn about bird conservation and habitats, the distribution of species throughout Europe (illustrated by attractive maps), the evolution and survival of birds, and a host of other topics.

The information is presented in some depth, accompanied by excellent illustrations. There are 90 video clips on the CD and recordings of more than 500 bird songs. Combine these with the illustrations and the fact file and you have a very good chance of identifying any birds you see when you are out and about with your binoculars in Britain and many European countries.

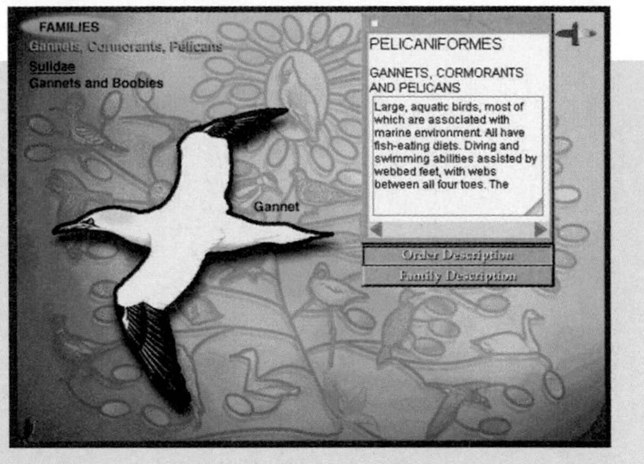

On the Birds of Britain and Europe CD-ROM, clear illustrations and information help you recognize birds. From here you can access more detail on the order and family of any particular bird.

The Jukebox (below) gives you access to bird recordings. The Habitats section on its right relates different environments to the bird life found in them.

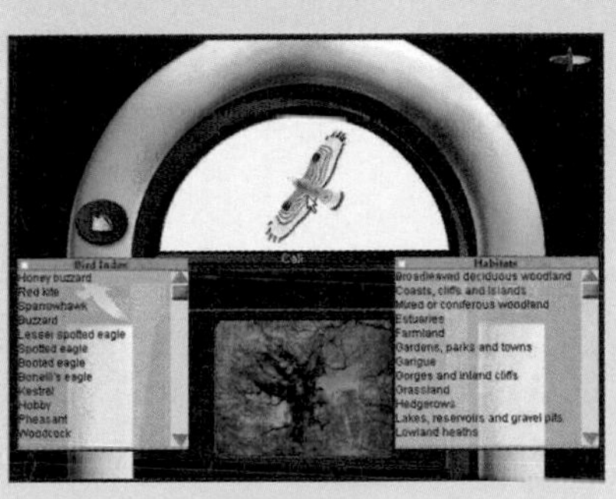

Also on Birds of Britain and Europe, you can get definitions of commonly used terms relating to birds, often with an explanatory diagram. Here (below) we discover what the Tarsus is.

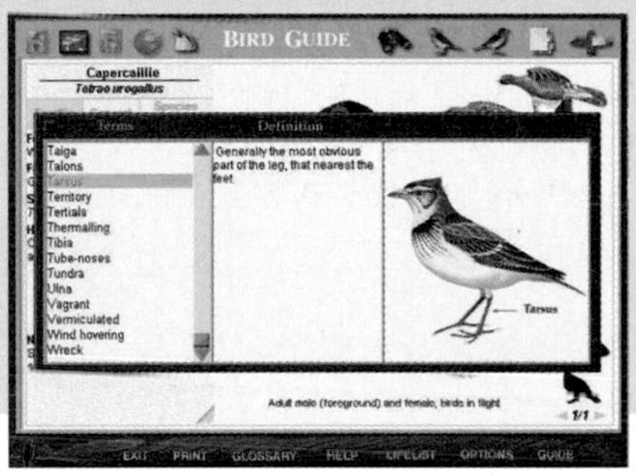

● Authoritative information

The series of CD-ROMs produced by BirdGuides ranges from a single program on common British birds, to a six-CD set of all the birds of Europe. This series concentrates on the presentation of authoritative information. However, this is not to say that the BirdGuides are not slick and professional products; far from it. The clear screen display allows quick and easy access to whatever you want to find. As well as looking up an individual species, you can even split the screen to compare similar birds side by side. You can also play a video, listen to a bird's song and view a distribution map – all at the same time. Illustrations, video and sound are all of extremely high quality, as is the depth of information presented on each bird – which, if you wish, can be listened to as a voice-over commentary. There are lots of extra features that will appeal to serious and non-serious birdwatchers, such as quizzes, a bird search facility and a log to record your sightings.

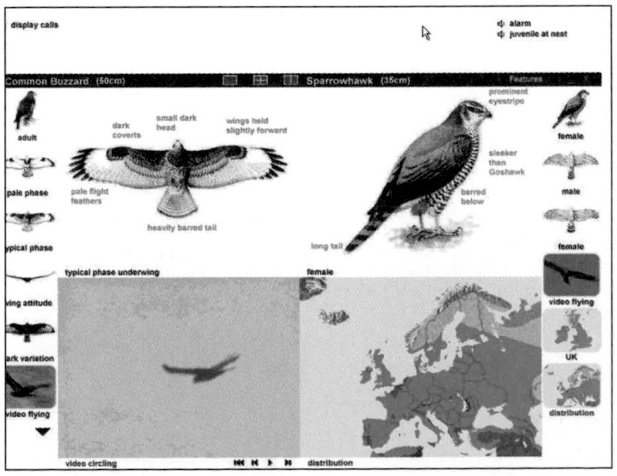

The split-screen approach of the BirdGuides CD-ROMs (left) gives you the opportunity to take in lots of information on one screen. Here we have two illustrations of a sparrowhawk, a video window and a map showing distribution throughout Europe. Further illustrations can be accessed from the list on the right of the screen, while two different sounds can be played by clicking on the speakers (top right of screen).

CONTACT POINTS

Birds of Europe
Focus Multimedia
Tel: 0780 840 4400
Price: £9.99*

AA Interactive Encyclopaedia to Birds of Britain and Europe
BTL
Tel: 0800 389 2795
Price: £19.99*

Beginners Guide to British Birds
Price: £24.95*
The CD-Rom Guide to British Birds
(2 CDs)
Price: £59.95*
The CD-Rom Guide to All the Birds of Europe
(6 CDs)
BirdGuides
Tel: 0800 919 391
Price: £149.95*

*UK prices

The Internet

Parental control programs

For concerned parents who are keen to monitor their children's use of the Internet, filter programs that screen access to certain sites and subjects are a useful aid.

Freedom – one of the Internet's most important assets – is also one of its biggest problems. Adults are at liberty to take advantage of the Net's policy on free speech and all that this entails for the content of Web sites, newsgroups and chat lines. As a result, the Internet offers easy access to plenty of material that is inappropriate for children.

It is highly inadvisable for any child to use the Internet unsupervised because of the danger that they will (intentionally or not) come across something unpleasant. There's no easy way around this problem: the best solution is, as always, to monitor your child's surfing habits personally. But, realizing just how difficult this can be, several companies have come up with filter programs to block access to sites where unsuitable material might be found.

● Filter programs

These filters are small programs that are run automatically whenever you access the Internet. Although they vary in scope, most of the filters can work with Web sites, but also with chat and IRC (Internet Relay Chat) channels, ftp (file transfer protocol) sites, newsgroups and email.

What the filters do is simple. As soon as you log on, they access a CAN'T GO list of 'banned' sites (or other areas of the Internet). They then check the address of any site that is requested against this list.

If the site is there, the user is blocked from entering and the site does not load. Similarly, access is denied if any site contains telltale words or phrases that appear on a master list of offending words.

Usually, each person who uses the family PC is given their own password. This allows the parents to set various levels of access for their children. Only the adult in charge has the authority to change password and access privileges. Using an Internet filter might not be perfect but it is currently the safest way to allow your children to access the Internet when using the computer unsupervised.

● What gets banned?

One problem with censorship is that the banned lists are all drawn up by groups of Americans you've never

FOREIGN LANGUAGE SITES

Since the Web operates globally, you might find yourself asking just how these Internet filter programs can cope with the problems of foreign languages. Not very well, is the answer, although (as usual) the programs err on the side of caution to cope with the problem. Most of the big filter programs do block areas with banned foreign words or phrases. But often these are not checked as thoroughly as English language sites, so many perfectly acceptable sites can find themselves banned as well.

Please enter
your password
to gain access to
this program
GATEWAY2000

Some Internet sites contain material unsuitable for certain surfers, but there are programs that can make these sites, or their content, unavailable.

met, and whose particular areas of concern you may or may not share. Concerns have been raised that many of the filters have a hidden political or religious agenda, although all the monitoring organizations deny this. Still, it has to be said that the tone adopted by some programs does seem to imply a certain moral superiority, particularly as they do not allow you to unblock sites of your choosing.

To counter these worries, some of the filter makers have set up country-specific sites with their own, slightly altered lists, so you can ensure that the censor is of your own nationality and language.

● Updating the filters

There are three ways in which filters are maintained. The first is the main way that most draft lists are drawn up and also the least accurate. The filtering company simply uses special Internet search engines to find sites featuring words or phrases which are deemed restricted, or suggest that restricted content exists on that page. In some cases (if the search engine shows that the site may be a marginal case, for example), the area will be checked manually. But they are often banned automatically until someone tells the list-makers otherwise.

The second avenue is through the creators of unsuitable sites sending notification of their areas' content to the filtering companies (see Self-censorship box, below).

> **SELF-CENSORSHIP**
>
> Not all of the hedonistic sites that are banned by some filter programs are entirely unprincipled. The more responsible sites are well aware that their content is not suitable for children and register themselves with filter lists. By doing so, the sites not only gain a degree of moral high ground, they also make it much harder for people to complain about (or sue) them.

The third system is to set up lists of areas known to be suitable for kids. These so-called CAN GO (as opposed to CAN'T GO) lists are becoming more reliable and more popular – not only with parents seeking to guide their children but also with adult Web surfers wanting to avoid web sites that are not of interest to them.

The problem with controlling Web access is that it's hard to tell, just by using a search engine, whether a site is merely discussing a delicate subject or actively promoting it. All filters block obvious categories such as sexual issues, illegal activities, drugs, bigotry, racism and pornography. However, a Web site that is dedicated to fighting racism or instructing about sexually transmitted diseases often may also end up getting automatically banned until someone updates the lists by hand.

Some, but not all, filter programs allow parents to update the lists themselves. This is perhaps the only really effective way to control what's going on, allowing you to ban sites that you think are offensive and to unblock those that are no problem.

● Monitoring messages

The topics discussed by newsgroups, chat rooms and the like pose another sort of problem. In an open forum, people are free to say anything they like. This can be a major drawback to letting your children participate.

Filter programs deal with such problems in a different way: they are equipped to spot the use of a banned word or phrase instantly. They will then protect the child in a way indicated by the parent – usually by breaking the connection. However, except for special areas designed for children, newsgroups and chat rooms are no place for innocent browsers.

Internet ratings

If you use your browser for filtering which Web sites can be accessed (see page 140), how does it know which sites to allow?

There are two main systems for rating the content of Web sites – SafeSurf and the RSACi. Both are American in origin. Internet Explorer and Netscape Navigator can make use of both systems. SafeSurf (www.safesurf.com) has been monitoring Web sites since 1995, and encouraging them to register with it. Its software, which blocks search requests using banned words or phrases, is used by many Internet Service Providers (ISPs) and a number of family-friendly search engines.

The acronym RSACi stands for Recreational Software Advisory Council, now managed by ICRA (the Internet Content Rating Association). Established in 1999, its goal is to set internationally recognized self-rating standards for Web content.

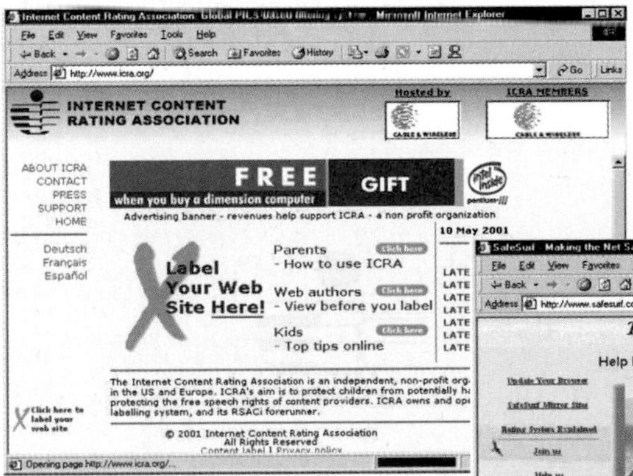

If you visit the ICRA site (left) at www.icra.org you will find tips on using the system in your browser, and also a sample questionnaire for those sites wishing to register.

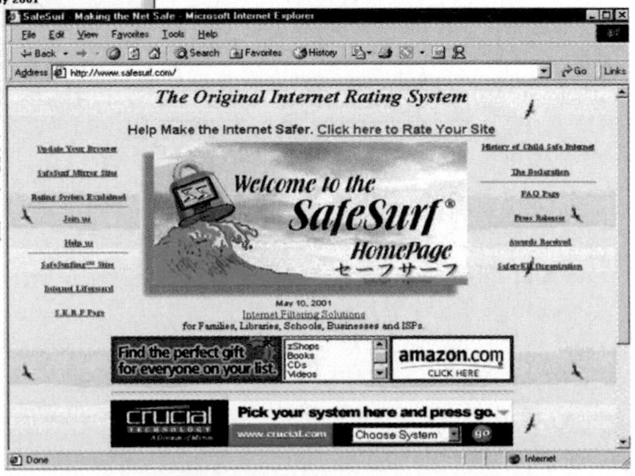

SafeSurf (right) takes a proactive stance, providing regularly updated lists of good, family-friendly sites on its own Web site.

Monitoring with a browser

Although not as good as filter programs, browsers have useful filtering options.

Internet Explorer

1 In Explorer, select Internet Options from the Tools menu, and then click on the Content tab. Click the Enable button in the Content Advisor box near the top of the window.

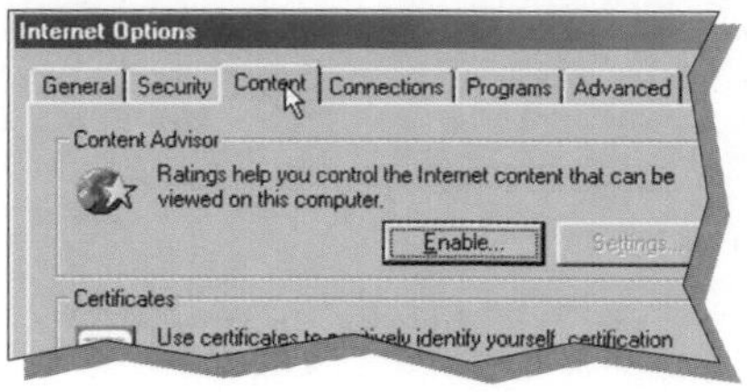

2 There are now four tabs for altering a variety of settings. The first uses the RSACi ratings (see Internet ratings, page 139) to set levels of acceptability for language, nudity, sex and violence. Just select one and move the slider to determine what is or is not allowed. Text in the bottom of the window tells you what you can expect to get at each level.

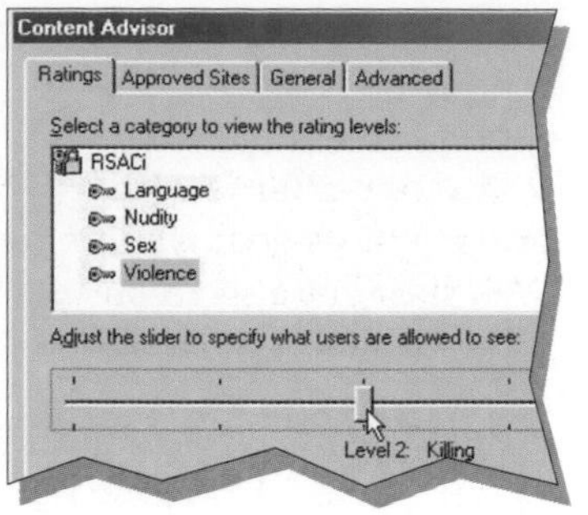

3 The Approved Sites tab brings up a window allowing you to set a list of sites that are always viewable or never viewable. Just type in the URL in the top window and then click Always or Never, as the case may be.

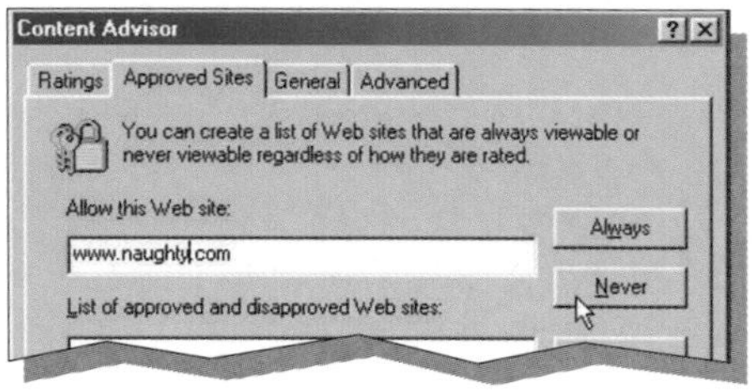

4 The General tab opens a window that allows you to set a variety of options, the most important of which is for setting the Supervisor password. You can change, or turn the content settings on or off at any time.

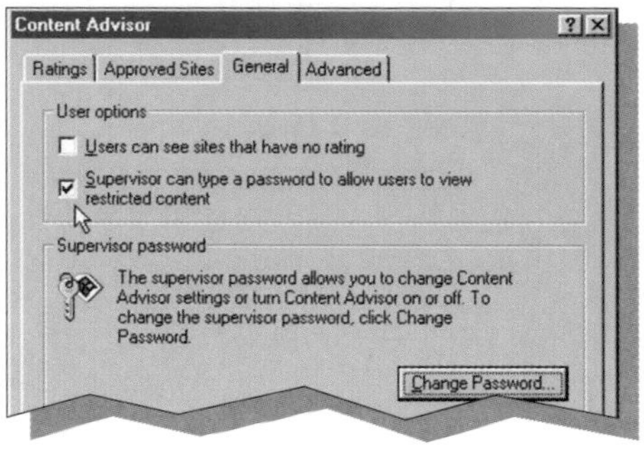

Netscape Navigator

1 In Navigator, connect to the Internet and then select the NetWatch option from the drop-down Help menu. Alternatively, visit www.netscape.com and follow the link.

2 You'll be taken to the Netscape NetWatch site; click the setup icon to continue and then on the next screen – assuming you are a new user – the New User button.

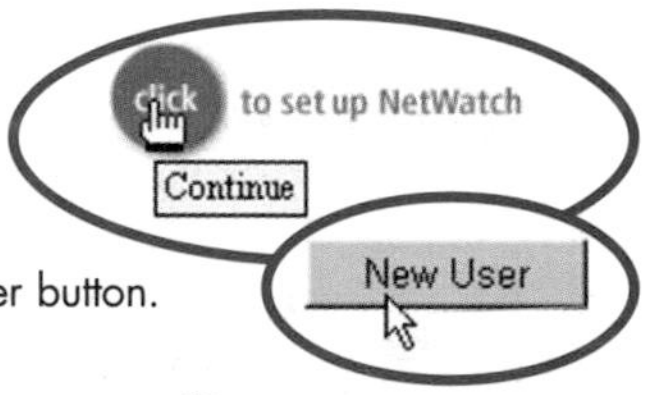

3 NetWatch needs to install a small program – a Java applet – on your computer. Click the Grant button on the pop-up window to allow the download.

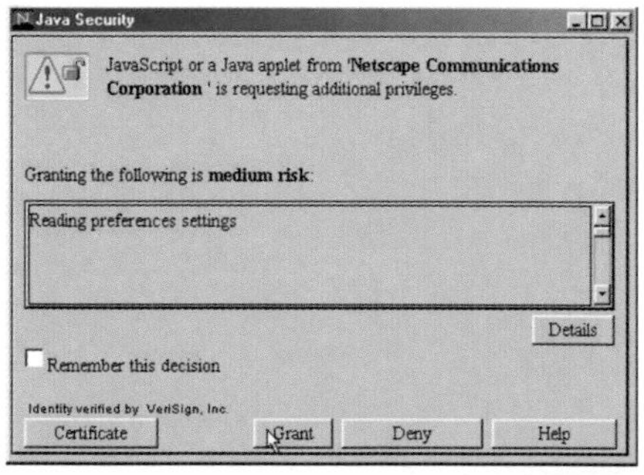

4 Now you are on a scrolling page several screens long where you set up your required options. In the RSACi Rating System area, make sure the Recognize RSACi Ratings box is checked, and then use the drop-down box to select the required level for the various categories.

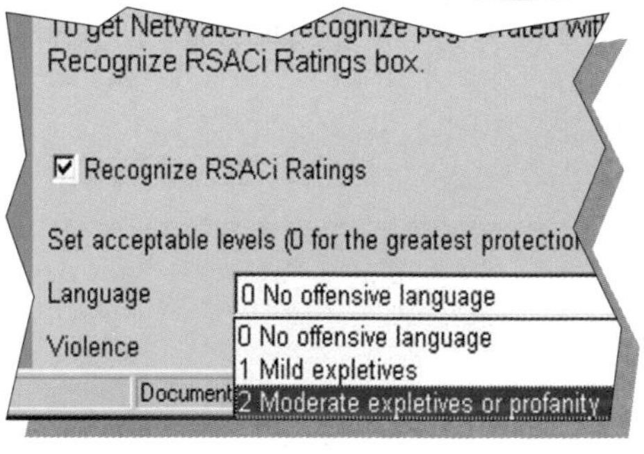

5 Scroll down to the SafeSurf Rating System area. It's a good idea to do the same thing here, to add SafeSurf ratings as well as RSACi.

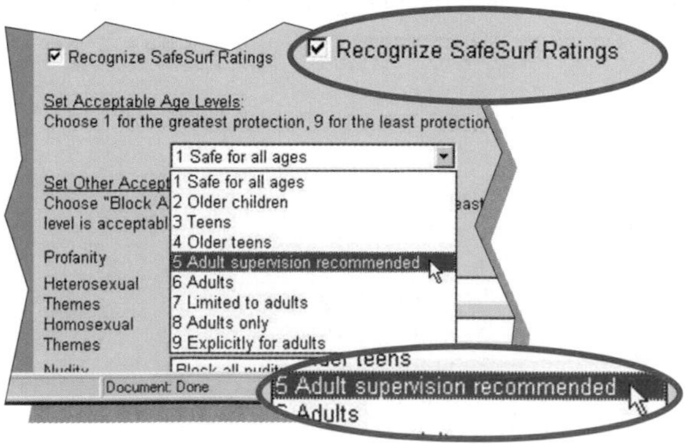

6 Finally, choose a NetWatch password and click the Radio button to turn the system on.

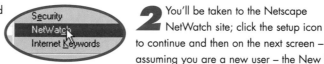

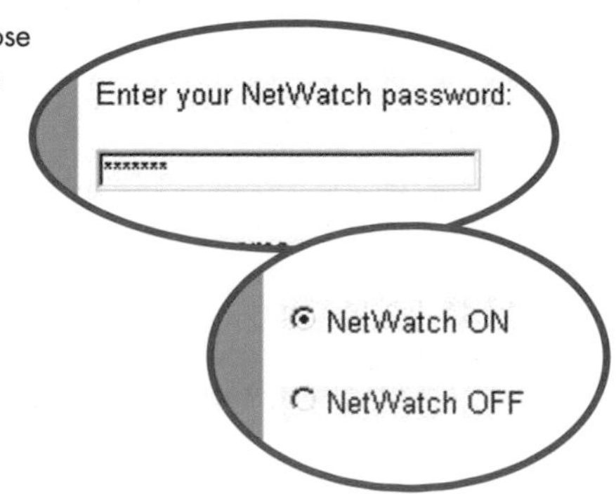

Popular filter programs

Many different filter programs are available for download; here are three of the most popular.

Cyber Patrol

www.cyberpatrol.com

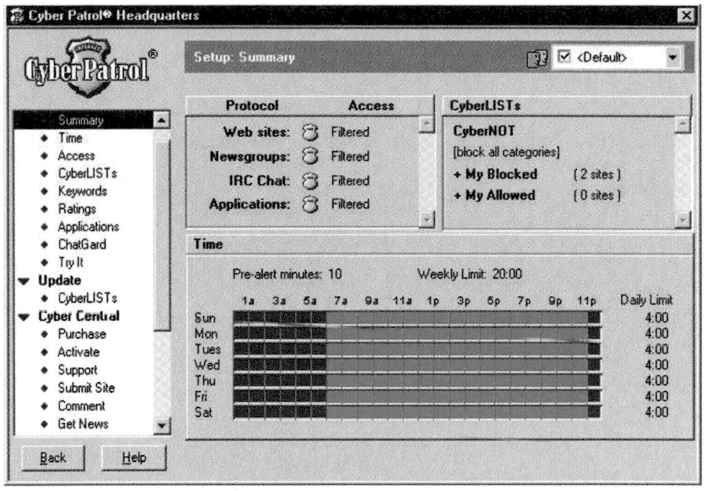

Cyber Patrol's motto is 'To Surf and Protect' and it manages to do so in a far less po-faced way than other such programs. Its goal is not only to prevent access to unseemly Web sites but also to limit when and for how long children can be online. Another subtle difference is that Cyber Patrol goes out of its way to be user-friendly. Some other filters may be just as effective, but they are often very complex and confusingly set out. Cyber Patrol is easier to use than most and comes installed with a set of default features, including YES and NO lists, which most parents can use immediately. The program can still be fully customized, using one of the most comprehensive sets of blocking tools around. You can ban whole categories of content, specific sites and even specific files.

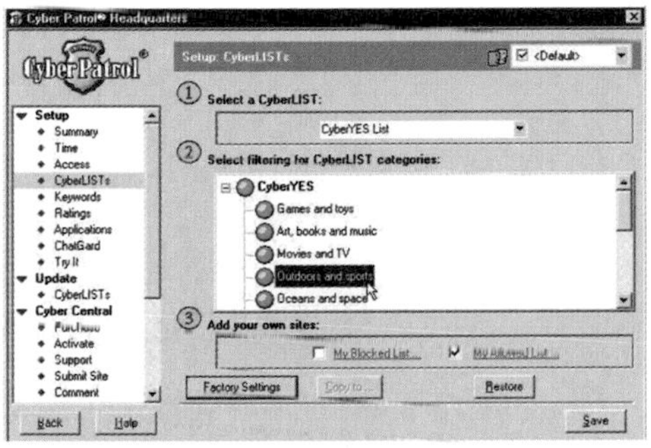

CYBERsitter

www.cybersitter.com

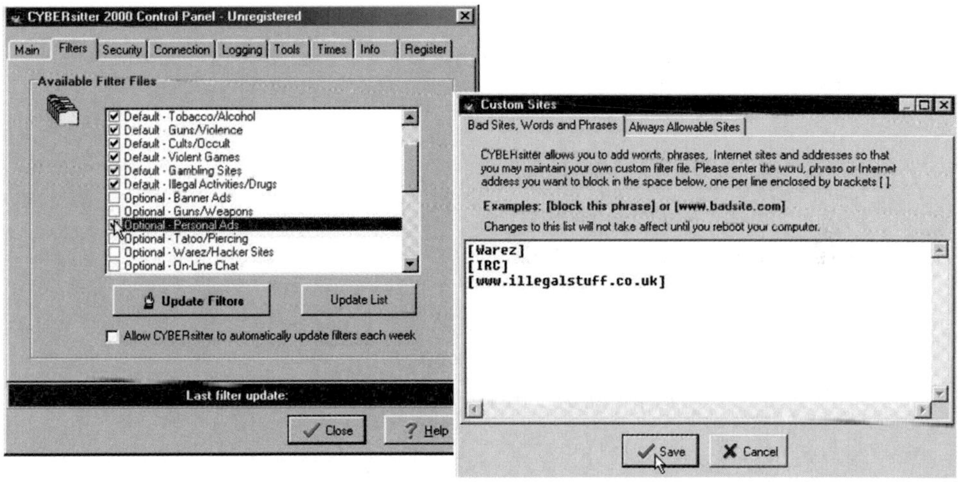

Earlier incarnations of this program came in for some criticism on the grounds of inflexibility; if a site was banned, there was no quick way you could reverse the ban. CYBERsitter is now much more amenable to user input, and you can alter the settings in an almost infinite variety of ways. But the program has lost none of its bite: it's extremely rigorous, allowing you to block just about every possible avenue of objectionable Internet use.

NetNanny

www.netnanny.com

NetNanny takes good care of you, monitoring not just Internet usage but also, if you want it to do so, any activity on your PC. In terms of the Net, it provides you with a number of lists containing blocked sites, as well as words, phrases, chat rooms and so on. You can edit these lists as you wish, adding or deleting sites as appropriate. Note that editing the lists must be the job of a mature adult, since the addresses themselves can be as offensive as the sites they headline. Separate databases of lists with unique passwords can be set up to cope with PCs with multiple users. If you come across a site which has escaped your reach, NetNanny will pop up a window telling you it has detected 'use of unacceptable Words and Phrases'. It's then up to you whether or not to continue regardless, or to add the site to the banned lists.

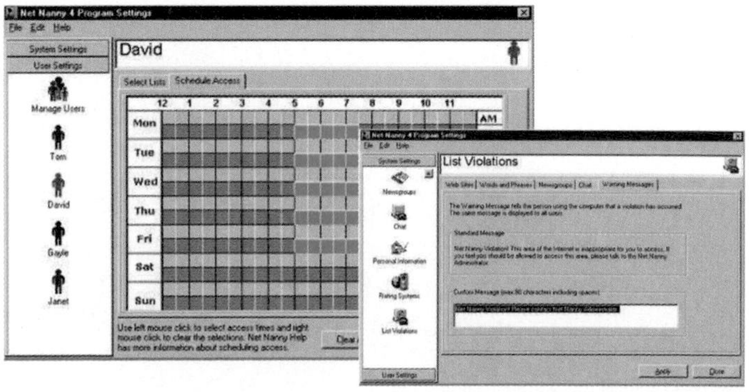

Introducing newsgroups

Where can you get the facts you need to settle a friendly argument? Where should you go when you need professional advice? How can you find new recipes for a dinner party? Newsgroups can provide the answers to all your questions.

You've already seen how to get to grips with two of the most popular uses of the Internet – email (see Stage 1, pages 150-153) and browsing the World Wide Web (see Stage 2, pages 134-137). But there's another popular part of the Internet that millions of people find just as interesting and useful – and that's newsgroups.

Newsgroups provide a way for you to make contact with people all over the world who share your interests. You can ask for advice, exchange experiences, pool information and even participate in debates. It's a little like writing and sending email. The difference is that when you write to a newsgroup (known as making a posting), your message is sent to special computers which everybody who participates in the newsgroup can access in order to read what you've written. Then the members can reply if they want – either by posting a comment to your message (this appears in the newsgroup for everyone else to see) or by sending a private email to you.

● A newsgroup for every interest

There are also newsgroups that specialize in just about every subject you can imagine. Some are devoted to academic debate, while others are for business people. There are also newsgroups for almost every type of hobby, sport and leisure activity. For example, there are newsgroups for gardening, music, cooking, football, UFOs, TV and cinema and keeping animals as pets – and these are just a few of the thousands of subjects.

It's easy to see what a great resource newsgroups offer and how much fun it can be to get in touch with like-minded people anywhere in the world. Newsgroups are free to join: all you need is access to the Internet and an Internet newsreader program.

● Joining a newsgroup

If you have an account with an Internet service provider (ISP), you probably already have everything you need to join a newsgroup. Sometimes the Internet newsreader program is a separate piece of software, but the latest email and Internet browser programs include the facilities needed to access newsgroups. It's simply a matter of taking a few moments to set up your software properly before you try it out (see page 144).

When you send, or post, a message to a newsgroup, it is transmitted to a special computer called a news server. There isn't one big central news server but many scattered all around the world. They are operated by different organizations, such as companies, universities and ISPs. These news servers swap messages frequently, so yours are initially sent to your

Q. How strong a wind can a 747 take-off in?
Q. I've been growing roses for three summers and they've always had black-spot. What can I do?
Q. Is it true there are no freezers in the Savoy Hotel kitchens?
Q. I am visiting Thailand. Which vaccinations will I require?

local news server and then passed on to all the other news servers across the world.

● Know your newsgroups

Each newsgroup covers a particular topic. But newsgroups almost always have cryptic names, so how do you find the right newsgroup for the subject in which you're interested? The first clue usually lies in the newsgroups' strange names. Typically, newsgroup names are made up of several parts, each separated by a full

Q. How strong a wind can a 747 take-off in?

stop. For example, rec.music.beatles is the newsgroup where fans of The Beatles communicate with each other.

As there are so many newsgroups (currently over 30,000, but this number is changing all the time), the Internet community has organized them into a hierarchical structure to keep them manageable. At the top level (the first part of the name), they are split into broad subject areas. For

ALTERNATIVE CHOICES

Newsgroups cover many different subjects and attract all sorts of people. Some newsgroups – especially those in the alt.* group – are aimed exclusively at adults and almost certainly contain material that could be unsuitable for children to see.

Be vigilant and, if you're not sure about a newsgroup, check it out yourself before you let children gain access to it.

FOR ADULTS ONLY

instance, comp contains computing newsgroups, biz has business newsgroups and, as in the previous example, rec (short for recreation) covers newsgroups for hobbies, interests and leisure activities.

● Family concerns

Another set of newsgroups you should be aware of – and wary of if you have children who share your computer – are the alt (short for alternative) newsgroups. These often discuss alternative lifestyle and/or adult material in a frank, sometimes explicit fashion (see Alternative choices below left).

Within each top-level set of newsgroups, you will find subsets. For instance, rec.music is the subset of the main rec heading that contains newsgroups about music. As music itself is such a huge area, you will find many newsgroups within it catering for particular tastes in music. We've already mentioned one example, and others of interest include rec.music.country.western for country music or rec.music.bluenote for jazz fans, plus many more.

● Take your time

Once you have found a newsgroup that seems interesting, the next step is to join it (see page 145). It's a good idea not to wade straight in and start posting messages, however. Read the postings other people make for a while – this will give you an idea of the sorts of things being discussed in the newsgroup. This will also give you guidance on the level of behaviour and politeness other members of the group will expect from you if you join in. Some newsgroups are informal, but others expect certain standards from their members.

When you first join up with a newsgroup, look out for a posting about FAQs (short for Frequently Asked Questions). This is a text file (often just a long message) which will explain the behaviour expected of the newsgroup members, including **netiquette**, and describe the subjects the

WHAT IT MEANS

NETIQUETTE

Netiquette – short for 'network etiquette' – is the widely accepted code of good conduct on the Internet. It has evolved with the growth of the Internet community and wasn't imposed by one individual or organization. It relies on peer pressure to encourage considerate behaviour and to discourage, or even punish, bad behaviour.

One example of poor netiquette is when some unscrupulous users post advertisements to newsgroups: they take advantage of the fact that their posting costs them just a few pennies, although most of their recipients will have to pay to download the message. For this reason, many newsgroups are advertisement-free zones.

newsgroup was set up to discuss. In particular, the FAQ file will provide you with basic information you might want to know. This will help you to avoid asking questions the newsgroup has answered many times before.

● Don't be intimidated

As a final note, some newsgroups can be a bit over-critical of newcomers' mistakes. Don't worry if you are 'told off' by any of the more experienced users. There are some fanatical people who take any breaks in convention or slips in netiquette very seriously. The best thing to do if this takes place is just refuse to be intimidated and use any criticism as a useful learning exercise, which will allow you to get the most out of any newsgroup you choose to join.

Q. I've been growing roses for three summers and they've always had black-spot. What can I do?

Setting up a newsgroup reader

Before you can read and post newsgroup messages, you must first spend a few minutes setting up your newsgroup software to communicate with your Internet service provider's servers and downloading the full list of newsgroups.

1 You don't need to splash out on extra newsgroup software because newsgroups rely on email messages to distribute postings. Windows' own email program, Outlook Express, is perfect for composing and reading newsgroup messages. Double-click on its Desktop icon to start the program.

2 When the program window appears, click on the news entry in the Folders panel on the left of the Outlook Express window. The exact name will vary depending on the ISP you have joined, but it should be at the bottom of the list. If there's no news entry on your computer, see No news? box, below.

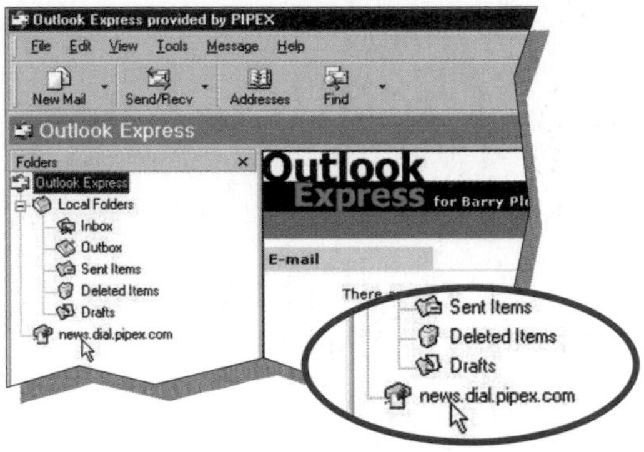

3 If you haven't used newsgroups on your PC before, Outlook Express has nothing to display and it suggests that you start by retrieving a list of newsgroups from the newsgroup server. Click the Yes button.

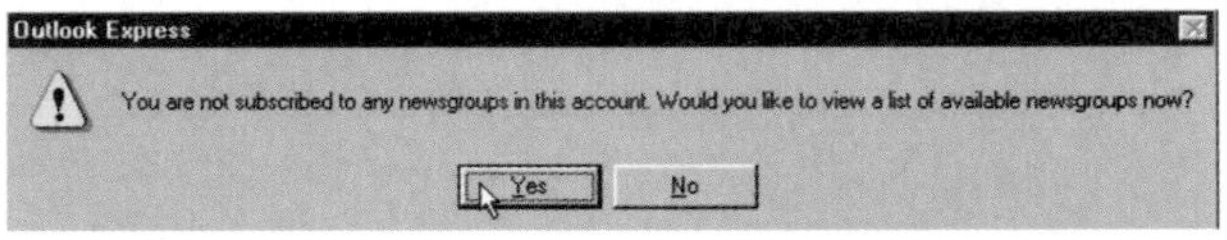

4 Now connect to the Internet when your ISP's dial-up dialog box pops up. When the connection is established, Outlook Express locates the server and starts to download the newsgroup list.

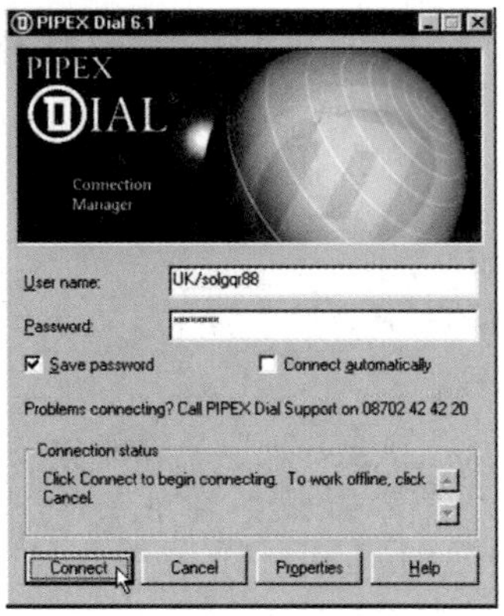

5 Because this is the first time you have connected to your ISP's newsgroup server, there's a lot to download, with over 30,000 newsgroups to choose from. However, at this point Outlook Express is only downloading the names of the newsgroups – not the messages – so the download shouldn't take more than a minute or so.

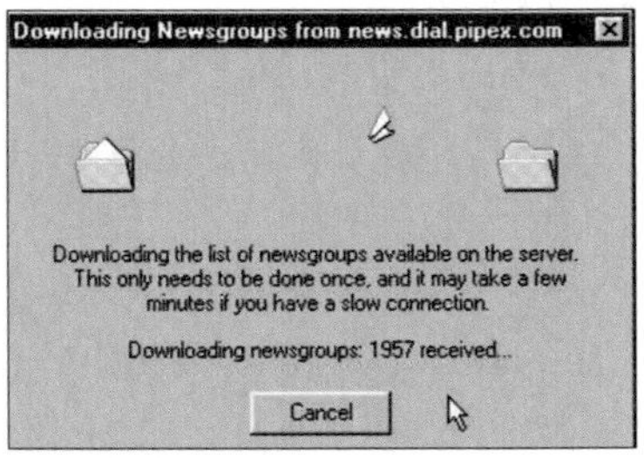

6 Once the list has fully downloaded, it appears in alphabetical order in the main panel of the Newsgroup Subscriptions dialog box. You're now ready to choose which newsgroups to join (see opposite). Note: if your children share your PC, you should be aware that there are lots of newsgroups that cater for adults, and many have very explicit names. Think about installing a parental control program (see pages 138-141).

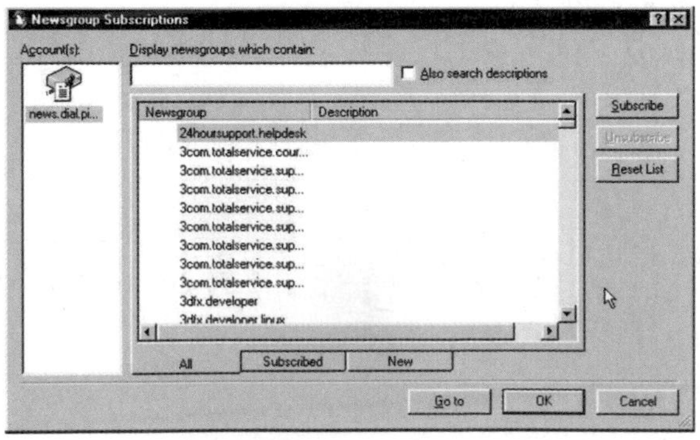

NO NEWS?

Most Internet service providers (ISPs) set up their software so that your PC displays an entry for their own newsgroup servers in the Folders panel (see Step 2). However, some do not, and you may have to set it up manually. To do this, first check your ISP's documentation or Web pages for information about its newsgroup servers. Select Accounts from the Outlook Express Tools menu, click the Add button in the dialog box and then News to enter this information.

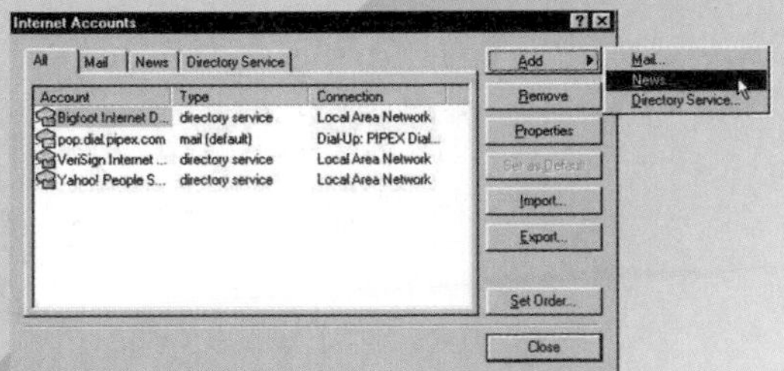

Subscribing to newsgroups and posting messages

There are newsgroups to cover every subject under the sun, and once you have subscribed to one, you can read messages and post your own for other people to comment on.

1 Once you have downloaded the list of newsgroups (see opposite), you're ready to subscribe. It takes too long to look through the whole list, so type one of your hobbies into the 'Display newsgroups which contain' box.

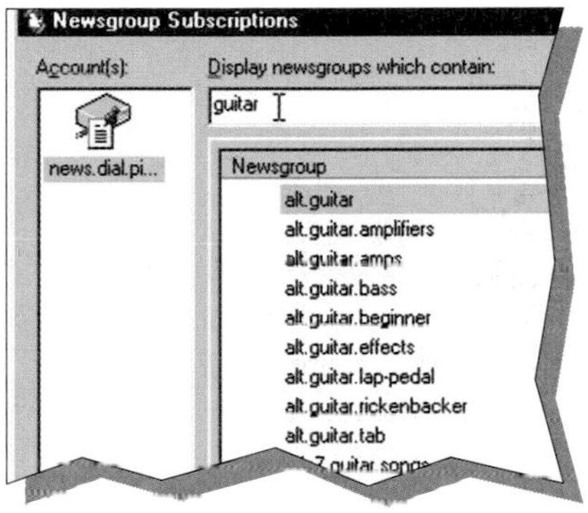

2 Now that the list is much shorter, scroll through and find an interesting sounding newsgroup. Click on it once and then click the Subscribe button. A small icon appears to show that you have marked it.

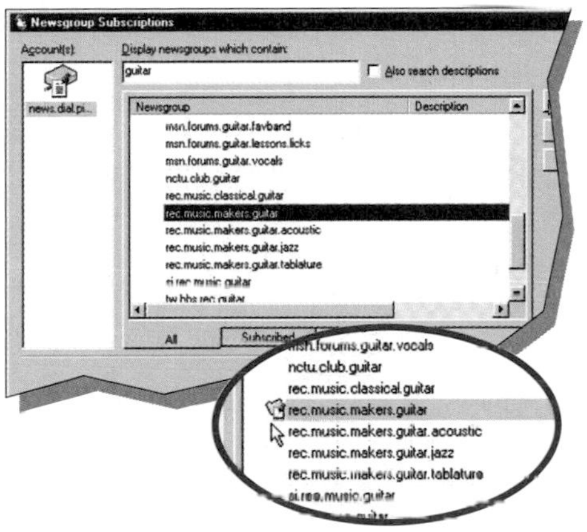

3 You can add more subscriptions, but for the moment, it's worth keeping things manageable by starting with just one. Click the OK button to go back to the main Outlook Express window. To read messages posted to your newsgroup, select your newsgroup, click the Settings button and select New Messages Only. Then click the Synchronize Account button.

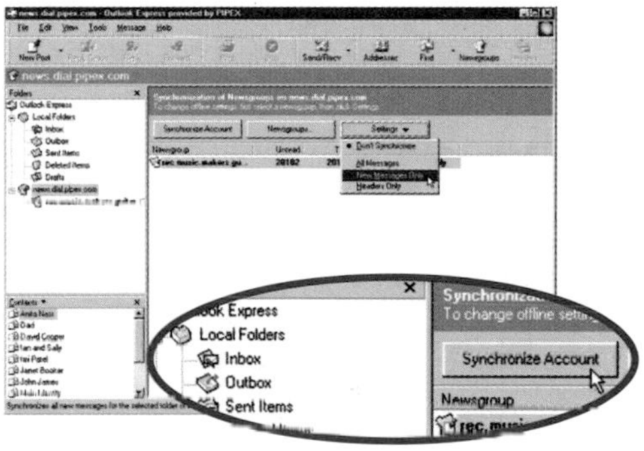

4 Outlook Express downloads the newsgroup messages and displays them. Click on the newsgroup in the Folder panel on the left and the right of the window changes: message titles appear in the top panel, with the text of the highlighted message in the panel below. Click on any message to read it.

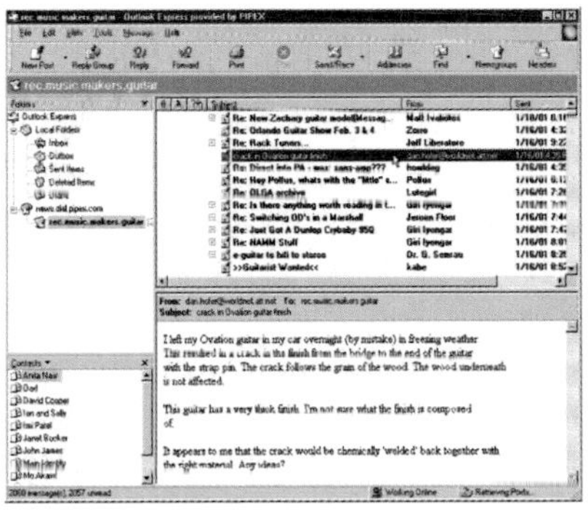

5 When you see a message you want to respond to, click the Reply to Group button on the Outlook Express toolbar. Use the message window to type in a reply just as you would type a reply to a normal email message. Click the Send button when you're done.

6 To start a completely new topic, click the New Post button instead. This pops up a similar message window. Type your message in the same way, but this time, remember to give the message a clear subject – this is vital in busy newsgroups where your message may be easily overlooked.

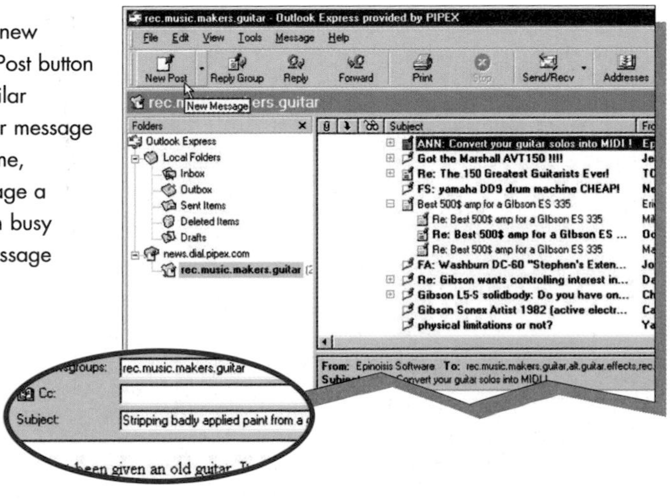

PC TIPS

Newsgroups

When you first subscribe to a newsgroup, there may be several thousand messages to download. This can take time, but it's a good idea to browse through these messages to get a feel for newsgroup netiquette – which can vary from newsgroup to newsgroup – before posting your own questions.

Climate change

Climate covers the underlying trends that make the weather what it is. Today there are many sites on the Web tracking the dramatic changes in both weather and climate that we are now experiencing.

Dramatic changes in the weather worldwide are a symptom of climatic change. The old certainties can no longer be relied upon and global warming may be responsible for shifting the familiar climate zones across the planet.

Recent years have put climate at the forefront of global concerns. The devastation caused by Hurricane Mitch in Central America was one of the most horrifying examples of what the weather can do. It's thought that the climate is changing, so events like Mitch might become more common.

Elsewhere, but particularly in North and South America, there have been droughts, deluges, heatwaves and great freezes which have caused enormous damage to both people and property. Even in Britain, spring 2001 brought extraordinarily high rainfall and flooding in many parts of the country. These examples of 'extreme' or 'severe' weather back up the climatologists' arguments that weather systems are changing and we need to take firm steps on a global basis to counter them.

● Global warming

There are plenty of Internet sites where you can find out about what dramatic weather events are taking place. While there is occasionally a ghoulish side to some of these sites, most present the awesome effects of climate for serious purposes.

The main cause for concern is, of course, global warming. The steady rise in temperatures during this century, largely caused by increasing CO_2 emissions leading to the 'greenhouse effect', is widely accepted to be the underlying cause of much of our extreme weather. Many sites deal with global warming and do so from various perspectives.

● Propaganda sites

Educational sites aim to present a clear explanation of the global warming phenomenon which will make sense to the general public, from schoolchildren to adults. In general, these sites do the job very well, using diagrams and animations and clear text explanations to get the main points across. However, these sites also have what might be called a 'propaganda' purpose: they want to stimulate public demand for more stringent and effective measures to manage global warming. One reason for this is that, despite a series of inter-governmental meetings over the past few years in which the nations of the world attempted to reach an agreement on just how CO_2 emissions could be managed, some countries are still rather reluctant to take the required action.

● Politics and environment

You can find plenty of Internet sites that analyse the agreements made at Buenos Aires and later at Kyoto and outline the progress – or lack of it – that has since been achieved. These sites can be heavy going, since this is a political issue as well as an environmental one. However, if you make the effort, you'll find yourself well clued up on just what we, the human race, are doing about this major change to our planet. While everyone now agrees that global warming is taking place, there are different opinions on how we should deal with it. On one side are those who argue for 'mitigation', believing that we should cut emissions and try to halt, or even reverse, the trend. On the other side are those who argue that we should go for 'adaptation', and learn to live with global warming, taking appropriate measures, such as limiting water use. Both sides are well presented on the Internet, so making your mind up can be hard. Scientists would never have been able to come to any firm conclusions about global warming (or other climatic changes) without a mass of historical climatic data to work on. Much of this data can be found on the Internet, and it's often very accessible and impressive – not always in its presentation, but in the facts themselves. You'll find a wealth of data on the Web for the world's hottest, coldest, wettest or driest places – so whether you are planning a trip or researching a project, the Web is bound to provide the information you need.

Action on climate change

Browsing the Internet will give you some useful background information on climate change, or if you want more detail there are many sites that deal specifically with this subject. Some of the best are featured here.

United Nations Environment Programme

www.unep.ch/conventions

The UN is at the forefront of just about every initiative on global climate change and the various environmental disasters it has caused. Here's where you can find out about the various programmes, such as the Convention on Climate Change, the Convention on Biological Diversity, and the Convention to Combat Desertification. It's all very clearly presented, both on screen and in downloadable .pdf files, which you can study offline at your leisure.

Climate Change Campaign

www.panda.org/climate

This sub-section of the Worldwide Fund for Nature site is both an education and a call for action. It presents a clear and elegant interface that makes it easy for you to get straight to the information you want. If you feel ignorant about the subject, check out An Intelligent Man's Guide to Global Warming (there's a very good reason for the apparently sexist title). Elsewhere on the site there is a comprehensive and constantly changing round-up of global news related to climate change, not all of it, thankfully, bad. The impact on ecosystems and individual species is also presented clearly and powerfully.

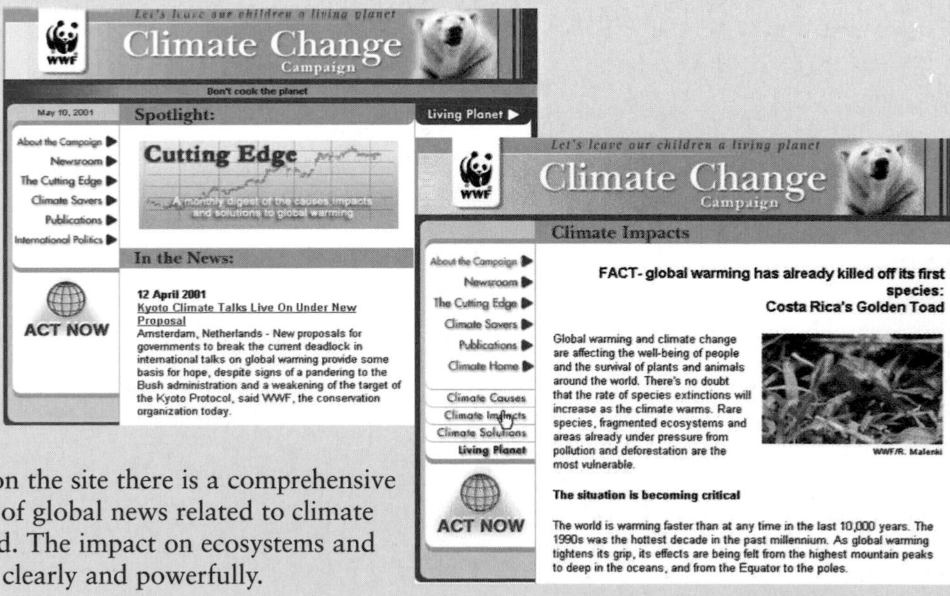

The Ozone Hole Tour

www.atm.ch.cam.ac.uk/tour

Brought to you by the Centre for Atmospheric Science at the University of Cambridge, this site is an object lesson in how to present the results of a scientific study to the general public in an easy-to-understand way. With a host of Multimedia aids, it tells the story of the discovery of the ozone hole in Antarctica and the continuing research into it. There's a lot of detail, but it's all explained with great clarity.

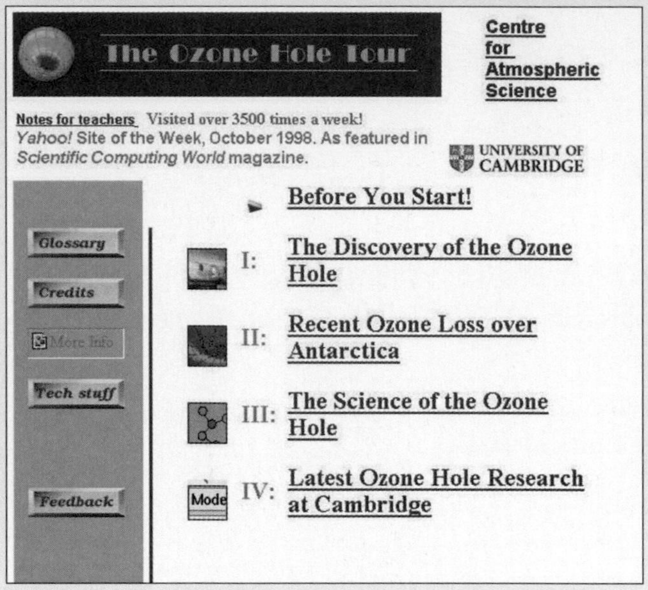

Death Valley

www.ivnet.net/usr/pupfish/default.htm

Death Valley, California, USA, is one of the hottest spots on Earth (see the World Temperature Extremes site at www.iinet.net.au/~jacob/worldtp.html for just how hot) and, as such, this largely tourist-orientated site gives excellent advice on how to cope with the heat for those driving, walking or even playing golf in the vicinity. It's well worth looking at if you're thinking of visiting the valley or any other very warm place.

American Petroleum Institute

www.api.org/globalclimate

If you want to hear a dissenting voice on global warming, this is one of the few sites to present it clearly. The US oil companies don't agree with the current prognosis or cure for global warming. They present their case without hysteria, and with lots of material about what they have done for the US public. They also provide good links to sites that present the opposing case.

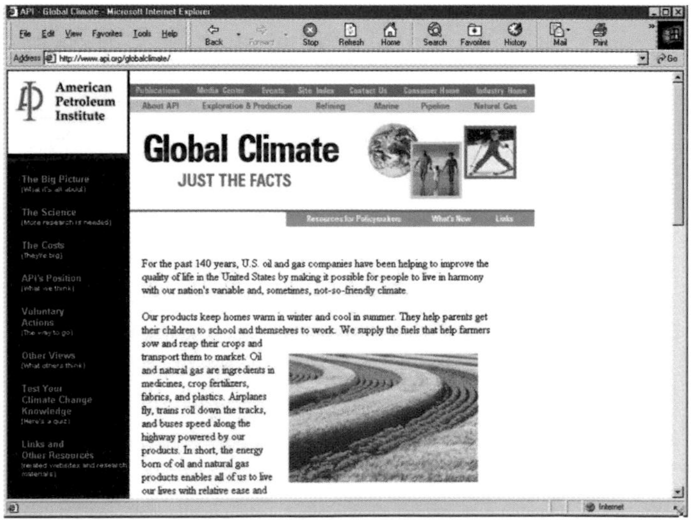

WorldClimate

www.worldclimate.com

This site provides the data that climatologists use to identify whether any long-term patterns are emerging. More than 85,000 records give you an idea of 'what the weather is normally like' – it's not concerned with extremes, but averages. Just type in the name of a place and up comes the relevant data. If you don't know where a place is, click on a link to have it displayed on a map.

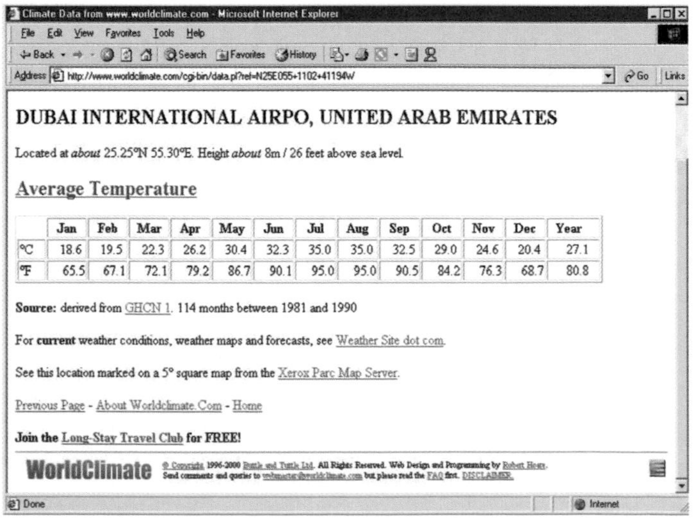

National Oceanic and Atmospheric Administration

www.noaa.gov

The NOAA is the USA's top climatic and weather research body, and has a rich Web site. It contains sub-sections that are worthwhile sites in their own right. You can get access to statistics and research from NESDIS – the National Environmental Satellite, Data and Information Service, and there are fascinating 3D diagrams showing visualizations of live climate phenomena one click away from the main page.

Weather Land

www.weatherland.com

A one-man site that, nevertheless, crams in a lot of weather and climate-related material in an attractive package. There's a great deal of material on the latest storms and hurricanes, a separate hurricane page and a special El Niño page. But perhaps the most attractive element is the live Web cams page, which features a range of sites as diverse as Mount Everest to New York City, so you can check the latest climatic conditions for almost every country in the world.

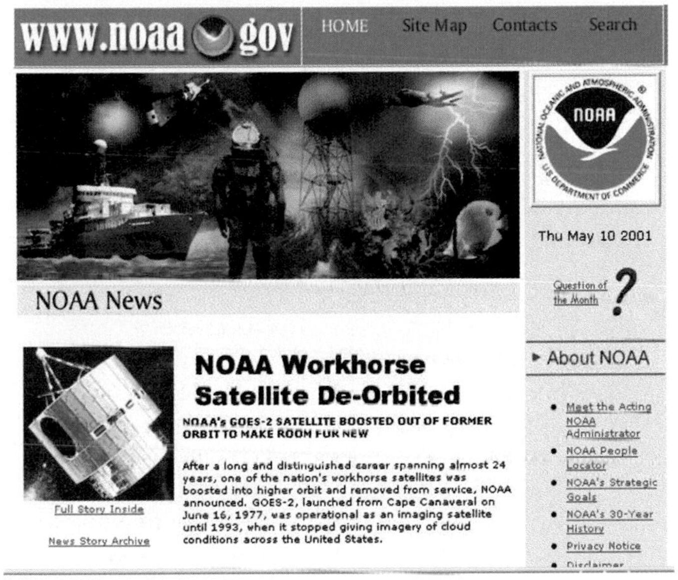

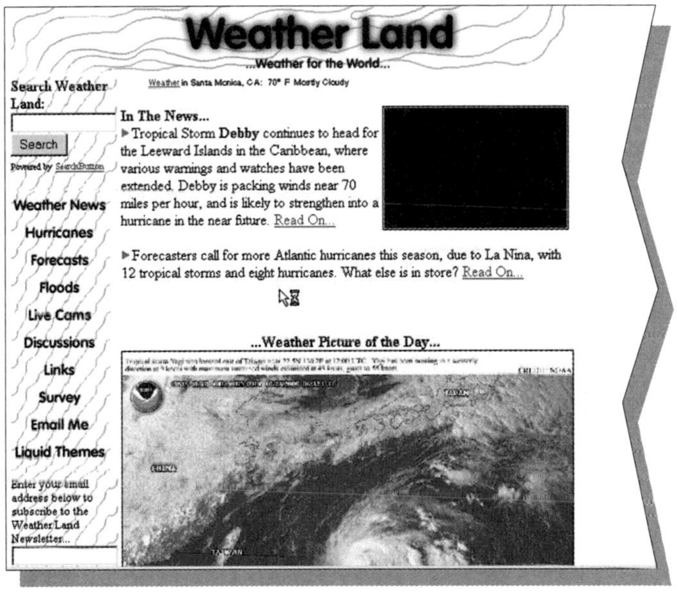

El Niño and La Niña

Many believe El Niño and La Niña are responsible for a wide variety of disastrous weather events in recent years. This Web site explains why.

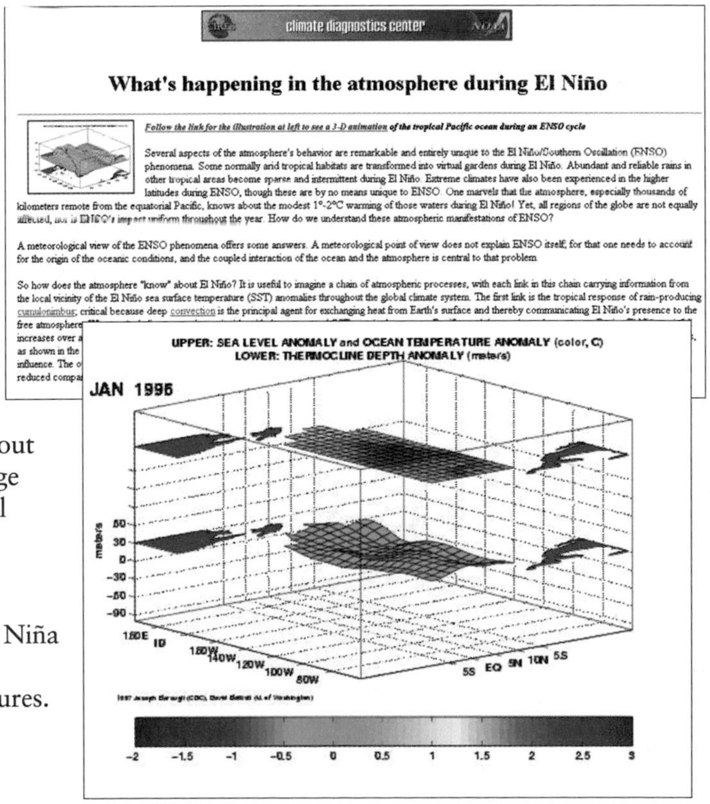

www.cdc.noaa.gov/ENSO

El Niño causes disruption of ocean-atmospheric patterns in the Pacific Ocean and is thought to be responsible for a wide variety of disastrous weather events in recent years. The El Niño page provides just about the best introduction you'll find on the Web to this strange phenomenon. There are excellent explanations of what El Niño is, together with colourful diagrams and maps, and there's even an animation that you can watch.

The NOAA (National Oceanic and Atmospheric Administration) does a similarly successful job on the La Niña phenomenon – which is comparable to El Niño, but is characterized by cold, rather than warm, ocean temperatures. This site tells you all you need to know about these fascinating forces, but it also provides excellent links to other sources of information.

Online shopping

Internet shopping has evolved rapidly in its brief lifespan as traditional retailers have moved from 'bricks to clicks' to challenge the Web's innovators.

If going to the shops drives you mad, try Internet shopping and you'll never have to walk the supermarket's aisles again. With secure means of ordering and paying, there's nothing to stop you going virtual shopping.

In the beginning of online shopping were the innovators, such as Amazon (www.amazon.co.uk), online sellers of books originally, but now selling CDs, videos, and just about everything else. From a standing start, such outfits grew incredibly fast, using the vast amounts of venture capital they had raised to launch sites in all major world languages and to offer tempting discounts on many items. They also developed the technologies, techniques and systems that make online shopping work for the consumer: easy registration, virtual shopping carts, safe transmission of credit card data and prompt home delivery of the physical item.

Traditional retailers were at first left behind, but it has not taken them long to catch up, and they are now beginning to dominate the online shopping universe. This is clearest in the field of groceries, where Britain's supermarkets have invested substantially in Web sites for home shopping, along with the delivery services to get your goods to you. In fact, Tesco claims to be the world's largest online grocery service.

Buying your groceries and drink online is a very attractive proposition for many of us, but before you rush to log on and order the baked beans and kitchen roll, you first have to check that you are eligible in terms of where you live. Such online services always begin in the heavily populated urban areas before spreading out to the regions and countryside. All the supermarkets have 'postcode checkers' so you can find out in a click if they can deliver to you.

Catalogue companies seem an even better fit with the Internet than supermarkets. And there are distinct advantages for them on the Web; as access to the Internet increases, fewer catalogues will need to be expensively printed and mailed. And the Web allows catalogue retailers to alter stock and prices almost instantly. Britain's traditional catalogue companies already have a strong Internet presence; but opposite we take a look at French giant La Redoute, too.

At the same time, high street fashion and clothing companies are also building Web sites that have something of a catalogue feel, as in the case of Top Shop and Marks & Spencer (see page 152).

● Techno beats

New technology implies radical change in both what and how we buy.

SECURITY

The security of any financial details you divulge online has been a major concern since the early days of the Internet, and it's not going to go away. All reputable online shopping sites use powerful data encryption techniques to scramble your data, and will make it clear on their home page that they do so; if there is no statement about security, then steer clear of the site. While encryption does not guarantee absolute safety, it is pretty effective, and makes online shopping no more dangerous than giving your card number to a salesperson over the telephone. What encryption cannot do, however, is insure against human error; most notorious breaches of Internet security occurred where someone made the mistake of putting a secret file (with customer names, addresses and credit card details) in an unprotected area of a Web site, where anyone could stumble across it.

This is particularly true wherever a product can be delivered digitally. For example, with shareware all you have to do is log on to a Web site, give credit card details and download a program straight to your hard disk. But it is in the field of music where this is having the most effect. The digital MP3 format (see MP3 sites, right) allows consumers to download an almost CD-quality song in only a few minutes, which has led to a boom in sites that sell (illegally) performers' work or let fans swap audio files.

● Is the price right?

Checking who has the best deal on an item can be a time-consuming chore. But a relatively new breed of site promises to take the legwork out of online shopping. You simply type in the item you want and the site's software gets to work, trawling the online retailers and reporting back with sites and price comparisons (see page 152).

MP3 SITES

MP3 stands for MPEG Layer-3, a compression technique that can reduce a CD music file to half its previous size. Because the resulting files are smaller, they are ideal for sending over the Internet. Despite court action in the US against some sites offering MP3 files, there are still plenty of legal sites around.

For example, iCrunch (www.icrunch.com) offers a huge range of tunes from independent labels at 99p per download. You can preview tunes online and then buy one at a time or get a collection. And there's plenty of additional content, such as chat rooms and a beginner's guide, to give the site more depth. BeSonic (www.besonic.com) isn't really involved in online shopping. Rather, it's more of a showcase site where unsigned artistes in pretty much every genre of popular music can display their wares. Downloads are free in return for your email address, which is used to compile the download charts.

Shopping lists

Some are born to shop, others tag along behind looking bored. But, with online shopping you can shop from the comfort of your home.

Haburi

www.haburi.com

If you want designer clothes and accessories without paying designer prices, take a look at the Haburi Web site. This site works like an international factory outlet store: you get a mix of designer brands with typical discounts of 25% to 60%. There are even greater savings to be had on the clearance sales pages. If you're worried that you may be tempted to spend more than you can afford, once you have chosen a clothing category, you can use the price range filter so that the high-ticket items are safely hidden from view. To get a fashion edge over your friends, join Club Haburi and receive advance notice of special offers and a personalized Haburi shopping page. As you expect with online shopping, there's a good returns policy and free shipping once you're spending £50 or more.

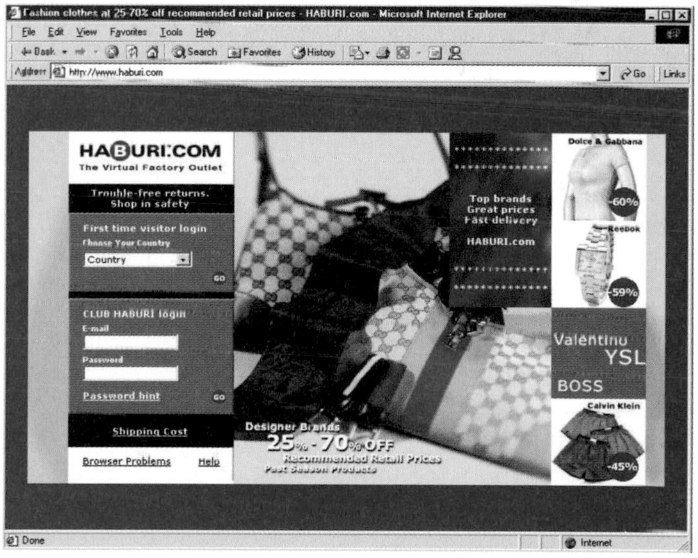

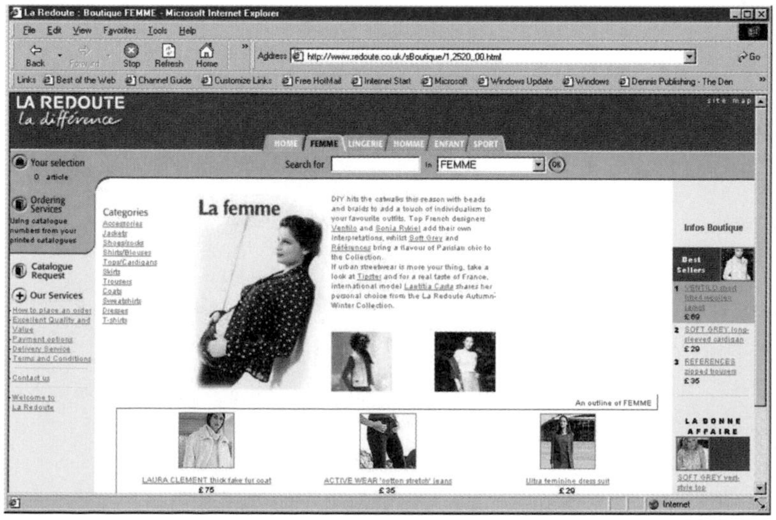

La Redoute

www.redoute.co.uk

Mounting a stylish French challenge to the UK's traditional catalogue powerhouses is La Redoute. Its online store is well stocked with clothes for all members of the family. Special discounts and prizes are also featured on the site, and the ranges are smart and tempting throughout, whether moderately priced or from swanky designers, such as Sonia Rykiel. Delivery takes 5–10 days and costs £2.45, no matter how many items are ordered. And – as should be the case for all clothing sites – returns are free.

Marks & Spencer

www.marksandspencer.com

As they have jazzed up their high street stores, so M&S have revamped their Web site to make for a more pleasing shopping experience. There's a good range of clothing on view for men, women and children. A particularly good point is that all images are enlargeable, so you can see exactly what you'll get. Delivery is promised in 48 hours for a £2.95 fee and all returns are free of postage (or you can take them to your nearest store). They'll also give you a full no-quibble refund.

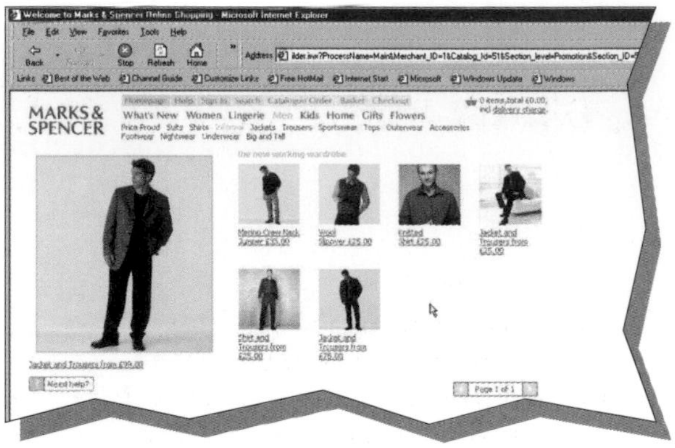

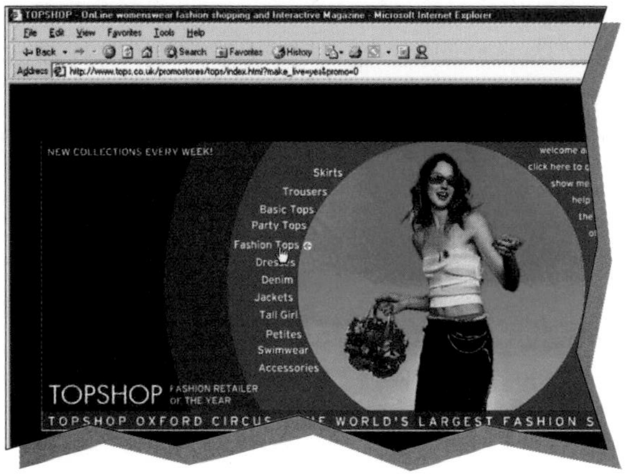

TopShop

www.tops.co.uk

The young follower of fashion on a budget is unlikely to find a more action-packed site than this one. Here you don't simply buy goods, you take part in a lifestyle experience. There's masses of fun content – interactive dating, guides to the latest trends, competitions and quizzes. In fact, there's so much on the site that it can be a bit of a trek to find your way to the clothes themselves. When you do, you'll find that they are presented in a fizzy youthful manner. The site is divided into categories, covering everything the party girl needs, from top to toe – including the all-important accessories. There's even a section to cater for taller girls. Older shoppers might find the site a little brash, but then it's not aimed at them.

Price comparison

Just key in the name or type of product and 'intelligent' software will scour the Web, reporting back instantly on who is charging what, where and for how much.

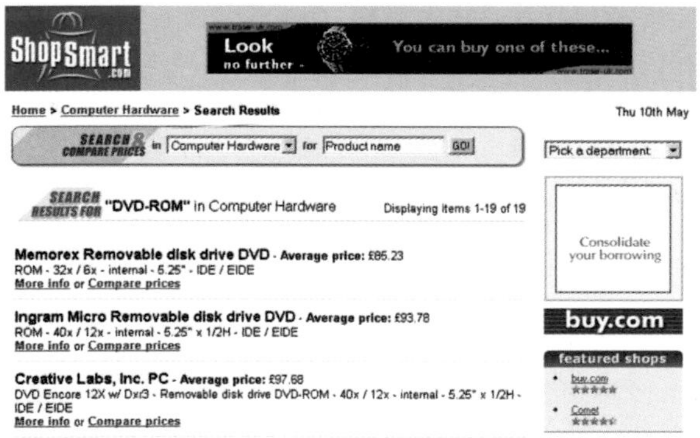

ShopSmart

uk.shopsmart.com

This is one of the longer established and higher profile UK sites. The price comparison side works well and quickly shows the prices of books, videos, CDs, computer games and consumer electronic items. Just go to the site offering the cheapest deal. ShopSmart offers more than just comparison – listing and rating hundreds of online stores in a wide range of categories. The comments are intelligent and far from uncritical, and browsing the site will inevitably throw up dozens of Net stores you'll want to visit.

Kelkoo

uk.kelkoo.com

This site also aims to offer both a shopping guide and price comparisons. There are product reviews as well as shop details, and its comparisons extend to include computers, hi-fi and some household goods, along with the other usual categories. As these sites mature they will be able to offer increasingly more serious and credible price comparisons on a huge range of goods and services. At the moment, they're limited in scope, but still very much worth using; you could save as much as £5 on a single hardback book.

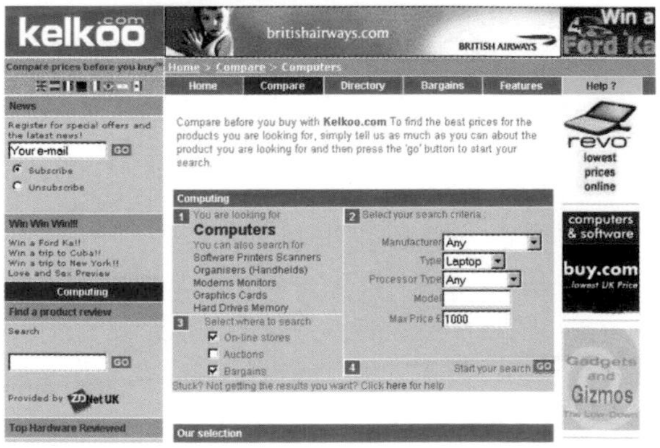

Supermarket sweep

After initial scepticism, the supermarkets have embraced online shopping in a big way, selling not just groceries but a wide range of other goods, too.

Tesco

www.tesco.com

Tesco offers the online shopper a vast range of goods in addition to its grocery range. You can buy books, videos, electrical equipment and even financial products. The site is colourful and easy to navigate and although there is a lengthy registration process, it does make return visits much quicker and easier. Delivery costs £5 and there's a wide range of time slots to choose from, up to 10pm on weekdays.

Waitrose Direct

www.waitrose.com

This site is a little peculiar, in that you can buy everything from organic vegetables and flowers to CDs but not, it seems, straightforward groceries. Nevertheless, if you are interested in organic food, their selection boxes are tempting. A 48-hour delivery service throughout the UK costs from £4.99 per box.

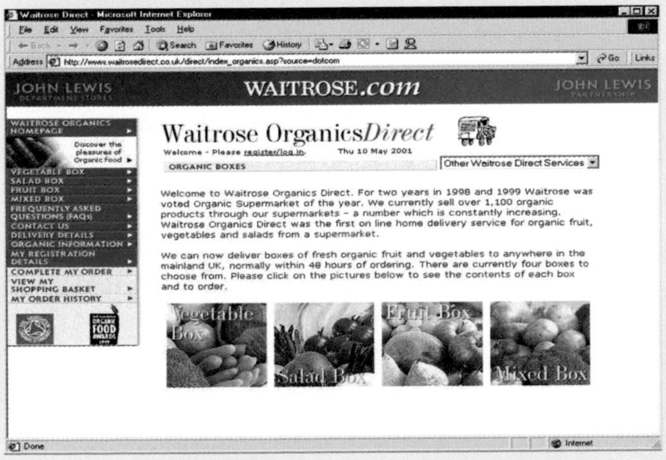

Asda@thome

www.asda.co.uk

Once you have registered, having inserted your postcode and chosen a PIN, you can look through the store's virtual aisles or search for particular items. Everything is listed in text, with very few graphics, which makes online shopping a quick, if rather uninspiring, affair.

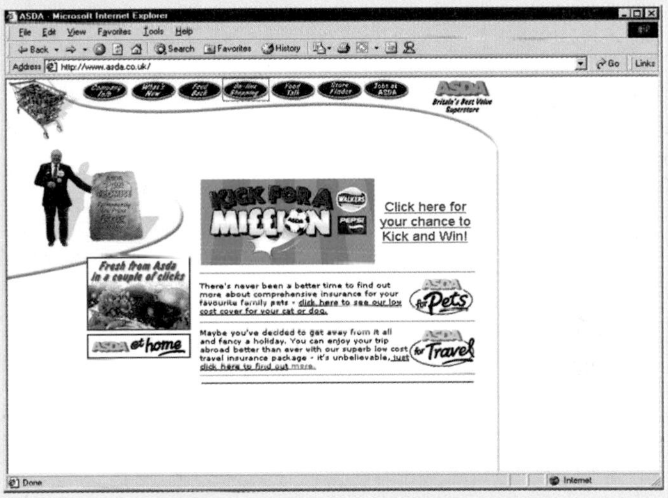

The Sainsbury's To You site

www.sainsburystoyou.com

It can take as long as four or five minutes to load but thereafter is easy and quick to use. There's a straightforward postcode check to see if you are in an appropriate area. If you don't have time to browse the extensively stocked virtual aisles, you can zoom around with a Sainsbury's List – a trolley of pre-selected popular items – and then modify its contents. And you can book a delivery slot up to three weeks in advance.

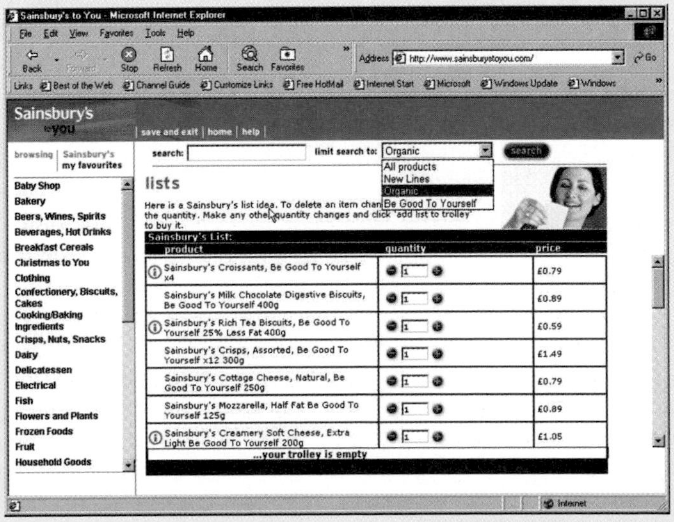

Antiques and collectibles

The current interest in antiques, collectibles and treasured 'junk' is phenomenal – and the Internet hasn't been slow to promote or exploit it.

Ever since the UK television show *Going for a Song* made a star out of the elderly antiquarian Arthur Negus, antiques have been a topic of enduring interest – even for those of us who don't have the necessary financial resources to buy a Meissen figurine or a Chippendale chair. That popularity has been reinforced by other British TV programmes, such as *The Antiques Roadshow* and *Lovejoy*, which make us all wonder if we haven't got something of value tucked away in the attic. This widespread interest is, unsurprisingly, strongly reflected on the Internet.

As it does with many subjects, the Internet offers you a range of opportunities with regard to antiques: you can further a practical – perhaps, professional – interest by buying and selling online; the casual antiques fancier can broaden his or her knowledge by tapping into the large amounts of expert information available; and the rest of us, the armchair fantasists, can simply indulge our idle curiosity, gawping at the beautiful, strange or simply very expensive objects on view.

WHAT IS AN ANTIQUE?

There's no hard and fast definition of what an antique is, but it's generally accepted that an object must be over 100 years old to qualify. Even then, however, we need to make allowances. There's a lively trade, for example, in antique or 'classic' wristwatches – and these didn't exist 100 years ago. Very old and rare items dating back many centuries – or even millennia – are known as antiquities. While there's a lot of excellent material about antiques on the Web, there's much less about antiquities, possibly because there are not so many about to buy.

Antiques dealers can provide a global shop window for their stock by using Internet Web sites.

● Things to collect

As well as antiques, there's a further category of objects which it is appropriate to include here – 'collectibles'. These are more modern items, often taken from popular culture, such as film posters, pop memorabilia, and even *Wallace and Gromit* spin-off merchandise from the animated films. The term refers to anything that people collect, since as soon as a number of people value a certain type of object, you can guarantee that lively trading will start in it. Nowadays, an Internet community will be formed seemingly overnight to support such an interest.

So whether your interest is at the Sotheby's or *Star Wars* end of the market, you'll be well served on the Web. The major international auction houses are there, with elegant and authoritative sites, offering everything from background material and historical explanation to, of course, exhaustive details of their present, past and forthcoming sales. The Sotheby's Web site is a good example.

Many smaller antique dealers have also set up Web sites which serve as a shop window for their wares. But because of the nature of the goods they sell, these online catalogues are often an excellent source of information about any given area of antiques, providing detailed descriptions of the object, and very often a photograph as well.

If you want to buy and sell, rather than window-shop, the Internet doesn't disappoint. Online auctions are increasingly popular, giving you the chance to get hold of objects that you might otherwise never have known about, from far-flung lands you would probably never visit. You simply type in your bid and wait to see if you are the winner. The Web is now so vast and so lively that, whatever the object of your collecting passion, you're sure to find it somewhere, either by using a search engine or by browsing among the antique sites.

Visiting antiques sites

No matter what your level of interest, you can still bid for an Old Master or find a missing Teletubby.

Architectural Heritage

www.architectural-heritage.co.uk

These days it's not just objects but entire buildings – or at least parts of them – that can qualify as antiques. This site sells 'original and antique garden ornaments, chimney-pieces and panelled rooms' for you to buy to create a noble country-house look in your home. Typical items include an English 17th-century oak-panelled room, a stone faun for the garden and a 17th-century limestone chimney-piece. It's a lovely collection of objects, all of them illustrated; a click expands each picture to give you a better idea of what it looks like – and what you might be buying.

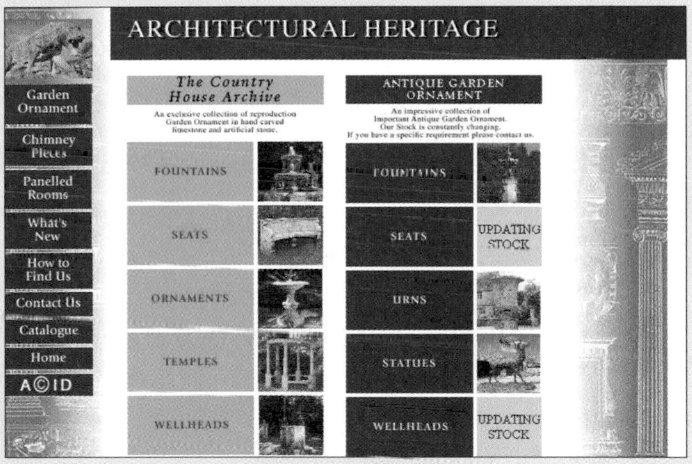

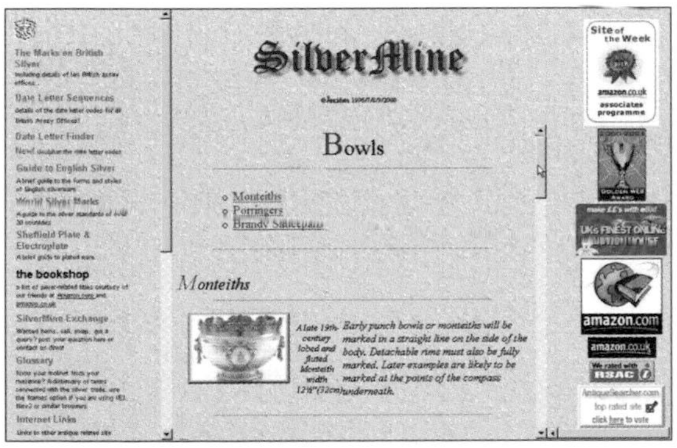

SilverMine

freespace.virgin.net/a.data/

If silver is your fancy, then you really should visit this informative site. Its core is a guide to British silverware, complete with historical overview and notes on the development of styles and forms such as cruets, teapots and so forth. There's a detailed listing of marks from the ten British assay offices, as well as information on silver marks from around the world. There's also an Exchange area, where you can buy, sell, swap, or merely ask questions. All the pictures are in black and white, but that doesn't detract at all from the quality of this site; after all, there's not a lot of colour in silver.

Antiqueweb

www.antiqueweb.co.uk

This is an umbrella site, bringing together a number of UK dealers and events under one roof. The main point of interest for the UK antiques fan is its comprehensive listing of antique fairs. Although the site is based in Lancashire and has a good coverage of the north, its listings also provide a comprehensive nationwide resource of what's on where and when.

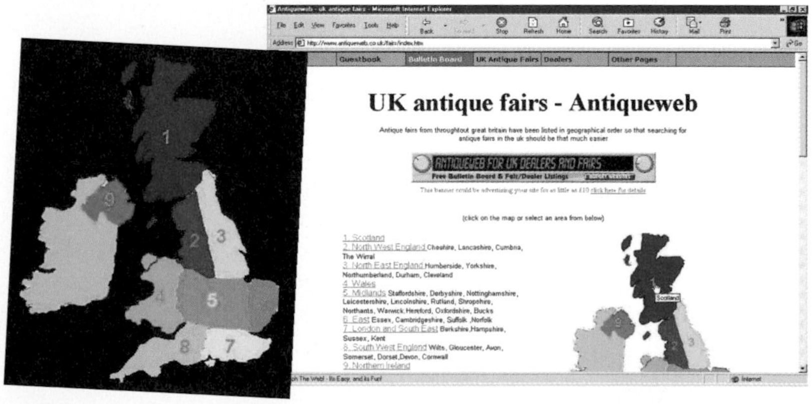

Antiques World

www.antiquesworld.com

The site 'where antiques and collectibles buyers and sellers meet on the Internet' is the claim, and it appears to be true to its word. The aim of the site is to put buyers and sellers in touch with each other, and its core is the Marketplace section, essentially a Wanted and For Sale classified advertising area. It seems to be very popular and the powerful search engine brings up plenty of good results.

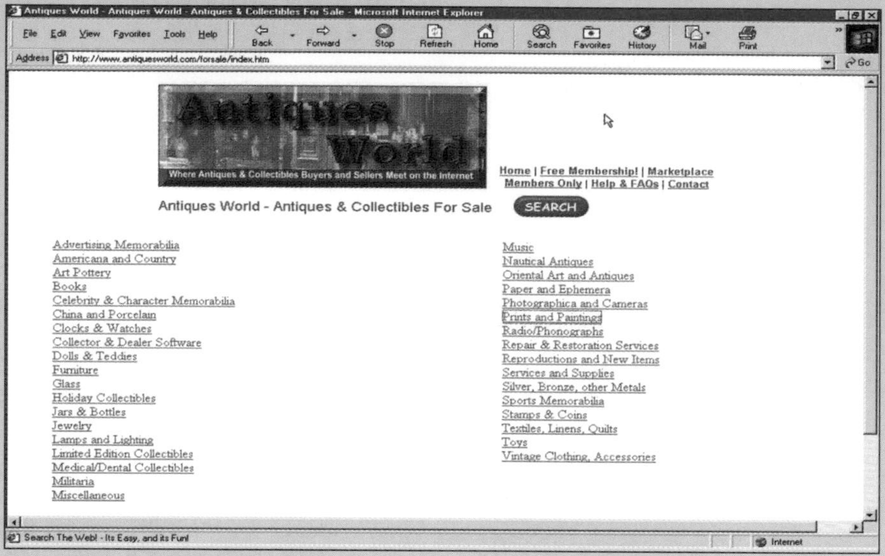

ONLINE AUCTIONS

Online auctions take place for all sorts of things, but they're particularly popular in the world of antiques and collectibles. Unlike a real auction, you don't bid against others in real time; instead, you examine the lot (which, of course, is not exactly foolproof if you're looking at a picture on a screen), and then submit whatever you think is an appropriate bid. On some sites – such as eBay – you can use a facility known as 'proxy bidding', whereby you submit the maximum price you're willing to pay and the increments by which your bid may increase; the software then ups your bid if others put in a higher one, until you reach your limit. Auctions are exciting ways to buy, but they can also be dangerous, because it's easy to get carried away in the thrill of the chase. It's wise to check out the site to assure yourself of its trustworthiness, and it might be worth emailing a request for testimonials. Also, remember that a bid at auction is a 'binding and irrevocable offer to purchase': if your bid wins, you have to go through with it.

Sotheby's

www.sothebys.com

This is a predictably impressive and suave site with a wide variety of online auctions of classy art and antiques. These are backed up by expert articles on collecting everything from art to fine wine, or even 1950s Italian jewellery. It also lists all the marks of eminent makers of silver and china.

Kool Collectables

www.koolcollectables.com

This UK company specializes in collectibles from popular movies and TV programmes – *Star Trek*, *Star Wars*, *Harry Potter* and the *Wallace and Gromit* films, to name but a few. The dolls, toys, laser wands and other bizarre spin-off merchandise from such productions rapidly become sought-after collectors' items. This site offers the ideal opportunity to complete your collection of, for example, *Star Wars* figurines, or simply to find out what the old junk in the toy-chest might be worth nowadays.

eBay

www.ebay.co.uk

eBay is one of the most successful of Internet start-ups. It's the original online auction business and is worth a fortune. It's not hard to see why it's so popular, and why it has spread its operations from its California base to many other countries. There's just so much stuff on eBay, in every possible category – and that holds true for the antiques and collectibles section. On the UK site there are thousands of items listed clearly under categories that range from writing instruments to fridge magnets, kitchenalia, and many other odd objects. It's fascinating stuff for the idle browser, but absolutely essential for the collector, whether buying or selling.

Objects are listed with a brief description, the closing date of the auction, and the current highest bid. Most also have a photograph. To bid for an item you first have to register, then simply go ahead and enter your price. eBay will even carry out 'proxy bidding' for you to your pre-set upper limit (which no other bidders can see).

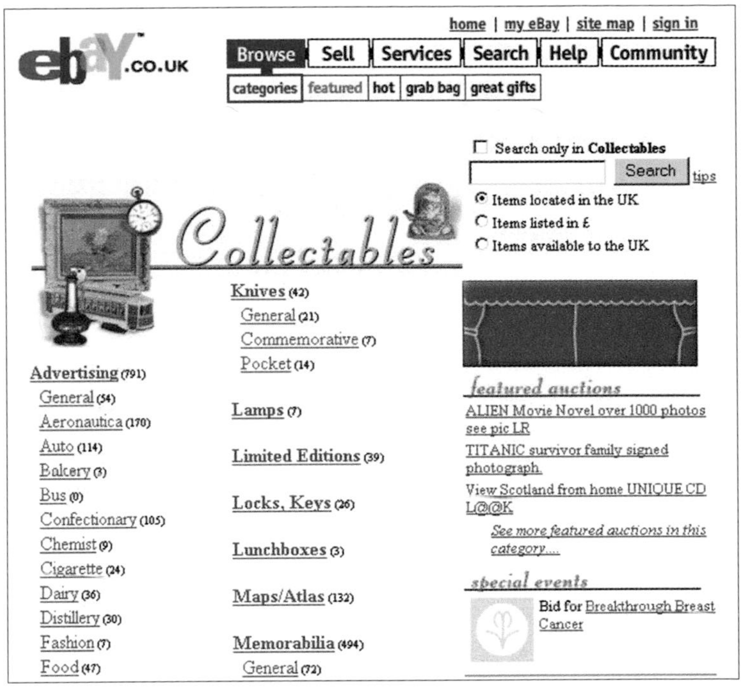

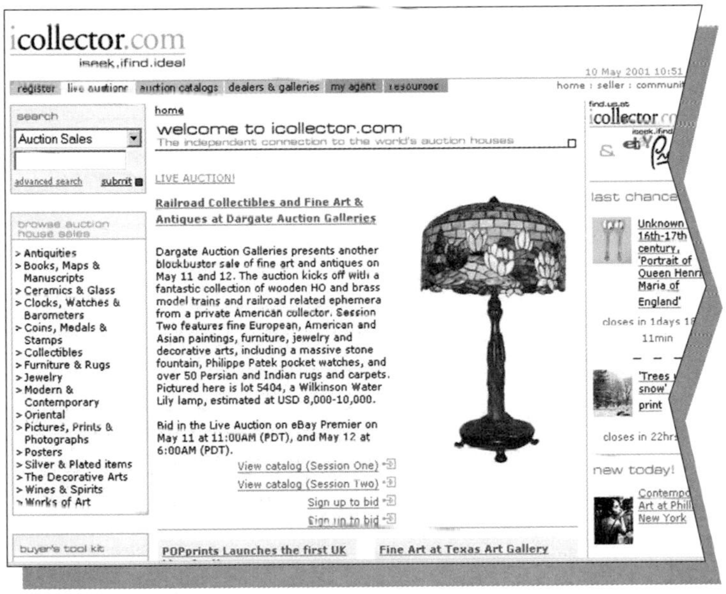

icollector

www.icollector.com

This site positions itself in an upmarket stratum of the online auction world: there are more Picasso lithographs and Georgian sideboards than fridge magnets. Nor does it stick exclusively to online auctions; there are some of these, but at least as important are the links to 'real-world' auctions around the UK. These give full details of what's on sale, with many photographs. Similarly, there are lots of links to dealers and galleries at the more expensive end of the market, together with special offers. Supporting the auctions are good histories and guides to various aspects of antiques and collectibles. This is a clean and smartly designed site that's well worth examining if you're looking for something a little bit special.

Postcards International

www.vintagepostcards.com

It's difficult to know if old postcards are antiques or collectibles. Perhaps the word 'vintage', as applied to cars, is the term that fits best. They're much sought after by an avid collecting community. This site has a well-illustrated online catalogue, covering topics from Art Nouveau to social history. It's fully searchable, and you can buy online or take part in online auctions. It's a fascinating site and well worth a browse.

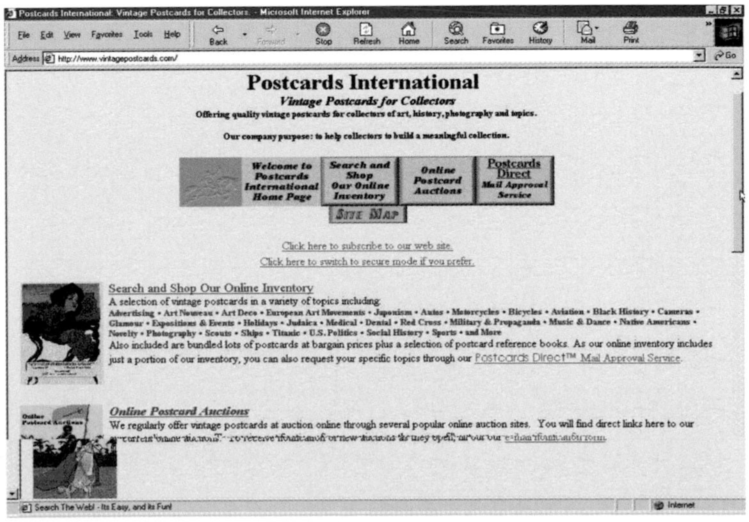

About the index

Text in italics is used for cross-references within the index (as in *see also...*). Page numbers in bold type denote the main entries for a topic.

A

B

C

D

E

F

G

H

I

J

K

L

M

N

O

P

R

S

● Acknowledgments

Abbreviations: t = top; b = bottom; r = right; l = left; c = centre; bkg = background. All cartoons are by Chris Bramley

8tr	Lyndon Parker/De Agostini
10t	Lyndon Parker/De Agostini
13br	Lyndon Parker/De Agostini
14	Lyndon Parker/De Agostini
18t	Lyndon Parker/De Agostini
18b	De Agostini
20	Warrender Grant/De Agostini
22	De Agostini
23all	Lyndon Parker/De Agostini
24b	Lyndon Parker/De Agostini
26	Corbis
44t	The Stock Market/Hose Luis Pelaez Inc
30b	Lyndon Parker/De Agostini
34	Lyndon Parker/De Agostini
36t	Lyndon Parker/De Agostini
38t	Lyndon Parker/De Agostini
64	Lyndon Parker/De Agostini
44t	Lyndon Parker/De Agostini
46t	Lyndon Parker/De Agostini
48tr	Lyndon Parker/De Agostini
50bl	Lyndon Parker/De Agostini
52tr	The Stock Market
54	MGM/Kobal Collection
56	MGM/Kobal Collection
58	MGM/Kobal Collection
60	NASA
62	Tony Stone Images/Olney Vasan
66	Lyndon Parker/De Agostini
70	The Stock Market
71cl	The Stock Market
73	The Stock Market
74	Lyndon Parker/De Agostini
78	Lyndon Parker/De Agostini
80	Getty Images
86	Lyndon Parker/De Agostini
87all	Lyndon Parker/De Agostini
88bc	MGM/Kobal Collection
88others	Lyndon Parker/De Agostini
89all	De Agostini
90	Lyndon Parker/De Agostini
93tl	Lyndon Parker/De Agostini
96all	Lyndon Parker/De Agostini
97t,b	Lyndon Parker/De Agostini
99	Lyndon Parker/De Agostini
100all	Lyndon Parker/De Agostini
101	Lyndon Parker/De Agostini
102t	The Stock Market
102cr	Olitec (courtesy)
103	ELSA AG (courtesy)
104	Lyndon Parker/De Agostini
106	Lyndon Parker/De Agostini
107all	Seiko (courtesy)
108bl	Psion (courtesy)
108cr	De Agostini
109tr	3Com (courtesy)
109bl	De Agostini
110	Canon
111t	Canon
111bl	Xircom
111br	Psion
112t	Xircom
112br	Lyndon Parker/De Agostini
113all	Lyndon Parker/De Agostini
114t	De Agostini
114b	Steve Bartholomew/De Agostini
115all	PMC Consumer Electronics Ltd
120	De Agostini
124	Tony Stone Images
126	De Agostini
127	De Agostini
128	De Agostini
130	Andy Teare/De Agostini
134	De Agostini
138	Lyndon Parker/De Agostini
142all	De Agostini
143all	De Agostini
154	The Stock Market